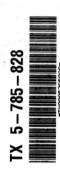

TX 5-785-828

A PASSION
— *for the* —
IMPOSSIBLE

SUNY series in Theology and Continental Thought
Douglas L. Donkel, editor

A PASSION
— *for the* —
IMPOSSIBLE

JOHN D. CAPUTO IN FOCUS

EDITED BY
MARK DOOLEY

STATE UNIVERSITY OF NEW YORK PRESS

Published by
State University of New York Press, Albany

© 2003 State University of New York

Printed in the United States of America

For information, address State University of New York Press,
90 State Street, Suite 700, Albany, NY 12207

Production by Judith Block
Marketing by Jennifer Giovani

Library of Congress Cataloging-in-Publication Data

A passion for the impossible : John D. Caputo in focus / edited by Mark
    Dooley.
    p. cm.—(SUNY series in theology and continental thought)
    Includes bibliographical references and index.
    ISBN 0-7914-5687-0 (alk. paper)—ISBN 0-7914-5688-9
(pbk. : alk. paper)
    1. Caputo, John D.   I. Dooley, Mark.   II. Series.

B945.C144 P37 2003
191—dc21

                                                            2002070714

10 9 8 7 6 5 4 3 2 1

To Laura, Madeline, and Kathy

CONTENTS

ABBREVIATIONS

Works of John D. Caputo

ME   *The Mystical Element in Heidegger's Thought*, (New York: Fordham University Press, 1978).

HA   *Heidegger and Aquinas: An Essay in Overcoming Metaphysics*, (New York: Fordham University Press, 1982).

RH   *Radical Hermeneutics*, (Bloomington: Indiana University Press, 1987).

AE   *Against Ethics*, (Bloomington: Indiana University Press, 1993).

DH   *Demythologizing Heidegger*, (Bloomington: Indiana University Press, 1993).

DN   *Deconstruction in a Nutshell*, (New York: Fordham University Press, 1997).

PT   *The Prayers and Tears of Jacques Derrida*, (Bloomington: Indiana University Press, 1997).

MRH   *More Radical Hermeneutics: On Not Knowing Who We Are*, (Bloomington: Indiana University Press, 2000).

Works of Jacques Derrida

Aporias   *Aporias*. Trans. Thomas Dutoit. (Stanford: Stanford University Press, 1993).

Cinders   *Cinders*. Trans. Ned Luckacher. (Lincoln: University of Nebraska Press, 1991).

Circum.   *Circumfession: Fifty-nine Periods and Periphrases*. In Geoffrey Bennington and Jacques Derrida, *Jacques Derrida*. (Chicago: University of Chicago Press, 1993).

Foi   "Foi et Savoir" in *La Religion*. Ed. Jacques Derrida and Gianni
         Vattimo. (Paris: Seuil, 1996) pp. 9–86.
GD   *The Gift of Death*. Trans. David Wills. (Chicago: University of
         Chicago Press, 1995).
Glas   *Glas*. (Paris: Galilée, 1974). Eng. trans. *Glas*. Trans. Richard Rand
         and John Leavey, Jr. (Lincoln: University of Nebraska Press, 1986).
Khora   (Paris: Galilée, 1993). Eng. trans. *Khora*. Trans. Ian McLeod. In
         On the Name, pp. 87–127.
OH   *The Other Heading: Reflections on Today's Europe*. Trans. Pas-
         cale Anne Brault and Michael Naas. (Bloomington: Indiana Uni-
         versity Press, 1992).
ON   *On the Name*. Ed. Thomas Dutoit. (Stanford: Stanford Univer-
         sity Press, 1995).
Psy.   "Psyche: Inventions of the Other." Trans. Catherine Porter, in
         Reading de Man Reading. Ed. Lindsay Waters and Wlad
         Godzich. (Minneapolis: University of Minnesota Press, 1989).
SoM   *Specters of Marx: The State of the Debt, the Work of Mourning,
         and the New International*. Trans. Peggy Kamuf. (New York:
         Routledge, 1994).
WD   *Writing and Difference*. Trans. Alan Boss. (Chicago: University of
         Chicago Press, 1978).

WORKS OF MARTIN HEIDEGGER

BT   *Being and Time*. Trans. John Robinson and Edward MacQuarrie.
         (New York: Harper and Row, 1962).
BW   *Heidegger: Basic Writings*. Ed. David Krell. (New York: Harper
         and Row, 1977).
GA 9   *Gesamtausgabe, vol. 9: Wegmarken*. (Frankfurt: Klosterman,
         1976).
IM   *An Introduction to Metaphysics*. Trans. Ralph Mannheim. (New
         York: Doubleday Anchor, 1961).
SZ   *Sein und Zeit*. (Tubingen: Niemeyer, 1962).

SAINTS AND POSTMODERNISM

Introduction

This book of essays on the work of one of the most exciting and controversial American Continental philosophers, John D. Caputo, attempts not only to put the latter's challenging ideas into context, but also to provide a context for some of the world's leading thinkers to discuss issues that are currently central to debates in the area of Continental philosophy and beyond. The issues that have preoccupied Caputo from his early work on Aquinas, Eckhart, and Heidegger, to his more recent ruminations on postmodern philosophers such as Levinas and Derrida, are so vast and wide-ranging that they have serious implications for philosophy and theology well beyond the purview of Caputo's particular specializations. His writings on ethics and religion, for example, while being indebted primarily to the insights of Jacques Derrida, are nevertheless ground-breaking in their own right; the implications for our understanding of the role of "God" in the contemporary situation, as well as the consequences for political debate of his claim that we have reached "the end of ethics," are indeed enormous. As such, this book seeks to tease out and test the efficacy of many of these contentious views that challenge not only many of the inherent presuppositions in recent philosophy but also in the humanities writ large.

My initial aim and aspiration in bringing together people as intellectually different from one another as Norris Clarke, Jacques Derrida, Lewis Ayres, and Tom Flynn, was to show the rich diversity of Caputo's writings, and to demonstrate how he himself has managed to reconcile traditions that ostensibly appear at variance but which prove to be much more congruous at a deeper level of inquiry. I am thinking here, for example, of how he has made a convincing case for the affinity between the Medieval mystics and deconstruction, about which I shall say more below. The result, however, is a book that far exceeds those initial aspirations. *A Passion for the Impossible* is not simply a retrospective appreciation, but a volume that launches us into new territory in the areas of ethics, religion, political philosophy, hermeneutics, deconstruction, post-structuralism, and of course, Medieval and mystical thought. In his extensive replies to each of the papers gathered here, Caputo not only defends his position on a host of vexed and complicated issues, but also brings the debate up a notch or two by vigorously testing the coherence of his critics' theses and claims. The result is an extraordinary dialogue that refuses to stand on ceremony and tackles the issues robustly but in a manner accessible to those with even a cursory knowledge of contemporary philosophical/theological thought. Indeed, it could be said that by way of his own original contribution to the volume, "God and Anonymity," and by way of his engaging rejoinders to each of his interlocutors, Caputo furnishes us with a book's worth of his most recent reflections.

One of the highlights of this confrontation between Caputo and his critics comes in the form of an interview that I held with Jacques Derrida in January 2000. The interview is noteworthy for the praise that Derrida heaps on Caputo for his work and commitment, but also for what it adds to the whole question of the relationship between religion and deconstruction, a question that has fundamentally preoccupied Caputo over much of the last decade. In the course of our exchange, Derrida addresses not only the nature of his "religion without religion," about which Caputo has so evocatively written, but he also reflects on how the name "God" functions for one who "rightly passes for an atheist." In many ways, this is the clearest statement by Derrida on God and religion to date, and I hope that it will act as a springboard, not only for further debate around Caputo's incisive reading of Derrida in this regard, but also for a much more comprehensive debate on these issues by all those influenced by Derrida from whatever quarter.

Moreover, thanks to papers by Norris Clarke and Tom Carlson, we not only get an insight into how Caputo reconciles his early interests with his latter day preoccupations, but we are also given a glimpse into the current general state of Thomism and negative theology. The same goes for those essays that challenge Caputo's readings of Heidegger, Foucault, Derrida, Levinas, and Rorty. In each case, the reader is invited to take sides in debates that are currently exercising scholars each of whom is at the cutting edge of his or her respective fields of research.

A Passion for the Impossible, therefore, provides a forum in which some of the more salient issues in the work of John D. Caputo as well as in the broader philosophical and theological scene, are subjected to rigorous and original appraisal, thus reinvigorating in surprising and exciting ways many debates that have long since become arid and stale. So much for the general profile of the book. In order to set things in context for the reader, allow me to devote what remains of this introduction to painting a general profile of Caputo and his intellectual formation and trajectory.

I think many will concur when I say that Jack Caputo is one of the most versatile, humorous, sensitive, and astute philosophers writing in the English-speaking world today. Caputo's intellectual adventure has taken him from Medieval to postmodern Paris, from Eckhart and Aquinas to Derrida, from mystics and magi to deconstructionists. Even today, steeped as he now is in the writings of Heidegger, Derrida, and Levinas, Caputo will invariably and fondly invoke the names and ideas of the scholastic masters to whom he owes an enormous personal debt. It was his early encounter with these saints and mystical scholars that inspired him to abandon life as he had known it in order to dedicate himself to learning and writing philosophy. Even his most "impish and impious" works, as he likes to describe his most recent output, bear testimony to his time studying the French Catholic intellectuals, like Jacques Maritain and Pierre Rousselot, writers who illuminated the texts of Aquinas for him in exciting and startling ways. In Caputo, the voices of "the Tradition" harmoniously intermingle with the rhapsodic ruminations of the saints of postmodernism.

It is this blend of the old and the new, of pre-Modernity and the post-Modern, which characterizes John D. Caputo's writings at their best. Unlike many "Continental" philosophers of his generation, he shirks the temptation to indulge in gratuitous esotericism, preferring instead to address his reader in a style reminiscent not only of the medieval monks, but also of his favorite proto-postmodernist, Søren Kierkegaard. In a recent exchange with Michael Zimmerman, Caputo remarks that "time and again I have succumbed to the temptation to make myself clear, which is, as someone once warned me, a very dangerous business. For nothing offers a philosopher better protection and a surer escape than an enveloping cloud of continentalist obscurity." He follows this up by saying that, as writers go, few can match his "not-so-secret hero" Mr. Either/Or: "For those who care about such things, it is not hard to tell that *Radical Hermeneutics* is a retelling of Constantine Constantius's *Repetition*, while *Against Ethics* is a postmodern version of *Fear and Trembling*."[1] Caputo's deployment of certain Kierkegaardian techniques—irony, clarity, humor and wit—have enabled him to render Continental philosophy accessible and intelligible to many who had long since abandoned ship. He has helped convince those of a more traditional persuasion that many of the themes being treated in contemporary European thought have their origins in the texts of Aristotle, Augustine, Aquinas, and Eckhart. He has shown how it is indeed possible to love both the pre-Moderns and the Postmodernists, how it is feasible, in other words, to talk of St. Thomas and Heidegger, the Bishop of Hippo and Derrida, in the same breath. Caputo's writings have served to debunk the myth that Continental philosophy is nothing short of fatuous and frivolous word play devoid of argument and reason. They bear witness to the fact that such philosophy can be as "serious" in content and tone, or as rich in argument, as any of its rivals.

So what exactly does this lover of mystics, saints, and maji, have to teach his reader? To what end does he aim the literary strategies borrowed from his not-so-secret Danish hero? I think Caputo's message is most poignantly encapsulated in the following passage from his most recent book, *More Radical Hermeneutics* (Indiana, 2000):

> . . . I cling steadfastly to Husserl's 'principle of all principles,' to stick to what is given just insofar as it is given, which has always meant for me a minimalist injunction *not* to put a more sanguine gloss on things than they warrant. I have always been both braced and terrified by Friedrich Nietzsche's demand to take the truth straight up, forgoing the need to have it 'attenuated, veiled, sweetened, blunted and falsified.' I readily confess that we have not been handpicked to be Being's or God's mouthpiece, that it is always necessary to get a reading, even if (and precisely because) the reading is there is no Reading, no final game-ending Meaning, no decisive and sweeping Story that wraps things up. Even if the secret is, there is no Secret. We do not know who we are—that is who we are. (*More Radical Hermeneutics*, 12)

Caputo's is a minimalist position to the extent that he is deeply suspicious of any maximalist philosophical, scientific, ethical, religious, or political structure that pretends to be more than a provisional formation. He steadfastly abides by the Kierkegaardian suggestion that we are, from the very outset, ineluctably situated in the rush of existence, caught in the grip of factical life, exposed to the merciless vicissitudes of time and chance. As "poor existing individuals" we are always already embedded in socio-linguistic frameworks, webs of beliefs and practices that determine how we view the world and how we relate to the others with whom we share it. This, of course, is not only Kierkegaard's belief, but also that of Nietzsche, Heidegger, and Derrida. As such, Caputo's *radical* hermeneutic turn, a turn that he took in the mid-eighties, has been dominated by these figures and their stress on historicity, the aleatoric flux of events, and the mediated character of experience.

The point of radicalizing hermeneutics in this way is to suggest that, whether we like it or not, we are unable to override interpretation, that there are no uninterpreted facts of the matter, and that the world is unavailable to us in any naked or raw sense. This is not to say that we are, as certain critics tend to argue, caught in a prison house of language, but simply that we have no way of knowing whether our interpretations accurately correspond to the way things are in themselves. Only those who believe that they can wash themselves clean of their socio-historical conditioning and assume a view from nowhere, would claim that their interpretations correspond to facts. To belong to a tradition means that one is claimed by a language, a language that is not one's own, but one which is comprised of multifarious voices and tongues. Languages are neither homogeneous nor univocal, but heterogeneous and plurivocal; they are contaminated from within by an assortment of dialects and vocabularies, all of which freely bleed into one another. Thus, when I speak I bear witness to the fact that purity is an illusion, that I simply cannot excuse myself from my heritage, and that I have no means of filtering out the words and signs that get closer to reality than the others with which I have been lumbered.

For Caputo, the upshot of this is clear: we must be prepared to face the worst, we must, that is, be prepared to go the distance with Nietzsche when he suggests that we are but clever little animals making our way in the midst of an anonymous rumbling which is devoid of sense and meaning. For we simply do not know if there is anything that acts as a firm foundation for our beliefs, values, judgments, and truths. We are not in a position, as factically situated beings, to fully unravel the various strands and threads that tenuously hold our traditions together so as to access some extra-contextual reality. Once you take history and context seriously, and once you realize that it is simply impossible to transcend one's time and place through an act of metaphysical bravado, then you will be more inclined to agree with Nietzsche that there is a distinct possibility that one day the little star will grow cold and the clever animals who inhabit it will have to die.

Caputo's radical hermeneutics endeavors, therefore, make trouble for those committed to the view that we can get out from under—either through metaphysical system building, or through the tools of theology—the network of finite structures and institutions into which we have been thrown, and through which we have been acculturated. It seeks to engender a sense of humility akin to that called for by Johannes Climacus when faced with Hegel's world-historical process. Like the pseudonym, Caputo contends that there is no *one* tradition, no *pure* language, and no history that is not already laden with heavy doses of fiction. There are, as stressed above, traditions, languages and histories, all of which are inhabited from within by even more complex traditions, languages, and histories. Consequently, the so-called "subject" is incapable, in a manner reminiscent of Hegel and Heidegger, of fully gathering itself up from a past that has never been present. This suggests that any attempt to spin a grand narrative of how we came to be where we are, is predicated upon the dubious assumption that there is a way of disentangling the disparate and highly convoluted linguistic and historical matrices in which we find ourselves. But such attempts at construing what Paul Ricoeur calls a "supreme plot," are always destined to fail, for there is simply no way that even the most skilled hermeneuts or historians can *fully* unfurl the manifold layers of history, no way that every trace of the past can be recovered from decay or deformation. There will always be a need, as Caputo repeatedly reminds his reader, to continually probe our texts and our histories in the name of those who never made it as far as the officially sanctioned record of events, those whose traces have long since turned to dust or ash. With Climacus and Derrida, Caputo stays on the lookout for the debris that falls from Hegel's desk as he crafts his systematic account of world-history.

For Caputo, thus, radical hermeneutics seeks to keep us attentive to the fact that we have to try to make sense of ourselves from where we stand. We cannot, he insists, circumvent the difficulties which existence presents by simply pushing aside the inordinate amount of traces, signs, tracks, and marks that constitute the past. As such, we are never quite sure as to *who* we are or whence we came. We are, as Derrida argues, always already lost (*destin-errant*), always already cut from the origin and forbidden access to the *terminus ad quem*. Our identities are, as Hegel suggests, constituted through a dialectical mediation of identity and difference. But, unlike Hegel, Caputo argues in favor of the belief that difference is not merely the antithesis of sameness, or something which, through a process of dialectical mediation, can be reconciled to the same. Rather, difference on this reading resists assimilation because it is synonymous with death and loss. Due to our being unable to fully recover the past, and due also to our being incapable of prying apart the multitudinous languages and traditions that feed into "our" own, we are somewhat alien and foreign to ourselves. We are, in other words, inhabited by many whose voices will never be heard either because they have been brutally suppressed, or simply because they have been lost to memory. Consequently, "we" should always be circumspect when "we" say "we," for no identity is ever pure and uncontaminated. What "we" call an "identity" is a highly miscegenated and contingent formation that has, over time, come to seem homogeneous and virginal.

Hence, Caputo's claim that "[w]e do not know who we are—that is who we are." For him, we are debarred from "The Secret," or from a supreme Truth of truths which could only be accessed after one had found a way of cheating time, language, and interpretation. The Secret is that which resists the overarching schemes that mortals try to erect in order to twist free of their mortality, or the sacred codes with which ontotheologists try to enter eternity through the back door. Being as we are always already severed from the origin, we can never—not at least if we have a certain degree of hermeneutic honesty and humility—bring to reality the dreams which the philosophers of self-presence have, since Plato, put forward for our consideration. The fact that one does not *know* The Secret is another way of saying that, try as I might, I cannot trace my ancestry back to some divine or infinite source. That is not to say, however, that some such source does not exist. Rather, it is a way of saying that if there is such a source, this poor existing individual is unable to reach it.

We are all, says Caputo in one of his most arresting phrases, "siblings of the same dark night," devoid of any privileged access to "God," "Being," or "Truth" (capitalized). There are no such master names in radical hermeneutics, no names that are not components of some natural or historical language. *All* names, thus, have a history, which means, in turn, that no name picks out a natural kind. Consequently, when you privilege a name by giving it a saving quality, radical hermeneutics urges you to undertake a careful genealogy or etymology of the name. It enjoins you take a closer look at the socio-linguistic cum historical matrix in which the said name is contextualized. In so doing, you will notice that names do not fall from the sky, that, *pace* Heidegger, there are no names which attach to reality more precisely than others. So we do our best to make our way through the dark night with the disconcerting realization that we shall not get any closer to cracking The Secret by invoking a name which has been, to employ a line from Nietzsche which Caputo loves, "enhanced, transposed, and embellished poetically and rhetorically, and which after long use seems firm, canonical, and obligatory to a people." (From "On Truth and Lie in an Extra-Moral Sense" in *The Portable Nietzsche*, Walter Kaufman ed., Random House, 1980, pp. 42–47).

But how precisely does all of this connect up with Caputo's formative training in such classical and traditional authors like Eckhart and Aquinas? How, in other words, does Caputo, as I contend at the outset, reconcile his love for both the philosophical and religious traditions, with his radical hermeneutics? Has he not thrown the baby out with the bath water? Has he not mercilessly sacrificed his beloved saints and mystics on Zarathustra's altar? I think the answer to these questions and concerns is revealed quite clearly in the course of the respective dialogues between Caputo and his critics in the remainder of this book. In nearly each case, Caputo responds by pointing out that his is not a negative or nihilistic position, but one full of hope, faith, and affirmation. Moreover, he tries to convey a sense of the *religious* spirit which drives radical hermeneutics, and this is, I think, what marks Caputo off from many of the so-called "postmodern" thinkers with whom he is normally associated. He convincingly shows us how we can preserve what we consider valuable in our traditions, while concomitantly cultivating a hermeneutic sensitivity towards them. Caputo's brand of hermeneutics, that is, does not set out to destroy or decimate tradition, but only to make it a little more honest with regard to its origins, thus ensuring that it does not become, in Kierkegaard's words, a "fossilized formalism."

He wants to keep all structures and institutions—political, theological, ethical, sexual, philosophical—from closing in upon themselves, or from becoming overdetermined.

It would, therefore, be a serious mistake to accuse Caputo of celebrating nothingness or nihilism. Quite to the contrary, his aim is to expose tradition to the voiceless and nameless that lie buried beneath its *constructed* foundations, and to show that even the most ostensibly determined structures have a hidden history. This is a process that is thoroughly affirmative, one that does not close off any possibility or any avenue of inquiry no matter how embarrassing to the tradition the findings of such inquiries might be. While we may never be capable, for all the reasons proffered above, of cracking The Secret, this should not prevent us from trying to unlock it as best we can. We should, according to Caputo, push against what seems closed off to us, even if, after having penetrated the outer layer, we find ourselves mired in even deeper and more complex layers. Radical hermeneutics invites us to go the extra mile, to push against the prevailing reading, even if we will never hit upon a final Reading which will still the turbulent currents of interpretation.

What we can take from this is that, in affirming tradition and the heterogeneous forces that disturb it from within, Caputo's work is not an exercise in irresponsible iconoclasm. Neither is it a philosophizing with a hammer simply for its own sake. It is rather an approach to questions of meaning and value that endeavors to keep us as attentive to the insuperable difficulties that human life has to contend with. It tries to take the steam out of any edifice that purports to be more than the product of human hands. As such, it signals a twilight of the idols of metaphysics, theology, science, and morality. It is in the moment when radical hermeneutics resists the seduction of the idols that it joins up with the Medieval and classical heritage out of which it emerged. Caputo's affirmation of his Catholic and scholastic training becomes manifest, that is, when he draws parallels between his deconstructive tendencies and those of his Medieval masters.

This is, of course, why Caputo's other not-so-secret hero is Jacques Derrida—the Rabbi Augustinus Judaeus. In Derrida, Caputo has found a radical hermeneut who shows how it is possible to love one's tradition with all one's heart, while at the same time subjecting it to penetrating critique and scrutiny. But even more importantly, Derrida's is not a violent critique, nor one that seeks to dance on the graves of our most hallowed certainties, but one that listens in a painstakingly rigorous fashion to the solicitations of those for whom the claim to greatness of the tradition has proved to be disastrous. Such attention to those whose memory has been erased is, on Caputo's reading of Derrida, a prophetic cum religious appeal for justice, for the type of mercy and justice demanded by the prophets Amos and Yeshua. For, like these prophets before him, Derrida encourages us to stay alert to the singu-

lar cries of those whose only desire is for justice beyond the law, or for a justice which exceeds that of the universal order. Such prophets enjoin us to
respond to those whose miserable plight shows up the deficiencies in the law.
This is Derrida's "religion without religion," about which Caputo writes so
movingly throughout his magisterial *The Prayers and Tears of Jacques Derrida* (Indiana, 1997), a subject to which Derrida returns in his interview with
me included in this volume.

The most significant point of convergence between Derrida and the
Medieval and scholastic traditions, according to Caputo, occurs when, in the
course of a remarkable confessional piece entitled *Circumfession* (Chicago,
1993), Derrida conjures up the spirit of St. Augustine as he asks, "what do I
love when I love my God?" In this moment, Derrida dons his tallith, falls to his
knees, looks skywards, and, as he weeps in anxious expectation, cries out
"Come! Please come!" This is the prayer of one who knows that there is no
escaping the hermeneutic fix in which we find ourselves, no way, that is, of
repairing to some neutral vantage point to determine the efficacy of our beliefs
and practices. But this ineluctable feature of our lot does not deter the radical
hermeneut from hoping against hope for the impossible dream of universal justice and democracy, or for a time when the law of unconditional hospitality and
forgiveness of the type preached by the prophets, will prevail.

This is what Derrida and Caputo call a "passion for *the* impossible," or a
passion for The Secret. As mentioned above, just because The Secret resists
decoding does not mean that we ought to abjure from trying to crack it. For
it is precisely when The Secret seems to have absolutely and totally con-
founded our cognitive grasp, that we are impassioned all the more to access
and disclose it. Such a passion prevents us from ever believing that we have
at last broken a sacred code, or that we have laid claim to the word of God,
Being, or Truth. It is what keeps us hermeneutically humble and what saves
us from our tendency to succumb to ontotheological hubris. It is that which
keeps faith alive.

These prayers and tears of radical hermeneutics, Caputo argues, are no
less passionate than those of the mystics. Indeed, Derrida's Augustinian
prayer—"What do I love when I love my God?" is structurally of the same
order as that beautiful line of Meister Eckhart, one so touching it could easily be mistaken for a verse from *The Cloud of Unknowing*: "Therefore I pray
God that he may make me free of God" (cited in Caputo, *More Radical
Hermeneutics*, p. 250). Both radical hermeneutics and mysticism share a love
of the impossible, or for that which challenges our most sacred certainties.
They both hope against hope for impossible dreams, dreams that revolve
around the name of "God." When Eckhart begs God to be rid of God, he is
engaging in, as Caputo suggests, "a sublime form of language which calls for,
which prays and weeps for, the other of language, for the incoming of the

other, *l'invention de l'autre*" (Ibid., p. 251). The silence that mysticism encourages is not a means of cheating language, but the means by which language assumes its most sublime form, not because it has, at last, corresponded with reality, but because it takes the form of a prayer for what is *wholly other*—The Secret, the impossible, or, as Derrida might say, the *tout autre*. Silence is a way of *saying* or *signaling* (both linguistic operations) that, try as I might, I cannot make the impossible possible.

Caputo admits, of course, that there are significant and undeniable differences between the Meister, a figure who has hovered over all of the former's writings since *The Mystical Element in Heidegger's Thought* (Fordham, 1982), and deconstruction. These divergences notwithstanding, however, it is more than credible to argue that Eckhart was a deconstructionist *avant la lettre*, that is, of course, if deconstruction is defined *a la Caputo*, as a prophetic/biblical appeal for justice. In a similar vein to Derrida, Eckhart does not contend that the *name* of "God," the signifier, can claim to have captured the essence of God, the signified; that is, for the mystic there can be no unmediated access to God-in-itself, no ideal cognitive or epistemic situation in which the knower apprehends the known in a purely factual sense. For, to repeat, it is impossible for a poor existing individual to bracket out interpretation in an effort to strike at the heart of the thing itself. For both the radical hermeneut and the mystic, the word "God" acquires its force and meaning through its relationship to other signs and names in the textual chain. There is simply no point at which we can disengage the sign from its context, and match it up to an extra-textual entity. Moreover, for Eckhart, to predicate something of God was not to describe the features and attributes of the thing we call "God," but rather a way of drawing that name further into a complex network of signifiers.

Like Derrida, Eckhart does not believe that there will come a point at which we will be able to dispense with the name of "God" because we will have succeeded in leaving language behind through some form of magical transcendental trickery. While he does contend that God is One, and while he does hold, *pace* radical hermeneutics, that beyond the anonymous rumbling of factical life there must be supreme signified (The Secret), Eckhart nonetheless insists that all our attempts at enclosing and circumscribing God through naming, pushes us further away from the "reality" of God. Once we name, as Derrida argues, the subject quietly slips away, and because we cannot but name we can never claim to *know* the subject through and through. To pray God to rid oneself of God, thus, is a way of staying alert to the ineluctability of interpretation, or a way of sensitizing oneself to the fact that no one sign is any closer to an uninterpreted fact of the matter than any other. It is a good deconstructive way of keeping us on the watch for the idols of self-presence.

The originality of Caputo's work is evidenced, therefore, in the way in which he deftly and convincingly shows how radical hermeneutics does not

seek to destroy or purge tradition, but tries rather to keep it open and sensitive to its *other* voices, the voices which, like Eckhart's, disturb it from within.
Caputo identifies in Eckhart the same type of joyful wisdom that directs Derrida's work, and the same type of critical vigilance that animates the most
responsible of postmodern thought. In Eckhart one hears the first great theological voice of dissent, the first great act of affirmative deconstruction.
Caputo opens up a space in which to hear the deeply religious tones of deconstructive faith, a faith that is not informed by knowledge of a Godhead, but a
messianic faith in a kingdom that is always to come. Like Eckhart, Caputo and
Derrida do not consider the inaccessibility of The Secret to be bad news, but
an opportunity to become even more intensely impassioned by the impossible. They each stand like the woman at the foot of the cross in Daniele da
Volterra's evocative painting reproduced by Derrida in his *Memoirs of the
Blind* (Chicago, 1993), and resketched by Kathy Caputo as the frontispiece for
The Prayers and Tears of Jacques Derrida; a woman whose prayer is punctuated by a faith (messianic, anchorite) without faith (in the strong determinate
sense epitomized by the concrete messianisms).

The faith of one who is impassioned by The Secret, thus, takes the form
of an admission that we, by virtue of our factical situatedness, are debarred
from predicting or programming the future, that we are at the mercy of the
aleatoric nature of events. As such, it is a passion not driven by knowledge (*la
passion du non-savoir*), for none of us knows the code to the absolute secret,
but by a much more indeterminate act of affirmation for what presently
exceeds our cognitive grasp. We are, as stated above, always already cut (circumcised) from the origin, always already a stranger to ourselves, always
already enmeshed in a myriad of linguistic, political, religious, and sexual net-
works that resist the disentangling prowess of even the most qualified and eminent historians, narrators, geologists, archaeologists, theologians, and
psychoanalysts. As such, there is no escaping the claim that tradition, history
and language make upon us. But we can hope, these obstacles notwithstanding,
that one day we may indeed *see* the truth. Faith is only faith when it longs for
what appears impossible, for what it cannot presently see. It is, as Kierkegaard,
reminds us constantly, a leap in the dark. Genuine faith is only for the blind.

Much of what Caputo debates in his responses to the many papers
assembled here, revolves around the nature and viability of this anchoral
religion without determinate religion, and especially around his contention
that the positive messianisms—Christianity, Judaism, Islam—confuse faith
with knowledge. Their reluctance to bite the bullet and admit that we simply do not know who we are, is what generates sectarian division, holy war,
and ethnic disharmony. For once a sect declares that it has been visited from
on high by a divinity, thus inferring that it now has a monopoly on truth
because it is in on The Secret, it sets off rival claims by its competitors,

which, in turn, culminates in a battle for possession of minds and souls. Caputo follows Derrida in arguing—and this I believe is the culmination of his long trajectory from Aquinas through Eckhart, Kierkegaard, Nietzsche, Heidegger, Levinas, and Derrida—that the call that issues to me from tradition might indeed be the summons of a supreme deity, but it might also be the anonymous forces of history appealing for justice, or for the realization of an ancient promise. The fact is that *I* simply do not know *who* or *what* calls. I am debarred from The Secret. But deconstruction shows that when the passage appears blocked, or when I can see no way through, the passion of faith becomes most intense. For at that moment the prayers and tears of one who is a little lost (*destinerrant*) flow like never before. At that moment one falls on bended knee and begs like mad for the impossible. As Derrida says, there is an undecidable fluctuation between God and the impossible. Longing for one cannot be separated from longing for the other.

"I can't go on. I must go on! It is necessary to believe (*il faut croire*)." Undecidability, Caputo has taught, is not to be confused with indecision or with paralysis, as many detractors maintain, but is rather that which sets the flames of faith alight. It is the point at which the wheels of hope and desire are set in motion, the point at which we press against the current in the belief that we will reach dry land. I do not know *what* it is that I love when I love my God— that is the spin that Derrida and Caputo put on Augustine's weepy supplication. The name of God does not cut nature at the joints, does not break through the network of traces and signs to some signified beyond language and temporality. It is rather the name of what I most long for. It is a longing for what exceeds the present order, what suspends the law in the name of the singular demand for justice. It is what disturbs the restricted economy of Hegelianism, an economy (*oikonomia*) predicated upon closure, in favor of the general economy that strives to give credit without the usual "terms and conditions." The name of God, for Caputo, does not signify presence, but that which shatters the illusion of presence in the name of what has been driven out of the present order, and for what challenges its borders from beyond. " 'My God'," he says, "is not addressed to a being or an essence, an explanatory cause or the solution of an epistemic cramp. When Moses starts to get nosey about God's meaning and name, Yahweh told him 'I am who I am, nothing you will understand,' the clear implication being that Moses should mind his own business, and keep his mind on the business at hand, which is justice, not ontotheologic" (*The Prayers and Tears of Jacques Derrida*, p. 335).

God, justice, unconditional forgiveness, unconditional hospitality, the democracy to come, the gift—these are the impossible names that shatter the orders of presence and law, as well as the overdetermined religious contexts that tend to embrace idols and golden calves before the suffering flesh of the lepers and the lame. The prayers and tears of Jack Caputo, his prayer to God to rid him of God, is a prayer for such justice. He has all the while been reminding us that religion and philosophy are not antithetical to one another, but that one nourishes the other. From his early invocation on behalf of the mystical element in St. Thomas' thought, to his book on Jacques Derrida's religion without religion, he has earnestly tried to show how important it is for the borders separating Athens and Jerusalem to tremble. Philosophy which is not guided by religion without religion, is one which risks favoring the call of Being over the gentle pleas for mercy issued by the widows, orphans, and strangers. Caputo's Derridean/Joycean belief is that there is no clear demarcation between the bloodlines of the Jews and the Greeks. Purity, we will remember, does not go all the way down. To silence the voice of the Jew, thus, would be to silence the prophetic call for justice, a call which stymies the totalizing tendencies of Greek ontology. That, in a nutshell, is Jack Caputo's *modus vivendi*; to keep reminding the Greeks that the Jews, the saints, and the mystics are never too far behind.

Let me conclude this introduction by expressing my sincere gratitude to Jack Caputo, not only for his indefatigable enthusiasm for this project, but also for his friendship and inspiration. I also wish to thank all those who contributed to this volume either directly or indirectly. I have been assisted throughout by a number of my current and former students, amongst them Liam Kavanagh, Mark Raftery-Skehan, and Barry Ryan. I owe to each one of them an enormous debt. This book had its genesis in a conference that both myself and Dr. Maureen Junker-Kenny organized at Trinity College, Dublin, in April 1998, entitled *From Aquinas to Derrida*. I wish to thank both Dr. Junker-Kenny for making such a successful event possible, and to all those who took part in the conference. A very special word of thanks is owed to my Editorial Assistant, Neil Brophy, for his untiring dedication to this project. Finally, I want to thank my wife, Laura, for her love, friendship, and support.

Mark Dooley
Dublin
July 2002

NOTES

1. John D. Caputo, "An American and a Liberal: A Response to Michael Zimmerman" in *Continental Philosophy Review* 31:215–220 (New York: Kluwer Academic Publishers, 1998), p. 215.

1 GOD AND ANONYMITY: PROLEGOMENA TO AN ANKHORAL RELIGION

MINIMALISTS AND MAXIMALISTS

"A wit has said that mankind can be divided into officers, servant girls, and chimney sweeps."[1] So says Constantin Constantius in Kierkegaard's *Repetition*. The Hongs, Kierkegaard's indefatigable, omnivorous English editors, have tracked down this wit, whose profundity Constantin cherishes, only to find that he chose to remain anonymous and hence unclassifiable (very fitting), signing his name with the initials "B.C.," upon whose significance we can only speculate. The point is this, and a profound point it is, Constantin thinks. Since speculative thought serves up classifications that pretend to exhaust their objects but never do, it is better to have an amusing, accidental, non-speculative classification than one we would have to take too seriously. Moreover, a classification, from the Latin *classicus*, originally had to do with the tolling of a bell (*glas*) to signal the order of rank, signaling who comes first. So classifications can be invidious and dangerous and we are better served deconstructing them, which is what Derrida's *Glas* is all about.

Having been thus duly warned in advance, having weighed B.C.'s admonition carefully, I will venture the following highly deconstructible working hypothesis for the present study: in the universe of discourse whose parameters I am here tracing out, the world divides neatly into minimalists and maximalists, knowing full well that most of us fall somewhere in between and that this entire distinction may fly up in my face.

Minimalists are what Johannes Climacus calls poor existing individuals, those who concede they do not know the "Secret," that they have no access to a secret beneath the surface of things, no secret or master name that holds the key to the most important doors of being, truth, or goodness.[2] So minimalists

1

are not inclined to overestimate what they know or to make more of things than they need to. They live with the uneasy suspicion that things might at any moment slump back into the chaos from which they are formed, and that it is only a matter of luck, time, and physics until that happens. Minimalists, who are wary of going too far, try to stick to the facts. They take themselves to be faithful heirs of father Husserl when he advises us to take things insofar as they give themselves and *only insofar as they are given* (*Ideas I*, §24). That "only" does not seem to them like a parsimonious restriction or an impoverishing constraint, just good advice. Minimalists think that what is given, what gives, does not quite give enough and that whatever is given requires a little supplementary interpretation. They worry about letting the principle of givenness, the principle of all principles, or any prestigious principle whatsoever, become so much sounding brass.

Maximalists, on the other hand, think there is always *more* to things than we think, and they tend to see the finite things around us as images, imperfect forms, and pointers to an unlimited plenitude, or perfection, or benignity from which all things emerge. Maximalists, who are wary of constraints, are taken with movements of excess, excellence, and overflow. For maximalists, the task in life is to learn how to open yourself up, how to expose yourself to this overflow, in order to tap into to it. They too take themselves to be sticking to the facts and to be heirs of father Husserl when he said to be as loyal as possible to what is given. But when it comes to givenness, they want to be more Husserlian than Husserl and they wonder what he was worried about when he added the "only insofar."

One way to see the difference between minimalists and maximalists is to see that for the minimalist, a "limit" represents progress, a perfection, an advance and an advantage, a temporary triumph things have made over the chaos, a shape inscribed in formless *apeiron*, so that it is always an achievement even to get as far as a limit.[3] Limit gives things determination, a definite and defined shape, a *finis* or border, like a property line that gives the owner a certain amount of privacy, a handle or a perspective or an angle of entry. For the minimalist, limit is a positive idea and the unlimited is a negative one, signifying that the limits have broken down, borders have been erased, and determination lost. For the maximalist, on the other hand, "limit" is an imperfection, a mark of finitude and constraint, a kind of stopping off or arresting of a *prior* and irrepressible infinity in things which seeks to burst out, if only given half a chance. For the maximalist, it is the infinite which is perfect, and it is in comparison with infinity that the finite things of ordinary experience are said to be limited. Infinity for them does not mean the formless *apeiron* but an infinite momentum in things, an uncontainable surge that will overtake and wash over us if only we let it be, let its infinite surge run through us and carry us off. That will require that we clear everything away that might block off infinity, that all the impediments the thinking subject throws up against the infinite be removed or reduced.

Maximalism is most clearly found in Neoplatonism and Christian Neoplatonism and it shows up in metaphysical theories that make a lot out of infinity, like Anselm and Descartes. Nowadays, on my telling, good examples of maximalism, which could also be called infinitism, are to be found in the work of Levinas, which cashes in Neoplatonic figures like *epekeina tes ousias* and a famous reading of Descartes' Third Meditation, and that of Jean-Luc Marion, who is a lot closer to Christian Neoplatonism. But what is so interesting and so very provocative about Levinas and Marion is that they are not Neoplatonists but phenomenologists (of a sort) who maintain that the infinite is something given or encountered, not a bit of metaphysical speculation. From the point of view of the minimalists they have, shall we say, let the nose of infinity under the tent of phenomenology, with the result that—wonder of wonders—God makes an appearance (of a sort) in phenomenology. That is an appearance that would have turned Husserl's head![4]

Minimalists are content with more modest, finite findings and are wary of infinite givenness. That is why, in the present study, I have inserted a certain phenomenology of "anonymity" as a kind of signature of minimalism, anonymity being part of the "factical" situation in which we find ourselves, part of the unadorned truth of our condition, which is to be severed from the Secret. By "truth" I mean neither correspondence nor unconcealment, nor anything unshakeable and well-rounded, nor any kind of Secret Truth about the Way Things Are, but the humble truth, the sort of thing one has to face, or confess, or circumfess, a bit of unpleasantness we would just as soon avoid. By a "condition," I mean the inescapable terms that always accompany our situation, so that whatever is given comes along with a catch, a spin, a reading, and you always have to read the fine print, including and especially if you think you have hit upon a positive infinity. Minimalists are inclined to think there is a catch somewhere in the small print and that you have to keep an eye out for the "teasers" that lure you into a deal that you would have otherwise avoided. There are always conditions. A *conditio*, from *con + dicere*, means the terms that are talked over, negotiated, and agreed upon when we enter into a contract, so that before agreeing you better be sure you know all the terms. Minimalists are conditionalists, who are always on the look out for the conditions that come attached to things, who have been burned enough times to know that there are always conditions. When they speak of the "human condition," which is a congenial expression to a minimalist, they mean that we are thrust into a situation *without* our asking, whose terms have been agreed upon in advance, prior to, and without our consent, terms with which we are just going to have to cope. Kierkegaard's Constantin Constantius was being very minimalistic when, speaking about being born into this world, he asked why he was not first consulted.[5] It was just this sort of Kierkegaardian idea that Heidegger had picked up on in *Being and Time* when he said that a "factical" being is thrown and hence not free, not its own, "from the ground up."

So in the spirit of a good minimalism, which is the spirit of poverty—*beati pauperes spiritu*—I begin by trying not to assume too much or to open the negotiations with too high a demand. I begin in a spirit of quasi-Augustinian circum-fession, a spirit of owning up or "fessing up" to an "elemental condition" that besets us all, that creeps over us like a fog, that threatens to swallow us whole or leave us lost for words (not to worry). I will describe a shadowy, formless penumbra that hovers over us, a demi-being or shade that haunts us and disturbs our sleep. This haunting figure, called the anonymous or anonymity, will serve as my point of departure, my first word, but by no means my last. It describes a lower limit condition, unformed and indeterminate, chaotic and confused. I have the advantage of beginning where Genesis begins, which has a lot to say about beginnings, with the "*tohu wa bohu*,"[6] from out of which are formed all the higher forms of life and history and culture, of ethics and science.

As other as the anonymous may be, God would be, on my construal, the *other* limit, another other or another wholly other. God is the upper limit, not of nameless anonymity but of eminent hypernymity, not of negative formlessness but of positive infinity, not of bottomless recess below being but of uncontainable excellence beyond being, not of humble truth but of the excess of Truth, not of cruel indifference but of benignity, not of cold uncaring unconcern but of loving care. But pray do not misunderstand me. The difference between minimalists and maximalists is not the same as the divide between atheists and theists. Minimalists are not, God forbid, against God, no more than maximalists (like Bataille) are for God, not necessarily, but they are dubious in the extreme about claims of infinite givenness, or positive infinity, or of a phenomenology of infinity, which sounds to them too much like the Secret. So it is not by God but by their "approach" to God that they differ from the maximalists, who think it is mostly a matter of breaking down (or deconstructing) the blocks we throw up against an infinity that will take us by surprise. But minimalists like Johannes de Silentio confess they simply have no "prodigious head"[7] for such big ideas as a positive infinity and they are more inclined to say that here, where the path is uncertain, the signs conflicting, the data confusing, here, *in hoc statu vitae*, as St. Thomas liked to say, we proceed by *faith* (which, significantly, Johannes Climacus called "the condition"). Faith, according to the Apostle, means through a glass darkly, leaving a more clear-sighted phenomenology, or hyper-phenomenology, for another time (or day, or day without time).

Paul Ricoeur was being a minimalist when, at the end of *Oneself as Another*, he made a confession about what philosophers should confess, a confession that I myself also make without the least resistance (that I know of), which he called the "aporia of the other:"[8]

> Perhaps the philosopher as philosopher has to admit that one does not know and cannot say whether this Other, the source of the injunction, is another person whom I can look in the face or who can stare at me, or my ancestors for whom there is no representation, to so great an extent does my debt to them constitute my very self, or God—living God, absent God—or an empty place. With this aporia of the Other, philosophical discourse comes to an end.

If the Other is really other, then it is the shore I cannot reach, the step beyond which I cannot make, the point at which my *voir, avoir, et savoir* breaks down. If the alterity of the Other is anything more than provisional—something that I will eventually take possession of, suppress, and make mine—then I have to say that when I am visited by the Other, I do not know what is going on. I cannot say whether it is God, or my mommy, or *khora* or *il y a*. That is what I call the anonymous, for the perfectly good reason that it keeps its own counsel and does not tell me its name.

To be sure, there is a perversity in undertaking a phenomenology that would be expected to accommodate itself *either* to anonymity *or* infinity. A phenomenology of anonymity seems perverse inasmuch as phenomenology is meant to be a philosophy of life, but anonymity threatens phenomenology with death. Anonymity is dark and menacing, impersonal and oppressive, a structure or non-structure that de-constitutes whatever has been constituted, that drains the meaning out of meaning-giving acts, drains the life out of the life-world, drains the existence out of the existent, the Being out of the being, drains the care out of Dasein, and takes the shine off *phainesthai* and *aletheia*. Anonymity is the structure or non-structure of the nameless no one. So if this is phenomenology, it is at best a quasi-phenomenology, an exhausted and burnt-out phenomenology, working at the lower limits of phenomenality, where things have not yet quite been constituted or objectified, and not yet managed to rise up into manifestness, or to shine or glow with *Sein*, or even in a certain sense to be at all. Not beyond but below being. Still, minimalists like me will often (especially when we are under attack), seek the protection that the word "phenomenology" or even "quasi-phenomenology" affords, because phenomenology is an honorable word with honorable associations. To begin with anonymity is to make a humble beginning and "phenomenology" lends it some dignity.

On the other hand and from the opposite end, a phenomenology of infinity, which would be quite a perfect phenomenology, a phenomenology of pure life without death, seems an equally daunting, unlikely, and suspect undertaking and for the opposite reason. Phenomenology is not made for such heights or depths. Pure, unconstrained, absolute infinity flies off the registers of phenomenological experience. But just like their minimalist friends, maximalists are also seeking the protection and respectability the word phenomenology affords, for they want to look like *strenge Wissenschaftlers* and not like spirit-seers. Jean-Luc Marion, writing of the "saturated phenomenon," which represents an excess of intuition over intention, complains that Husserl spent too much time scrutinizing "impoverished" phenomena, like pure formal geometrical intuitions, and "ordinary" phenomena, like the sound of a melody or the sides of a building, while never going in for anything exciting.[9] Marion is one of the best possible examples of a maximalist; I cannot conceive of a better one. Marion goes for big phenomena. Husserl, however, was a centrist, a middle of the roader who was more comfortable around medium size objects and manageable intuitions.

Phenomenology itself seems to function no more easily in the absolute white light, the white ecstasy, of infinity than in the shadowy blackness of anonymity. Phenomenology is neither *blanche* nor *noire*, neither white hot nor burnt out black, but a phenomenology of color that depends upon the shadings and differentiations that help define determinate things and objects. Phenomenology is best fit for medium size things, for the more manageable, intermediate shapes of ordinary experience, and one wonders how well it can function when pressed to the limits of experience, to either limit; that of infinite surges or flows, on the one hand, or that of the still, barely detectable rumblings of anonymity.

UNDECIDABILITY

A central hypothesis of the present study is that these two formless limit-states tend to run together, on the sound principle that two things so similarly other, so similarly dissimilar to ordinary experience, must be similar to each other. So, once again we find ourselves bending to the wisdom of the anonymous wit B.C. Different as they may be, if they be, these extremes of underdetermination and overdetermination tend to meet somewhere behind our backs, so that the dark night in which all cows are black and the bright light in which all spirits are white tend to be phenomenologically indistinguishable. My hypothesis is that, if we stick to the phenomenal facts, the borders between the negative infinite of the formless *apeiron* and the positive infinity of *aliquid quo major nequit*, between the formless *tohu wa bohu* of *il y a* and infinite givenness, tend to blur. We have no sure way of differentiating them, and that is because their *phenomenal* traits tend to be the *same*: nearly everyone who has been there, as we shall see, reports back that these limit states are indefinite, formless, nameless, unforeseeable, unknowable, and from time immemorial, to mention but a few of the best known reports. So it is no wonder that these states or conditions tend to overlap and converge, finally reaching what Levinas calls "the point of possible confusion" of God and *il y a*, or even, to play up a little alliteration, of *il y a* and illeity.[10] *Phenomenologically* speaking, how are we supposed to tell the difference between the *il* of *il y a* and the *il* of illeity? So it is a part of this hypothesis that maximalists, being good and true phenomenologists, will always end up reporting this blur and confessing this confusion, will always let the cat of confusion out of the bag of the infinite, and so will always end up conceding that the minimalists may be right.

To be sure, it is easy enough to keep these two, God and anonymity, apart *conceptually*. That is why Thomas Aquinas criticized David of Dinant for being so "foolish" as to say that God and prime matter are the same—*qui stultissime posuit Deum esse materiam primam*, the angelic doctor said, in a rare moment of devilish ill temper.[11] (David saw that neither God nor prime matter have defining, determinate form.) The difficulty is not conceptual but phenomenological, to tell the difference between them experientially, phenomenologically, that is, once you say you are not just differentiating concepts, which is as easy as reading a very clear map in your easy chair, but are reporting back experiences to the rest of us, which is like actually being on the road and traversing a confusing terrain. Then the reports start to sound alike and the travelers begin to report a "possible confusion" as to where they are and what is going on.

That phenomenal finding of a point of possible confusion I take to be *a central phenomenal fact* and proof positive of the *undecidability* that besets our lives, the undecidability that works its way into the interstices of our beliefs and practices, our ethics and religion, and this in virtue of *différance*. Enter Derrida and deconstruction, those old nemeses of the Lovers of the Good and the True. But do not misunderstand me. I count myself among the lovers of the impossible, fired by a passion for things to come, so that for me undecidability and deconstruction are good news, even evangelical. Undecidability adds spice to life because it makes decisions possible, and indeed constitutes the very condition of possibility of decisiveness. The opposite of undecidability, it must be insisted, is not "decisiveness," as the Defenders of the Good and the True contend, but *programmability*, deducibility. A real decision requires undecidability, requires being in a situation where the deck is not stacked in favor of one option, where the conclusion is not contained in the premises, where the only way a situation can be resolved is through *judgment* and *decision*. Undecidability is an account of judgment, not an attack upon it.

Good minimalist that I mean to be, I am not here to heap jeremiads upon our heads, to curse the day I was born, or even to complain about the taxes I have to pay (which seem to us all like an expenditure without return). I am, in the spirit of a certain phenomenology, and certainly of a certain deconstruction, here to affirm this undecidability and to try to show that it is good news. *Oui, oui.* Undecidability is good news for philosophy, religion and art, for politics, law, and architecture, and quite a few other things. Above all, and this is my concern here, it is good news for religious *faith*. Such undecidability, I will argue, is a way to define faith, not to undermine it, to situate faith within the limits of the finitude, *différance* and undecidability within which belief must function. For belief is always through a glass darkly (through the *glas* of unclassifiability darkly). Undecidability is not necessarily good news for infinite givenness, I concede, or for being visited by the infinite plenitude of the saturated phenomenon. One might even say, in the spirit of a certain Kant, I have found it necessary to deny givenness in order to make room for faith (even as the phenomenology of infinity has to watch out for looking like spirit seeing). If faith is, following Johannes Climacus, the "condition," undecidability is the condition of the condition, the reason *the* condition is a condition, the quasi-transcendental condition under which faith is possible and also a little impossible.

Undecidability, I will constantly argue, keeps things safe. To see how this is so, consider the fact that the debate that I am trying to stage between minimalism and maximalism has a political coefficient, everything always being political. Inscribing faith within *différance*, making faith a decision within undecidability, should promote a sense of tolerance and restraint among believers toward those whom they regard as infidels. For the point is that everybody is an infidel vis-à-vis somebody's faith. We are all in this together, divested of the Secret, siblings of the same "possible confusion," doing the best we can, construing traces and reading signs, practicing a certain radical hermeneutics in the midst of undecidables. We are all forced to make our way where the path has not been cleared, where the maps are bad and the roads are worse. That is our "condition," humble as it is. The secret is, there is no Secret, none that we *know* of. That is where we are and I always make it a rule to begin where I am, which is an honorable minimalist axiom. The most presuppositionless beginning is to begin with the supposition that we are always situated in the midst of an uncontrollable mix, always already posited, de-posited, post-posited after the fact in the midst of one pre-understanding or another (*Sauf*, 43/ON, 49). We always arrive too late, after the Secret has offered its excuses and made an early departure.

IL Y A

All that being said, let us introduce our little phenomenology of the anonymous. This is by no means a Big Ontology of How Things Are, but a humble description of an experience that I wager everyone from the author of Genesis to Jacques Derrida has from time to time undergone. It is not a thing in itself, but a perspective, one more perspective, which was given a voice in *Against Ethics* by Felix Sineculpa.[12] I beg to be excused for lapsing into Franco-English in what follows. But if I am right, this is not just a little idiomatic structure deeply embedded in a highly idiomatic language like French, but a general condition that besets us all to which we must own up.

Il y a is an idiom that has been meditated upon at some length for us by Levinas, Blanchot, and by Derrida, in *Feu le cendre*, which is nicely translated as *Cinders*, where Derrida meditates the phrase *il y a là cendre*, "there are cinders (or ashes) there." For Derrida, *il y a* resonates with cinders or ashes, which are an excellent and even biblical sign of the humility (*humus*) of our condition and for the anonymity from which things arise and into which they return. *Il y a* is, I hope to show, not just a shibboleth confined to French, but a token of a more widespread condition that is as old as Genesis. *Il y a* is an idiom for "there is," like the German "*es gibt*," which taken literally does not mean "it gives" but something starker, like "it has there." That is why it is to be understood idiomatically, not literally, and why I who am being a bit perverse intend to torture it half to death by taking it literally to see what happens, and why I pray you to be patient with me. I will soon enough return to American English.[13]

It (*il*) is older than I can say. It has been there (*y*) from the beginning, from before the beginning, from time immemorial, from time out of mind, a timeless time. It is not something I have; rather it (*il*) always has (*a*) me. There (*y*). Always and already. As soon as I come to be, and before that, it is there, and it waits patiently for my return after I cease to be, when it, the neuter and neutralizing, will separate existence from the poor existent that I am when they scatter my ashes. It humbles the pretension of the ego, like death itself.

It (*il*) is nothing I do, but more a matter of my undoing; it is not at all a matter of an I or an ego. I do not posit it, but I find myself de-posited, deposed, destituted, by it, before I can posit myself and take up my position. It will not allow me to take my leave and quietly excuse myself. It holds me. There. It traps me, fixes me, "without remission," as Levinas says. The I is at best an afterthought and an adverb, thrust there (*y*) adverbially, after the fact.

I cannot say what it (*il*) is. How would I know that? I was not there (*y*), at the beginning. I have been cut off from all originating beginnings. I was not there (*là*). It is older than any thing that is, older than essence, which is already a very advanced formation for it to assume. It is older than Being, before Being's time, and mine, the time of the I. It was many years ago (*il y a de plus ans*). Being and essence have been reduced to ashes, their substances consumed, by *il y a*.

It is older than objects in their objectivity. It has (*il a*) them before they form themselves into determinate unities, well formed and determinate objects. Objectivity is already a late formation, very advanced, too complex and exalted for the humble state of *il y a*. It is that from which objects are formed, out of which they emerge, the indeterminacy that antedates the determination that objectivity supplies, there from of old, from before the time of objects and the constitutive acts in which objects are forged.

In the beginning, there was a formless void, *tohu wa bohu*, and darkness covered the face of the deep.

All that (and more) is confessed when the I, taken by surprise, blind-sided, having never seen it coming, is forced to say *il y a*. It is not a matter of what I constitute or project, or what I let be. It is nothing I own, nor anything by which I am owned. Owning and ownness have been scattered to the four winds, like ashes. It is something to which I must own up—that is as much *er-eignen* and *ver-eignen* as I admit.[14]

It does not care about me or need me. If I call out, it does not answer. If you say that it calls me, that it calls me to be, that it calls me by my name, from before my time, that would be to say too much and more than we know. All I know is that I call out to it and it does not answer. Anonymity has the structure of the "no one there," above all when I need someone. The structure of the "someone," of someone who calls, is a very advanced formation, very late, from which, if one makes a humble beginning one must need to make reduction.

Anonymity is the heartless thought that no one is there, that in some distant time, when the earth has fallen back into the sun, and the sun has burnt itself to ashes, no one will be there to notice, no one will have been there, and the forces will simply play on.

That I cannot say what it is, or who. It is a structural limit, a mark of our facticity, not of our stupidity. It has me before I come to be, before I come to say *il y a*, to say or know anything at all. It eludes my grasp and humbles my pretensions. I cannot say from what dark place it starts out, by what dark force I am held in place. There. There where "it'" never becomes "I," since the I would represent an advanced and high level formation for it to take, there where the I sinks into the it. What can I say of a place that withdraws from view, always and already, structurally, in principle, *in prin-cipio*? How am I to fathom a bottomless depth? What am I to make of that (*ça*), of it?

In principio erat id. In principio, erat. That is not blasphemy, but a certain humble, minimalist phenomenology, with a heavy borrowing from Genesis I:1.

The anonymous haunts me, like a ghost that never really is or is not.[15] I cannot get back before it and disarm it of its eerie phantasmic quality. The haunting is the unknown, the ungraspable, the fear of being swallowed by an abyss.

Imagine a great endless cosmic space, and a camera to end all cameras panning the endless horizon. Nothing but great stretches of darkness and silence, until it catches sight of a small and distant light and sounds, ever so faint. The camera moves in closer to find a blue planet, moist and noisy and living, and then closer, to find a small house, a fire burning within, and laughter. Then the light goes off and all is quiet again and the camera resumes its endless silent sweep of the abyss.

It is neither masculine nor feminine (*ne uter*), and both masculine and feminine. It is more motherly, more embracing, more enveloping and uterine, like a vast embryonic sea on which I am tossed. Or like mother *khora*. Even so, it is a fierce father, a harsh law, an interdiction, angry and impervious to my pleas. It is both, and neither, a namelessness that absorbs every proper name like a great dark star, a black hole, absorbing the light of the smaller bodies around it.

"There is (*il y a*) *khora* . . . But what *there is*, there (*il y a, là*) is not; we will come back later to what this *there is* can give us to think, this *there is*, which, by the way, *gives* nothing in giving place or in giving to think . . ."[16]

I have for a very long time been haunted by the idea that what is there (*il y a*) is a vast starlit night of endless skies, a dark expanse of stars flickering in a void. I am kept awake at night by the thought of a sprawl of endless space and time, punctuated here and there by celestial fires of astronomical proportions, massive spheres of flaming gases, burning furiously. Fires burning from time immemorial, from long before my time. They burn and burn. They burn because they burn, in a stretch of endless space. Until they burn out. Meanwhile, off on a distant star, by now all cool and blue, in an obscure corner of the universe, clever little animals invent for themselves proud words like "being" and "truth," "ethics" and "knowledge." In time, the little blue star, which is no more than a little planet made of dust, all out of breath, loses its momentum and sinks back into its sun, where it burns to a crisp. Thus the clever little animals have to die, leaving behind nothing but ashes and the fading echoes of their now dead languages reverberating in the void.[17]

I am visited nightly by the thought that this is what there is, what is there, *là*, that this is what has us (*il a*), there (*y*). What then?

CALLING ON ABRAHAM

Now let us turn a few pages and interrupt this silent anonymity of the *tohu wa bohu* with the calling of proper names in a very famous story from a few chapters later in Genesis.

"Abraham," the Voice called out, in Hebrew (I assume).

"*Me voici*," Abraham responded.

"*Du sollst*," the Voice commanded, in its best German-Jewish.

"*Me voici*," Abraham repeated, sticking to the French.

If Heidegger thought you had to be German to understand Greek, I, perversely enough, prefer to follow Levinas's French translation of the Hebrew. If the Hebrew *tohu wa bohu*, the chaos and confusion, the originary chaos into which God spoke his word in Genesis 1:1–2, shows up phenomenologically in *il y a* and its hubbub, its *remue ménage*,[18] here the Hebrew *hineni* comes out as *me voici*, all of which brings out something Jewish about the *il y a* or the anonymous. *Hineni/me voici* provides the terms for the minimalist reading of the binding of Isaac that I here propose.

The French language has the advantage here of bringing out what we might venture to call the grammar of obligation. It puts Abraham in the accusative, on the receiving end of a command, a call, an obligation, turning him inside out from a nominative I (who can take charge) to an accusative me (who is given a charge). The grammar of the obligatory phrase, the performative force of the commanding categorical call that comes over us and will not take no for answer, is to put us in the accusative, singled out and accused. *Me voici*,[19] see me here, in the accusative; here you will find me, which is also what Mary said to the Angel Gabriel (Luke 1:38). So even though it is a communication from God, there is something of the structure of the *il y a* in Abraham's situation, something of the "it has me, there, something, I know not what, has overtaken me, has taken charge of me." Levinas thinks that with the *me voici* one surmounts or transcends the *il y a*, whereas I am inclined to give him an argument on this point and to say that *il y a* constantly reasserts itself, that the anonymous voice of *il y a*, of something I know not what, has slipped in even here on the road to Moriah, so that while Abraham is sure enough that he has been summoned, he cannot say by what or whom.

See Abraham there, *still* caught up in *il y a*. It, *il*, has him. But *what* has him? What is this Voice, this mysterious force that comes over him and drives him to such an extreme? That question, of course springs from an *identitarian* impulse, about which we must be cautious in the extreme. But must Abraham not make sure of what it is, sure of what is there, when it demands so much? Still, if it is an obligation, there can be no question of testing the Voice to see if it is true. That is something the Voice would never abide. It has Abraham and puts him in the accusative; it will suffer no counter-accusation or cross-examination itself, and it is not about to trade places with Abraham so that Abraham can see what is going on. It has come to put Abraham to the test, not to be tested itself. In the Hebrew scriptures, as Urs von Balthasar points out, we do not have an experience of God, but God, has an experience, makes an experiment, with us, puts us to the test.[20] Abraham has been sent a message from who knows where and now it is up to Abraham to do what he must do.

This was surely none of Abraham's doing, not his idea, no egological project of his own. He would rather give his own life (death) to the Voice, would gladly have laid his own body down upon the altar instead. The Voice comes from afar, from on high, from a time before his time, from across the mountains, from beyond the stars. It seizes Abraham and sends a tremor through his body, rending his heart, confounding his mind. Abraham cannot grasp it, cannot ground or found it, cannot engage it in a dialogue. The Voice has not come to argue.

Why was he not first consulted about this order, this man who had served the Voice faithfully for many years? Why was he not given the opportunity to state his case, to make his own counter-proposals, to do a little bargaining, to negotiate the terms and conditions, to cut a deal with the Voice, as he had been able to do over Sodom and Gomorrah? Why is he unilaterally stuck on the receiving end? The Voice always has him. The deals it cuts are always one-way streets. This is always how it is with the Voice.

For three days they rode together, side by side, sleeping under dark skies illumined only by an occasional star. Abraham wondered whether the Voice lived on one of those stars. Which one? Does anything live on those stars? Are there stars out beyond those stars, without beginning or end? Are the stars filled with gods who hold them mightily in their hand and steer their course and who look down on us mortals, keeping a watchful eye? Or do the stars simply wend their way through a void and then burn out, all the while utterly unmindful of us and of our cares? Are we alone, with no one watching, utterly unseen, unheeded by anyone, he asked himself?

Who or what calls Abraham? What is the voice that calls? Well, that is impossible to say. If Abraham actually *knew* who or what the voice was, knew its identity, if Abraham knew what he was doing, the whole thing would not have been a trial and he could have been assured of a good outcome. But the whole point of the story is that Abraham was blind, that he did not know or see, and that this transaction does not transpire in the domain of knowledge. That is because it is an ordeal, a trial, a test not of what Abraham knew to be true, but a test of faith, of not knowing, the test of one who must proceed, as Derrida says, *sans voir, sans avoir, sans savoir*. Kant's critique of Abraham is that he should have cross-examined the voice a little more closely, asked a few more questions. Kant was an *Aufklärer* who wanted to shed a little light on the situation, not the father of faith who was content with blindness and seeing through a glass darkly. The whole idea here is that the Voice is the voice of I know not what, it comes *je ne sais pas d'où*.

But that means, if we let us ourselves think about this, that for all we know, for all Abraham knows, the Voice could have been nothing more than the result of a bit of undigested meat and sleepless nights, as an impudent Nietzsche might have speculated. Or the Voice might be some blind impulse in Abraham's subconscious that obsessed and tormented him half to death because of something, long ago, that he will not let himself remember. As Paul Ricoeur said above, the philosopher as philosopher just does not know the source of the injunction, does not know whether it is the voice of my ancestors or of the living God, or the absent God—or an "empty place," like a *khora*. With this "here I am," philosophical discourse runs into a dead end.

Abraham is flat up against the "possible confusion" of *il y a* and *illeity*. We never quite know what is coming down upon us. This is risky business. If the Voice comes from on high from out of nowhere, it is *no less* imbedded in the anonymous, from way below. That is my hypothesis, the hypothesis of undecidability. If Abraham knew where it was coming from, if he had been able to get his bearings long enough to identify the Voice, to bring it within the scope of his cognitive reach, make it an object for his subjective powers, then the ordeal would have been over. Then he would have been able to calculate whether this was a good investment, something he was of a mind to do because it was a good idea, and thereby economize on the fear and trembling. But then he would not be the father of faith but of good investments and estate planning.

But if the Voice described by de Silentio is *structurally unknowable*, then on a minimalist reading, does that not mean that the voice is as much a *what* as a *who*, an *it* (*il*) as a *he* (*il*). Indeed it is not already too much to say a *Voice*, because to say a *Voice*, to call this call a *call*, is already to have anthropomorphized it, to have called it by a familiar name, to have brought it close, to have destroyed its distance and made it into something we know how to name. We know what a voice is called, we know what a call is called; to speak of a voice or a call is to have domesticated *il*, to have brought it within the horizon of language with which we are comfortable. That robs it of some of its surprise and gives us the time to catch up with it, to get our bearings. So on the most rigorously minimalistic reading, which does not read too much into it, which tries to stick to what is given insofar as it is given without making too much of it, Abraham would not know *what* is going on here, including even whether *il* is even a voice that calls.

ANKHORAL RELIGION

For Johannes de Silentio, this is the story of the teleological suspension of the ethical. But for Derrida it is an allegory of a "hyper-ethics," so that the paradox is the paradigm of the situation that envelops every "obligation." As Derrida shows, *ethical* obligation in Levinas is *structurally* the same as de Silentio's telling of the story of Abraham as a teleological suspension of ethics, which is the *religious*. On Derrida's rendering, God stands for the *tout autre*, the wholly other, the one who has us before we have him/her, whose secret interiority and hidden motives we do not comprehend. Isaac stands for all the other others, the ethical community at large, everybody else who *also* need us and to whom we are *also* obliged. Abraham stands for us all, for every ethical subject when *the subject is faced with a real decision*; so we have the honor of standing, allegorically, in the shoes (sandals) of the father of faith. A real decision, for Derrida, requires the *undecidability* that comes of not knowing everything that is going on, as Abraham's situation saliently illustrates, to excess. Obligation means cutting something off, *giving* oneself completely *to* the other, responding with "unlimited responsibility," in a moment of decision and madness, to the other who lays claim upon us, while *giving up* the other others, which is the spot on this grid that Isaac occupies. By reproducing the very structure of obligation, responsibility, or substitution in Levinas, the story shows that the rigorous distinctions between the ethical and the religious of which both Levinas and Kierkegaard are fond are suspect.

The story of Abraham illustrates the Lyotardian point in *Against Ethics* that "obligation happens." The Other takes me by surprise, lays claim to me, and I respond. That is so above all when the Other comes to me from on high precisely by being laid low, as the biblical leper and the lame, the widow, the orphan and the stranger, which throw me into an irrecusable accusativity, accused and responsible. The other is hungry and naked and we are called upon to feed and clothe the other.

Now it may turn out that, later on, we will find ourselves saying, "Lord, when did we see you hungry and feed you, find you naked and clothe you?" And it may turn out that the Lord will say "whenever you fed or clothed the least of mine, you fed and clothed me." It may turn out, and this is the Jewish version of the same point, likewise very beautiful, that the face of the orphan is the trace left by illeity as it withdraws from the world. The mark of the Lord is on the face of the neighbor and the stranger. Maybe, maybe not. But that at least is the religious, or one mark of it. Then the *me voici* is the response to the solicitation of God who calls to us from the face of the neighbor or the stranger.

The interesting thing, I dare say the crucial thing, is that we would not have *known* that this was the Lord. If we had, we would have fallen all over one another in our rush to lend Him a hand, and that of course that would have ruined everything! Structurally, we do not know what is going on; we do not know what has us. The essential thing is the non-knowing, the veil of ignorance. So now we can see the salutary effect of the possible confusion over the *il* in *il y a* and *illeité*, the saving factor in the dangerous bit of grammatical undecidability between he/it. For all we know—which is not much—the stars twinkle in a void and the little planet made of dust will one day fall back into the sun. For all we know, the universe will yawn and stretch its limbs and take another turn. Then all of our little obligations, truths, verities, institutions, structures, etc. (whatever inflames your heart) will be reduced to ashes, forgotten in a time beyond time, lost in a space beyond space. Without a trace. Maybe, maybe not.

The anonymous has a productive role to play. The thought, the suspicion, the anxiety, the unnerving premonition that overtakes us as we lay awake at nights, or as we wend our way down a long and empty highway, that behind it all there is nothing behind it all, nothing to prop up the beliefs and practices we most cherish, nothing that underwrites them, nothing we *know* of—that is the condition of the faith. We are not directly wired to the Infinite, or to the Secret; we have to get through one day at a time; sufficient for the day is the confusion thereof. We do the best we can to cope with the difficulty in life, the possible confusion. But that is the condition of faith, of hope, of love. Faith is most required when it all seems incredible, even as hope is really hope when everything is hopeless and we hope against hope. Love is loving what is most unlovable, the enemy, even as the test of forgiveness is to forgive the unforgivable.

I would go so far as to say that the anonymous, the Secret that there is no secret, is what keeps us *safe*. For if there were a Secret Truth, who could we trust with it? Who would not spill blood in its name? It is better that the Secret remain a secret and not be *given*. The best gift the Secret could give would be to disappear and not make a spectacle of itself. If the Secret were given, there would a terrible fight, a war to the death, over who would get to have it, administer it, interpret it, protect it, speak in its name, rule in and rule out distortions of it. There would surely be a war over which city would be its capital, which language would be the official language, and even over who would have the rights to the T-shirts. If the Secret were given, this gift would quickly turn to poison. Thus a proper wariness about having too much given, this minimalist suspicion of unlimited givenness, arises in the name of public safety, and it is not to be confused with an insistent, dogmatic, atheism. It is just good minimalism, an austere but humble quasi-phenomenology of undecidability that creeps over our decisions—and keeps them safe, i.e., keeps everybody else safe while we take the beautiful risk of a decision. Through a glass/*glas* darkly.

Undecidability is what makes decisions possible, what makes decisions responsible. Undecidability is what makes *faith* possible. Service to the neighbor is nothing more than servicing oneself, nothing more than enlightened celestial economics, if we are all convinced or have somehow learned that this beggar is the Messiah or the Lord God traveling incognito, who will certainly reward us handsomely when he comes into the kingdom. The crucial thing is that we do not know it is the Messiah or the Lord dressed in rags. The best we can do is believe it, and *even that* might interfere with the service, might inspire the service that the poor beggar is a means to celestial ends, which is why it is necessary to deny knowledge, and sometimes even to deny faith, in order to make room for (a more radical) faith. For it belongs to the structure of the Other to be *tout autre*, which means the Other is a shore on which we are not going to land, a beach we will never reach, structurally unknowable, inconceivable, beyond the reach of our *voir, avoir, savoir*, so we do not know who the Other is.

UNRAVELINGS

The wisdom of B.C., the anonymous wit who advised us to be wary of distinctions, is now visited upon us. Beyond seeing to it that we do not *know* that this is the Lord God traveling incognito, and that the best we can do is believe it, beyond making faith possible, undecidability has the further, perhaps unnerving consequence of rendering undecidable the very distinction between believers and non-believers. As Amos has the Lord God say to him: I don't care about your sacrifices, your festivals, and your songs, I care about justice, about service to the neighbor and the stranger, whoever they are, *tout autre est tout autre* (my favorite Hebrew prophets keep slipping into French, the way Heidegger's favorite Greek prophets keep slipping into German). I don't care about your doctrines—or maybe even about your "religion"—but about justice. Justice precedes religious doctrines or beliefs. Of course, justice is *also* a faith, a practical faith in service to the Other, whom I do not know, in whom I believe. Belief in justice does not require the least belief that someday the Lord will pat me on the back and tell me there are more things stored up for those that serve the neighbor than we can dream of. In fact, it even seems to bracket or suspend such eschatological promises. The much vaunted "expenditure without return" upon the neighbor or the stranger seems to require *not knowing* who the stranger or the neighbor is, whose mark he bears.

What if you serve the Lord but do *not* believe that it is the Lord you serve, if you "rightly pass for an atheist"? What if you do not believe in the Lord but you do believe in the madness of the gift to the Other? What if you believe that after we shuffle off these mortal coils the *il y a* will recall us all, the *il y a* being all in all, if you believe the universe will draw another breath and forget we were ever here?

What if the most religious thing you can do, service to the neighbor and the stranger, requires that we not think or believe *at that moment* anything religious at all, so that the religious doctrine, the thematic religious content, would actually get in the way of the religion? What if the most religious thing of all, the greatest passion of religion, its passion for the impossible, requires a moment of atheism, structurally, so that if you knew or firmly believed that this is the Messiah dressed in rags before us, that would ruin everything? What if religion can be itself only if it is a "religion without religion"? What if religion turned out to be an ankhoral operation, wandering in a desert, awash in anonymity and the *tohu wa bohu*, where the one thing we can and must do is offer hospitality to the stranger, open our home to his knock at our door? What then becomes of the distinction between religion and irreligion, belief and unbelief, believer and infidel?

What, then? Well, then, it would turn out that the minimalist is beginning to look like a maximalist, and minimalism the most effective means of being a maximalist, someone who makes an expenditure without return, who gives a gift with no expectation of a reward. Minimalism is a maximalism not of givenness but of giving, according to the incalculable logic of the gift. The gift, if there is any (*s'il y en a*), requires the *il y a*, the cloud of anonymity, the inexpungeable confusion, which lends profundity to the anonymous wit "B.C.," who warned us about all classifications (*glas*). We are better served to drop these classifications—between maximalist and minimalist, believer and non-believer in the various messianisms—and to meditate upon the profound maxim that humankind can be divided into officers, servants, and chimney sweeps.

NOTES

1. Søren Kierkegaard, *Kierkegaard's Works*, Vol. VI, *"Fear and Trembling" and "Repetition,"* trans. H. Hong and E. Hong (Princeton: Princeton University Press, 1983), p. 162.

2. This is the theme of my MRH. On the secret, see Derrida, ON. "Passions" and my PT, 289–291 et passim.

3. See W. Norris Clarke, "The Limitation of Act by Potency: Aristotelianism or Neoplatonism?" *The New Scholasticism*, 26, 2 (April, 1952): 167–194, which shows that "infinite" first became a perfection in Neoplatonism; and John Izzi, "Proximity in Distance: Levinas and Plotinus," *International Philosophical Quarterly*, 38 (1998): 5–16, which shows the Neoplatonic sources of Levinas, including the work of Levinas's teacher Victor Yankélévitch on Plotinus.

4. For the ins and outs of that debate see Dominique Janicaud et al., *Phenomenology and the "Theological Turn": The French Debate* (New York: Fordham University Press, 2000).

5. *Kierkegaard's Works*, VI, p. 200.

6. This magnificent Hebrew word is the formless confusion from God that forms the world in Gen.1:2. *Tohu* can also mean a wilderness or desert.

7. *Kierkegaard's Works*, Vol. VI, p. 7.

8. Paul Ricoeur, *Oneself as Another*, trans. Kathleen Blamey (Chicago: University of Chicago Press, 1992), p. 355.

9. See Marion, "The Saturated Phenomenon," in Janicaud, *Phenomenology and the Theological Turn.*

10. Levinas, *De Dieu qui vient à l'idée* (Paris: J. Vrin, 1992), p. 115; "God and Philosophy," in *Levinas: Basic Philosophical Writings*, eds. Robert Bernasconi et al. (Bloomington: Indiana University Press, 1996), p. 141.

11. *Summa Theologiae.* Part I, Question 3, Article 8, c.

12. John D. Caputo, AE, chapter 8, pp. 134 ff.

13. In what follows I run together Nietzsche, Levinas, *Existence and Existents*, trans. Alphonso Lingis (The Hague: Martinus Nijhoff, 1978), pp. 57–64, and Derrida, *Cinders (Feu le cendre)*, by way of a certain improvisation upon Derrida's phrase—if it is his—*il y a là cendre*. I offer not an explication of this text, which is very personal, very idiomatic, and hard to explain, even for him. I offer instead a certain extension of it, in an effort to become part of its momentum, to join in its dissemination and its play, in order to set the stage for the question of God.

14. On owning and being owned, *On Time and Being*, trans. Joan Stambaugh (New York: Harper & Row, 1972), 1–24.

15. Derrida says a feminine phantom haunts the homophone *là/la*, even as a feminine proper name (Cinderella) haunts the common noun (cinder). *Cinders*, p. 33.

16. Jacques Derrida, ON, p. 96.

17. See Nietzsche, "On the Truth and Lies in the Non-moral Sense," in *Philosophy and Truth: Selections from Nietzsche's Notebooks of the Early 1870s*, trans. Dan Breazeale (Atlantic Highlands: Humanities Press, 1979), p. 79; and Martin Heidegger, *The Principle of Reason*, trans. R. Lily (Bloomington: Indiana University Press, 1991), p. 113. I am also improvising upon Derrida, *Cinders*, p. 21.

18. Levinas, *De Dieu qui vient à l'idée*, p. 115; "God and Philosophy," in *Levinas: Basic Philosophical Writings*, p. 141.

19. For Derrida's gloss on *me voici*, see "At this very moment in this work here I am," trans. Reuben Berezdivin, in *Re-reading Levinas*, eds. Robert Bernasconi and Simon Critchley (Bloomington: Indiana University Press, 1991), pp. 17 ff.

20. Hans Urs von Balthasar, *New Elucidations*, trans. Sister Mary Theresilde Skerry (San Francisco: Ignatius Press, 1986), p. 23.

2 THE BECOMING POSSIBLE OF THE IMPOSSIBLE: AN INTERVIEW WITH JACQUES DERRIDA

MARK DOOLEY

JD–Jacques Derrida; **MD**–Mark Dooley

MD: You once remarked that Jack Caputo reads you the way you love to be read. Why is that so?

JD: I have many reasons for saying this. Firstly, he reads me the way I not only enjoy being read, but also in the way I strive to read others—that is, in a way which is generous to the extent that it tries to credit the text and the other as much as possible, not in order to incorporate, replace, or to identify with the other, but to "countersign" the text, so to speak. This involves approving and affirming the text, not complacently or dogmatically, but in and through the gesture of saying "yes" to the text.

What I love in Jack Caputo is this willingness to say "yes," as well as his willingness to countersign and to try and understand what he reads. He does this without giving up his own demanding rigor, his own culture and memory, as well as his singular relation to other texts that I don't know. So even when he is apparently reading me I learn from him because he illuminates my text with his own culture and insight. To take an example, because he knows the work of many theologians, such as Meister Eckhart, Luther, and Kierkegaard, better than I do, he is able to write his own text according to his own trajectory and his own desire without, at the same time, betraying me. So that is why I don't really consider him simply as a commentator or interpreter. It is another kind of gesture.

21

MD: He's doing something new. . . .

JD: He is doing something new that, in turn, enriches my own text and gives it a wider scope. From a narcissistic point of view, I like being read in this way. Caputo sends me back an image of me and my texts that, of course, I enjoy. I would not, however, be so pleased if *his* text was not original in a certain way, if it was not very different from mine. For example, his book *The Prayers and Tears of Jacques Derrida,* helps me to understand how deconstruction is indebted, on the one hand, to Heidegger, and, on the other hand, to the Lutheran tradition. In so doing, it helps me understand what is Christian and what is not Christian in my own text. This I could do only through Caputo, which is why he is for me a teacher in a certain way. It is very precious to be read by someone that I benefit from reading in my own turn, which is to say, that in reading him I am not simply looking at the reflection of my text in his. We write very different texts. No one will be surprised when I say that we have very different histories, very different backgrounds. It is not only a question of language and religion, but also our training is very different. Consequently, this encounter between Jack and myself is all the more surprising and, for me, a stroke of luck.

Another reason why I am so grateful for his writings is because when he reads my texts, which is especially the case throughout *Prayers and Tears*, he is the first one, and so far the *only* one, to bring the most philosophical and theoretical of my writings together with those which are most autobiographical. As some recent texts show, the two are for me sometimes indistinguishable. Jack has both the generosity and the competence to read these texts together, to pay attention to the *philosophemes*, so to speak, which are sometimes buried, sometimes embodied in an argument, as well as to the most idiomatic and singular references. He pays attention to tiny details which are very significant for me, and he is the only one who really pays attention to significant motifs, details, metonymies, or subtle tropes and connections, which, as far as I can say, go unnoticed even by my most generous readers, my most friendly readers. These are the reasons why I am so grateful.

MD: From *Radical Hermeneutics*, his first major book to deal with issues raised in your work, to *The Prayers and Tears Of Jacques Derrida*, Jack Caputo has tried to highlight an ethico-religious impulse which he sees at the heart of your ideas. How do you react to people like Jack, Richard Kearney, and others, who interpret you in this way?

JD: Don't forget that Jack Caputo speaks of religion *without* religion!

MD: I'll come to that!

JD: I am very grateful to Jack in that regard also, because he doesn't try to transform me into a pious person. He respects the fact that I may be an atheist, and of course he takes into account all the complications which this suggests. I think he is right to mention this because my relation to religion is a very complicated one, and he respects how complicated it is. Without trying to attract me back to religion, he attempts to understand what I am struggling with myself. He is capable of appreciating this because of his background and probably because of his proximity to his religious tradition. That is, he appreciates the intimate relationship there is between faith and atheism, between radical doubt and faith. And not only does he do know this in terms of discursive arguments and traditional discursive programs, but also in terms of the pathos and the effects it tends to engender. I must say that I am always so surprised by this because we are so different personally. But despite these differences, Jack has never shared certain prejudices about me or my work. For there are those who say that what I am doing is really a hidden or cryptic religious faith, or that it is just skepticism, nihilism, or atheism. He has never shared these prejudices.

MD: In fact, he has publicly defended you against such charges. He has never failed to come up with a paragraph every so often to trounce your detractors. . . .

JD: For which I am also very grateful. From the point of view of the cultural and academic wars that are going on, he is a very precious ally because he is not simply someone who takes sides with me because he is my friend, but is someone who courageously and lucidly, in situations which I imagine are not always that easy for him, engages in the problems themselves. As you know, it is not easy for me either, because there are battles all the time, there are enemies, and a lot of hatred. So I can imagine how difficult it is for him in his own social and academic *milieu*. It requires great courage of him, and that's the reason why I am so happy not only to be with him and to discuss with him, but also to attend the conferences he organizes at Villanova, a place where they are open and not reactive in the way other universities and other philosophy departments sometimes are. It is thanks to Jack that this *milieu* is open to these things. In the course of these conferences he does a wonderful job in terms of putting people together, people who come from different traditions and religious backgrounds, as well as from non-religious backgrounds, and he organizes an ongoing discussion which goes far beyond myself and my own small contribution. His conferences should, I hope, change the situation in philosophy and theology in the States and beyond.

MD: Is it a surprise that an American theologian, such as Mark C. Taylor, and an American philosopher of religion, such as Jack Caputo, have probably done more in recent years to promote your work than any other figures in the States? Are you surprised that you command such popularity amongst American theologians and professors and students of religion at this stage of your career?

JD: My answer would be a "yes" and "no" answer. I have been happily surprised in certain ways, but not so surprised in other ways. I should try to explain why I say "yes" and "no." Yes, because for someone like me who is French, a Jew, and so on, to be read and received that way by a Protestant theologian and a Catholic philosopher in the United States, is, of course, something which might seem unpredictable. In a certain way, I am still surprised by this, happily surprised. On the other hand, I think there was from the very beginning good reasons to foresee this series of events. For long before the works by Mark Taylor and Jack Caputo, which were of course very impressive developments, there were signs of interest on the part of theology. It was discreet and it had to be interpreted, but I was nevertheless attentive to it. Indeed, long before I met Mark and Jack, I had asked myself why is this so? What is there in my own texts and my own gestures which draws the attention of American theologians? I knew from the very beginning that deconstruction, in the manner in which I was trying to elaborate it as deconstruction of theology or onto-theology, could be considered as a help to, or a model for, theology and theologians. I knew, for instance, that there had been in Germany, and in other places too, a similar gesture to deconstruct a certain type of theology, a certain philosophical theology, in order to uncover or unveil, so to speak, an evangelical Christian message. I also knew that around Heidegger there had been something similar. I felt that deconstruction, from the very beginning, could be considered as a good strategic lever for theologians. On the other hand, I was aware that the deconstruction of metaphysics or onto-theology didn't simply mean attacking God, the Divine, or the Sacred.

I was aware also that in the United States, much more than in France or Europe, there was a strong and vibrant life in theology, and, consequently, that they might be interested in something which could appear both threatening and appealing at once. Due to the strong role which religion plays in the life of the United States, deconstruction could appear as an enemy and as a fascinating ally. During the very first years I was writing and publishing in the States, however, I was aware that for my detractors this was just one more "sin" of deconstruction. They would say that deconstruction's allies are theologians, and that it is a hidden form of theology and religion. Deconstruction is, on the one hand, nihilistic, relativistic, skeptical, and, on the other hand, a left wing anarchic radical movement, or, it is a hidden or cryptic religious sect. . . .

MD: You just can't win!

JD: Or one wins on all sides!

JD: This situation prevails not only in the States, but also in Europe. However, while the matrix is somewhat the same in Europe, the symptoms are nevertheless different. In the States it is more spectacular and visible.

MD: Even as early as *Glas* you seemed to be preoccupied with various "religious" themes, motifs, and problems, themes which Jack Caputo and Mark Taylor would later take up, such as the gift, speculative economies, the nature of the host and the Holy Family. Have you always had an interest in the phenomenon of religion and the religious?

JD: My interest in religion, as developed in *Glas* and elsewhere, is simply an interest in something that is in our culture, in our philosophy. From the very beginning I was interested in religion without, I must insist, having any *serious* religious context. My own family, even though we were more or less observant, had no religious culture. I knew very little of such things. Even when I was growing up as a student and a young professor, I knew in principle that I should read the Bible seriously, something which I had not done up to that point. You see, on the one hand there is this orientation towards these religious problems, but on the other hand I am really ignorant of such matters. Each time, on the occasion of seminars, I learn just like a young student. This year, because I am giving a seminar on the "Death Penalty," I had to read and reread texts in the Bible, the Old Testament, and the gospels, and, in so doing, I just happen to discover things. That is what differentiates me from Mark Taylor, Jack Caputo, you, and others. While you were trained and grew up in a religious environment and context, I did not. My situation in this regard is strange; it's a mixture of, on the one hand, incompetence, and, on the other, a terrible hunger to learn. This is just the way I work.

MD: Are you comfortable, therefore, with Jack Caputo's description of you as a Jewish Augustine from El Biar, one which he formulates on the basis of your own remarks in *Circumfession*?

JD: In a certain way, yes. *Circumfession* is both a tragic and an ironic text. I am constantly laughing in a way that is tragic throughout this text. At the same time, this mixture of tragedy, laughter, and irony is something which Jack manages to capture in a very lucid way. I always play with my religion, Judaism, in a serious way. When, for example, I say that I am the "last Jew"— meaning both the worst one and the last one—it is a play or a game, but a serious game nevertheless. Jack understood that he had to do the same with me. He understood that he had to make serious jokes. It is true that I was a young Augustinian Jew from El Biar. I could not deny this. I was born Jewish, I was circumcised, and I tried to understand what was going on with circumcision. This happened in a very specific and singular situation historically, that is, in a Jewish community in the colony of French Algeria in the thirties and forties. This is irreplaceable. Not only am I a Jew, but a Jew of this generation, of the suburb of Algiers, one who was ten years of age when the war broke out, one who was expelled from school, and one who read Saint Augustine one day and felt that he *had* to write this text, *Circumfession*. I knew, of course, for many years that I wanted to write a huge book on circumcision, and I accumulated a lot of material with that purpose in mind. Then this book was commissioned with Geoffrey Bennington, and I had to write one hundred pages approximately. But I don't remember how I decided to write the text with that particular structure, that is, with the references to Saint Augustine, the various layers, etc. At the time, as far as I can remember, I was reading Saint Augustine for other purposes. I was, for many years before I wrote *Circumfession*, fascinated by Augustine without reading him very seriously. But I cannot explain the precise chemistry which gave birth to this text. I cannot account for what happened there. The same is true of *Glas* and *The Post Card*, which, along with *Circumfession*, are the texts which are closest to me. These are the most fictional and autobiographical of my works. The three of them were written very spontaneously and artifically, in a very brief period, as if I was compelled to write them urgently. If you were to ask me what texts I would keep, I would say this kind of text.

MD: Jack Caputo has tried in his recent work to underscore the "prophetic" and "messianic" nature of deconstruction. I am interested to know if you were aware of this "prophetic" strain in your work before you thematized the idea of the undeconstructable notion of a "justice to come" in the early nineties, or was this something of a "turning" in the spirit of Heidegger?

JD: I don't think this is a turning. If I may over-simplify a little again, I would say that from the very beginning, from *The Introduction to the Origin of Geometry*, with its emphasis on the "end of history," "the telos" and so on, the project had what sounded like a prophetic tone. So the prophetic, the eschatological, or the apocalyptic tone, could be heard in my work from the very beginning. This could be shown very rigorously. At the same time, however, I was so vigilant and so anxious not to give into or accept this tone, that I multiplied the signs of irony.

Let us look at an example. In the text, "Of an Apocalyptic Tone Recently Adopted in Philosophy,"[1] I speak apocalyptically, while, at the same time, denouncing the strategy, the mystification, and all the abuses of this tone. I write as an *Aufklarer* in a certain way. There is both an apocalyptic tone and the tone of someone who denounces this, and both voices are intertwined. The theme of a multiplicity of voices within one voice is thematized in this text. So, from the very beginning, there was both this very prophetic, messianic, mystical tone, and its opposite. This is why I think that if there is an idiomatic tone in my texts, it is a mixture of the two—that is, the one who plays at being prophetic while laughing at himself. I know that my tone is prophetic, but I am not a prophet.

If I may make a confession here: I have always had the feeling, even more so of late, that my destiny as a writer and as a thinker has something prophetic about it, even though I know that I have no particular prophecy to make, nothing to foresee, nothing except catastrophe. Sometimes prophets foresee catastrophe. In fact, almost all of them foresee catastrophe! So this is a permanent *Stimmung*: I am a prophet without prophecy, a prophet without being a prophet.

Against the background of this permanent *Stimmung*, it is true to say that during the last ten years or so, something in the content of the texts—especially in the theme of the "to come," the reference to messianicity, and the reference to justice as different from the law—is more explicitly recognizable as being intrinsically or structurally prophetic, that is, pointing to what is "to come," which is not the future, in a certain way.

Is this original? There is something like that in Levinas, in Heidegger, in Nietzsche. Heidegger says somewhere that thinking is eschatological; when you think, you think the extreme, that is, the eschatological, the apocalyptical. The truth is apocalypse or, what he calls, "unveiling."

So if I wanted to address these questions in a non-improvised way, I should, of course, begin by analyzing the relationship between philosophy, thinking, poetry, and prophecy. Even if you don't say this in Heideggerian terms, you have to admit that there is no thought without the inscription of "the new." You have to think poetically in order to think something new. The difference between poetry and prophecy is difficult to determine because there is something prophetic in every poetic gesture. There is a strong relationship between poetry and prophesy. Of course, in a very dry and cold way, when, like the speech-act theoretician, you pay attention to "the promise," you will see that the promise has something prophetic in it, that the theory about the promise is a promise itself. The promise in language is in itself prophetic. Language is prophetic. You don't have to be a Messiah or to believe in one to say that the structure of language is messianic. I am simply saying, in a theoretical way, that the experience of language is messianic, and it is part of the experience of the messianic that the Messiah may come at any time. I am working on this limit between describing a prophecy and performing a prophesy without prophecy.

MD: Caputo suggests, in both the Introduction and Conclusion of *The Prayers and Tears of Jacques Derrida*, that there is an endless translatability, or an undecidable fluctuation between the passion for *"the* impossible" and the passion for God. He says that we will never be able to decide which is an example of which. How do you respond to this?

JD: If I had to react quickly, I would say that the difference between the passion for *the* impossible on the one hand, and the passion for "God" on the other, is the *name*. *"The* impossible" is not a name, it is not a proper name, it is not some*one*. "God"—I do not say divinity—is someone with a name, even if it is a nameless name like the Jewish god. It is a nameable nameless name, whereas *the* impossible is a non-name, a common name, a non-proper name. "God" is a proper nameable nameless name. *"The* impossible" is a common non-proper name, or nameless common name. Now, you cannot and you should not translate one into the other. If there is a transparent translatability "the faith" is safe, that is, it becomes a non-faith. At that point, it becomes possible to name. It becomes possible because there is some*one* whom you can name and call because you know who it is that you are calling. Not only can I not say this, but I would not and should not say this. If I were sure that it was possible for me to replace *"the* impossible" by "God," then everything would become possible. Faith would become possible, and when faith becomes simply possible it is not faith anymore. So I see a danger for faith and for something which is the abyss of faith. This danger consists in stating, or in believing in, the mere translatablity between these two things. I keep oscillating between the two.

MD: So you would concur with Caputo's contention that for you there is an endless or undecidable fluctuation between the two?

JD: Yes, absolutely. Once again, to be in undecidability does not mean simply that I don't *know*. It means, firstly, that it does not belong to the order of knowledge, and, secondly, that I don't *want* to know. I know that I should not know. If I could rely on this translatability there would be no God anymore.

Now, when the God comes, when the Messiah comes, we will see! But I cannot foresee and program this. That is why I am an atheist *in a certain way*—a faithful one! I am faithful to this sort of atheism. So I agree with Jack Caputo when he says there is this undecidability, but to say that there is such undecidability doesn't mean that the two terms are replaceable one for the other. That is the problem of God.

MD: So when you appropriate the name of God in your text, are you *using* this name or are you just *mentioning* it?

JD: Do you think I can answer such a question?! This is an interesting question about the "use-mention" distinction. If I knew if I were using or simply mentioning the name of God, the answer would be given. Most often, I am sure that I am just mentioning it. God is a name which is in use everywhere, so I am always mentioning it. When I write I am not addressing people in a church. I am just reading texts, writing fictions and philosophical treatises. So I am constantly in the situation of *mentioning*, of using by mentioning; I am always referring to what others say, what the Bible says, what Hegel says, what Heidegger says, what Jack Caputo says, what my mother says about God. So it is difficult for me to to use the word God.

Now, when and if I pray—Jack Caputo's book has to do with prayer, and I refer to my own *secret* experience of praying—I am not sure that even in that situation I would simply *name* God; you do not have to *name*, you can address someone, not knowing who this other one is, or how to name him or her. This is very interesting, but, in a certain way, it is impossible to answer such questions improvising before a tape recorder. On the other hand, you are compelled to say things that you might not say if you had more time. So what I should not say, but what I will say, is that beyond all the situations in which I probably just *mention* the name of God, as when I borrow it, read it, or analyze it in different situations, if I *use* it, or if I use something which looks or sounds like the name "God," it refers to the becoming possible of "*the* impossible"—that is, and here I come back to something which in my text I usually question or criticize, a saviour, a redeeming someone, someone who would save, not only myself, but save everything I am attached to exactly when I think nothing can be saved. So when I refer to some power, some saving power in which I don't believe in a certain way, God would mean this. The one who could finally make possible what I am sure is impossible. For me, God is precisely the one who would share my desire for the impossible, even if he doesn't respond to, or satisfy that desire. This is a dream.

I am not very happy with what I am saying here because I have a number of relations with God or divinity. I have the one I just tried to describe, but I also often think, not in a pantheistic fashion, that God is what puts in motion the question, is the fabric of existence. God is everywhere. To take the example of demythologization, once you have pushed this gesture as far as possible by psychoanalyzing or deconstructing everything in religion, you can still say God is not some*thing* else or some*one* else, that is, the product of a phantasm or a desire. God is precisely what produces this neurosis or this pathology. That is what God is.

MD: Neurosis?

JD: Once you account for religion through neurosis, then you have to account for neurosis. "God" is the name of what produces this neurosis, of what produces religion. Religion is fabulation, it is mythology. I remember once, when he was a young boy, my elder son was asked by my father: "Do you know what the Bible is?" Pierre, who was then five years old, replied "Yes, it is the mythology of the Hebrews!" So the force by which this mythology was produced is what I call "God."

Let us take the existence of "the secret," or the possibility to hide something, to spiritualize, or to interiorize. You can, of course, scientifically follow the evolution of animals and biological organisms, and you will see that a cat can hide something behind the door. He has a way of hiding. When, however, you climb up the scale you find that there are more subtle ways of hiding. Finally, we are brought to what we call consciousness—or that by virtue of which you can hide something in your head by lying. So hiding or keeping a secret is a long story of life. Nietzsche would say that "the ruse" or "the lie" is a part of life. You can also see the secret at work in Christianity, as in the case of Abraham on Mount Moriah. Christianity teaches that God can see into your soul.

Once you have reduced all this to a movement in life, to an evolution in a very flat positivistic way, you realize that this does not serve to deny the existence of God. It is God. This lie, this hiding, this transformation of life, from the most elementary forms of life to the more sophisticated forms of secrecy in religion and in the unconscious—this is God, we could call this "God". . . .

MD: Why?

JD: Because how else could you account for this progressive spiritualization which produces ultimately the idea of sharing a secret with God? Who could prevent me from calling this *unique* adventure "God," the power of God. This does not contradict the most scientific positivistic approach. Let us call life, and the ruses in life, "God." On the one hand, you can go as far as possible in the direction of this reduction, this scientific reduction. To do so is necessary. I am, from that point of view, an *Aufklarer*, in that I think we have to reexamine and question the limits between animality and humanity. We have to be as scientific and as reductive as possible. Such a reduction is not, however, incompatible with faith, divinity, and the sacred.

MD: Could you not call it, as you have in the past, *khora*, or *differance*, or anonymity? What you are describing sounds a lot less like God, and more like *khora* or *differance*. . . .

JD: Yes, but *khora* has something which *resists* historicization or revelation. *Khora* has something which is irreducible to any anthropo-theological revelation; it is something which is absolutely cold and which doesn't give anything. *Khora* would be, nevertheless, not part of the process, but that out of which, not as an origin, but on the impossible background of which, something like God, man, and animal, take shape. *Khora* is not God. Non-God is part of this experience of the sacred and divinity.

You see, I have the feeling that no name, as such, is indispensable, and especially not in my texts. That would be true for the name of God also. I could have written almost everything I wrote without the name of God, and even without the name, *differance*. Yes, I could do without it. This would not change the stakes and the content of what I am saying essentially. Of course, it would change both the strategy and the economy. *Differance*, for instance, is a way of describing, more economically, the economy itself, the principle of economy. So it is a better economy. Perhaps the word "God"—with all the precautions we have taken a moment ago—is also a metonym, or a more economic way to express something else. In using it, we are naming in the quickest and briefest way a lot of things: God is *the* impossible, the singular, what makes *the* impossible possible, the gift, forgiveness, pure hospitality. These are different names, and, at some point, I encounter the name of God at these limits. "God" is the name of the limit, the *absolute* limit, *absolute* transcendence, *absolute* immanence. Each time I write "the absolute" I think of "absolution," the moment when the debt is remitted absolutely. Each time I write "absolute," I could, of course, replace this common attribute with "God." So, I can imagine a transformation of my texts in which the words "God" and *"differance"* would simply disappear without causing any damage. This may mean either that the name "God" is useless, or because it is so powerful it can be replaced by any other. It is everywhere. It is a useless, indispensable name.

Now, given this very general axiom, why do *I* use the name "God" here and not there, more in this text than in that one, later rather than earlier, or earlier rather than later? I have no general answer for this, I have no criteria. It would be too simple to say that, for instance, I refer more frequently to God in the most recent texts. I don't know if I do. It is probable, but that is a matter of socio-historical analysis. During the last decade or so, mainly because both the scene and the way people now read me has changed, I have felt a greater freedom to use the word "God" than I did at the beginning. To good readers, my texts attest to the fact that I am not simply a dogmatic, religious person, and that when I say "God," it is said with tongue in cheek. Levinas once said to me that when you say "God" you have to add "so to speak," or, as we say in France, "allow me, if you will, to speak that way." He was complaining, with a smile of course, that the name of God is so obsolete that when you use it you have to apologize. So I know that today when I use the word "God" I don't have to apologize, because I assume that people know that when *I* use it I do so with tongue in cheek.

MD: Why do you say in *Circumfession*, that you "rightly pass for an atheist," instead of simply stating that you are an atheist?

JD: Once again, I am being ironic. Firstly, I prefer to refer to what *they* say, even if they are right in saying so, and even if they have good reasons for saying this, it is still what *they* say. So I feel free because *I* am not saying this. Even when I say that *they* have good reasons for saying this, *I* am not saying this of myself. *I* am just referring to them, to what *they* say. It is, however, not that simple. For I am more than one: I am the atheist they think I am, which is why I say that I "rightly" pass for an atheist, but I would also approve of those people who say exactly the opposite. Who is right? I don't know. I don't know whether I am or not. Sometimes it depends on the moment or the hour. It is not a matter of knowledge. I would prefer not to say who I am myself.

MD: But you are comfortable saying that you have a "religion without religion"?

JD: Yes.

MD: Caputo would say that it's a religion of justice, an openness to the other. . . .

JD: That is true. I try in more "scholarly" texts to explain what religion is or is not, and to explain the difference between faith and knowledge. So in a certain sense of "religion" I am religious. I am a very religious person, not because I pray or because I go to church or the synagogue, but in my relation to others, in my behavior as a citizen, as a father, and so on. I am obsessed with the problem of "perjury," and someone who is obsessed with the problem of perjury is someone who hates perjury, who wants to respect the other and the sacred. I have a religious temper without piety and practice.

MD: Would you say that if there is a word you privilege above others in your work it is "justice"?

JD: No. It is true that it has prevailed throughout the last eight or ten years. I felt that it was my duty, my responsibility as a professor, a writer, and a philosopher, to give *some* privilege to this word in this context for some time. I would not, however, privilege it absolutely, because even when I say that justice is not reducible to the law, and that justice is always to come, there is still something totally enigmatic for me in justice. Some day I would like to do a very patient work on the history of this concept, of this name, *dike*. So while I have a strong feeling of some necessity in this distinction between justice to come and the law, its meaning remains very obscure. I would not transform such an obscure meaning into a master name.

Furthermore, I would be very slow to suggest that mine is a novel sense of justice. It is much more complicated than that. As Nietzsche taught, you may be on the side of the weak because the weak will prevail. In other words, I may be interested in the margin, the minority, the minor text, because I suffered myself and I want to exact revenge. If so, you are not doing this simply and purely out of a sense of justice. I think I have to do what I am doing with the word "justice" in this context, and this "I have to" is something which I would not, and cannot, deny, is something that is absolutely universal. You can, of course, translate this "I have to" into a call for justice or for duty. But, as you know, I interpret duty as something which should go beyond duty, beyond debt. These are the aporias.

MD: Can you say a final word on Jack Caputo's legacy?

JD: I think that people will consider Jack Caputo's work as a major contribution because of the way he has provided a powerful interpretation, not just of my own work, but also of the texts of Meister Eckhart and Heidegger. His legacy will be the legacy of someone who has transformed the picture in the United States, in the English-speaking world, transformed the relation between religion and philosophy through a confluence of the most radical attempts of the twentieth century—Heidegger and deconstruction. He has left behind a field in which thinking, writing, and religion have a new relationship, where religion would not be enclosed in a dogmatic field of revelation, but open up to radical deconstructive questioning, open, without being threatened, to the naked minimal experience of faith. So that will provide a field in which new ways of reading and teaching will become available. While these new ways of reading and teaching will happen first within the American academy, my hope is that they will extend far beyond. My hope and prediction is that Jack Caputo's work will some day be translated into many idioms, many other idioms.

NOTES

This interview was recorded in Paris on January 15, 2000.
1. tr. J. P. Leavey, *Oxford Literary Review*, 6, no. 2 (1984), pp. 3–37.

A GAME OF JACKS:
A RESPONSE TO DERRIDA

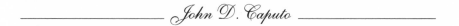

John D. Caputo

It is impossible to avoid vertigo here. I have so often written about Derrida, stretched out his texts on the analytic table and dissected them, that I am unprepared for the dizzying effects of the reversal, of the inverted world produced by Derrida discussing my texts. I never thought he would look back, talk back, get up off the table and analyze back, agree and disagree, as Mark Dooley has made him do. No one has prepared me for this, or warned me that this could happen, now in *my* fifty-ninth year. I meant to give him a gift—and I did not expect a return. I thought it was impossible. Still, if it were impossible, I should have known.

He is absolutely right that we are so completely different, with such utterly different cultures and memories—El Biar, a suburb of Algiers, and southwest Philadelphia; a Franco-Algerian Arab-Jewish atheist and a mono-cultural third generation Italian-American Catholic; an internationally famous philosophical celebrity of prodigious intelligence and—well, enough of these differences. For there is this thing about the name. Everything is different—save the name: Jackie/Jack. He actually has an American name and, what luck, it is "my" name, my "nick"-name, "Jackie" being what I was called in child-hood, now just "Jack." This is a name that neither of us ever "signs" because it seems a little silly for the printed page; it is strictly confined to use among friends and family. So just as he let "Jackie" slide into "Jacques" I had recourse to the formality by which I was addressed only in school, "used" only by the religious sisters by whom I was taught in grade school: "John" always reminds me of nuns. When someone calls me "John" it is because they do not know me well. "John D." is meant to put still more distance from "Jack."

"Jack" is the name of a felicitous congruence, of a great "stroke of luck," just as Jacques says, that spans oceans, continents, cultures, languages, liter-ary traditions, religions, who knows what else. "Jack" is a token of certain inner sympathies—of "this mixture of tragedy, laughter, and irony," of the mix of play and seriousness, laughter and tears, hope and despair, faith and doubt, propriety and impropriety, piety and impiousness, not to mention a common love of St. Augustine, to give just some examples. Or one more example from the interview, which is more than an example: ". . . one who plays at being prophetic while laughing at himself." Who said that? Did he? Or did I? And if it was I, was I speaking about him or myself? If I found that scribbled on a loose note on my desk I would not know how to reconstruct its source. That is why there were times when I was writing *Prayers and Tears* that it was quite literally true to say that "I do not know where to draw the line in this game of Jacks" or "whether it has to do with his religion or mine" (PT, xxix).

His religion—I am still reeling from the shock of that phrase—his religion without religion, according to the strange logic of the *sans*. I do not know if G. was surprised, but I will never forget the "surprise," the salutary shock of sitting on a plane one day, soaring off to another conference, reading *Circonfession* for the first time, coming to the words "my religion about which nobody understands anything," with the result, he says, that he has been "read less and less well over almost twenty years" (Circum., 154). That, I promised myself, then and there, some thirty thousand feet above the earth, up among the angels, *s'il y en a*, is the first paragraph of a new book that I therewith resolved to write. I will write a book about Derrida's religion and it will scandalize everyone, or so I hope and pray. (I had just written *Against Ethics* and was in search of new materials for scandal.) On the one hand, the secularizing deconstructors will not want to hear a word about it. The pious, on the other hand, will say—as a distinguished philosopher of religion indignantly protested to me in a session on *Prayers and Tears*—"I have nothing to learn about religion from Derrida and I will thank him not to expose his circumcision!" They will all cup their ears and cover their eyes. Still, if any one reads it, this book will set the record straight about Derrida, exposing the heart of a supposedly heartless deconstruction. It will also give me still another chance to scandalize the pious, another chance to prove my impious piety, another opportunity to needle the orthodox and to sound an alarm about fideistic violence.

Maybe also, I thought, if I can fit this in, I will speak about *my* religion. I can slip my religion in, in pockets, like the windows in *Glas*, in little asides, *apartés*, like commercial, "words from our sponsor," or what my hero Johannes Climacus called "edifying divertissements." His religion and mine, intertwined in a kind of unscientific double helix, all along trying to keep them straight. For they are very close, almost indistinguishable, yet they are mirror opposites, constituting thus a mirror game, a *mis en abîme*, a game of Jacks, that is found in the interplay between the main text and the "edifying divertissements," if these borders can be maintained at all. The game of Jacks, which differs from the game being played with G., goes like this: we each quite rightly pass for the opposite of each other, he quite rightly passing for an atheist (*je passe à just titre pour athée*), I quite rightly passing for a Catholic, *je passe à just titre pour Catholique*, and the question is, what is the difference? He told me once, on one of his visits to Villanova, a Catholic campus where he always gets a huge and warm reception, that when he was growing up the word "Catholics," *les Catholiques*, was used by Algerian Jews to mean *everybody* who was not Jewish. So you can see the extraordinary irony, the high stakes, of this game. It enters a terrain that is filled with tensions—the Vatican and the holocaust, centuries of Catholic anti-Semitism, Edith Stein, in short, the war between the Christians and the Jews. The key to the game is to see that "rightly passing for" this or that is as much as one can hope for in life; it is not a regulative ideal but a compromise forced upon us by life itself, which is a tough bargainer. Exploring the aporetic logic, of "rightly passing for," is—though I never put it that way in the book—pretty much what *Prayers and Tears* is all about.

So before Mark Dooley traveled to Paris for this interview I urged him to draw Derrida out, to get him to make one more move in the game of jacks, to ask him, among other things, *why* he said "I quite rightly pass for an atheist" (Circum., 155), instead of just saying he *is* an atheist. My whole hypothesis in *Prayers and Tears*, as I now see, turned on that. So I prodded Dooley to let the text of *Prayers and Tears* be but a pretext to wring still more circumfessions from him—about his religion, his God, his faith, his atheism—so that I could also, by applying the law of the mirror game, thereby learn more about mine. That Dooley has succeeded admirably in doing so speaks for itself in the interview, and for this we are all grateful. For there is something deeply religious about Derrida's atheism—that is what I love—even as there is something atheistic about this religion, a bond existing between them that is "without continuity and without rupture," which I also love. That is why, as he quipped about the first Villanova conference on "religion and postmodernism" (a phrase he really dislikes), his atheism plays very well in the churches.[1] It does in some churches, at least.

My hypothesis in *Prayers and Tears* is that the key to understanding deconstruction is also the key to understanding religion, viz., that *both* are brewed from a devilish mix of "faith and atheism," "radical doubt and faith," as he says to Dooley. That makes for a delicate and scandalous blend, an exquisite commingling that requires a trained palate. It is easily misunderstood—as the violence with which Derrida is denounced *both* as a nihilist and a negative theologian testifies. It allows deconstruction to seem to the faithful now like an enemy, now like an ally, even as its secular critics will say that it consorts with religious fanaticism. Deconstruction is accused of nihilism by the radically orthodox and of constituting a "cryptic religious sect" by the *Aufklärer*! No wonder I, who love scandal, love deconstruction so much! Something that would create both impressions, both illusions, at once, that is what I always dreamed of! It must be the source of my recurring dream of a Dionysian rabbi, my dream of opening a seminary that would train students in Dionysian rabbinic studies. My impudent hypothesis, my impious piety, calculated to scandalize the faithful and the secularists alike, is that deconstruction gives words to something close to the heart of religion and of faith, but it is a faith that is but a heartbeat removed from heartless, radical doubt. We require the heart to have a faith that is really faith rather than a rod with which to thrash the infidels or to bewail the decline of the middle ages. "When faith becomes simply possible," he says, then "it is not faith anymore." That is high theology! In what seminary was Derrida trained?

What he and I have in common is a faith *sans* faith, both of us loving to pose as prophets but without prophecy, as he says to Dooley. To understand this question of prophecy, he says, we would need to study "the relationship between philosophy, thinking, poetry *and prophecy.*" This a reference to Heidegger, who is also part of our common story, and it isolates exactly the innovation that he has introduced on Heidegger. For Heidegger leaves out prophecy or, when Heidegger does mention it, he does not mean the prophetic call for justice at all, which is my argument with Bill Richardson later on in this volume; it is just another word Heidegger uses for *Denken* and for waiting for his Hölderlinian gods to spread their wings and save Greco-Europe (i.e., everybody who is not Jewish, *les Catholiques*). When Heidegger gathered his two hands into one in prayer, if prayer it be, he was not praying for justice for the least among us. The messianic promise promised in and by Heidegger's *Sprache* is not "prophetic justice" but the shine of *Germania*. I wandered about in those Schwarzwaldian woods for a while, but I have since found my way out.

One irony of my relationship to Derrida is that, despite the fact that he treats Heidegger with more filial *pietas* than I do, he more than anyone else helped break the spell of Heidegger over me. I have by now had quite enough of Heidegger, even as I recognize that we will never be done with Heidegger; he is too important. But I think that what Karl Jaspers said to the De-Nazification committee is still true today: Heidegger produces an "unfree" relation with students. Heidegger holds them under a mystifying spell, which thus induces in them—and this is very ironic—an epigonal thoughtlessness. I myself think that Derrida's deepest tendencies are quite antagonistic to Heidegger, more spell-breaking and more thought-provoking, though he will doubtless disagree with me about this. To put it all too simply, I think that things in Heidegger and Derrida are organized around deeply antagonistic tropes. In Heidegger the tropes turn on home and homecoming, the economy of *Heimlichkeit* and *Un-heimlichkeit* and mystery (*Geheimnis*), the mother tongue, the fatherland, and the autochthonous. But in Derrida everything is different because everything is turned toward the immigrant, the exile, excluded, homeless, dispossessed, those deprived of fatherland and mother tongue, the disjointed and uprooted—in short, the prophetic. Derrida will criticize Heidegger about "Gathering" but he does not see this criticism through to the end out of respect for Heidegger. Then there is the utter humorlessness of Heidegger, the utter absence of laughter, which is why, though Heidegger stole some of his best lines in *Being and Time* from Kierkegaard, he never saw what Kierkegaard was doing. The fertile mixture of laughter and the prophetic in Derrida—and in Kierkegaard, a great comic master cum melancholic—that would be my regulative ideal, if I still had one. I dream of a dance between Kierkegaard and Derrida, two great comic masters, and Meister Eckhart, a master of *Leben und Lesen* the tradition says—but I would add of *Lachen*, too, of life, the letter, and laughter, a certain mystical laughter.

The strategy of *Prayers and Tears* is at work in the way the "Introduction"—"A Passion for the Impossible"—and the "Conclusion"—"A Passion for God," literally enframe the book so that everything turns on what I call the thesis of exemplarity. Tom Carlson has expounded this quite marvelously in his essay below. We would never be able to tell which is an example of which, whether God is an example of *the* impossible, as someone might think whose passion does not take the form of a confessional faith, or whether *the* impossible is an example of God, which is what St. Augustine thought, who said that whenever we love anything, however base or noble, we love God, even if we do not know that it is God whom we love. Whence the endless translatability of one name into the other, the endless substitutability and irresoluble fluctuation, the "undecidability" between them. "I keep oscillating between the two," God and *the* impossible, Derrida says to Dooley. That also produces a mutually destabilizing effect upon philosophy and religion, neither of which can stand on its own as an autonomous, exemplary discourse *into which* the other one may be translated. Deconstruction, we might say, to adapt a Lyotardian trope, is incredulity toward meta-languages.

In the course of his discussion with Dooley on this question, Derrida introduces a useful qualification on the thesis. There cannot be a "transparent translatability" made possible by the fact that "there is someone whom you can name and call because you know who it is that you are calling." There certainly cannot be a stable and *one-way* translation of the impossible into God. That would make everything possible, everything easy, and drive faith out of the element of the undecidable and *the* impossible. If "God" is a name that has become transparent and secure, if the name of God is a logical constant, if it is held firm and kept proper, if it is a properly proper name and we know exactly what we are saying, then it would be destructive—destructive even of faith itself—to translate the impossible into God. But of course everything interesting about "my God" in *Circonfession* is found in the fact that there the name of God is not the name of a stable and transparent answer but rather of a question, indeed of the most question-worthy of all, "what do I love when I love my God?"—a question Derrida says he has been asking all his life. But it is precisely there, in that loving un-knowing, not a *docta ignorantia* let us say but an *ignorantia amans*, where the name of God throws everything into question, that I would say that the name of God is most at work, glowing white-hot, endlessly disturbing the "powers that be," the powers that pretend to be present, *ousia* and *exousia*. That is why there is, as Derrida goes on to say, "absolutely" an "oscillating" between the two, which is the hypothesis of *Prayers and Tears*, an absolute passion for *the* impossible whose coming cannot be precisely determined. Who would have the authority to stop this oscillation? Where would we get the resources? Where would we be standing when we tried?

The whole power of this passion is to be a passion of unknowing. I do not deny that there is a place for passion when we know full well what we are impassioned about; that is *also* an important part of life and we will not get far without it. But in deconstruction we discover a more disturbing, more restless passion, one which takes Augustine's *inquietum est cor nostrum* very radically. That, I would say, is an even more impassioning passion that is driven precisely by the un-knowing and one that is very important for those of us with a religious tradition, who quite rightly pass for believers. In the end, as Derrida says here, there would not even be a question of ever acquiring knowledge; this passion would belong to a different order, the order of what Augustine calls, *"facere veritatem,"* not knowing the truth but doing it, where the issue is not knowledge but witness, not orthodoxy but justice, loving truly, which is truly to love God.

When Dooley asked Derrida whether he uses the name of God or just *mentions* it, Derrida winces at the question and he protests the injustice of putting a tape recorder under his nose and making him answer such things. He fears what the madness of the moment of the tape recording will elicit from him. So his first answer is cautious, that the question is unanswerable, as it is, and this *unanswerability* is that which Derrida rightly pleads goes hand in hand with the thesis of exemplarity or undecidability. All the secularizing deconstructionists are hanging off their seats on this question, praying (if they pray at all) not for undecidability but for a decisive answer, keeping their fingers crossed and hoping that he will pound on the table and insist that he only mentions the name of God, that he never uses it. But he does not say "never" but "most often." Most of the time he is just analyzing what is said about the name of God in the Bible or by the philosophers. But he goes on: the title of the book refers to the *prayers and tears* of Derrida, to "my own secret experience of praying," as he says. Now the secularizing deconstructors have begun, if not to pray, at least to sweat; they are brought, if not to their knees, at least to the edge of their seats. What, they ask themselves, will the madness of the tape recording induce Derrida to improvise next? Well then, when Derrida prays, does he not pray to God and hence use the name of God?

That provokes another question (no surprise): Is it possible to pray without knowing to whom you are praying? Indeed, that is another impossibility whose possibility comes into view in a religion without religion. In *Circonfession*, the readers do not know whom "you" refers to when Derrida confesses to "*tu*," whereas in the religion of St. Augustine *te* clearly refers to God. But would not such a prayer paradoxically constitute the most profound, the most passionate prayer of all, with all the passion of non-knowing (*la passion du non-savoir*)? Is that not good theology? When I pray, am I not also praying that there is someone to hear my prayer? Praying is the sort of thing that requires that we are already praying in order to get started. When I pray, I am also praying to be able to pray, praying that my prayer "has a prayer," has a prayer of a chance, that it is not left without a prayer. I am praying that there is something to prayer. I am praying for prayer itself, for its efficacy, and for the gift to keep on praying, just like when I pray "Lord, I believe, help thou my unbelief." Just as the unbelief is structured into the faith, so the prayer that there is someone to pray to, the prayer on behalf of prayer itself, is structured into the prayer, and that is what reduces the one who prays to tears.

Then, when he prays, what does he say? If he does not say "our father, who art in heaven," what *does* he say? I put a prayer in the mouth of one "Rabbi Augustinus Judaeus" in *Prayers and Tears*, in the 6th Edifying Divertissement (PT, 308) which turns on the *viens, oui, oui*, giving it both a slightly Jewish messianic tone and a slightly Christian tone, like the "come Lord Jesus" with which the Book of Revelation ends. That is a prayer for the coming of *the* impossible, of the Messiah, who will never show up, the coming of justice or the gift, which is *the* impossible, so it was a prayer for *the* impossible, by which something *tout autre* begins. Here, in this interview, face to face with Dooley and his devilish tape recorder, Derrida says that in his secret experience of prayer, he is praying for the coming or the "becoming possible of the impossible":

> So what I should not say, but what I will say, is that beyond all the situations in which I probably just mention the name of God, as when I borrow it, read it, or analyze it in different situations, if I use it, or if I use something which looks or sounds like the name "God," it refers to the becoming possible of *the* impossible . . .

I do not know how to improve upon that improvisation before a tape recorder. It would not be improved by turning off the tape recorder and taking more time. It is very precise and even very biblical. Consider how often the name of God is associated with the impossible in the Scriptures. When, in Luke's story, Mary receives the surprising news from the angel Gabriel that she is with child, Mary says what any virgin expectant mother might be expected to say:

how is that possible? To which Gabriel replies with angelic assurance: nothing will be impossible with God (Luke 1:26–38). This association of God and the impossible occurs frequently in the Scriptures, both Jewish and Christian. The becoming possible of the impossible is what we "mean" by God, but with this proviso on the improvisation: we must remember that we do not exactly know what we mean; we do not exactly know which is an example of which and we cannot stop the oscillation between God and *the* impossible. For the becoming possible of the impossible is *also* what Derrida means by the gift, forgiveness, hospitality, and justice.

So whenever Derrida finds himself in the same situation as the Virgin Mary, figuratively speaking of course, whenever he needs a "savior" who will "save everything I am attached to exactly when I think nothing can be saved," a "saving power" "in which I don't believe in a certain way, God would mean this. The one who could finally make possible what I am sure is impossible." That is pretty much what Mary and Gabriel mean by God, too. And if I may add myself to this unlikely list—of the angel Gabriel, the Virgin Mary, and Derrida—which is stranger than anything Borges could come up with, I gladly do so. When the situation is impossible, then, God help us, Derrida *uses* the name of God. Then, when he is dreaming of the impossible, praying and weeping, "hoping sighing dreaming," he *uses* the name of God. God forbid, the religious right wails. That devil of a tape recorder made him do it. The secularizing deconstructors complain, get that thing away from him! But, of course, as he says later on in the interview, he uses the name of God *ironically*, because he quite rightly passes for an atheist. I will come back to that shortly, because it is part of the mirror game of Jacks and it has implications for those who quite rightly pass for the faithful, for Catholics or Jews or whatever, "rightly passing for" being the most one can hope for in life.

Still, there is something in this interview for the secularizing deconstructors to seize upon, a morsel tossed to the neo-*Aufklärer* who wants to use deconstruction to drive a stake into the heart of the old God, to treat it as the final stage of the death of God. God, Derrida says, somewhat like William James in the opening lectures of *The Varieties of Religious Experience*, is what produces the religious neurosis or pathology, and so we should not hesitate to go as far as possible in the direction of a demythologizing exposé, a scientific reduction of religion, that will expose its fables, its myths, its unconscious desires, the way it is embedded in the very structure of consciousness, subjective interiority, the interior secret, etc. When Augustine prays to God, to "you" (*te*), for example, might he not just be talking to himself? Might not "God" be precisely how the inner space of the interior self is hollowed out? Might that not *be* what God is? We must undertake a psycho-pathology of religion, and in a kind of hermeneutics of suspicion, *sicut leo rugiens*, ruthlessly rooting out all the ways, and they are innumerable, that religion has devised to deceive us, to make us ill, to destroy the *joie de vivre* by way of the destructive guilt it produces, in the analysis of which Nietzsche is an unsurpassed master.

But still, when all this is done and redone, and it is always happening, and we should take it as far as we can, we will not have finished with God, or with the name of God, just because we would never be able to reach a point where we could say that this is what God *is*. Deconstruction is happy to have demythologizing critiques at its disposal, as many as possible. But the last thing that would ever happen, or that Derrida would ever permit, is that deconstruction would sink into a simple scientism, allowing itself to be identified itself with Freud's positivism and scientific reductionism. Freud's attitude to religion, which seems particularly hostile, is as good an example of the "metaphysics of presence" as one will find. Deconstruction, on the other hand, is not reduction; it does not close things down, but opens them up, keeping them in motion, unfinished, open-ended, and what is more openended than the name of God? We can never be finished with God, because we can never be finished with history, with justice, with the future. The *pathology* of the impossible is just what we must expect from the *passion* for the impossible. The lovers of the impossible are disturbed, out of joint, unhinged, while those whose sights are set on the possible remain eminently sane, in danger of becoming what Johannes Climacus calls "mediocre fellows." When religion effects a divine madness, as opposed to just making us ill, then it represents a neurosis or quasi-neurosis arising from our most profound affect, a neurosis without neurosis, without a destructive pathology, a pathology that impassions rather than debilitates. Religion is like the *mal d'archive*, which means "to burn with a passion . . . No desire, no passion, no drive, no compulsion, indeed no repetition compulsion, no '*mal de*' can arise from a person who is not already in one way or another *en mal d'archive*."[2] To suffer from the religious neurosis is to burn with a fever for the impossible, to be in a bad way over the impossible, *en mal d'impossible*, like being love-sick or like a woman in labor.

As with every pathology, the religious patient must see a doctor and tell her about his dreams, all of which have been written down in the Book. The mythology of the Hebrews, as the five-year old Pierre Derrida called them (I am not sure I believe a five year old said that), is their oneirology; their myths are their dreams, the stories of their dreams, the stories in which they dream, not simple wish-fulfillment dreams, but dreams of the impossible, where desire means the affirmation of the *tout autre*, of the coming of the *tout autre*. God is the name of what produces religion and produces these dreams and stories. When we are stretched out on the couch of deconstruction and tell the doctor our dreams, the one dream that keeps recurring, for which deconstruction can offer no single interpretation, the one for which an interpretation is both necessary and impossible, the one dream that most demands and resists interpretation, is the dream of the impossible. This dream can be "read" only in what I like to call a radical hermeneutics, which begins by confessing that we do not know who we are or what we want, for which its endless readability is a function of its unreadability. Literature will have always begun in our dreams; we are always already interpreting and we will never be done with it. We are delivered over to the archive of our dreams while the *arche* itself slips away. But the *mal d'impossible* is a neurosis that we do not want to cure, for that would ruin everything. It is an infinitely productive neurosis that produces an endless stream of prayers and tears, which fly up like sparks, like one interpretation after another, like the multiple senses of Scripture in Augustine: we want as many as possible, Augustine says, so long as all of them are true. Wittgenstein said that philosophy is the illness of which it should be the cure, but for deconstruction, the impossible is the illness that does not want to be cured. We are sick with love and we love it. The cure would be like the Messiah actually showing up, and while that would in a way solve everything, it would do so by spelling the end of history such that the cure would kill us.

So now we come to the central question, the one about the logic of *"passer à just titre,"* quite rightly passing for-an atheist. Why not simply say he *is* an atheist, Dooley (rightly) presses him? Why has he written in that wonderful passage that he "quite rightly passes for an atheist," instead of just (circum)fessing up? Rightly passing for has a certain wobbly ring about it, like the sort of answer you would give a grand jury if you were trying to *hide* something, trying to keep something *secret* from the jurors. He is an atheist, of course, if we say so, as we can rightly do. There are good reasons to say that. His interest in religion is an interest in one more cultural fact arising "I must insist, without having any serious religious context." He is, for all the world, by the usual mundane and confessional standards, an atheist. By the standards, say, of the local pastor, of the Pope or Jerry Falwell, of conservative mullahs and radical rabbis, he is an atheist, and also by the standards of his mother, too, who suspected it but was afraid to ask him for fear of what he would answer. Notice that early on in the interview with Dooley he says that he is glad that in *Prayers and Tears* I "respect the fact that [he] *may be* an atheist" (my emphasis). Always the *"peut-être"*! For Derrida could never, nor indeed could anyone who has ever drunk deeply of his deconstructive well, *be* an atheist, no more than one can *be* a theist, or a pantheist, which would break the undecidability too decisively and ruin everything (again). He is what people say he is, an atheist, but he is "more than one."[3] He is not identical with himself. Who is? But then, if no one is, then what about the faithful, *les Catholiques*, can they ever *be* the faithful, full of faith all the way down? Are the faithful not a mirror image of him? That is the question to keep on pressing, the question at stake in the game of jacks.

So it is proving not to be so simple, theism or atheism, either/or, one or the other, which is why, as he says to Dooley, he also approves of people who say the opposite of him (that he is *not* an atheist). Now he may mean me by this, but I would never simply say the opposite—of him or of me, I too being caught up in this non-identity of being more than one. How could I? No, what I have said in *Radical Hermeneutics* is "I do not know who I am or whether I believe in God or not" (RH, 331). I, who quite rightly pass for a Catholic, one of *les Catholiques, ex corde ecclesiae,* said that. That is also pretty much what Derrida says to Dooley: "Who is right? I don't know. I don't know whether I am [an atheist] or not . . . it is not a matter of knowledge. I would prefer not to say who I am myself." *Oui, oui,* I say, amen. So then what is the difference between quite rightly passing for one of the faithful and quite rightly passing for an atheist? It is getting difficult to tell the difference.

I myself would go further than Derrida does here, for there is still too much fence-sitting in putting it this way, which I was content to do in *Radical Hermeneutics*. In *Prayers and Tears* I recommend adding a supplement or two: "I do not know whether what I believe in is God or not," which sounds a little more like someone who intends to get something done, and then finally, "I do not know what I love when I love my God," which is when the passion for the impossible has really kicked in, for love is not a matter of knowledge (PT, 331–332). Derrida—and I—fall on the Augustinian side of the ledger in the old debate between love and knowledge. Unlike the intellectualists, who think that love follows upon knowledge, Augustine thought that you need to love something enough in order to understand it. Before his conversion, Augustine knew exactly what he was after; it was only after his conversion that God, whom he had been seeking without knowing it, became a question, even as he himself became a question unto himself, with the result that he wanted to know what he loved when he loved God, which is a search that cannot be undertaken outside the love. The love will help you understand what you love, and it will drive the search, but love is not a matter of understanding. It is not a matter of knowing the truth but of doing it, in spirit and in truth, whether you call it God or justice, the impossible or the Most High, in Greek or Hebrew, in Arabic or Farsi, in any of innumerable forgotten languages from times and places out of mind, or whether you are lost for words. Or lost in the desert.

Dooley is not going to turn his tape recorder off without hearing about *khora*. *Khora* is not God, or the Messiah, or justice, or democracy, or any name, proper or common, drawn from any "natural," that is, historical language. *Khora*, as Derrida uses it, is not the name of any historical entity, of a person or a thing, in a time or a place. *Khora* is a surname for *différance*, for the originary or quasi-originary, quasi-transcendental "spacing" called the play of differences, which supplies the time and the place (the possibility of spatial and temporal grids) for things in time and place, and it is given to us in a "figure" in Plato's *Timaeus*. *Khora*, like *différance*, is an economic expression—a shorthand, we would say in English—for the very economy of words, of social relations, of whatever is differentially constituted—and what is not? The very idea of a differential economy is such that it is constituted by the internal relations of its elements in which no *one* element in the economy commands the other elements. So there is no master name, not God or man, not even *khora* or *différance*, which are not even names, strictly speaking. They are simply "indicators" of the process by which names are formed. Even that is only true, as Rorty points out, the first couple of times they are used, after which they start to form into names, by virtue of repetition, that is, by virtue of the very thing Derrida is pointing out by *différance*. Then we would need *other* names, which is why Derrida says "I could do without" *différance* and nothing would change. No name is indispensable; there would always be other ways to say all this.

Then all hell breaks lose! Anything goes! Nothing is true, nothing but a play of traces, nothing but a void veiled over by a veneer of fictions. God is dead, let us dance on his grave! Everything is permitted! Not quite. Stay calm. That all sounds like the hysterical letter to the Cambridge faculty, like John Searle or William Bennett, or Allan Bloom or Gertrude Himmelfarb wringing their hands over the decline of the west, or Radical Orthodoxists wringing their hands over the decline of Neoplatonism. I will have the occasion to discuss some of these issues in more detail in my comments on some of the papers that follow (Kearney, Ayres, and Westphal), but let me say only one thing here. When, flying thirty thousand feet above the ground, I decided to write about Derrida's religion without religion, I resolved to show that the *point* of what is variously called *différance* or *khora* should now be plain for all who have the eyes to see. Put in Kierkegaardian terms, the "undecidability" of the play of traces, which implies the contingency and provisional stability of meaning, is not a form of "aestheticism," which is governed by the "rotation method," but a form of the "religious" stage, which represents its own version of leap of faith, *sans voir, sans avoir, sans savoir*. *Khora* or *différance* refer to the inescapable conditions under which all our beliefs and practices are formed, the unavoidable "necessity" to forge meaning under the conditions of *différance*, which means that there is an uncircumventable contingency attached to them, a structural reformability or deconstructibility.

That contingency, that deconstructibility, that quasi-transcendental conditionality constitutes the context, the situation (within which messianic expectation, the affirmation of justice, of the democracy to come, the name of God) are all variously forged and formed. That keeps things loose, and by keeping them loose keeps them open, and by keeping them open, keeps hope alive, as Jesse Jackson likes to sing and shout, and well he should.

Deconstruction is not nihilism but a radical affirmation of something to come, something unforeseeable, one of whose best analogues is the religious affirmation of the messianic age. But in deconstruction no one name, including the name of the Messiah, or God, or justice, can assume the role of a Master Name that arrests the play and gives us all a good night's sleep, and Derrida can do without any and all of them. They are all replaceable names because we are structured by an expectation so radical that we do not know what to expect. That is why, in another interview, when pressed on why he is attached to the word "democracy," and how he knows that the justice to come would take the form of a democracy, Derrida admits that in the phrase "democracy to come" the "to come" is more important than "democracy" (whereas Rorty thinks that democracy is the last word, despite all his talk about the contingency of our vocabularies).[4] Even the word "justice," as his answer to Dooley makes plain, has a strategic value in the politics and ethics of our times that can be easily turned inside out, since a great deal of injustice—of revenge, for example—is committed in the name of what some people call justice. Such deconstructibility and open-endedness are not nihilism, which the rash critics of this sort of thing suppose, but the very conditions of faith. Faith is really faith when faith faces the incredible, just as hope is really hope when it is hope against hope, hope in the face of despair, and love is really love when it is faced with the impossible situation of loving the unlovable, viz, the enemy. That is not nihilism, but something like Pauline religion. But it is a religion without religion, because the concrete religions are attached to the specificity and propriety of their own proper name, the name transmitted to them by their traditions, in a way that deconstruction, if there is such a thing, cannot be.

Derrida, who quite rightly passes for an atheist, uses the name of God with a sense of irony and tongue in cheek, which belong to the very structure of rightly-passing-for. That is because he is, on the one hand, judged by public and conventional standards, an atheist, but, on the other hand, being more than one and having more than one hand (unlike Heidegger), he does not give up on the name of God, on the love of God, on what goes on under that name. Derrida, who quite rightly passes for an atheist, "is" an atheist, still he does not know if he believes in God. By a symmetric and correlative operation, having to do with the other way of rightly-passing-for that is being played out in the "edifying divertissements," *which is what my mirror game of jacks is all about,* I want to say that the faithful—*les Catholiques*—by which I mean all the faithful, are those who quite rightly pass for believers in the several historical religions, those who, judged by public and conventional standards, believe in God. Accordingly, in virtue of the law of the mirror, they *too* should also confess that they are more than one, that they lack identity with themselves, and hence that they do not know if they are atheists. I am arguing that the faithful should come to respect and suspect the atheist within their breast, and that is a condition of their faith in God, just as Derrida respects and suspects the believer within his breast. The faithful need to build-in a similar sense of contingency and irony into their faith. They ought to respect their own atheism, for the faithful, too, may be atheists, and have their atheist moments; they do not know who they are, are never sure that their faith goes all the way down. They do not know what the future holds or under what name they may in the future expect the future.

If I were asked to run my local church (never fear), I would form a hospitality committee whose charge would be to recruit deconstructors into the parish. I would look for ways to admit a deconstructive effect into religion, just as Derrida admits a religious effect into deconstruction, in virtue of which believers would always understand the historical contingency of their vocabulary and the provisionality of the historical form their faith assumes. In the same way that Derrida puts his atheism in doubt and makes ironic use of the name of God, the several religious traditions must put their faith in doubt and recognize the contingency of the name to which they are absolutely attached. I want faith and atheism to become more porous, more exposed and intermingled with each other, two strands of a deconstructive double helix, all along circumfessing that you can at best *rightly pass* for one or the other. If I am thereby accused of having admitted the fox of irony into the hen house of faith, I will admit that that is true. But it is true with what I called in *Radical Hermeneutics* the "cold" truth—which is why I like what Derrida says to Dooley when he calls *khora* "cold." Cold truth is the truth you have to "face up to" or "confess," the inescapable play of differences, which is for me what constitutes the radical hermeneutical situation.

Now we come to the point of what difference it makes, what sort of difference is there between rightly passing for an atheist and rightly passing for a believer? The answer turns on answering another and obvious question: how can someone be *ironically committed*? How can someone "witness," even "unto death," how can someone be on fire with love, with the cold breath of irony breathing down their neck? Is not an "ironic witness" a form of iron wood, a square circle, like that mediocre fellow Climacus warns us against, a half-hearted lover who keeps his fingers crossed behind his back even as he takes the marriage vows? Well, let me remind everyone that we have squared the circle on the cover of *Radical Hermeneutics*, and then again on the cover of *More Radical Hermeneutics*. Why persecute square circles? Besides, the irony belongs to the order of *knowledge*, of coming up with some fixed cognitive determination or other, with something we can definitively nail down, while the witness has to do with *love*, generosity, and the gift. If we wait for the results of the search for the historical Jesus to come in, Johannes Climacus rightly thought, we will never lift a finger to bring about the kingdom of God. The name of Jesus does not belong to the order of objective historical information for Climacus, but to the order of passion, action, loving one's neighbor and loving God, "in spirit and in truth," whether it turns out that Jesus was born in Bethlehem, Nazareth, or New Jersey. Our love of God and neighbor, our hope for the coming of the messianic age, remains firm, *whatever name* we use. "Jesus" is not the "transcendental signified," the name that stills the flux of names in the epistemic order, which is a dangerous triumphalism—whence the ominous sound of *"les Catholiques"* if you happen to be Jewish—that rightly makes a lot of *other* people nervous and has sometimes cost them dearly.

To be sure, as Paul says to the Ephesians, his is a name above all other names, at the sound of which every knee shall bend, and that is true, so long as you have heard this name and recognize its sound, in short, so long as you belong to the Greco-European-Christian tradition. But that does not mean that God gave Christians some epistemic advantage that he denied to everyone one else because he prefers *les Catholiques*. So if you are Jewish or Islamic or something completely non-Western, your knee will bend at the sound of some other name, which is for you the name that is exalted above every other name, a name that would sound a little "bar-bar-ous" to non-Greco-Europeans ears. (A whole generation of younger Americans want "the Force" to be with them and are filled with fear and trembling at the very mention of the "dark side.")

Wending its way through the several religions is a religion without religion, whose faithful labor in the name of a nameless something to come, justice or the gift, the Force or something, depending on the economy in which it is deployed. Something to come, for which we pray and weep, a name for which we have no one name, in which there is an endless substitutability, according to the aporetic logic of exemplarity. A passion for God? Or for the impossible? We do not know who we are and we are always asking what we love when we love the name of God. All those who love God are born of God's name, or of *the* impossible, I am not sure, no matter what name they use, including names now long forgotten in dead languages of which we no longer retain a trace. Even if they quite rightly passed for atheists.

NOTES

1. See Catherine Malabou and Jacques Derrida, *La Contre-Allée, Voyager avec Jacques Derrida* (Paris: La Quinzaine Littéraire, 1999), p. 99.

2. *Mal d'archive: Une impression freudienne* (Paris: Galilée, 1995), p. 142; *Archive Fever: A Freudian Impression*, trans. Eric Prenowitz (Chicago: University of Chicago Press, 1995), p. 91.

3. See the delimitation of identity at the beginning of *The Other Heading: Reflections on Today's Europe*, trans. Pascale-Anne Brault and Michael Naas (Bloomington: Indiana University Press, 1992), pp. 9–11.

4. See "Politics and Friendship: An Interview with Jacques Derrida," trans. Robert Harvey, in *The Althusserian Legacy*, ed. E. Ann Kaplan and Michael Spinker (London: Verso Books, 1993), pp. 18–231.

3   REFLECTIONS ON CAPUTO'S HEIDEGGER AND AQUINAS

W. Norris Clarke, S.J.

I am indeed grateful to have been invited to make a contribution to this *Festschrift*, principally because I am truly grateful to John for creating this book. It has been at once one of the most challenging and most enlightening books I have read in my philosophical life. In choosing my topic I decided not to comment on the later chapters in the author's own history, the deconstructionist ones. I have had a modest exposure myself to postmodernism and deconstruction, but I came to the conclusion that what was going on there was far more concealing than revealing, more *lethe* than a-*letheia*, and I do not wish to descend into that somewhat murky arena again. I much prefer to dwell in sunny rather than foggy climates. What I would like to do, therefore, is to reflect on John's earlier seminal book, *Heidegger and Aquinas*, in a free-wheeling personal reflection. I do not want to get into detailed scholarly arguments about exactly how accurate is his portrayal of Heidegger—that is a whole cottage industry in itself, a maze into which it is certainly worthwhile to shed as much light as possible, but one beyond my competence and interest.

I accept—for good reasons, I think—Caputo's Heidegger. My reflections, therefore, will be avowedly on Caputo's Heidegger and indirectly, of course, on Caputo himself as personally endorsing—at least at the time, in 1982—the Heidegger story of how it is with Being and the stories he says it is telling us. My reflections, therefore, are intended to be only indirectly historical, but directly trying to come to grips with the profound philosophical problem of the authentic meaning of Being and beings—which is exactly what the author himself says is his own basic objective in his own book.

POSITIVE CONTRIBUTIONS OF THE BOOK

1. The first is Caputo's positive exposition of Thomas's own metaphysics of being in its own right, as seen from within Thomism, in Chapter 4. I find this—not his later Heideggerian interpretation of Thomas, but his own exposition in Chapter 4—amazingly accurate and insightful. (Of course he has taken some good Thomistic interpreters as guides, but he has used them well.) He has sorted out well the main themes in Thomistic metaphysics: St. Thomas's own creative existentialism, plus the knitting together of Neoplatonic participation and Aristotelian act and potency as a framework for expressing it.

2. Secondly, I think Caputo has done a masterly job of presenting in all its strength Etienne Gilson's famous interpretation of the history of Western philosophers' understanding of the meaning of being, from Plato to the present, in *Being and Some Philosophers*, which turns out to be in Gilson's eyes mostly, outside of Aquinas, a repeated overlooking of the act of existence as the core of every being and substituting essence for it in various forms of essentialism—truly a forgetfulness of being, as Heidegger himself charged. He really has Gilson right, I think, and makes him almost convincing by his very exposition. Caputo is someone who really listens to other philosophers as they speak, as he clearly does here, and for this I take off my hat to him. There are not too many who are willing to listen carefully to other philosophers, especially in the case of a philosophy they do not themselves share. There is an admirable self-discipline and asceticism here, as John well knows.

3. I think he has expounded very clearly just how Heidegger differs from St. Thomas and exactly what his fundamental criticism of Thomas is. He has put his finger right on the principal neuralgic spots, and shown clearly how all the attempts of contemporary Thomists to make a rapprochement between Thomas and Heidegger, to show that Heidegger is really saying something quite close to what Thomas is saying, are off the mark, missing the distinctive new turn of Heidegger, and that this is true not only of the later Heidegger, which is patent, but also of the earlier—the one I have the most sympathy for. This of itself is a valuable contribution, warning us against a well-intentioned but too facile concordism that can only obscure the revolution that is really going on in Heidegger and in the history of modern thought that follows the path of Heidegger. His criticism of the principal contemporary Thomists who have most sympathetically tried to carry out this rapprochement, and whom Caputo takes quite seriously (Chapter 7), covers Johannes Lotz, S.J. *Martin Heidegger und Thomas von Aquin* (1975), Bertrand Rioux, *L'Etre et la verite chez Heidegger et Saint Thomas Aquin* (1963), on truth and being in both,

John Deely, *Tradition via Heidegger: An Essay on the Meaning of Being in the Philososophy of Martin Heidegger* (1971), and Gustav Siewerth, *Das Schicksal der Metaphysik von Thomas zu Heidegger* (1959) together with Max Muller, *Existenzphilosophie im Geist-igen Leben der Gegenwart* (1964) as the most Heideggerian of all these Thomistic commentators. I think he is on target in each, insofar as they have missed or glossed over the radical differences between the two, not as regards the efficacy of their own critiques of Heidegger himself, which I think are often quite on target too.

4. In his final Chapter 8: The Mystical Element in St. Thomas' Thought: A Retrieval of Thomistic Metaphysics, Caputo makes the daring attempt to "retrieve" the hidden best, the closest to Heidegger, in St. Thomas' personal thought by appealing to his final direct mystical experience of being in God and his subsequent going into silence and refusing to do metaphysics any more—all of which John interprets as a final "overcoming of metaphysics" by going beyond the whole rational superstructure of metaphysical reasoning, and simply leaving it behind. This is similar in its general direction to Heideger's own final overcoming and deconstruction of metaphysics, although, as Caputo points out, Heidegger ends up not with a mystical experience of God but of something quite different, as we shall see. He does not point out quite as clearly, however, that St. Thomas went into silence, beyond metaphysics, because "All that I have written now seems to me like straw, compared with what I have seen," and gave up his own doing of metaphysics for something better. He never claimed that he never should have done what he did, or that well-made straw cottages, sculptures, and signposts are not helpful, even necessary along the journey, nor that he had put an end to all Western metaphysics and its usefulness for everybody else along the journey, as a propaideutic for the mystical and final heavenly vision. In fact, John kept needling me for a while after his book to follow St. Thomas's example, give up metaphysics, go into silence (i.e., shut up for a while) and get going on the road to a mystical experience! I did think about this for several moments, but then decided it is not a good idea to try to pursue a mystical experience of God on one's own initiative, but that one must wait for a call, a gracious free reaching out of God to "touch" the soul from within as a gift, and that I had not yet received such a call; on the contrary, I was receiving at present quite a different call, to actively go about constructing the best and most illuminating metaphysical expression of the world of being in its total meaning as I could, and that in fact is what I have done: I have just sent off to the University of Notre Dame Press a manuscript entitled *The One and the Many: A Contemporary Thomistic Meta-Metaphysics*. And far from frowning on me, St. Thomas himself seems to be giving me some much-appreciated help along the way.

But back to St. Thomas! I think Caputo has done a very insightful job of showing how Thomas can be drawn out from the metaphysical to the silent mystical mode through the inner dynamism of the mind itself, to move beyond the inferior mode of discursive knowledge we have to put up with on earth most of the time, towards *intellectus*, the more direct intuitive mode of knowing, which we do have intermittent flashes of even in this life, such as in the knowing of first principles, in sudden intuitive metaphysical insights emerging from or leading into streams of discursive metaphysical reasoning. For metaphysics, Thomas claims, has more moments of intellectus in it than any of the other sciences. Caputo develops this well, inspired strongly by the seminal book of Pierre Rousselot (the brilliant young Jesuit philosopher cut off in the prime of life while doing his mandated military service during World War I), entitled, *Intellectualism of St. Thomas* (1935, English translation).

But Caputo also points out quite honestly that this fulfilment of human knowledge for St. Thomas in mystical vision (perfected in the next life by the gift of the "beatific vision" from God) is a mysticism of light, where what is finally seen is God as pure Being, pure light with no darkness; this is quite different from the Heideggerian version of mysticism, if it can be called such, which is still incorrigibly the play of revealing and concealing, light and darkness, given by the *Ereignis*, the mysterious and inscrutable ultimate sender of all messages, sent through Being about Being and beings, and beyond which it is not given to us to go. This not a vision of the pure light of Being, but rather of "the end of metaphysics," waking up to the fact that the game is over, as regards metaphysics, at least, and in fact a passage more into darkness than into light. In fact, the final message of the later Heidegger as to the mysterious faceless and impersonal *Es gibt* (There is given) behind the play of Being in history is that the most appropriate image with which it can be referenced is that of Heraclitus: a child playing, playing simply because it plays, and all why's (*warum*) must be finally given up—indeed a somber and not at all person-friendly end to metaphysics!

But here Caputo, admitting that there is yet no real bridge from Thomas to Caputo, wonders if there can found something more like a bridge or closer rapprochement by turning for guidance to the most radical declared "follower" of St. Thomas, Meister Eckhart, the metaphysician turned mystic, with his daring—and highly dubious, to my mind and that of the Church—message of an ultimate darkness or formless desert of a Godhead behind and deeper even than the Trinity of Persons—an abyss which we can with the proper discipline of letting go to God (*Gelasssenheit*) enter into intermittently ourselves. Here, I think, Caputo has taken a wrong turn. The Church itself condemned—and Eckhart humbly renouced any unorthodox interpretation of this—any doctrine that tries to distinguish betwen the Trinity of Persons eternally in communion and a deeper hidden nature of God beyond this, introducing a kind of quaternity in God. The estalished and very ultimate nature of God is the Trinity itself; there is nothing beyond or deeper than that. The Father is always fully manifested in the Son and both in the Holy Spirit; there is no dark unmanifested state of the Father somehow prior to his manifestation in the Son. The Buddhists love to say that beyond any manifestation in personal communion there must ultimately be the Emptiness (*sunyatta*). That is why they love Meister Eckhart, and take him as the highest and most authentic peak and paradigm of Christian mysticism. But as the Church with its intuitive sense of what Revelation is revealing to us—and as Donald Mitchell (a convert from Buddhism to Catholicism) puts it, in his deeply illuminating book, *Christian Spirituality and Buddhist Emptiness*—the emptiness does not come from the Trinity, as the ultimate stage; rather it comes before, and the last word is the Trinity itself, Persons-in-communion, where there is indeed no shadow of difference between the Persons, but there is distinction, coming uniquely from their relations of origin, as totally self-communicating knowing-lovers. That is the magnificent message of the revelation of the true God as Trinity: the last word about the ultimate perfection of being itself is Persons-in-communion. So Caputo's attempted move from Thomas through Eckhart towards Heidegger is more obscuring than illuminating, I fear. Eckhart, if this particular teaching of his is taken literally, which the Church wisely has vetoed, is not truly the paradigm of Christian mysticism, beloved though he may be by the Buddhists, but rather something of a maverick. Some even think that what he is really doing here is not direcly reflecting on an authentic mystical experience—which he may also well have had—but rather exploring all the way to its limits a Neoplatonic metaphysical teaching of God as beyond being itself—a profoundly un-Thomistic doctrine! In fact, it has been pointed out that there are a number of other positions in Eckhart, such as on analogy, etc., that indicate that, although declaring himself (perhaps quite sincerely) to be a follower of Brother Thomas, he is really following the call of an older, and not a Christian, master. Here, for the first time, John and myself part company.

THE EARLY HEIDEGGER'S CRITIQUE OF THOMISM

Now let us turn to the other partner in this confrontation or dialogue, Heidegger, and his critique of Thomism and of all Scholasticism. His first criticism, as posed by Caputo, Heidegger's very capable and articulate spokesman, is this: Thomism and the Scholastics are too naive in their objectivistic realism of beings and our knowledge of them. Modern man is not satisfied with just knowing that something truly is. Rather, he wants to know *how* it comes to pass that we humans on the one side will come to be truthfully acquainted with being on the other, in a word, the genetic question

about how we come to know being. This question is not even raised by
Thomas or the Scholastics, but taken for granted as already presupposed,
taken care of somewhere else, or not even needing to be taken care of. They
go on directly to analyze the real world, as veridically delivered to us, in all its
objective relations of properties, causal explanations, etc. They take for
granted what we moderns want to know, incorrigibly curious and suspicious
as we are, after Descartes, about the origins of everything that appears in
consciousness, taking nothing for granted, as far as possible. In a word, what
is needed is not just an objective metaphysics of what is, and how it is related
to other real things, but a genetic phenomenological being that comes to us,
is revealed to us. This we cannot find at all in St. Thomas or in any Scholastic. They do have an objective metaphysical analysis of the process of knowing, with respect to what we do with being when it is presented to us. But
there is nothing explicit about the unnoticed first step or preamble to all subsequent analysis of the process of human knowing, namely, the shining forth
of beings to us, the self-presentation of beings to us.

There is not a little truth in this charge. Thomas and the other Scholastics take this preliminary step, before any objective analysis can take hold,
simply for granted, as already obvious, or presupposed as already done by us
as part of our ordinary common-sense knowledge before we begin philosophy proper, whose job is explanatory, not phenomenological, or descriptive.
Thus there is no critical problem, properly speaking, in Thomas or the early
Scholastics, of how to bridge the distance between subject and object, mind
and being, that modern Scholastics have been forced by their peers to take
up—although Gilson has resolutely refused to do so, since for him even to
raise the problem is already to have lost the key to its solution. The union of
subject and object, mind and being, is simply given before we can go any further, a gift to be gratefully accepted, not first suspiciously analyzed by the
very tool we are trying to certify—a futile task!

I think Heidegger is making an important point here that Thomism has
not paid enough explicit attention to: how real beings shine forth to us—
enough, that is, for modern man. I would like to suggest a partial excuse, however, for St. Thomas as a medieval thinker. They lived in a whole enveloping
atmosphere of faith, in which they saw all created beings as intentionally and
lovingly thought-created by an Infinite that is fully intelligible to all minds,
although never exhaustively intelligible by human minds because the thought-
creations of an Infinite Mind pose as images of itself. But this means that God
has deliberately made all creatures as intelligible and apt to be understood by
us, and hence for us, waiting to be fulfilled by being brought into the light of
our intellects and spoken forth truthfully, revealed or unveiled, as they are.
Thus real beings are for us. On the other hand, the same God has also made
our human minds precisely as apt, adequately equipped for knowing these

same beings, imperfectly and incompletely but truly, and in a way that also reveals their Maker. All this has been beautifully brought out by Josef Pieper in the luminous Chapter 2 of his *The Silence of St. Thomas*, in the section "Creation as the Hidden Key." As Maritain puts it beautifully too, the relation between created minds and created beings is "a nuptial relation." And God is the one who has prepared the marriage and introduced the bride (the human mind) and the groom (created reality) to each other, given the bride away, so to speak, to the groom. So when a new human knower comes on the scene in the midst of other created beings, the two have already been introduced to each other in a prearranged marriage and no further explanation is needed as to why beings should shine forth to us. This is clearly implied in the tersely stated but inexhaustibly rich metaphor Thomas uses to describe the role of being in the universe: that of light. The act of existence in each real being is "like a light" (*quoddam lumen ipsius*) within it—not pure light itself, like God, who is pure *subsistent Esse*, but "lit-up" so to speak, because they are only finite participations in the Infinite pure of their Source:

> Each and every thing is known by that which it is in act, and therefore the very actuality of a thing is like a light within it (*ipsa actualitas rei est quoddam lumen ipsius* Expositio in Librum De Causis, lect. 6, n. 68).

As much as a thing has of form and act, just so much does it have of light (Expos. in Timoth., lect. 3, n. 268). Caputo has tried to brush aside this light-aspect of actual existence as another merely objective aspect of being, unrelated to mind, but this is clearly biased, as the first text shows: the whole point of light outside of a scientific context is that it lights up beings so that they can be seen, appreciated. Thus, for Thomas, the Being of Heidegger, the shining forth of beings to us, is already built-in by God as an active potentiality in every being possessing an act of existence, the shining forth like a light made to be seen by the world of minds, ready to light itself up for those for whom it is finally made. This is the implicit background of metaphysics for Thomas and his peers.

This may be fine and satisfying enough—though a more fully explicit statement would be even better—for the medieval mind. But modern man has lost (either never known, or forgotten, or rejected) this enveloping and illuminating atmosphere of faith which medieval man had available before coming to philosophize. Hence we need today a new preamble on how beings appear and shine forth to us today. Heidegger has undertaken to do this for our day by calling attention to the primal shining forth of real beings to us, which he calls "the Being of beings." The difference between Being and beings he calls "the ontological difference"—a not entirely appropriate naming, it seems to me, given the danger of confusing it with the older meta-physical—also called "ontological"—meaning of "being." This Being of beings should in no way be confused with the essence-existence distinction in all created beings propounded by St. Thomas, as Caputo clearly shows. The latter is an objective distinction within created beings in themselves, quite independent of whether they shine forth to us or not (which we can uncover, however, by a classical metaphysical reflection on the necessary conditions of possibility of their manifesting themselves as they do to us, guided by the suf-ficient-reason principle that Heidegger later so unmindfully turns up his nose at). Heidegger's Being of beings, on the other hand, is only the shining forth of beings, which has no independent being of its own but is only the shining-forth-of-beings-to-us, the Dasein, the there-being, placed, or rather "thrown" into the midst of beings with the mission to pick up this shining forth or rev-elation of beings and speak it out truthfully. In a word, it is precisely the "between" linking beings to us. This whole kind of phenomenological analy-sis Heidegger calls an "alethiological analysis," based on the original Greek word for truth, *aletheia*, with its rich connotations of *a-lethe*—the un-con-cealing or un-veiling of something. Hence, of course, such an unveiling of beings depends on us to receive them and let them shine forth as they are.

Taken as such, in the role it is supposed to play, this interpretation of Being should in no way exclude the further metaphysical analysis through causes that sets in a broader, more ultimate horizon; just how this whole "marriage" of mind and beings comes about in the first place and why—a task that genetic phenomenology itself is incapable of doing. So the two types of analysis are complementary, not competing or mutually exclusive—although Heidegger himself has too often "overlooked" this complementar-ity, and even talked himself into denying it, as we shall see.

Now it seems to me—as a contemporary Thomist, trying to listen care-fully to the immensely rich implications of Aquinas's dynamic metaphysics of being as self-communicating, self-manifesting through action, and bring these into the light by what I call a "creative retrieval" of St. Thomas—is that in its large lines this whole alethiological analysis or genetic phenomenology of the early Heidegger can be fruitfully assimilated into the existing meta-physical perspective of Thomas as a rich complement to it—not substituted for it. It is indeed a typical perspective congenial to modern man, who always insists now, since Descartes, on seeing where the subject stands in all this and giving it a central place; yet this does not necessarily make it a relativistic or anthropomorphic outlook in the bad sense, but an explicit opening out of Thomistic metaphysics to what is already implicit in it, namely, that the human person as knower is absolutely central to the understanding of being itself. I have gathered the key texts expressing Aquinas's dynamic and intrin-sically relational understanding of being in one of my own articles that has

proved to be very revealing to many, entitled, "Action as the Self-Manifesa-
tion of Being: A Central Theme in the Thought of St. Thomas," and developed futher its application to persons as the highest expression of being, in
my *Person and Being*. Let us listen for a moment to these eloquent and too
little known texts:

1. From the very fact that something exists in act, it is active. Active
    power follows upon being in act: for anything acts in consequence of
    being in act (Sum. c. Gent. ch. 43; II, ch. 7).

2. Each and every thing abounds in the power of acting *abundat in vir-
    tute agendi*) just insofar as it exists in act. De Potentia, q. 1, a. 2).

3. It is the nature of every actuality to communicate itself insofar as it is
    possible. Hence every agent acts according as it exists in actuality. It
    follows upon the super-abundance proper to perfection as such that
    the perfection that something has can be communicated to another.
    Communication follows upon the very intelligibility [or meaning] of
    actuality (De Potentia 2, 1; Sum. c. Gent. III, 64).

4. Natural things have a natural inclination not only toward their own
    proper good, to acquire it if not possessed, and, if possessed, to rest
    therein; but also to diffuse their own goodness among others as far
    as possible. Hence we see that every agent, insofar as it exists in act
    and possesses some perfection, produces something similar to itself.
    Hence if natural things, insofar as they are perfect, communicate
    their goodness to others, much more does it pertain to the divine will
    to communicate by likeness its own goodness to others as far as pos-
    sible (Sum. Th., I, 19, 2).

5. The operation of a thing manifests both its substance [essence] and its
    existence. The operation of a thing shows forth its power, which in
    turn points to [or indicates] its essence (Sum. c. Gent. III, 79; II, 94).

6. Every substance exists for the sake of its operation. Each and every
    thing shows forth that it exists for the sake of its operation; indeed
    operation is the ultimate perfection of each thing (Sum. Th. I, 105, 3;
    Sum. c. G. III, 113).

7. The substantial forms of things, as they are in themselves unknown to
    us, shine forth to us (*innotescunt*) through their accidental properties
    [of which the primary ones are their actions] (Sum. Th. I, 77, 1 ad 7).

8. Sometimes a created intellect does not arrive at the essence of what
    it knows directly through itself (as do the angels), but only through

the mediation of what surrounds the essence, as though through doors placed around it; and this is the mode of apprehending in man, who proceeds to the knowledge of the essence of a thing from its effects and properties. Hence in this knowledge there must be a certain discursive character (Expos. in Lib. Sent. II,2,2, sol. 1).

This is an astonishingly dynamic conception of actually existing being as intrinsically oriented toward action, toward connecting up with other beings through action—and an action that is also self-manifesting, self-revealing, and self-communicative. Furthermore, the whole point of beings, of substantial natures, is precisely to pour over in such self-communicating, self-manifesting action to others, whether such action is material or spiritual in nature (e.g., toward God). The perfection and fulfilment of every real being, therefore, lies precisely in this overflowing into "operation," or self-communicating action, thus joining up with others through interaction to form a "universe," as Thomas says (from the Latin *universum*—turned toward unity). The real world, therefore, for St. Thomas, is not one of static, congealed substances, resting in their splendid isolation as simply being in themselves—the "naive Scholastic realism" that Caputo's Heidegger complains against—but a profoundly relational world of beings which express their full being only in self-manifesting interaction with each other, sharing with each other, joining together to form a unified community of existents—a "universe" where "to" necessarily means together, given the self-communicating dynamism that is woven into the very nature of every real being as existing in act. Since it is impossible to know any being as it is itself apart from, or unmanifested by, any action proceeding from it, as Thomas explicitly tells us in his text #7—which always astounds Kantians when I show it to them—then the only truly realistic realism of human knowledge, which expresses how beings are in themselves, i.e., what is really going on in the world of real (actually existing) beings, is a relational realism of beings always in self-manifesting relation to some other, and, for a human knower, always in some way in relation to me, being insofar as it manifests itself to me by its action, according to the measure and mode of my capacity to receive: "Whatever is received is received according to the mode of the receiver," as St. Thomas never tires of reminding us. Hence by the nature of our knowing process, whenever we know some real being, it is never a knowledge simply of some isolated "it," subsisting in itself apart from any relations of action, but always, at least implicitly, of a "we-being," the universe and me dialoguing together. And since I as a conscious knower am an abiding receiving set for all the real beings surrounding me, with a memory, I can gather up over time the self-manifesting actions of a constantly expanding number of actors, each distinct in how it expresses itself to me and how it expresses to me as interacting with others, and thus gradually form a unified horizon of a community of beings open to human knowledge, and then project out all that I know as situated within this universal community, the unified horizon that only I possess as thus gathered, not artificially made up by me, but gathered together by me—pretty as much as Heidegger himself has said. This is not idealism, or relativistic anthropomorphism, as some Thomists have thought; for the human person is the only conscious knower in our part of the universe that can do that as a service to the community of non-conscious beings who cannot do this for themselves. It is precisely part of my human mission to speak out the meaning of beings, to be the voice of my material universe. As many poets have said, and the Dalai Lama has put it beautifully recently, "The universe has no voice; but it needs to speak. We are the voice of the universe" (spoken at the Interfaith Meeting in Assisi). St. Thomas would add, "our God-given mission."

So far we have gotten on well with Heidegger, welcoming his genetic phenomenology—early style—into our Thomistic horizon as an enriching complement. Now the real trouble begins.

HEIDEGGER'S ATTACK ON THE CAUSAL METAPHYSICS OF AQUINAS

Here we begin to differ sharply with Caputo's Heidegger. We shall consider two main aspects of Heidegger's critique of Thomistic metaphysics. The first begins with the early Heidegger and perdures throughout all his work: that is the sharp opposition he draws between his own alethiological approach to being and the causal metaphysics of Aquinas. The first is the contemplative approach that focuses with wonder on the nature (*physis*) of beings as they blossom forth in their own being, shining forth to us. This began with the primordial wonder and openness to being of the Presocratics and was already beginning to fade away into something else with Plato and Aristotle. The causal type of metaphysics, which St. Thomas brought to perfection, focuses rather on the explanation of beings, because of their deficiency in being, by something else outside of them, their causes. This corresponds to the genius of the Latin language, as opposed to the Greek, which in turn manifests the distinctive Roman spirit, with its emphasis on efficient causality—*causa efficiens*. This is an aggressive, extraverted, activist spirit, focused on making things outside of it, explaining things by something else outside of them, in a word, the spirit of builders rather than contemplators.

Response

Whatever may be the partial truth in the contrast between the Greek and Roman psychologies as cultures, it is quite unfair and oblivious of the evidence to impose this rigidly on the Latin language, as forged into a new technical tool by Christian thinkers thirteen hundred years later, deeply influenced not only by Christian ideas of all creatures as images of God, mirroring, however imperfectly, their Source, but also by Greek Neoplatonic ideas of participation tending in a similar direction. This is particularly true with respect to the enrichment of the notion of efficient causality, which is the particular *bete noire* of Heidegger. It should be clear from the texts of Thomas cited above that when real beings act upon each other they do not merely produce something different outside of themselves; they also by this same action are self-manifesting, self-communicating, producing an image of themselves in those on which they act, according to that key axiom of Thomistic efficient causality: every effect in some way resembles its cause.

It is also the case that when the real beings of the world act upon others endowed with appropriate cognitive receiving sets, the latter are not simply changed into something other than the agent; rather, these cognitive receiving sets, both in the order of sense and of intellect, offer themselves as very sensitive receptive fields which allow the beings acting on them precisely to express in them their own self-images, to act out their own natures on the stage of consciousness provided by these receptive knowers. What Heidegger has forgotten, or overlooked, is one of the central aspects of the causal doctrine of St. Thomas, namely, that action is the self-manifestation, the self-revelation of being itself. In fact, upon closer examination it turns out that far from there being any opposition between the alethiological dimension of being—its shining forth to us—and the active dimension of efficient causality, the latter is the mediator, and the only possible one, of the very alethiological unconcealing of being itself of which Heidegger is so justly proud of emphasizing. Take the example of vision, at once the richest and most sensitive in information of all our senses, and at the same time the one where the causal dimension of its transmission to us is the most completely submerged below consciousness, and so the least open to discovery by conscious phenomenological analysis. As soon as we open our eyes the surrounding visible world immediately (apparently) appears as simply present to us, without any discernible mediation. Yet science tells us quite clearly and we could even infer this from reflecting on other experiences of light and darkness—that this apparently immediate presence is actually mediated by light rays bouncing off the surrounding physical objects, molded actively by them to carry the form and color of these objects, and then physically acting on and affecting our eyeballs to transmit the messages to our brains, where they appear almost

instantaneously as images of the outside world. But this whole causal mediation system, what we might call the delivery system of sight, has been, somewhere in the course of evolution, completely submerged with astonishing
efficiency just below consciousness, so that awareness of it will not distract us
from full attention to the rich content being conveyed from the outside
world. A simple phenomenological analysis, necessarily confined to what
appears in consciousness, cannot possibly pick up this skillfully hidden causal
delivery system. But this in no way justifies opposing the two dimensions of
the knowing experience—the alethiological unconcealment and shining forth
of being to us and the mediation of the causal delivery system of the same—
as though one excluded the other, forcing an either/or choice. The two
dimensions are complementary but absolutely inseparable. To my mind this
whole sharp, emotion-laden opposition between the two approaches, with its
obviously biased disparagement of the Thomistic causal one which runs
through all of Heidegger's career, early and late, and which also seems to
have been picked up with uncritical enthusiasm by Caputo himself, at least in
this book—is a prime example of inauthentic metaphysical thinking with
respect to the great classical tradition, but one that I have found, to my surprise, echoed over and over with similar emotional overtones, by most other
Heideggerians I have known. An illuminating example of how this attitude
can lead one to overlook clear evidence to the contrary is given when Caputo
himself, trying to co-opt Thomas to some degree for the Heidegger side
against Thomas's own usual causal approach, cites with enthusiasm a well-
known text of the latter where Thomas speaks of the wonderfully intimate
presence of God in all creatures (Sum. Theol., I, q. 8, art. 1; Caputo, p. 283).
But in a puzzling "forgetfulness," Caputo also leaves out the key sentence in
which Thomas identifies the root of this intimate presence precisely in the
act of efficient causality by which God constantly feeds in actual existence at
the very roots of every being! What Thomas explicitly joins, Heidegger and
his followers insist on splitting apart, sometimes even, as in the present case,
in the very interpretation of Thomas himself!

  This same radical opposition between the alethiological phenomenology
of Heidegger and the causal metaphysics of Thomas comes to a head and is
expressed most clearly and powerfully, with the strong undertone of feeling
characteristic of Heideggerians on this point, in Chapter 6 of Caputo's book:
"Presencing and the Act of *Esse*." A few samples (HA, 200–201):

> St. Thomas' is a metaphysics of power. . . . It conceives of being in
> terms of power, efficiency, action, force, making . . . Greek thought
> is epiphanic; Thomistic thought is causal; . . . Under the invisible
> influence of the Roman language St. Thomas translates the phe-
> nomenology of presencing into a metaphysical dynamics, a system

of limited and unlimited acts and *actualities*, of finite and infinite causes. Actualitas is the measure of *causalitas* as causalitas is the sign of *actualitas* . . . The whole conception of Being here is in terms of producing. . . . The doctrine of *esse*, arising on the horizon of creation, gives us access not to the splendor of presencing, but to a world of metaphysical production. . . . The metaphysics is basically at odds with the meditative savoring of the original sense of Being as presencing.

To me and to many other Thomists who have read this eloquent chapter, which really does capture the Heideggerian spirit in its deep antipathy to the Thomistic approach, this seems like a reading through dark glasses, or perhaps better, through a prism which lets through only a highly-selective range of light wavelengths. *Actualitas* in Thomas is not just a function of action, an efficient making of something else. It means the first act of a being, which is precisely presence, an act, not an action; the second act of the being, presupposing the first and flowing from it, is action; and one of its primary functions is precisely the being's own self-manifestation. And one of Thomas's key insights is that all self-manifestation, all shining forth of one being to another is through action, limited on the part of the receiver and most of the time on the part of the actor too, and thus both revealing and concealing. Of this causal mediation Heidegger and his followers seem blissfully or deliberately ignorant, opposing the two, which are necessarily complementary, and reluctant to admit that their phenomenological method by its very nature is incapable of taking in the causal "delivery system" that is the hidden root of every self-presencing of one being to another. It is all very well to admire the child-like wonder of the early Greeks in their openness to the splendor of being; not so, to keep presenting as a virtue their child-like unawareness of the whole causal delivery system making possible—both in its revealing and concealing—what Caputo calls "the simple splendor of presencing."

A similar incomplete reading of Thomas occurs, it seems to me, when John confronts the challenge of Aquinas's doctrine of truth (i.e., ontological truth: the intelligibility of being) as a transcendental property of every being as such, inseparable from and convertible with being itself. He interprets this as meaning that truth is not identical with being itself but something added onto it from outside, so to speak, by a relation to minds as something extrinsic to it. Being in itself says nothing about this relation, but remains locked in its pure objectivity. Admittedly, it is easy to misinterpret this technical doctrine. But in fact what Thomas takes pains to assert is that this property of intelligibility is something added on from the outside but is identical with the very being itself, built into its very nature; but in the order of our concepts it makes explicit as a distinct concept what was already implicit in our concept of being but not expressed therein. Being is thus intrinsically ordered to all spiritual minds and wills as knowable and lovable, is made for them by God, but it cannot express all this relational richness in a single concept. It is Kant who is primarily responsible for the splitting off of the transcendentals from being, holding that unity, truth, and goodness have to be imposed on being from the outside by our minds.

THE LATER HEIDEGGER'S TEACHING ON BEING

I have left very little space for this important topic, so I must be very terse here. To be frank, I (with others) consider this famous "turn" (*Kehre*) in Heidegger a philosophical disaster, not only in the order of metaphysics but of phenomenology as well. I think it implicitly undermines the whole rich aletheiological dimension of his previous thought, in addition to further downgrading the causal metaphysics of St. Thomas. Consider what has happened. The center of gravity has now shifted from Being as the shining forth of beings themselves, manifesting to us the truth of what is, to Being as taking the initiative on its own for what it will reveal and conceal about the world of beings in its succcesive "missions" (or messages "broadcast" to us humans). This process of always partial revelations is an essentially historical process, determining the different epochs of Being, since Being in itself has now become thoroughly temporalized in its own being: being and time have now been fused together. But a number of strange and oddly inconsistent consequences follow, if this new historicized view of Being is thought through:

1. It turns out that Being itself is now responsible for telling us a series of half-truths about the world of beings and its significant meanings, differing significantly with each epoch; and this not because beings themselves have not yet revealed themselves to us or we have not been ready on our part to receive their self-revelations, but due to the initiative of Being itself. Yet it is dangerous to tell people only half-truths, especially if the concealed part is important for people to know at a given period. And Being itself, it appears, is a faceless, impersonal "agent," not accountable for its actions. Furthermore, since we have memories, we can compare these varying messages, and we discover that some of these messages contradict each other over the years. Now it is true that none of these messages, as both revealing and concealing, will contain the full truth; nevertheless, what each one reveals is supposed to be a revelation of what truly is. Caputo praises St. Thomas, in that his genius was to listen carefully to what Being was revealing in his own time. But what Thomas taught about the reduction of all things to one Infinite Source transcending all time and change, the time-transcending character of

truth, etc., is quite contrary to the story also supposedly revealed by Being itself about its own self as well as the truths it reveals as radically temporal. They can't both be true. The troubling consequence now turns out to be that Being itself can no longer be taken as a trustworthy storyteller or reliable guide for humans to follow—thus undermining the whole alethiological function of Being that was Heidegger's basic contribution in the first place.

2. Who is telling the story about Being as radically temporal in its own nature—which necessarily implies, if it means anything, that this is a trans-temporal state of affairs that has prevailed throughout the whole of history? But if Being really is radically temporalized in itself, it cannot possibly tell any story about itself as trans-temporal without contradicting itself. Who then is telling this story, if not Being itself? Has some human spokesman arrogated to himself the right to put these words into the mouth of Being? By what right? Note well that this declaration about Being as temporal is by no means the result of any phenomenological description, since phenomenology can unveil only what is actually present in consciousness now, or personally remembered, not what is present throughout all of history. In a word, this is but another old-style metaphysical hypothesis projected onto very limited data, subject to critical judgment for its lack of cogent evidence.

3. Suppose one inquires further, how can any human tell what Being is actually revealing to us at any given time? Being has no press releases of its own, no statements in any given human language. Must not its messages, then, be interpreted by a spokesman? Who has the right to do this? What are his credentials, and who has the right to appoint him? Is it Heidegger? Why trust him? Why Heidegger, and not Aquinas? And who is to say that one message or epoch of Being has ended and a new one begun? All these quesions turn out to be unanswerable. It becomes clear that it is we humans, and only we, who are responsible for interpreting all "messages" purportedly sent out by Being, the mysterious faceless Storyteller has no voice of its own and yet no authorized human prophet. The dark suspicion arises that we have been had, that we are being told a series of half-truths and inconsistent stories put in the mouth of Being—which could not make up such stories itself (as radically temporal)—by some merely human figure behind the scenes, a self-authorized prophet who, exposed to the light of critical reason, turns out to be no more than another modern myth-maker!

4. When this myth is pushed all the way, as it is obscurely by the later Heidegger, it points ultimately to a mysterious, faceless, impersonal and inscrutable "figure" of an *Es gibt*—an "It gives," behind the scenes of all time and history, dispensing both Being and apparently its succession of epochal

stories: what is to be revealed and what concealed. And the most appropriate metaphor Heidegger can find to point obscurely to It is the ancient image of Heraclitus, that of a child playing (with human history of course). And if asked why it is thus playing, we are told, "It plays because it plays," and all our anguished human questions of "Why?" must be finally surrendered, in a blackout of the very radical unrestricted drive to know that constitutes us as human, as embodied spirits! But clearly this myth is not at all a message of Good News for us humans on a hope-filled journey toward ultimate self-fulfilment in communion with the Ultimate Source of our being and of all history. It is more like a regression to the ancient Greek myth of an ultimate inscrutable impersonal Fate governing all history, which it took the Greeks themselves such time and trouble to work their way out of. This is a man-made myth, with no sufficient reason supporting it. Why should we accept it as a revelation of what truly *is*?

In conclusion I must now come clean and reveal that most of the main seeds of this severe criticism of the later Heidegger have been inspired by John Caputo's own insightful and unsparingly critical earlier criticisms, or questionings, of the later Heidegger, "Time and Being in Heidegger," Modern Schoolman (1973), 325–349—one of the best things John has written, in my opinion.[1] I should also hasten to add now that all this by no means prevents me from recognizing the many profound and insightful analyses of modern culture and aspects of human living that Heidegger has put forward over the years on his own authority as critical commentator on human history. I am quite willing to accept these on his own authority, open to human criticism; what I will not accept is purported messages from some mythical independent, unreliable, impersonal, and unaccountable Story-teller called "Being," whose "messages" must all be interpreted to us by some self-authorized human prophet behind the scenes—and whose basic message to us humans is a myth that is not at all good news to boot! Why should we accept such a man-made myth as revealing what truly *is*? I prefer the simpler and non-mythical explanation of St. Thomas: Being is not an independent Storyteller on its own initiative, but simply the shining forth of all real beings to us, insofar as we are attuned to receive it, by their own power of active self-manifestation, built into their very being as the power to light up all human minds, in participation with their Infinite Source, at once the active presence of pure Subsistent Light, that lights up all else.

Thanks, John, for the stimulus and the challenge to let all this unconceal itself for me!

NOTES

1. I just learned, after writing this (courtesy of Sarah Borden, Stein specialist), that Edith Stein, a brilliant Husserl student and phenomenologist who converted to Catholicism and to Thomistic metaphysics as a necessary underpinning and corrective to Heideggerian phenomenology, has made a similar (though gentler) critique of Heidegger's temporalization of Being, in "Martin Heideggers Existentialphilosophie," Appendix zu Edith Steins Werke, (Louvain: Nauwelaerts, 1962).

NUPTIAL REALISM:
A RESPONSE TO CLARKE

John D. Caputo

Before reaching my present impudent state of mind, I was steeped in two masters, first Thomas Aquinas and then Heidegger, both very sober. My first published work attempted to articulate Heidegger—himself a sometime student of medieval thought—in terms of the medieval masters, Meister Eckhart and Thomas Aquinas. Then, in *Radical Hermeneutics*, I tried to articulate Heidegger's work in terms of Derrida, who was neither medieval nor, as I then thought, very religious. Then I finally twisted free from Heidegger and found my own voice, remembering always the sage maxim that originality consists in forgetting where you read it.

So it is with some trepidation that I "respond" to Norris Clarke, for if Thomas Aquinas was my first master, and his Latin the first experience I had of learning something in a foreign language, Norris Clarke is one of the magisterial figures in the Thomistic tradition in which I was nurtured. I have been learning from the life and writings of Norris Clarke—which span half a century!—even as I have learned from the present study by which I am immensely honored. Of course, my response will be complicated by the fact that I have not only strayed from the path of Thomism, which Norris Clarke continues to widen and deepen, but also from the path of Heidegger, so that to a certain extent I am now on *neither* side of the divide between "Heidegger and Aquinas." But if that complicates my response it does not lessen its urgency. The philosophical issues raised by Fr. Clarke are current and crucial and I can hardly plead that I am not involved in them. I have hardly washed my hands of phenomenology. In *Heidegger and Aquinas* I had seized upon Thomas's saying, reportedly made at the end of his life after a mystical experience, "Everything that I have written seems to me as straw compared to what I have seen and has been revealed to me." I used the legend as a wedge to "delimit" St. Thomas's more causal, metaphysical mode. So the question turns on what this *"non possum"* ("I am not able") means and what St. Thomas meant by straw!

Norris Clarke identifies very nicely the point of contact between phenomenology and Thomism when he speaks of a "relational realism." As I showed in *Heidegger and Aquinas*, Heidegger came to phenomenology from

Aristotelian and scholastic realism, which is why he resisted the Neokantian and idealizing tendencies of Husserl's phenomenology after the *Logical Investigations*. True, Heidegger also rejected "realism" (*Being and Time*, §44c) but only insofar as this was an epistemological position that allowed the question of the existence of the world to get off the ground, a question which, when it is posed by a being whose being is being-in-the-world, makes no sense, which is also Gilson's position on realism.[1] Aristotle said that the knower in act and the known in act are the same, and Heidegger's phenomenology situates itself there, in that precise point of contact or even identity (*idem fieri*), where knower and known make for a "nuptial unity," as Fr. Clarke so happily says. Indeed, phenomenology does not even need to situate itself there because that is where we always and already *are*, and it would always be an abstraction to extract ourselves from that point of contact. It would always be something of a construction—not false or illusory, but an abstract construction—to take leave of this point of union (to arrange a "temporary separation," to stay with the nuptial metaphor) where knower and known are joined, and to speak of how it is with them "in themselves," outside this interactive field that Norris Clarke explains so insightfully. What phenomenology has found together, let no epistemology put asunder. Phenomenology is the attempt to settle into the primal nuptial setting and to give the lovers words. Phenomenology's insights then are never far removed from Aristotle and Thomas—who, it should not be forgotten, get five of the first seven footnotes in *Being and Time*.

But these insights are developed in St. Thomas "objectivistically," "from without," like a doctor (a very angelic one), giving an analytic account of being, the soul, and its faculties, and using principles like act and potency. Phenomenology, on the other hand, works "from within," in terms of the lived structure of experience, feeling about for the texture of our encounter, rather more like Augustine's deeply personal and poetic prose in the *Confessions*, which sounds more like a patient than a doctor, more like prayers and tears than Thomas's cool, majestic *scientia*.

So I agree that the deep divide between phenomenology and St. Thomas is just where Norris Clarke says it is—over the status of causal accounts. Phenomenology is a descriptive undertaking that resists engaging in speculative, deductive, and causal reasoning, which it regards not as false but as second order and "founded" upon the "sense" of experience. Even God enters into phenomenology in terms of experience—whence the importance of the work of Jean-Luc Marion today and his notion of the "saturation" of intentionality by an "unconditional givenness." Concerning God as the *prima causa*, Heidegger and the phenomenologists concur with St. Paul, who scolded the Corinthians about the vanity of their speculations, which is a deeply biblical complaint that continues through Pascal and Kierkegaard right on up to our own day. Arguing that the very self-revelation of being described by Heideggerian phenomenology requires a causal back up, Norris Clarke offers what a phenomenologist would consider a baldly "reifying" account of knowing in terms of the causal influences that the thing known has upon the knowing thing, so that knowledge in this relational realism comes down to a relation between things.

The nuptial embrace, it turns out, is the issue of an arranged marriage, where the parent/causes are behind everything and the romance is over. For phenomenology causality is precisely a relation between things (*res, quod*), while the whole idea behind "intentionality," which is not a *quod* but a *quo*, is to seize upon the unique relationship between knower and known, as the nuptial scene in which things emerge into presence *for* knowledge. Causality then is one of the ways that knowers have of connecting "things," but knowing itself is something simpler or older than causality. To take the example of sight that Fr. Clarke picks out, Husserl would say that perceptual life is not "caused" but "motivated" to constitute things into unities of visual meaning by the harmonious flow of appearances. The phenomenological account of "constitution" clings close to how visual things take shape for us, an account that precedes and gives meaning to the various causal accounts we may subsequently offer of vision. Accounts in terms of light waves and synapses or impressed species, or whatever variety of "causal delivery system" you favor, would always have the status of secondary causal explanations and they would always presume that we have already settled into and experienced by a kind of phenomenological *nous* or *Anschauung* the very "meaning" of color, perception, remembering, reasoning, etc. of which we now seek a causal rendering. So it is perfectly true, as Fr. Clarke argues, that phenomenology is *not inconsistent* with a subsequent causal account. But rather than forming a true and "absolutely inseparable" "complementarity," as he argues, I would say that the phenomenological account keeps its nose close to the surface of the lived experience and settles in as close as possible to the texture and phenomenality of things, heeding the words the nuptial lovers whisper in each other's ear, and practicing an ascesis, an *epoche*, which resists intruding on this scene with an explanation. But the causal account will always have a *separable*, secondary, explanatory, and contingent character, constituting a kind of *commentarium*, a second word, which fluctuates with the state of scientific knowledge. That is why hardly anybody makes use of "impressed species" in their "causal delivery systems" nowadays, preferring instead to employ more sophisticated state of the art, neuro-physiological explanations—while Augustine's prayers and tears ring as true as ever.

As for Heidegger's famous "*Kehre*" after *Being and Time*, Norris Clarke considers that a "disaster" and the later Heidegger a "myth-maker." I have tried to show in some detail in *Demythologizing Heidegger* just what the "disaster" was that engulfed the later Heidegger, to spell out just what the "myth of Being" was that he had up his sleeve, and to explain how this myth tended to undo his best insights—into *Gelassenheit* and the blossoming of the rose "without why." (It is for that, that the other sometime Fordham Jesuit contributing to this volume has made me pay!) Norris Clarke and I will certainly not want to abandon the later Heidegger when he says that in the mystics we find not confusion but the most extreme depth and sharpness of thought. *Heidegger and Aquinas* belongs to my own "early" work, before my own *Kehre*, before I reached a much more severe judgment of Heidegger. It was good detective work on the part of Norris Clarke to have found an article that I wrote back in 1973 when my concerns about Heidegger first began to surface. He is certainly right to criticize a certain unguarded enthusiasm about Heidegger in this book and I am grateful for his analysis, which, here as elsewhere, now as always, is so clearly and deftly executed.

NOTE

1. Etienne Gilson, *Thomistic Realism and the Critique of Knowledge*, trans. Mark Wauck (San Francisco: Ignatius Press, 1986).

4 HEIDEGGER'S FALL

_____ WILLIAM J. RICHARDSON, S.J.

"Lethe is Schwarzwald black, not Buchenwald black."

With this succinct remark, a widely-respected philosopher (and good friend of many years) John Caputo, crystallizes his reaction[1] to an attempt I had made[2] to discuss the tragic debacle of Heidegger's involvement with Nazism in terms of Heidegger's own conception of the negativity of truth: *aletheia*. Thereby hangs a tale.

The symposium that occasioned my proposal was entitled "Heidegger and Politics," and I have taken as a springboard for the essay an earlier reflection of John Sallis, commenting on Heidegger's then recently-published *Beiträge zur Philosphie (Vom Ereignis)*: "What if Truth were monstrous? . . . What if there were within the very essence of truth something essentially other than truth, a divergence from nature within nature, true monstrosity?"[3] Seizing on the theme of negativity of truth as suggested by Sallis, I stressed the concealment (*lethe*) quality that remains interior to the process of non-concealment (*aletheia*) as Heidegger conceives truth, focusing particularly on a secondary modality of that negativity (after "mystery"), namely "errancy" (*Irre*):

> Errancy is the primordial counter-essence to the primordial essence of truth. Errancy opens itself up as the open region for every opposite to essential truth. . . . Every mode of comportment has its mode of erring. Error extends from the most ordinary wasting of time, making a mistake, and miscalculating, to going astray and venturing too far in one's essential attitudes and decisions. The errancy in which any given segment of historical humanity must proceed for its course to be errant is essentially connected with the openness of *Dasein*. By leading him astray, errancy dominates man through and through.[4]

73

I tried to argue that Heidegger's philosophical experience (the Being-ques-tion, eventually Being as *aletheia*) did not lead to his capitulation to Nazism but did not prevent it either. It may be that he himself became victim of the errancy of which he wrote. Truth that tolerated this would be monstrous indeed. To situate this thesis in a literary context, I wove it into the story line of Joseph Conrad's *Heart of Darkness*,[5] where I suggested that Kurtz sym-bolized the victim of this darkness that Heidegger calls "errancy."

Caputo would have none of it. *Lethe*, the concealing of concealment that distorts truth and seduces a human being into forgetting its conceal-ment, may indeed lie at the heart of *aletheia*, but for Caputo that is not where Kurtz's problem lay. The darkness was not in Kurt's head ("his intelli-gence was perfectly clear," says Marlow) but in his heart, in the hardness that had over taken it. This, then, was not a matter of truth, whether as con-cealment or unconcealment, but of something "otherwise than truth." "It had to do with faces, with his utter nullification of the face of the other." Hence, for Kurtz "there was no Other, no Law of the Other." He was a sim-ple murderer, with all the in-vunerability, in-sensitivity, im-passivity that this implies *vis-à-vis* the "niggers" that he "decapitated." "The darkness of *lethe* is not old enough, not ancient and anarchical enough, to envelop murder." "*Lethe* belongs to the economy of shining temples and emergent *physis*, . . . of the silent fall of snowflakes outside the cabin and tinkling cowbells . . . "But this is "Schwarzwald black." "Buchenwald black" is the black of mur-der; its interdiction derives from an "immemorial past" whose signification signifies over and beyond the manifestation of being, that is otherwise than being—*lethe* and all.

This criticism that Caputo makes of my position is trenchant and com-pelling. It demands a response, whether by way of defense or of withdrawl. I shall indeed attempt to defend it, if only as a form of discernment in order to decide whether or not to abandon it completely.

Clearly Caputo is condensing into a few pages here the fundamental the-sis of his full length critique of Heidegger as articulated in the imposing work of recent vintage, *Demythologizing Heidegger* (1993). There he argues that Heidegger's original posing of the Being-question ("what is the meaning of Being in its differentiation from beings, " i.e., question about the ontological difference") as formulated in *Sein und Zeit* (1927) was sabotaged in the 1930s by what Caputo calls a "mythologizing" of Being under the aegis of Greek thought that allowed Heidegger's seduction into the orbit of National Social-ism. Accordingly, multiple turnings notwithstanding, Heidegger never recov-ered from this fall. Caputo's own project in the book is to demythologize that Greco-German myth by retracing very critically the evolution of Heidegger's thinking of being from beginning to end. He insists that the initial experience of being must be not simply Greek but "jewgreek" (Joyce's word), i.e., also non-

Greek, or, more specifically (in the Judaeo-Christian West, at least), also biblical, with its special regard for the poor, the victim, the disenfranchised. In a
rousing final chapter Caputo formulates his own approach to these problems in
terms of what he calls "Hyperbolic Justice," an intriguing synthesis of his own
reflection as filtered through Emmanuel Levinas and Jacques Derrida.

In the midst of all this, Caputo takes time to address my proposal, which
he first summarizes ("*Irre* is not evil but it is the condition of possibility of
evil") and then observes:

> . . . That sounds to me like a conflation of *Irre* with original sin.
> But *Irre* is something very Heideggerian-Greek, and it has nothing to
> do with sin or evil, not even as a condition of possibility. It is a myth
> of a different sort than the myth of original sin. For *Irre* means the
> concealment, the forgetfulness that being is withdrawn, and that is a
> strictly phainesthetic matter. It has to do with the look that being has
> . . . not with human justice or mercy or love. If mortals slaughtered
> one another under the sky and on the earth, in the name of the
> advent of the gods, and all this with handmade swords, then the
> thought of Being could but smile approvingly. . . . *Irre* does not lead
> us into evil, but into going along with the occlusion of being as *physis*
> and *logos*, and that has at least an indirect and at worst a downright
> inverse relationship to history of ethico-political emancipation.[6]

Since this is a fuller statement of Caputo's critique, I shall take it as the context
for this reflection and polarize my remarks around three separate foci: A) *a
mise au point* of the issue that divides us; B) a clarification of the notion
of "original sin" that Caputo introduces into the debate; C) a return to the
question of the possible relation between Heidegger's thought and original sin.

ISSUES AND NON-ISSUES

What is not at stake here is the debacle of Heidegger's personal history as we
know it, particularly with regard to his association with Nazism. At issue only
is the nature of the thought that could permit it, and the possible usefulness of
this thought for the Christian thinker. Nor is there any way to gainsay the fact
that his thought was not concerned with the poor, the widow, and the orphan,
any more than it was concerned, as such, with the problem of God. This simply was not his gift. But how many of the great thinkers of history (including
Thomas Aquinas) could pass the test of concern-for-the-poor-the-widow-and-
the-orphan as a criterion of their philosophical value? The issue is whether
their thought excludes the possibility of such concern, i.e., concern for every

human individual precisely in terms of their humanity. In the present case, the question is whether Heidegger's fundamental conception of human being (*Dasein, Mitsein, Mitdasein,* care, solicitude, etc.,—in short, his entire anti-metaphysical humanism) excludes the possibility of developing an anthropology that accommodates the dignity of the individual as such, or at least some kind of "ethico-political emancipation." Until that is done, the question of the intrinsic value of Heidegger's thought (not of his personal history), hence of its eventual utility for Christians, must, I think, remain open. Finally, not at issue here is Caputo's full-scale assault on Heidegger in *Demythologizing Heidegger,* which serves as context for his criticism, except to say that I agree wholeheartedly with the reproach that Heidegger failed to take account of the jewgreek experience. The rest must be left for another venue.

1. What is at issue is the matter of "phainesthetics." This term is Caputo's confection from the Greek word *phainesthai* ("to show oneself," "to appear") and characterizes one of the fundamental ways that Heidegger experiences the meaning of Being among the Greeks, particularly in the form of *physis*. Thus, from the very beginning of his way Heidegger conceived of Phenomenology as the logos of *phainesthai*, and the conception of truth (*aletheia*) as unconcealment is but another modality of the same experience. All this is beyond dispute. But when Caputo speaks of "a phainesthetic matter," the term becomes pejorative and refers to the alleged "essentialist" use of *phainesthai* in Heidegger's later period as the shining forth of earth and sky, gods and mortals, etc., that is, in Caputo's reading, an indifference toward the suffering of real flesh and blood. As for an "essentialist" reading of the later Heidegger, this is one of Levinas's critiques that I consider a gross distortion but cannot deal with properly here.[7] The implication of "phainesthetics," however, is that the conception of Being as *phainesthai* is too intellectualist to include the wealth of the genuinely jewgreek experience of the Is of what-is, and this I deny. If being as *phainesthai* is a characteristically Greek experience, it is not exclusively so. Surely the prominence of the "light" (and, of course, darkness) motif in the bible needs no argument here: e.g., "let there be light" (Gen. 1:3), "by your light we see light" (Ps. 36:9), "I am the light of the world" (John 8:12). And about the metaphysics of "light" throughout the middle ages Caputo surely needs no reminder from me.[8] The experience of Being as *phainesthai*, then, is far more profound than the word "phainesthetics" would suggest.

2. *Irre* ("errancy"), furthermore, is not quite the "look that Being has." For "look" here I take to translate *Ansehen/Ansicht*,[9] i.e., the way

Being "looks," the visage it offers when it reveals itself in beings as beings. Being, then, withdraws behind the "look," and it is this withdrawal/concealment/negation that is in question when Heidegger talks about mystery and errancy. In compounding this concealment and seducing us into forgetting it, errancy is precisely what has not to do with the look of Being but the distorted self-presentation of beings. It drives *Dasien* hither and thither, dominating it through and through so that *Dasein* misperceives the look of Being in beings and falls victim to this distortion.

3. In presenting errancy as a "look," Caputo suggests that this "look" appears to a *Dasein* that is, as it were, at a distance from Being, looking at being as a subject looks at an object. This impression is confirmed by the analogy soon introduced: "If mortals slaughtered one another under the sky and on the earth, in the name of the advent of the gods, and all this with handmade swords, then the thought of being could smile approvingly. Clearly, Being here for Caputo is an object and "thought" the thinking subject, suggesting that being is to be understood as intelligibility, and *Dasein* as intelligence. But this is a travesty. Whatever it is, *Dasien* is not a subject: it is transcendence; it is Being-in-the-World; it is the There of Being among beings, in which and through which the revelation of beings comes-to-pass; eventually it becomes the clearing where the light of Being is diffused among beings; as such, in the later period, *Dasein* functions as the thinking of Being, where "of" is to be understood as both subjective and objective genitive.[10] All this adds up to saying that if *lethe* is something much more profound, more hidden, more pernicious than simply the "look of Being," then it penetrates *Dasein* to a correlative depth as well. The question is: what does that really mean in the concrete?

What it really means in the concrete is that *Dasein* is fallen, but fallenness is only one modality of *Dasein's* existential structure as being-in-the-world, structure whose proper function is to disclose the world. Other existential components of this movement include the power to illumine projectively (understanding), the power to disclose affectively (state-of-mind), and the power to bring the process to articulation through language (discourse)—all equally original—all unified in the process of care. These existential/ontological structures are, of course, instantiated on the ontic/existential level, and it is through the analysis of the ontic appearances that the ontological structures are discerned. The whole task of *Being and Time* was to probe the ultimate ground of that unity (time) in order to gain access to the larger question—the first and, ultimately, only question that

really interested him—the question of the ontological difference. All the
analyses were selected in function of that unique concern. But Caputo will
not have it. He will not let Heidegger be!

Heidegger simply should have had more "heart" (*kardia*), which is "not
so much an insight as a giving into the needs of the other,"[11] (331) "a sensitivity to afflicted flesh."[12] Kurtz's problem, after all, lay not in his intelligence
but in the darkness/hardness of his heart. But: "In Heidegger's 'everyday
world,' there are no beggars, lepers, hospitals, homeless people, sickness,
children, meals, animals . . . Yet the 'kingdom of God' (*basileia theou*) is a
kingdom of flesh, of banquets and of hunger, of cripples made whole, dead
men made to live again, a realm of bodies in pleasure and pain."[13]

But these are ontic phenomena, just as idolatry, blasphemy, filial impiety,
murder, adultery—in short, all the prohibitions of the Law of Moses—are
clearly ontic phenomena. Their sheer onticity is the focus of Caputo's concern,
not of Heidegger's. As a matter of fact, Caputo gives no thought to the possibility that ontic matters of this kind *might*, indeed, be thought through in a
Heideggerian perspective if some phenomonologist as astute as himself
explored the implications, say, of solicitude (*Fürsorge*: "care for the other").
Clearly, however, Heidegger himself, having analyzed the ontological structures that underlie such phenomena, heard no call to develop a regional ontology (anthropology)—Mosaic, Christian or otherwise—to deal with them. His
unique concern was the difference between such phenomena and the Being
that lets them be what they are: the analyses of *Being and Time* were but a
step along the way. To refuse him the ontological difference as his problematic
of privilege, the way Caputo seems to do,[14] is like depriving Plato of his ideas
and then bludgeoning him for not being Aristotle. Single-minded preoccupation with the ontological difference, even when grossly insensitive and tasteless (e.g. "Agriculture . . . atom bombs.") does not make Heidegger guilty, like
Kurtz, of ontic "murder." Language of that kind Caputo may find rhetorically
satisfying, but, philosophically speaking, it is not just misleading, it is meaningless. The bottom line is that Heidegger was not what he was not: if that, in
itself, be a crime, "who will 'scape whipping?'"

More to the point, how is errancy to be understood? My argument for seeing in errancy the foundation in Being itself for what the early Heidegger
described as the fallenness of *Dasein* (its There) in *Being and Time* has already
been made.[15] A comparison of the language describing errancy (*sich-vertun*,
sich-versehen, *sich-verechen*, *sich-verlaufen*) in "On the Essence of Truth"[16]
and *Dasein's* untruth (*verschleissen*, *verbergen*, *verdecken*, *verstellend*,)
grounding its fallenness in *Being and Time*,[17] makes clear that each is the correlate of the other. The common denominator between them is manifest in the
use of the inseparable prefix *ver-*, suggesting: removal, loss, untoward action,
using up, change, reversal—in other words, negativity of one form or another.

One form of this negativity is *Dasein's* fallenness, part and parcel of its facticity: "Because *Dasein* is essentially falling, its state of being is such that it is in 'untruth.' . . . To be closed off and covered up belongs to *Dasein's* facticity."[18]

This theme of negativity in Being returns again and again in Heidegger's thought over the years, but it occurs with special force in *Beiträge zur Philosophie (Vom Ereignis)*, a relatively recent publication (1989) of a text that dates from the years 1936–1938, while "On the Essence of Truth" was still gestating.[19] There he speaks of a "not" as indigenous to the emerging of the ontological difference itself (*Seyn: beon*), "and thus to the event that appropriates (*Ereignis*)."[20] What are the consequences of this for life as we know it? Heidegger speaks of *Dasein* (Being-there) as also *Weg-sein* (Being-away), and the latter takes two forms: the first is the endemic structural tendency of *Dasein* to fall away from itself, so that "Being-away is the more primordial name for the inauthenticity of *Dasein*"[21]; the second is Being-unto-death, the ultimate modality of *Dasein's* Being-away from itself.[22]

One should recall, too, a little known comment reported by Medard Boss as having been made during one of Heidegger's visits to Zurich in order to offer seminars to the psychiatrists of Switzerland. Speaking of what psychotherapists call "projection" (that phenomenon by which the patient attributes to another feelings [usually negative, e.g., anger, hate] that one has oneself), Heidegger observed:

> Psychologically, we say, someone projects an evil side of himself onto an enemy, consequently hates him as the evil one and thus avoids seeing the evil in himself. . . . But that does not have to be, by any means, a projection. For in ascribing evil to another, one is merely warding off the recognition that I too belong to evil [*zum Böse gehöre*], like all men . . . To each *Dasein*, also, always already belongs the power to be evil (*Böse-sein-können*) in relation to what it encounters, whether this power be genuinely brought to fulfilment or not. . . . Evil is not first of all there as an abstract possibility that then somehow or other is "actualised," but the power-to-be-evil belongs to my power-to-be, that is, already in quite original fashion. It is [always] already coming-to-presence.[23]

Power-to-be-evil, then, is for Heidegger part of *Dasein's* existential structure. If this, too, is another mode of the negativity of *Dasein* that is grounded in the negativity of *aletheia* (one mode of which is *lethe*), surely we are dealing with something more serious than simply a "look that Being has." Be that as it may, this leads me to question Caputo's claim that errancy "has nothing to do with sin or evil, not even as a possibility." That is the heart of the matter.

ORIGINAL SIN AND HUMAN FALLENNESS

When Caputo speaks of "original sin," presumably he refers to the old, old story, too familiar to bear repeating: Adam and Eve . . . privilege bestowed . . . command disobeyed . . . privilege withdrawn . . . fringe benefits, too . . . for them, for us . . . but *felix culpa* . . . the "Christ-Event" . . . and after . . . gotcha!

Now, this account is based upon a literal interpretation of the story of the Fall as told in the *Book of Genesis*, Chapter 3. Curiously, however, no one ever heard of "original sin" until the fifth century of the Christian era. It was St. Augustine who invented the terminology of *peccatum originale originatis* (personal sin of Adam) and *peccatum originale originatum* (its effect on human kind). It had emerged in his polemic against Pelagius (circa 400 AD), who had maintained, in strictly Stoic fashion, that free will, supported by ascetic practices, was sufficient for the living of a full Christian life. As for sin, its origin was extrinsic to the will, i.e., contracted through the imitation of the bad examples of others (e.g., Adam and Eve). Augustine insisted that the source of sinfulness was interior to human beings, an intrinsic corruption in them, passed on through generation, indeed in the very lust involved in the procreative act. For Augustine, the nature of the sin lay precisely in the unruly passions ("concupiscence") that turned humans away from God. It was Thomas Aquinas who developed a more sophisticated conception of the nature of sin as consisting in the loss of the original privilege, the special intimacy with God ("sanctifying grace"). This enabled him to distinguish between the formality of the sin and concupiscence as its consequence, thus explaining how the sin could be eradicated by baptism though concupiscence remains. Luther reappropriated the Augustinian position that identified original sin with concupiscence, and it was with him in mind that the Council of Trent insisted on the distinction between the two. The Council's Decree on Original Sin is considered a definitive statement on the matter for Catholics.[24] When Caputo claims that I conflate errancy with original sin, I assume that he means that I identify errancy with the congenital tendency toward evil that Christians consider to be part of the burden of inherited guilt, and he cries "Foul!"

But the twentieth century has given rise to a new style of thinking about the Fall. For one thing, the evidence of cultural anthropology for the evolution of the human species forced a re-thinking of the Garden of Eden story, and in Catholic circles, the work of Teilhard de Chardin added momentum to this effort. At the same time, burgeoning research into the literary and cultural sources of the text(s) of the Bible enabled scholars to reinterpret Genesis 3 in terms of the broader context of which it is a part. The consensus of scholars now seems to be that Chapter 3 is only one part of the first eleven chapters of Genesis that belong to a special genre all their own. They have as their function to express in symbolic narrative form plausible versions of how the world began, and how things turned out to be the way they are. As such, they are accounts of what the scholars call "primeval events." In the language of linguists, their significance is synchronic rather than diachronic, i.e., they present an aetiological account of the narrators present in terms of a storied past rather that a chronological account of the *de facto* history of a given people. For Israel, the chronological history begins with the story of Abraham and the Patriarchs (Gen. 12–50). To situate Gen 3 properly, then, we must keep in mind the following:

1. Chapters 1–11 are to be read as a whole. For example, the account of creation of flood go together to suggest that the power to create is the power to destroy. Other stories exemplify the whole gamut of human experience from birth to death. In particular, the stories of Adam and Eve, Cain and Abel (along, no doubt, with the flood and the tower of Babel) are to be taken together as the saga of transgression: crime and punishment. In describing the fall of Adam and Eve, then, the narrator would be describing the phenomenon of sin in his own time and projecting backwards a parable to explain how it began.

2. Along with many parallel neighbouring cultures, these stories implied true universalism. The word *"adam"/"adamah"* was a common noun ("earth creature") before it became a proper name (Gen. 4:25). In such a context, "Adam" could be taken to refer to a group, indeed the entire human race. His sin, then, would be "original," not because it had some mysterious, quasi-physical force that could contaminate the rest of human kind but because it was considered first in the order of time, i.e., the head of a series.

Thus:

> The account of crime and punishment in the primeval story is depicted primarily as part of the human condition. Sin, guilt and revolt are not the results of a long encounter with God as are the sins of Israel which are condemned by the prophets. . . . They belong to human existence as such and are common to all people in all places.[25]

Many questions remain unanswered in such an interpretation of the Genesis account, but two things are clear: the creator invites his human creatures to collaborate with him in bringing to fulfilment the work of creation ("Be fruitful, multiply, fill the earth and subdue it" [Gen. 1:28]); this power to collaborate is of such a nature that human beings must answer for what they do

("God called to man: 'Where are you,' he said" [Gen. 3:9, 10]; "Yahweh asked Cain, 'Where is your brother Abel?'" [Gen. 4:9]). Let that say that human beings are endowed with some kind of freedom, however limited it may be, relative to the level of consciousness achieved at a given period of the evolutionary process. The bottom line: humans are responsible enough to collude in their own perversity.

By mid-century, these developments affected a sea-change in the way theologians thought about original sin. Fresh readings of Romans 5 underscored the Christo-centrism of such statements as "Just as by one man's disobedience many were made sinners, so by one man's obedience are many made upright" (Rom. 5:18). Vatican II's Pastoral Constitution, *Gaudium et Spes*, shifted emphasis from Romans 5 to Romans 7, where Paul speaks of the human being divided against itself. All this liberated theological speculation, and some theologians began to speak of original sin in existential terms, relating it to man's "situation" in the world.

Piet Schoonenberg, for example, explored this situation in terms of the Johannine notion of the "sin of the world" (John 1:29), intending the formula to sum up the social nature of, or solidarity in, the sin of all humanity. Humans are affected by the sins of others, whether by reason of bad example, group pressure, socio-politico-economic structures, or simply the general obscuration of values—all of which combine to form a *communal* rejection of the Christ-Event. He asks whether original sin may not be understood in this globally social way, wondering whether transmission by "generation" is not sufficiently accounted for by the fact that what is transmitted by "generation" is essentially the human situation itself.[26]

Gustav Martelet, taking full account of the evolutionary process, underlines the frailty of human freedom in the early stages of humanity—frailty that *precedes* any exercise of it. "This is the first sense of the sin that we call *original*, because it is *anterior* to the liberty of each individual that finds itself objectively marked by the fact that she enters a world that is historically sinful."[27]

Karl Rahner's formulation is more complex. The universal experience of crime and punishment he calls our "existentiell" situation, according to which the exercise of individual human freedom is "codetermined" by the guilt of others with whom we share the world.[28] On the existential level, he postulates the functioning of what he calls a "supernatural existential." By this he intends to signify a structural element of every human being by reason of the Christ-Event, through which every human is always already destined to share in the divine life. This destiny is not merely external, something still to come, but is always already inscribed in the very ontological structure of human beings, i.e., prior to any act of choice to accept or reject the gift involved— gratuitously, to be sure (because "supernatural"), but nonetheless really there. Presumably, this supernatural existential would have been present in

Adam (whether an individual or group)[29] in virtue of the divine plan of creation/redemption that was always already effective from the beginning, in proleptic anticipation (humanly speaking) of God's self-communication in the Christ-Event. Salvation would consist in the acceptance of the gift as offered, personal sin in its refusal. If the gift is not bestowed even though "proffered" in virtue of the supernatural existential there is a lack of holiness that ought not be present (in terms of God's salvific will), and it is this lack, marking the human race from its beginning, that is called "original sin." The supernatural existential that abides along with the absence of grace it signifies constitutes precisely the ontological "guilt" of original sin—*de facto* part of human being, hence part of the historicity of its Being-with-others-in-the-world. It is the *de facto* history of this sinful historicity that Rahner conceives to be the "sin of the world."[30]

To conflate errancy with original sin in these terms would be to see it as analogous to the "sin of the world"—a secular paradigm for the universal experience of perversity in human behavior, i.e., solidarity in sin. The question is: may someone do that ? If so, is it worth doing?

HEIDEGGER AND ORIGINAL SIN

Let us return to Heidegger and ask what correalation, if any, is possible between errancy and original sin, at least in its expanded mode as "sin of the world." I have already made the point that errancy in the later Heidegger serves, from the perspective of Being, as the ontological ground of the fallenness of *Dasein*. Thanks to the exhaustive researches, recently published, of Theodore Kisiel (*The Genesis of Heidegger's Being and Time*)[31] and John Van Buren (*The Young Heidegger: The Rumour of the Hidden King*)[32] we now have a better appreciation of what "falling" and "fallenness" meant to him from the very beginning of his attempt to develop the "hermeneutics of facticity" (from 1919 on) that would eventually evolve into *Being and Time*. There is no need to repeat their meticulous analysis. I shall only consider the very beginning of the process to get a fresh sense of its import for the *Dasein*-analysis of *Being and Time*.

Van Buren is especially helpful here, for he emphasizes the religious background of Heidegger's early thinking. It is common knowledge that Heidegger's religious roots were Roman Catholic. Van Buren recalls how Heidegger's student years (1909–1915) were marked by the Neo-Scholasticism of his day, how at one point he had ambitioned appointment to the Chair of Catholic philosophy at Freiburg, how his initial teaching years, interrupted by military service (1917–1918), brought a dissaffection with the metaphysical tradition that this heritage represented.[33] By 1919 he felt the need to abandon it completely, even to destroy it in favor of a new beginning of thought that would be radically non-metaphysical. This included the felt need to abandon Roman Catholicism, too, whose dogmatic formulations were encrusted with metaphysical overlay. He turned rather to the Christianity of Martin Luther, with its anti-metaphysical bias that Heidegger then found much more congenial. His conviction was that the acute sense of immediacy and historicality that characterized primitive Christianity lost its freshness when it became burdened by the apparatus of metaphysical speculation. The first task would be to attempt to retrieve that original freshness by examining phenomenologically the experience as articulated by St. Paul and interpreted by the tradition that retained this sense of immediacy (e.g., Augustine, Luther, Pascal, Kierkegaard et al.). The result was an attempt to develop a phenomenology of religion that took the form of courses on "Introduction to the Phenomenology of Religion" (1920–1921) and "Augustine and Neoplatonism" (1921). Both courses would be followed by a turn to the practical philosophy of Aristotle. I shall limit my attention to this early work.

In the first of these courses, the keynote is sounded by Luther in his *Heidelberg Disputation* (1518) with his distinction between the "theology of glory" and the "theology of the cross." The former is based on Scholasticism's use of Aristotle's metaphysics to develop a notion of God in all his glory as first cause and supreme good, manifested through created works (e.g., the object of the human will as good). The latter is based on the humiliation and shame of the cross, scandal to the Jews, and absurdity to the Greeks (I Cor. 1:23). For Luther, the "theology of glory" must be crucified, and the "blind pagan Master Aristotle" unmasked for the "swindler" that he was. This would obviously mean the dismantling of Aristotelian metaphysics in order to return to historical consciousness of primitive Christianity, for which life is to be lived from day to day in the awesome shadow of the cross. "The young Heidegger saw himself at this time as a kind of philosophical Luther of Western Metaphysics."[34]

With Luther carrying the torch, Heidegger turned to the examination of primitive Christian texts, especially those of Paul (e.g., I Thessalonians). If he subsequently devoted an entire course to Augustine ("Augustine and Neoplatonism" [1921]), it was to show how Augustine, for all his sensitivity to the Pauline experience, was the prime example of one who contemplated it by filtering it through Greek (Neo-Platonic) philosophical concepts.

Van Buren spells out Heidegger's debt to the Christian religious tradition in great detail.[35] Concepts such as care, understanding, mood, anxiety, death, authenticity/inauthenticity and kairological time all have their antecedence in it. Fallenness, in particular, has a long history. Paul speaks, for example, of those who have "fallen from grace" (Gal. 5:4), and Heidegger himself takes the distinction between the "fallen and the redeemed by Christ" as the benchmark of Christianity. Augustine describes the condition as marked by temptation, dispersion, entanglements, flight from self to find contentment, and the "curiosity" that is a sign of the "lust of the eyes." For Luther, sinners are their own "obstruction" (*obex*) against the divine light, and, whether by excess or defect, life itself "goes to ruin."[36] Pascal adds the elements of diversion and restlessnes to the syndrome. In Kierkegaard, the theme returns under the guise of flight from self, or at least from anxiety over the self/God relationship, and Kierkegaard's description of the inauthentic life is taken over almost verbatim.

In sum, Heidegger's experience of facticity and fallenness in the early Freiburg years was conceived and nurtured in the Christian religious tradition of what that tradition understood as "original sin." At one point Heidegger even wrote to his student, Karl Löwth, "I am not a philosopher. . . . I am a Christian theologian."[37] Rudolf Bultmann went so far as to claim that in the twenties Heidegger's perspective was "no more than a secularized, philosophical version of the New Testament view of human life."[38] This is a bit much, of course, as the turn to Aristotle makes clear, but at least it suggests that Heidegger's effort to discern the formal indications of factical life was clearly compatible with the Lutheran conception of original sin. This would remain true even after Heidegger himself, in the name of the increasingly a-theistic character of his own philosophical endeavor, lost interest in the religious tradition as such.

But these religious preoccupations (1920–1921) yielded the following year to a more enduring interest in Aristotle in a course entitled *Phenomenological Interpretations of Aristotle: Introduction to Phenomenological Research* (1921–1922).[39] There he found in Aristotle's practical philosophy some of the themes that had interested him in the phenomenology of religion. After devoting the first half of the course about broader questions about the nature of philosophy and its role in the university, Heidegger cites a single text of Aristotle that serves as a hook on which to hang his reflection on factical living (*das faktische Leben*): "It is possible to fail (*harmartanein*) in many ways (for evil belongs to the class of the unlimited, as the Pythagoreans conjectured, and good to that of the limited), while to succeed is possible only in one way (for which reason also, one is easy and the other difficult—to miss the mark easy, to hit it difficult); for these reasons also, then, excess (*hyberbole*) and defect (*elleipsis*) are characteristic of vice, and the mean of virtue (Nicomachean Ethics, II, 1106 b 28ff.)."[40] (GA, 61:108)

Without regard for the ethical context of Aristotle's remark, Heidegger describes the "many ways" of failure discernible in ordinary, everyday (i.e., "factical") human living, marked as it is by myriad forms of "excess" (the "hyperbolic") and defect (the "elliptical").

The fundamental characteristic of human living for Heidegger is Aristotle's *kinesis*, which he translates as "animation" (*Bewegung*) or "animatedness" (*Bewegtheit*). Thus, the "animatedness is such that, as animation in itself, it comes to its own aid; it is the animatedness of factical living that fashions (*macht*) itself in such a way that factical living (*Leben*), as living (*lebend*) in the world, does not properly (!) make the movement itself so much as the world, as the wherein, whereupon and wherefor of living, is [itself] alive (*lebt*)" (GA, 61:130).[41] This suggests how intimate is the relationship between factical life and the world with which it deals that Heidegger already describes as "caring" (*Sorgen*). "Living is in the broadest relating-sense: caring about one's 'daily bread.' [Luther had used the same phrase.] The latter is to be taken in a very broad, formal-indicative sense. 'Privation' ('*Darbung*,' *privatio*, *carentia*) is the . . . fundamental how (*Grundwie*) . . . of living" (GA, 61:90). At another moment, Heidegger describes this basic poverty as consisting in the fact that "in one way or another something is always missing" (*ständig irgendwie etwas fehlt*) (GA, 61:155). In any case, this experience is not just a solitary one (*Selbstwelt*) but one shared with others (*Mitwelt*) in the world.

This indigenous poverty of life by reason of which it lives from the world and out of it (*von und aus*) is marked by the following characteristics:

1. Tendency (*Neigung*) or tendentiousness (*Geneigtheit*). This appears as a kind of weight (*Gewicht*) or gravitational force that drags (*drängt*) life into the world so that life represents itself and builds itself up (*ausbildet*) in terms of the world, indeed is taken up by the world (*Mitgenommenwerden*), and yields to the pressure (*Druck*) of its world. The result is an inevitable, and ever-increasing, dispersion (*zerstreut sich*) of its energies among the things of the world, so that life is forced to find what satisfaction it can by responding to the demands of life in terms of the world, experiencing itself as a kind of reflection (*Reluzenz*) of the world (GA, 6:100–102).

2. Equally original with this tendency is another component that is inclined to cover up (*verdecken*) this tendency by annulling (*Tilgung*), even suppressing (*Abdrängen*), the distance (*Abstand*) between life and the world, so that, caught up by its distractions (*Zerstreuungen*) life tends to make mistakes (*versieht sich*) and miss aim (*vermisst sich*) in all its ventures. Here are the roots for life's search for success, prestige, advantage, influence, etc., that (in a later analysis) feed into its eventual sell-out to the domination of the They. This is the characteristic that inclines life towards excess (*hyperbolisch*) (GA, 61:102–105).

3. A third component of this same structure is more obscure still. Preoccupation with all its distractions leads life to bar itself off from itself (*Abriegelung*), to lose all sense of its proleptic (*vor-*) character. (Luther had spoken of the sinner himself as an obstacle to the divine light.) "In caring, life bars itself off against itself, and in this barring becomes unfree (*nicht los*). In every new distraction, life is always in search of itself and encounters itself precisely where it doesn't expect, and for the most part in a masking of itself" (GA, 61:107). Thus caring becomes a non-caring (*nicht Sorgen*) in an endless round of misapprehensions (*Sich-immer-neu-Vergreifens*) and misdemeanours (*Verfehlbarkeiten*) of many kinds—life becomes blind, gouging out its own eyes. It is this barring function that makes life miss the mean by reason of defect (*des Elliptischen*) (GA, 61:105–108).

4. A fourth component of factical living is its inclination to lighten its burden by finding the easy (*leicht*) path of excess or defect rather than the "hard" way of the mean between the two. The result is a search for comfort and security, flight (*Flucht*) from whatever would make it look at its masks and perhaps make some basic decision (*Urentscheidung*) in their regard (GA, 61:108–110). All these categories of life as animatedness are examined in detail (GA, 61:110–130) and life finds its unity in a form of temporality (*einheitliche Zeitlichkeit*) that Heidegger, in the spirit of Paul, calls "kairological" (GA, 61:137–140).

This self-constructive, always accelerating animatedness which "as such is always fashioned by its world" (GA, 61:130), Heidegger designates as a "plunge" into the world (*Sturz* or *ruina*) to which he gives the name "ruination" (*Ruinanz*), a term that will eventually be replaced by "fallenness": "the animatedness" of factical living, which fatical *in its* self *as its* self *for its* self *out of its* self and in all this *against* its self "comes to pass," i.e., 'is'" (GA 61:131). Note the built-in counter-movement to the movement as it becomes increasingly involved with its concerns (*Steigerung der Besorgnis*).

Heidegger identifies four characteristics of this process of ruination: it has built-in corruptibility that makes it prone to temptation (*Verführerische*), not from without but from within, because it is so exposed to, dependent on, its world (GA, 61:141–143); it includes a built-in negative character, for the direction of the plunge is toward a nothing (*Nichts*) that is a kind of empty space (*Leere*) where it can come forward no further (*Nichtvorkommenkönnen* [*Vorkommen* normally translates *physis*]), a mark of its ineluctable poverty (*Darbung*) (GA, 61:143–148); at the same time the plunge is into the context of real objects of the world-about without any mediation to buffer them—hence, there is an object relatedness (*Gegenständlichkeit*) that is proper to life that is at once both alienating (*das Entfremdende*) and tranquilizing (*das Beruhigende*) (GA, 61:148–151); the plunge toward the immediacy of object-relatedness that is at the same time into the nothing of an emptiness leaves the movement eminently questionable (*die Fraglichkeit*) from a philosophical/phenomenological point of view (GA, 61:151–155).

Later that same year (1922), when, in order to apply for a new position in Marburg, Heidegger was forced to submit an account of his work-in-progress, he drafted an introduction to a proposed book to be entitled *Phenomenological Interpretations of Aristotle*, which Kisiel carefully summarizes.[42] Here, "falling" (*Verfallen*) replaces the term "ruination" but the essentials of the analysis remain the same. Added, however, was the notion that factical life, though lived by the individual, is absorbed by the average everydayness of the others with whom it lives. Thus, "it is *the* 'one' who in fact lives the life of the individual who is 'no one.' . . . The tendency of falling is the way life evades itself."[43] The most striking manifestation of this movement appears in the way life deals with death, but it is not feasible to follow the death problematic any further here.

How does all this add up? Three remarks are in order. In the first place, the plunge of factical living into the world and the consequent movement/countermovement of its ruinous condition anticipates already, I suggest, the *insistent-eksistent*, to and fro dynamism that constitutes the basic structure of errancy.[44] Moreover, the addition of "the They" problematic (*das Man*) adds a social dimension to the lostness of the individual in the world. David Krell (in reference to Nietzsche) speaks of the analysis as the "genealogy of masquerade and ruinous self-deception."[45] Perhaps. But, given the context out of which the analysis has emerged, could not a Christian theologian use this conceptuality (without distortion) to suggest, at least in part, the underlying structure of the solidarity in perversity that theologians have called the "sin of the world?"

Again, Krell observes, *à propos* of the negativing (*Nichts*) ingredient in ruination, that this anticipates the point in *Being and Time* (# 58), where Heidegger speaks of "guilt" as the "ground of a being that is determined by a not—i.e., being the ground of a nullity."[46] He continues:

> [This analysis] after an extraordinary itinerary of ruinance—through plunge and masquerade, through kairological time and the instant of a counterruinance that is always gnawing at life's false securities, always boring and burrowing, always subverting life's complacency, through the necessity of a phenomenological destruction of all interpretative seductions (particularly those of the ethico-religious sort)—culminates in an account of the "whither" of ruinance (GA, 61:143–148).

> Where does factical life land when it falls? Nowhere.
> When does ruinance strike home? Never.
> What rises to break its free fall? Nothing.
> The fall is nothing but unrestricted fall, uninterrupted crash
> (*Sturz*). Thus the very animatedness of factical life is nihilation.[47]

This is a tough read, especially since it implies (gratuitously, it seems to me) that ethico-religious experience cannot survive a phenomenological destruction (demythologizing) of its myths. That claim should be challenged, but this is not the time or place. I only wish to raise the question as to whether there is structure enough in a *Dasein*, trammelled by ontological guilt, to sustain Rahner's hypothesis of a supernatural existential. And how are we to understand Martelet's conception of a frailty of freedom before any exercise of it?

To be sure, factical life as described here did not get the technical name of "*Dasein*" until 1923, or the designation of "existence" until 1925–1926 (before then, "existence" was only one possibility of life that might function as counterpoise to its downward plunge), but enough is evident to raise the question for the theologian: how much must be postulated about *Dasein* to sustain the Rahner hypothesis? If we forego the literal reading of Genesis 3 and favor an evolutionary conception of human origins, how are we to understand the priority of the great gift as proffered *vis-à-vis* the always already fallen character of the existentiel situation in which the first humans found themselves? What kind of priority of recipient over gift (logical? chronological? ontological?) would be necessary? Obviously these are theological rather than philosophical issues and not really our concern, but the very fact that they can be raised suggests that at least these Heideggerian structures are still useful for pondering the nature of this mystery. And these are the structures, I claim, that anticipate what the later Heidegger calls errancy.

Finally, Krell calls attention to the restiveness (*Unruhe*) of factical living in terms of the "power of the timing process" (*Zeitigungsmächte*) under the guise of what he has called the "daimonic":

> Heidegger's restiveness marks the first appearance of the daimonic, of the powers of process, the might of maturation, and the potency of timely growth. In a word, die *Zeitigungsmächte*. Somewhere beyond the traditional categories of soul and body, animation and movement, ensoulment and auto-motion, somewhere between ancient lineages and succeeding generations, between self and other, between life and its sphere, its environs, and its generations— daimon life disseminates.[48]

For whatever it is worth, the otherness implied in the "powers of process" (i.e., daimon life) I take to be an anticipation of what eventually will appear as the power of errancy to dominate *Dasien* through and through. (49)

I wish to come now directly now to the problem of errancy. By way of transition, let me note that as Heidegger's interest in Aristotle continued to develop, the focus on factical living remained constant. This led to repeated attention to the *Nichomachean Ethics*, and in particular to Book VI, where Aristotle discusses both the role of *phronesis*, the habit of practical wisdom that discerns the mean between excess and defect (as analyzed above), and where he speaks of truth as a process of nonconcealment (*aletheuein*). The task of life is to live well (*eu prattein*), but through the passions (especially the love of pleasure), human beings may become concealed from themselves, hence perverse and self-destructive. It is the task of *phronesis* to help the human being to discover itself in truth. In this sense, Heidegger takes *phronesis* to be the voice of conscience, with all that means for the call to *Dasein* to acknowledge its ontological truth.[50]

As for *aletheia*, when Heidegger began to meditate on it explicitly, it was clear that concealment was ingredient to the process: disclosedness of the world is at once its concealedness (*Verdecktheit*) (GA, 63:85). To the extent that speech (*logos*) is also a part of daily factical living, this too, as uncovering/covering, contains the virus of its own perversion. In *Metaphysics*, Book V, 29, Heidegger finds three forms of falsity (*pseudes*) (false thing, false speech, false human), but the source of this falsity is the facticity of speech itself. The very manner of speaking and repeating in the style of the They (*das Man*) multiplies the possibilities of deception. "Add to this the possibilities of deception in speaking that derive from the world itself: its 'circumstantiality' of manifold aspects *kata symbebekos*, always allowing the world to 'give itself out' to be something other than it is; its 'recessibility' or elusiveness, as a kind of reverse side to the accessibility of the world through language. For the fleetingness or transitoriness belongs to the world as much as light and dark, day and night."[51]

But all of this is said from the viewpoint of the early Heidegger, where the focus is on *Dasein* rather than on Being. It is striking to see what happens to the same themes when we move ahead almost twenty years, to the time when "On the Essence of Truth," after gestating for thirteen years, was finally being readied for publication (1943). Rather than look at that familiar text one more time, I propose to consider selectively the lecture course that was being given at the same time, *Parmenides* (WS, 1942–1943).[52]

This course meditated on the *Poem* of Parmenides, I, 22–32, in which the goddess, *Aletheia*, appears. The process of unconcealment is considered in terms of the transformation of its "counteressence" (*Gegenwesen*), *lethe*. As we have just seen, the counterpoise to *aletheia* is normally taken to be *pseudos*, in the sense of "the false." Here Heidegger argues, though, that for the Greeks it meant a cover-up (*Verdecken*), a mode of concealment (*Verbergen*) (GA, 54:45/30)—a letting-appear, to be sure, but in the form of dissemblance (*Verstellen*), hiding (*Verhehlen*) (GA, 54:48/33), deception (*Täuschen*) (GA, 54:61/41) or detour (*Abweg*) (GA, 54:87/59). But such distortion does not have its source in human subjectivity; rather its source is something like an event (*ereignishaft*) that proceeds from something other (GA, 54:55/38), i.e., the *lethe* component of *aletheia*. If *pseudos* had this ontological meaning for the Greeks, however, how did it come to mean "the false?" By a kind of serendipity for which the Romans were at fault. The German *falsch* would be a latinization of *falsum*, derived from *fallere* (to fall), which in turn is cognate with the Greek *sphallo*, meaning to overthrow, bring to a downfall, make totter, etc. Heidegger continues:

> But this Greek word *sphallo* never became the genuine counter-word opposed to *aletheia*. I deliberately say "genuine", because the Greek *sphallo* can sometimes be translated "correctly" by "deceiving;" what is meant, however, thought in the Greek way, is "making totter," "making stagger," "letting stumble into erring." But man can be led into such tottering and falling in the midst of the beings appearing to him only if something is put in his way obstructing beings, so that he does not know what he is dealing with. First something must be held forth and set forth, and then something else entirely must be delivered, so that man can "fall for" what is presented that way and thereby fall down. Bringing to fall in the sense of misleading first becomes possible on the basis of a putting forth, dissembling, and concealing. (GA, 54:57/39)

Notice that we are dealing again with falling, that it is precipitated by *aletheia* itself (as *lethe*), and it precipitates a stumble into "erring." To be sure, it is human being that becomes errant, but this is as an effect of *lethe/aletheia* whose There it is. "Concealment places the entire essence of human being in hiddenness and tears it away from the unconcealed. Man is 'away' from it. He is no longer with it. He neglects and forsakes what is assigned to him. Concealment comes over man and draws and drags him away from the *pragmaton orthan hodon* [the right path of what is to be done]" (GA, 54:122/83).

Note the recurrence of the *Dasein* as Weg-sein theme of the *Beiträge* text. What is important to note here, however, is that the effect of concealment (Heidegger also calls it "forgetting," as if it were a kind of compound self-forgetting on the part of *aletheia* [GA, 54:104–107/71–73]) is not simply on the cognitive level but affects the entire range of human action:

> We are tempted to say the Greeks conceived forgetting not only in relation to cognitive comportment but also with regard to the "practical". But when we speak this way then we already think in a non-Greek way, for concealment concerns at the very outset man's entire being-alongside-beings (*Dabeisein*). Only because this is so does forgetting concern at once and equiprimordially "theoretical" and "practical" comportment. (GA, 54:123/83)

Note that the effect of *lethe* on *Dasein* is not a purely noetic phenomenon but affects the whole of its Being, practical as well as theoretical.

This has serious consequences when *lethe* affects *Dasein* in its dealings with others in the political arena, or at least in the world of the *polis*:

> The *polis* is neither the city nor the state . . . but the settling of the place of the history of the Greek experience (*Griechentums*). . . . The *polis* is the abode gathered into itself, of the unconcealedness of beings. If now, however, as the word indicates, *aletheia* possesses a conflictual essence, which appears also in the oppositional forms of distortion and oblivion, then in the *polis* as the essential abode of human being there has to hold sway all the most extreme counter-essences, and therein all the excesses (*Unwesen*), to the unconcealed and to beings, i.e., counter beings in the multiplicity of their counter-essence. Here lies concealed the primordial ground of that feature Jacob Burckhardt presented for the first time in its full bearing and manifoldness the frightfullness (*Furchtgarkeit*), the horribleness (*Grauenhafte*), the atrociousness (*Unheil*) of the Greek *polis*. Such is the rise and the fall of human being in its historical abode of essence—*hypsoppolis-apolis*—far exceeding abodes [yet] homeless, as Sophocles (*Antigone*) calls human kind. It is not by chance that human being is spoken of in this way in Greek tragedy. For the possibility, and the necessity of "tragedy" itself have their single source in the conflictual essence of *aletheia*. (GA, 54:13–134/190)

There are several remarks to be made about this passage. It supplies a context for a similar passage from the "Letter on Humanism," where he speaks of the "malice of rage" (*Bösartigen des Grimmes*) as deriving from the fact that Being itself is contested (*das Strittige*), i.e., the struggle between *lethe* and *aletheia*. Is the *lethe* the blackness of *Buchenwald*? Probably not—very few things are quite that black, except, perhaps Good Friday. But it is not *Schwarzwald* black either. We are dealing with real malice here and real evil, and we are talking about the ontological ground of it in the negativity of Being itself. That is black enough.

In such a context, one can understand why Heidegger feels justified in using the words "monstrous" (*Ungeheuer*) and "daimonic" to describe the emptiness of the place where *lethe* comes to pass: "The not-ness of the emptiness is the not of withdrawal. . . . The place of *lethe* is the Where, in which the monstrous comes to presence in a unique exclusivity. The field of *lethe* is in a special sense 'daimonic'" (GA, 54:176/119). Note, too, the striking resonance of this formula describing the most extreme form of errancy as proceeding from the *lethe* of *aletheia* with the nadir of the plunge of ruination (*Ruinanz*)—the emptiness (*Leere*) of the not (*Nichts*) of factical living (GA, 61:143–148).

How does human being make do with all this? Heidegger speaks only for the philosopher, whose task is the exercise of phronesis: insight "into what is properly discernible and unconcealed" (GA, 54:178/120), a kind of saving effort of the unconcealed from the concealment of distorting withdrawal" (GA, 54:179/121). Indeed, the course ends on an almost lyrical note, celebrating *aletheia* as the Open and the Free, and the journey of the thinker to the dwelling place of the goddess. Enough already!

CONCLUSION

What, then, is my claim? I maintain that the fallenness of *Dasein,* a mode of its facticity that accounts for the untruth ingredient to its very structure as the disclosedness of the world, is a theme that dates from the very beginning of Heidegger's work. Initially analogous to an Augustinian-Lutheran conception of original sin, the notion was elaborated with the help of categories drawn from Aristotle's practical philosophy (discernment of the mean through phronesis) into a non-religious, non-ethical, radically secularized conception of one of the existential components of *Dasein's* ontological structure. When the notion of truth as unconcealment (*aletheuein*) (likewise discovered in Aristotle's practical philosophy) was explored, a negative element of concealment (*lethe*) was discovered as intrinsic to it. In *Being and Time* both themes coalesced to yield the formula, "Because *Dasein* is essentially falling, its state of being is such that it is in the 'untruth'. . . . [This condition] belongs to *Dasein's* facticity." After the major turn in Heidegger's thinking that marked a shift in focus from *Dasein* to Being, the negativity that had marked *Dasein's* fallenness now appeared to be grounded in the negativity of *aletheia,* whether as mystery (concealing of the concealment) or errancy (seduction of *Dasein* into forgetting the mystery). It was in this guise that in the *Parmenides* course, *lethe,* both as mystery (*Vergessen*) and as errancy (*Verstellen, Verhehlen, Täuschen*), was seen to precipitate the downfall (*sphallo*) of *Dasein,* making Dasein correspondingly errant, not only in its thinking but in its practical action. It was *lethe,* too, that made ontologically possible the "frightfulness," "horribleness," and "atrociousness" of the Greek experience. It was this, too, that made Greek tragedy both possible and necessary. The task of *phronesis* now would be to discern deceptive concealment within revealment and deal with it as best errant *Dasein* could. In light of all this I have asked whether Heidegger's fall into the Nazi experience might be accounted for by his own failure to discern the deceptive distortions of that particular phenomenon to end up very errant indeed.

This is the proposal that Caputo dismisses as a conflation of errancy and original sin. If he means by that that I have mistakenly identified a philosophical concept with a religious myth based on a literal reading of Genesis 3, that is incorrect. The only conception of original sin I would consider relevant to this context would be one that would interpret it somehow in terms of the "sin of the world," a conception I have no reason to believe he has in mind. If he means that I have failed to recognize the difference between the Greek genius (gifted for vision, hence for philosophical reflection) and the Hebraic (gifted for hearing, hence for religious faith), that is also incorrect. The fact is that both use the same word to express human fault (*hamartia*) and both understood it basically in the same way ("to miss the mark"). If time permitted, this would be the moment to compare the different ways in which each culture actually used the word in order to highlight the profound differences between the two experiences. But for my present purposes, that would be beside the point.[53] All I wish to claim is that Heidegger has discerned in Being itself a pernicious negativity that permeates *Dasein,* its There, and I have asked what consequences this may have had for Heidegger himself who writes about it.

If Caputo means that I seek some soft-headed way to exonerate Heidegger by offering him the chance to say "the *Irre* made me do it," this is patently incorrect. Heidegger was as responsible as Adam/Cain was in the Yahwist's account. "Where is your brother Abel?" is as compelling a question today for Heidegger (and everyone else) as it ever was. I am not trying to excuse Heidegger's fall, I am trying to explain it—and, indeed, in his own terms. So if, to be done, Caputo means only that I have traced Heidegger's effort to disengage (under the guise of facticity and fallenness) the formal indication of what Luther (after Augustine) saw to be the basic condition of human being (the "state of original sin"), traced it through the turn in his way to the focus on Being itself in its negativity (*a-letheia*) as the source of that fallenness, then Caputo is correct. But this is hardly a conflation.

If that is all I can hope to show, why these labors of Hercules? I see two advantages to be made by making this case. In the first place, this examination takes Heidegger seriously on his own terms. Van Buren, in his powerful chapter of conclusion, enumerates all of Heidegger's sins of thought one by one. The author recasts the relevant material in terms of a series of configurations: existential-transcendental, primitivistic, antihumanistic, essentialist, speculative, Hellenic/Germanic, Helleno-Christian religious, gendered, anthropocentric, authoritarian—and adds in the "stories" of Being, to boot. The final pages say "what it comes to." I have no quarrel with this portentous balance sheet. I only insist that this shows better than any argument I could make that the revelation of Being as *aletheia* to Heidegger was trammelled with darkness too. All of the dissemblance, distortion, and deception that mark the hesitancies, inconsistencies, and ambiguities of his effort proceeded from the same source that marked his genius: the experience of truth that, as finite, includes its own counteressence: enthralling, but darkly mysterious . . . and potentially monstrous, too.

But there is a much broader reason for engaging in an enterprise of this kind. Heidegger remains (arguably) the most influential philosopher of the twentieth century, and his experience of *aletheia* raises all over again questions about the nature of truth as such, especially when conceived under the guise of revelation. On one hand the Incarnate Word says "I am the Truth"; on the other, the long history of the evolution of dogma in general (and of original sin as a particular case in point) is evidence enough of the need of Christian thinkers for conceptual tools to deal with the historicity of that finite truth. As the world moves into the twenty-first century and Christians must operate more and more effectively within parameters of the "postmodern" experience, Heidegger's notions of truth and the retrieval of it out of mystery, errancy and the unsaid of its articulation, may prove, if taken seriously, very useful indeed. How that might come about is another chapter that cannot be opened here, but at least the viability of such ideas should not be foreclosed because of the apparent failures of the one who proposed them. For Christians believe that the blackness of *Buchenwald* and the blackness of *Schwarzwald* are not the ultimate symbols of human tragedy. Both dissolve in the blackness of Good Friday that yielded to an Easter dawn. When all is said an done, this is the mystery of the Christ-Event: that to the unremitting need of our own redemption, it remains in continual advent. That is why we can hope.

NOTES

1. John D. Caputo, "Dark Hearts: Heidegger, Richardson and Evil," in *From Phenomenology to Thought, Errancy, and Desire*, ed. by Babette E. Babich (Dordrecht: Kluwer, 1995).

2. William J. Richardson, "Heidegger's Truth and Politics," in *Ethics and Danger: Essays on Heidegger and Continental Thought*, ed. by Arlene Dallery and Charles Scott (Albany, N.Y.: SUNY Press, 1992), pp. 11–24.

3. John Sallis, "Deformatives: Essentially Other then Truth," in *Commemorations: Reading Heidegger,* ed. by John Sallis (Bloomington: Indiana University Press, 1993), pp. 29–46.

4. Martin Heidegger, "On the Essence of Truth," BW, pp. 133–134.

5. Joseph Conrad, *Heart of Darkness* (New York: Penguin Books, 1983).

6. John D. Caputo, DH, pp. 166–167.

7. See Marlène Zarader, *La dette impensée. Heidegger et l'héritage hébraïque* (Paris: Éditions du Seuil, 1990), pp. 152–162.

8. See Josef Kieninger, *Das Sein als Licht in den Schriften des hl. Thomas von Aquin* (Citta del Vaticano: Libreria Editrice Vatican, 1992).

9. See Martin Heidegger, IM, pp. 98–115.

10. Martin Heidegger, "Letter on Humanism," BW, p. 218.

11. John Caputo, "*Sorge* and *Kardia*. The Hermeneutics of Factical Life and the Categories of the Heart," in *Reading Heidegger from the Start,* ed. by Theodore Kisiel and John Van Buren (Albany, NY: SUNY Press, 1994), pp. 327–343.

12. Ibid., p. 338.

13. Ibid., p. 332.

14. In private correspondence (cited with permission), Caputo writes: "If you are going to draw an ontological/ontic map, I think that *all* phenomenon are ontic and it is just a question as to what ontological phenomena—*Verstehen, Befindlichkeit,* etc.—you are going to valorize when you start calling certain things ontological. I think that the existential analytic proceeds from distinct, definite, historically datable existetiell ideals to which Heidegger is attached and which then get ontological valorization. I don't think that anybody has ever been to the ontological promised land."

15. Richardson, "Heidegger's Truth and Politics."

16. Martin Heidegger, "*Vom Wesen der Wahrheit,*" *Wegmarken* (Frankfurt am Main: Klostermann, 1976), GA, 9:197.

17. Martin Heidegger, *Sein und Zeit* (Frankfurt am Main: Klostermann, 1976) GA, 2:294/222.

18. Heidegger, BT, pp. 264–265.

19. Martin Heidegger, *Beiträge zur Philosphie (vom Ereignis),* hrsg. von F.W. von Herrmann (Frankfurt am Main: Klostermann, 1989). GA, 65.

20. Ibid., p. 338.

21. Ibid., p. 324.

22. Ibid., p. 324.

23. Martin Heidegger, *Zollikoner Seminare.* hrsg. von M. Boss (Frankfurt am Main: Klostermann, 1989). GA, 65:208–209.

24. H. Denzinger, Enchiridion Sybolorum. Definitionum et Declarationum de rebus fidei et morum, (Freiburg im Breisgau: Herder, 1958), pp. 787–792.

25. Claus Westermann, *Genesis: An Introduction,* trans. by John Scullion (Minneapolis: Fortress, 1984), pp. 66–67.

26. Piet Schoonenberg, *Man and Sin. A Theological View,* trans. By Joseph Donceel (South Bend, IN: University of Notre Dame, 1965), pp 186–187.

27. Gustav Martelet, *Libre réponse à un scandale. La faute originelle, la souffrance te la mort* (Paris: Éditions du Cerf, 1986), p. 71.

28. Karl Rahner, *Foundations of the Christian Faith, an Introduction to the Idea of Christianity*, trans. William Dych (New York: Seabury, 1978), pp. 106–115.

29. Ibid., p. 110.

30. Karl Rahner, "Original Sin" in *Sacrmentum Mundi. An Encyclopaedia of Theology* (New York: Herder and Herder, 1968), p. 110.

31. Theodore Kisiel, *The Genesis of Heidegger's Being and Time* (Berkeley: University of California Press, 1993).

32. John Van Buren, *The Young Heidegger, Rumour of the Hidden King* (Bloomington: Indiana University Press, 1993).

33. Ibid., pp. 133–156.

34. Ibid., p. 167.

35. Ibid., pp. 170–202.

36. Ibid., pp. 180–181.

37. Cited ibid., p. 134, p. 154.

38. Cited ibid., p. 152.

39. Martin Heidegger, *Phänomenologische Interpretationen zu Aristotles, Einführung in die phänomenologische Forschung* (Frankfurt am Main: Klostermann, 1985). GA, 61.

40. Aristotle, *Nichomachean Ethics*, ed. by R. McKeon (New York: Random House, 1941).

41. Heidegger, M. 1921–1922 *Phänomenologische Interpretationen zu Aristotles, Einführung in die phänomenologische Forschung*, hrsg. von W. Bröcker und K. Bröcker-Oltmanns (Frankfurt am Main: Klostermann, 1985). GA, 11, 61.

42. Kisiel, *The Genesis of Heidegger's Being and Time*, pp. 248–271.

43. Ibid., p. 297.

44. Heidegger, "On the Essence of Truth," BW, pp. 132–134.

45. David Krell, "The 'Factical Life' of *Dasein*: From the Early Freiburg Courses to *Being and Time*," in *Reading Heidegger from the Start. Essays in His Earliest Thought*, ed. by Theodore Kisiel and John Van Buren (Albany, NY: SUNY Press, 1994), p. 376.

46. Heidegger, BT, p. 329.

47. Ibid., p. 378.

48. Ibid., p. 371.

49. Heidegger, "On the Essence of Truth," BW, pp. 132–135.

50. See Kisiel, *The Genesis of Heidegger's Being and Time*, pp. 305–306.

51. Ibid., p. 280.

52. Martin Heidegger, *Parmenides* (Frankfurt am Main: Klostermann, 1982). GA, 54. Trans. André Schuwer and Richard Rojcewicz (Blommington; Indiana University Press, 1992). Reference in the text will be given to the English pagination after the German.

53. The limits of the present perspective also make it impossible to address formally an objection raised by Caputo in private correspondence (cited with permission): "You keep arguing . . . that you can find a place for malice after the clearing is cleared, which is of course better than just forgetting it altogether, whereas I am saying: 'don't

bother, you're too late, it's already there.' I don't see you addressing that criticism in this piece." Indeed I do not. By "already there" I take him to mean that the "place for malice" is already found in the traditions that date from "time immemorial" out of which the aetiological accounts of the Yahwist editor of Genesis, 1–11, (shared with neighboring cultures) are woven. I made reference to these accounts in a longer version of this paper that had to be excised for reasons of available space. These traditions antedate by far the emergence of philosophical thought in Greece (circa seventh century BC) and do, indeed, deal with (ontic) issues "otherwise than truth—as the Pre-Socratics began to conceive it philosophically. Claus Westermann (*Genesis, An Introduction*, p. 109.) writes suggestively: "In the creation declaration, people for the first time conceptualized the origin of mankind and the world as a whole. To speak of the creator is to speak of the whole. . . . This concept of the world and humanity as a whole . . . has, in Greek thought, been detached from the creator and become ontology; the Pre-Socrartics mark the transition. The Idea of the whole and of 'origin from' into being. . . . There is ontology only because people once understood their world as creation." Given the opportunity to address Caputo's objection properly, I would attempt to argue that ontological structures are "always already there" in ontic phenomena, even though the discovery (postulation?) of them may be subsequent to the chronological experience that records them. (Cf. Aristotle, *Physics*, I, 184a, 1–21.) In Heideggerian terms, the clearing makes possible such a discovery—it is the *clearing* that is always "already there."

THE HEART OF CONCEALMENT:
A RESPONSE TO RICHARDSON

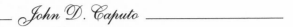

John D. Caputo

The guest editor of the special "Heidegger" issue of *American Catholic Philosophical Quarterly* in which "Heidegger's Fall" originally appeared described Bill Richardson as "the dean of American Heidegger scholars, generations of American students having cut their teeth on his *Heidegger: Through Phenomenology to Thought*," and that he is here responding to the complaints of an "impudent admirer."[1] Very well said indeed. I could not have said it better myself. I am indeed one of those teeth-cutters, my worn out copy of his Heidegger book having practically fallen apart from overuse. If I spent a lot of time learning Aquinas from Norris Clarke, I also spent a lot of time learning Heidegger from Bill Richardson, so that if I am at present in a bad way it is very much the doing of two Fordham Jesuits. Indeed, if I persist in being ornery about Heidegger even after reading Richardson's erudite and moving "Heidegger's Fall," I hasten to add that my orneriness goes hand in hand with a bottomless gratitude to someone who has shown a generation of American Catholics the way to fuse their faith with a creative engagement with the cutting edge of continental European thought. In the present piece, I am indebted to Bill Richardson once again for his searching analysis of Heidegger's thought, and for his response to my criticism which, coming as a contribution to this volume, is not only an occasion of further instruction but a very great honor for me.

The basic point of disagreement between Richardson and me is that no modulation of "errancy" (*Irre*) can account for moral evil because evil is not a deviant modality of what Heidegger calls "truth" or "unconcealment," but a deviancy in another order, in "justice" or the "heart," where malice, murderousness, and hatred reside, which are otherwise than what Heidegger calls truth. Accordingly, even if truth is rethought as *aletheia*, as Heidegger has so brilliantly done, and as Richardson so brilliantly explained to English readers, as the emerging of things from the heart of concealment, that lethic heart is not to be confused with the heart of darkness, in Conrad's phrase, which has to do with what Levinas calls the hatred of the other one, hatred of the "face" of the other. Levinasian "faces" never register in Heidegger's history of

being—although the faces of the slaughtered black natives are central to
Conrad's tale—and consequently the whole register of evil is missing from
the history of Being.

Richardson holds that while Heidegger was tending other fields he did
not exclude and indeed was supplying the basis upon which one could subsequently develop such an account, were one so minded. But I reject the claim
that in *Being and Time* Heidegger is tending to the ontological foundations of
evil and in the later writings to the "clearing" that precedes and makes possible the concrete good and evil that people do. I deny the *primacy* Heidegger is giving to something that somehow or another got there before the
command issued by the face of the other not to kill, which I would say is at
least as "primordial" as anything Heidegger can come up with. Furthermore,
I go on to deny Heidegger's logic of sorting out the originary from the derivative, which seems to me just more essentialism or hyper-essentialism, not of
the *hyperousios*, to be sure, but of his Greco-European *Ereignis* which gath-
ers its propriety to itself and wants to "own" Being and thinking to each other,
to use the jargon of the ridiculous English translation of the *Beiträge*. As I
said in the letter that Bill Richardson cites in note 14, one man's "ontology" is
another man's (or woman's!) "ontic" prejudices. The ontology you end up
with will always be a function of the ontic phenomena you prefer. The onto-
logical/ontic distinction ends up valorizing the ontical things to which you are
attached, putting what you favor first, jacking them up a notch or two, and
then declaring them "ontological" or "originary." (When the facts are staring
you in the face, you say that is "merely correct" but not "originary.") I have
been too much bitten by the bug of *différance* to put any stock in this distinction or to be drawn into that game. I sit and wait for someone to say
something ontological so that I can show them why it is ontical. Then, in a
gesture whose brazenness surprises even me, I went on to say to this eminent
Jesuit, that if you want a "story" about something "original" that explains
"evil," try the opening chapters of Genesis! But don't confuse that with *lethe*.
That I have not yet been struck down by lightning for such impudence is a
sign of a merciful Providence.

Let me say that I have never thought that what is at issue here for me or
for Bill Richardson is what lay in Heidegger's heart or private conscience.
That really is none of my business. What concerns the both of us is the heart
of "Being," or of concealment, that is, the relationship of the thought of
Being to the malice of murder, murder being what *The Heart of Darkness*
and the Nazis are all about. Does the thought of Being provide some ultimate
ground for malice or hatred or does it just *neutralize* any consideration of it?
Is the command that issues from the face of the other something "ontic" that
requires a prior ontology to illuminate it, or does it go to the heart of our relationship with the other and so does not need to wait upon Being's opening?

Heidegger's first cut (1920–1921) at building such a ontological table took its point of departure from Christian (but not Jewish) texts. But Heidegger did so, in my opinion, in a very one-sided way. Heidegger's "existentialia" reflected St. Paul's love of a good fight, the *bellum quotidianum* in Augustine's *Confessions*, and Luther's *theologia crucis*. He sketched the "ontology" of a macho Christian soldier, which he then fused with a reading of an equally combative Aristotle, for whom everything turned on the "difficulty" of hitting the mark of virtue. In the 1922 lectures Heidegger valorized the virtues of struggle (*Kampf*) and "difficulty" (even his "Socrates" was a warrior), not making things easy (*Leichtmachen*). All of that made him a sitting duck for Ernst Jünger's bombastics in *Der Arbeiter*, which provided the transition from *Being and Time*, where the trace of Aristotle and Kierkegaard are still to be found, to his Nazi period, where Jünger and Nietzsche get all the best lines. But Heidegger completely omitted the defining and touchstone phenomena of mercifulness, forgiving, healing, etc. in the New Testament. Furthermore the implicit embodiment in *Being and Time* is of an active, hale and whole agent body, never a "flesh" laid low by pain and suffering.[2] So the reading was selective; he picked the ontic phenomena he favored and treated them as formal indicators of the ontology that he then said, retroactively, founded them. Thus if someone comes along and protests that this or that is left out, he simply says that is "ontic" and can be covered later on by one of those researchers down there in the valley of the regional ontologies who engage in backfilling and joining the dotted lines.

Consequently the "ontological" structure of "Dasein" and "temporality" to which these phenomena serve as "clues" took its clue from the ontical phenomena selected in advance by Heidegger. They reflect a very Pauline attempt to fight the good fight, projected into the future ahead, the *vita ventura*, but not the beatitudes, say, which emphasize peacefulness, taking each day as it comes, *not* having any "*Bekümmerung*" about the future, and *having* concern for the suffering of others. That is why the "ruination" (from Augustine's *ruina* in the *Confessions*) in the 1922 lectures discussed by Richardson is never the ruin that the other suffers or the ruinousness of my own freedom, but a matter of how loyal I am to my authentic self. Heidegger's conception of the ontological difference is wrong-headed in principle, because nobody gets to the high ground it requires, and distorted in practice, because it leaves us with a one-sided and highly slanted account that, however interesting it is, only hears what it wants to hear in Aristotle, St. Paul, and Augustine. It takes what Heidegger himself would call "existentiell ideals" and jacks them up into a so-called "fundamental ontology," which then declares everything else that he has not selected as founded or derivative.

I do agree that the fascinating text reported by Medard Boss on *Bösesein-können* that Bill Richardson cites from the Zollikon seminar addresses my concerns. But had Heidegger built that bit of *sein-können* thematically into the "existentialia" of *Being and Time* he would have had to go back to the drawing board, for that would have spelled the "ruination" of the whole idea of *sein-können*! He would then have had to ask himself what *Böse* is and, to get it right, in my opinion, he would have to have seen that it had to do with the command issued from the face of the other, the prohibition of murder, the "first word" from the other. That in turn would have meant that the so called *da* is not my doing, my projective work, and that my own "freedom" and *Sein-können*, the whole sphere of *my power*, is the source of the problem, not the solution. Accordingly this "*da*" is already the work, not of *physis*, but of the other one who by coming over me opens up the world for me, if you want to talk like that.

Now, impelled in no small part by the disastrousness of the massive voluntarism of the early 1930s, Heidegger did in fact come to see something like that; he did subsequently displace Dasein's projective understanding, freedom, and transcendence. That is what is called the "later" Heidegger or what Bill Richardson called "Heidegger II." But the results, while deeply satisfying in terms of what Heidegger has to say about *physis* and "letting be" (*Gelassenheit*), are deeply mystifying as regards the face of the other, above all the face of suffering. We get a clue to that in the utterly tasteless utterance about murder and agriculture, which give us some idea of how much light is thrown on concrete ethical situations by occupying the standpoint of "thought." Thinking *neutralizes* murder; it does not disclose it in advance. The extent to which *Gelassenheit* is stone deaf to flesh, to suffering flesh, has been artfully developed, by the way, in Luce Irigaray's *Martin Heidegger: The Forgetting of Air*, which takes "the rose is without why" as an epigraph and then documents a systematic oblivion of "flesh" in Heidegger which, to summarize too quickly, is also my complaint in *Demythologizing Heidegger*.

So the later Heidegger makes things worse. I agree that there is a lot that a Christian theologian like Karl Rahner, and any theologian interested in a theology of sin, can do with the early existential analytic. That is because in no small part Heidegger has borrowed, however selectively, a good deal of these structures from Kierkegaard, Luther, Pascal, Augustine, and Paul, to begin with, and then formalized them, so that when the theologian looks into the early texts of Heidegger he often finds his own image looking back.[3] These analyses remain in touch with the factical situation of concrete human beings in a way that is, however, weakened in the later, more mystified and mythologized writings from the *Beiträge* on, where it seems to me Heidegger's thought, in particular of *Ereignis*, began to lose touch with reality. However beautiful the later writings on the Fourfold, they are insensitive as regards the sufferings of concrete, historical human beings, which are swallowed up in a myth about Being that took root in the 1930s when Heidegger became harshly critical of Christians, kept Karl Rahner and other Jesuit students at arm's length for "not doing philosophy,"[4] and began celebrating what the biblical tradition would call faceless pagan gods.

If we find in *Being and Time* a very Pauline-Augustinian figure, when we turn to the later writings we find a *Seinsgeschick* where the concerns of factical life are engulfed in what Lyotard would call a *grand récit*, Being's big story as it ducks and weaves through Greco-European history. Being grows darkest of all in the age of "subject-ism" and of the advent of modern democracies, just when men and women began to break out of the crust of the top-down onto-theo-politics of antiquity and the middle ages. Like Nietzsche, Heidegger had nothing but contempt for democracy and could not see a difference that made a difference ("ontologically," "essentially," *im Wesen*) between Stalinist Russia and the western democracies, painting them, along with National Socialism (when the Nazis stopped listening to him), as all the "same" in his *Seins-geschicklich* grey-on-grey! To give us an idea that Heidegger is settling into the concrete weal and woes of real people, Richardson cites the text from the *Parmenides* course on the *polis* as "the abode gathered into itself of the uncon-cealedness of beings." Now if you want to see what talking like that about the *polis* actually *means* for Heidegger read some *other* passages from the *Parmenides* lectures that Bill Richardson does not cite, where Heidegger reduces American democracy to technology (64), which is also the essence of the Russian (86), warns us that it would be a big mistake to confuse *limos* and hence *lethe* with "hunger," which was of no interest to *his* Greeks (71–73), and then, most stunning of all, tells the Germans (it is 1942–1943) that this historical people is invincible and has already won the victory, provided they stick with the "essence" of history (77), which is Germany, as the land of poets and thinkers, over all.

What then, in God's name, does *lethe* mean? What is being concealed or distorted? What is the monstrous? What is Dasein's "downfall"? What is un-concealed when something is wrested from *lethe* in the struggle between *lethe* and *aletheia*? On his best day Heidegger is saying that we need to rec-ognize the self-withdrawing character of nature, that natural things ought not to be reduced to "objects" of our domination but experienced as "things" that emerge into presence from out of their own grounds, like the "rose" which is without why in Angelus Silesius. But this beautiful idea of the "thinging of the thing," which is a completely ontic and particular phenomenon that Hei-degger has singled out for special nurturing and caressing, does not at all merit the grandiose name of "Being," or of the event in which Being is appro-priated unto itself (*Ereignis*). Heidegger does not see or admit the "equipri-mordiality"—to say the least!—of other phenomena, like the sphere of the sufferings of wounded flesh, of injustice, murder, which deserve at least as much fuss. Suffering is simply not what *lethe* means for Heidegger, which he regards as an "entirely" *ontic* matter, and Bill Richardson would agree. So do I, actually, but that is because I think that *everything* is ontic, and everything depends upon which ontical fields you have chosen to labor, which is your business, so long as you do not then declare everything else as "ontic," or "founded," or "derivative," of the work you are doing in your field. I myself want to savor the blooming of the rose *and* heed the imperatives of justice, in what Lyotard calls a "polytheistic" pluralism, and not get into a game about which is the ontological foundation of which.

So I reject the idea, which Bill Richardson is arguing, that what Heidegger calls *lethe* or the battle within *aletheia* could supply some sort of "ontological ground" upon which one could subsequently develop an account of justice, even though it is not directly about justice, because *Irre* somehow leads us (and may have lead Heidegger) into evil and because un-concealment could somehow lead us out (*sed libera nos a malo*). I reject this because (1) I do not think questions of justice require such second order accounts like Irre—as I argued in *Against Ethics*—and because (2), were they needed, Heidegger would be among all major contemporary continental philosophers singularly unequipped to supply them, as I argued in *Demythologizing Heidegger*. For his *lethe* leaves good and evil largely untouched. It has next to nothing to do with the ethical and political conditions of human flourishing, with concrete human freedom and individual dignity. For "modernity," the age in which such conditions are recognized at least in principle, is considered by Heidegger to be the age of the most extreme removal and withdrawal of Being, *lethe*'s darkest night. As ethico-political circumstances wax, the fate of Being wanes. What then is "frightful," "horrible," "atrocious," and "monstrous" for Heidegger? How about the injustice and misfortune of people who are out in the cold? Not so, for that does not belong to the essence of homelessness, which concerns the occlusion of the poetic essence of dwelling. Well, then, how about the fact that the whole race could be incinerated in a nuclear attack? Wrong again, for that does not belong to the "*essence* of destruction," which concerns the occlusion of the poetic essence of building.[5]

The only light thrown by what he calls *Wesen*, *Ereignis*, or the *Seins-geschick*—which are grossly presumptuous and inflated designations of the particular phenomena he is in fact describing—on evil and injustice, on the malice and murderousness of war, for example, is to differentiate its pre-technological and technological forms, "hand to hand combat" (see the hand-wringing about the decline of handwriting and the rise of typewriters in the *Parmenides* lecture),[6] for example, from technologized war. Now that is a tremendously important distinction, to be sure, but not under Heidegger's "hand." Because for Heidegger it is the *technology* of war that is a matter for thought or concern, not the technology of *war*. Technologization, whether of war or of cooking pasta, point to the occlusion of the poetic essence of *physis. If war did not assume technological form it would not even show up on the screen of the history of Being.* It would not be a matter of essential" thinking. Just as, on his reading, Trakl could not possibly be considered a "war poet" because Trakl is concerned with something "more essential" and "infinitely greater" than thousands of slaughtered young men and women— viz, a personal and idiosyncratic view of western history which Heideggerian hybris absurdly magnifies into the "history of Being."[7] War *as war* is no part of Being's sending or withdrawing; nor is hatred or starvation, not *as such*. Technologized murder does show up, of course, but only to be declared "in essence the same" as technologized agriculture because they are *both technological*. By implication, hand to hand killing and handwriting must also be "in essence the same" because they are both done by hand, not by machines.

Far from supplying some prior *ontological ground* that provides a basis for explaining evil and injustice, as Bill Richardson would have it, justice and injustice, war and peace, murder and feeding people, are *ontologically neutralized* by thinking, bracketed by a phainesthetic reduction of good and evil. They are just not matters of thought. Not only does "thought" not have much to say about them, but when it does, we are so embarrassed by what is said that we wish it had kept quiet!

I am in sympathy with the first part of Bill Richardson's "conclusion," about the proximity of conscience and its formal indication in *Being and Time*—although I do believe Heidegger is only "formally indicating" half-heartedly and that he is leaving out the "heart" in these texts, the heart of these texts. But if that is true of the early Heidegger, after the 1920s I think Heidegger fell out of touch with the movements of factical life that he had so promisingly begun to analyze in the 1920s, and so I think Richardson, who is deeply concerned with good and evil, is being too good, too generous, in his reading of the later Heidegger. That is what I meant when I said, so brassily, that he was running Heidegger's *lethe* together with the Hebrew story of the first sin. Richardson is giving the later Heidegger too much credit, trying to make what I take to be a mystified, romanticized, and essentialistic account of the technological concealment of a poetic experience of *physis* and treat it as if it threw some light on the malice within the human heart or explained the "monstrous" things in human life. The fallaciousness of that assumption can be multiply documented in Heidegger's texts, as I have tried to do in *Demythologizing Heidegger*: what Heidegger's calls the withdrawal of Being grows *deepest* in modernity, the age of "subject-ism," just when the aspirations for freedom, emancipation, and human flourishing begin to break out of pre-modern binds; the recognition of the value of individuals begins to emerge just at that point that he considers the beginning of the end, the dark night of the West, of the *Abend-land*, read "democracy", what is truly monstrous about modernity—that *killing* has now assumed unthinkable proportions, that the annihilation of the human race is now possible, that homelessness and displaced peoples now roam the earth in unprecedented numbers due to incessant global and local-ethnic wars—is *not* a matter of thought. The faceless darkness of *lethe* is a poetico-technological darkening, not the darkness of a murderous heart, not directly, as we both agree, and not as some sort of prior ontological ground, as Richardson argues. To that should be added another and very fundamental disagreement between me and Bill Richardson, which has to do with allowing the very idea of a "clearing" to get off the ground, and to suppose that someone can come along and be in a position to say something "essential" about the *Wesen* of the *Lichtung*, as if there were one (as if there were *one*). That I think is a mistake and an illusion, and it can even be a dangerous idea.

NOTES

1. John D. Caputo, "Presenting Heidegger," *American Catholic Philosophical Quarterly*, 64 (May, 1995): 130–131.
2. For my reading of the lectures on Paul and Aristotle in the first Freiburg period, see DH, chs. 2–3.
3. That is the argument of DH, ch. 9, "Heidegger's Gods."
4. See Hugo Ott, *Martin Heidegger: A Political Life*, trans. Allan Blunden (New York: Basic Books, 1993), pp. 274–76.
5. I have analyzed these texts with more care in DH, ch. 7, "Heidegger's Scandal."
6. *Parmenides*, pp. 80–81.
7. For my interpretation of Heidegger's reading of Trakl, see DH, ch. 8, "Heidegger's Poets."

5   *KHORA* OR GOD?

RICHARD KEARNEY

In an essay entitled "Dark Hearts: Heidegger, Richardson and Evil," Jack
Caputo has this to say about his debt to the great American Heideggerian,
Bill Richardson: "If, as Heidegger says, thinking is thanking, then one can
offer a work of thought as a bit of gratitude. Derrida, on the other hand,
repeats the warning of the circle of the gift according to which, in all gift-giv-
ing, something is always returned to the giver. The giver always gets a pay
back, a return on the investment, if only (or especially) in the most oblique,
the most indirect form, of gratitude. Therefore, the purest gift-gifting
demands ingratitude, which does not pay the giver back and therefore pay off
and nullify his generosity. Since I am in the highest degree the beneficiary of
William Richardson's work and friendship, and more grateful than I am permitted to say, I have undertaken to protect his generosity with a certain
ingratitude, precisely understood, with an utterly ungrateful bit of disagreement, not only with him, but also with Heidegger, to whom I have accumulated a life-long debt. So I offer what follows in the spirit of the deepest and
most loyal ingratitude, cognizant always of the unworthiness of my ungift,
which comes in response to what in a simpler world I would call the richness
of the contribution that William Richardson has made to philosophy in
America."[1] Replace the names Richardson for Caputo—and Derrida for Heidegger—in the above citation, and you will have a reasonable idea of my own
"loyal ingratitude" to Jack Caputo here today. Or as Nietzsche put it, in more
graphic terms, the best way to thank a mentor is to be a thorn in his flesh.

So here goes. I want to concentrate here on Jack Caputo's intriguing
analysis of the notion of *Khora* in *The Prayers and Tears of Jacques Derrida:
Religion without Religion*.[2] Though this analysis is deeply indebted to Derrida, and especially his essay of the same name,[3] there is, I submit, something
uniquely suggestive and provocative about Caputo's reading.

The first mention of *khora* in *Prayers and Tears* occurs in the second
page. It arises in the context of Caputo's discussion of Derrida's distinction

between the *Differance* of deconstruction and the "God" of negative theology. This is how Caputo unpacks the distinction: "However highly it is esteemed, *differance* is not God. Negative theology is always on the track of a 'hyperessentiality,' of something hyper-present, hyper-real or sur-real, so really real that we are never satisfied simply to say that is is merely real. *Differance*, on the other hand, is less than real, not quite real, never gets as far as being or entity or presence, which is why it is emblematized by insubstantial quasi-beings like ashes and ghosts which flutter between existence and nonexistence, or with humble *khora*, say, rather than with the prestigious Platonic sun" (PT, p. 2). Caputo concludes with this typically teasing inversion: Derrida's *differance*, he suggests, "is but a quasi-transcendental anteriority, not a supereminent, transcendent ulteriority" (PT, p. 3). So far, so good.

Later in this opening chapter, entitled "God is not *Differance*," Caputo adds another telling inflection to the point at issue. If God is higher than being, *differance* is lower than it. If God, like Plato's *agathon*, has gone beyond us, *differance* is more like Plato's *khora* in that it hasn't yet reached us. It is beneath us, before us, behind us: anterior rather than ulterior. This is how Caputo, paraphrasing Derrida, puts it: "God does not *merely* exist; *differance* does not *quite* exist. God is ineffable the way Plato's *agathon* is ineffable, beyond being, whereas *differance* is like the atheological ineffability of Plato's *khora*, beneath being (Khora 30/ON, 96)" (PT, p. 10). In other words, unlike the God of theology, Khora is radically anonymous, amorphous, aleatory and errant—or as Derrida would say, "destinerrant" (PT, p. 11).

In a subsequent section of the book entitled "Three Ways to Avoid Speaking," Caputo revisits Derrida's landmark intervention in the negative theology debate "How not to Speak: Denials" (Psy., 563).[4] The apophatic tradition of negative speaking—extending from the Greeks to Eckhart and Heidegger—begins with Plato. But Plato was complex in that he pointed to two different "topics of negativity" (Psy., 563). On the one hand, the famous Good beyond being (*epekeina tes ousias*), that so influenced the Christian neo-Platonic heritage of negative theology; on the other, the infamous *khora* before being. Or as Derrida himself observes, *khora* is without being in that it "eludes all anthropo-theological schemes, all history, all revelation, all truth."[5] Whereas one is obliged with *khora*, as with *agathon*, to unsay what one has said, the former differs from the latter in that is not a form, or the Form of all Forms, but precedes both form and sensibility. Reinterpreted by human language, *khora* can only be expressed in a series of tentative analogies or "didactic" metaphors—for example, in Plato's *Timaeus* (47e–53b) as space, nurse, mother, matrix, imprint, receptable, winnowing basket, essence of perfume, etc.,[6] or within philosophy itself as a series of approximative notions such as *hyle* (Aristotle, Husserl), *extensio* (Descartes) or *magma* (Castoriadis).

What interests Derrida—and by extension Caputo—is not, however, how *khora* came to be said, albeit inexactly, *within* the language of the logo-centric tradition of metaphysics and metaphorics. It is rather how *khora* manages to escape this tradition of language, appearing instead as an abso-lute stranger to it—or, to quote Caputo, as an 'outsider with no place to lay her/its head, in philosophy or in mythology, for it is the proper object of nei-ther *logos* nor *mythos*' (PT, p. 35). Caputo claims that this second (more elu-sive and external) tropic of negativity is anterior to both being and non-being, the intelligible and the sensible, without being analogous to either. Citing Derrida's reading of Plato's reading of *khora*, Caputo makes the following suggestive stab at a description of the indescribable: "*Khora* is neither pre-sent nor absent, active nor passive, the Good nor evil, living nor nonliving (*Timaeus*, 50c). Neither theomorphic nor anthropomorphic—but rather atheological and nonhuman—*khora* is not even a receptacle, which would also be something that is itself inscribed within it" (PT, p. 36). Nor, insists Caputo, is this discourse metaphoric, "for it does not have to do with a sensi-ble likeness of something supersensible, a relationship that is itself within *khora* (Psy., 567–68). *Khora* has no meaning or essence, no identity to fall back upon. She/it receives all without becoming anything, which is why she/it can become the subject of neither a philosopheme nor a mytheme ("*Khora*" in ON, p. 102). In short, the *khora* is *tout autre*, very" (PT, p. 36).

Now while we might be tempted to think that the Platonic metaphors of matrix, mother, and nurse in the *Timaeus*, imply a certain act of benevolence or benificence, of nurturing or engendering, Caputo and Derrida are adamant that *khora* is no giver of gifts. One cannot say of *khora*, as one might say of God or the Good, that it "gives." *Khora*, Derrida tells us, is "this 'thing' that is nothing of that to which this 'thing' nonetheless seems to 'give place' (*donner lieu*)—without however, this 'thing' ever *giving* anything" (Psy., p. 568). And even if one can say that *khora* "gives place" to something it does so "without the least generosity, either divine or human" (Foi, p. 86). Giving place is simply a letting take place that has nothing to do with producing, cre-ating, or existing as such. One cannot even say that *khora* is, or is not; only that there is *Khora* (*il y a khora*). But this *il y a*, as Derrida again insists, "gives nothing in giving place or in giving to think, whereby it will be risky to see in it the equivalent of an *es gibt*, of the *es gibt* which remains without a doubt implicated in every negative theology . . ." ("*Khora*" in ON, 96; cited Caputo, PT, p. 36).

In sharp contrast, therefore, to the neo-Platonic/Christian/mystical/metaphysical tradition of One-Good-God beyond being, *khora* is not only a-theological but a-donational. It even eschews the more contemporary idioms of transcendence and mystery—the Levinasian idiom of infinity (oth-erwise than being), the Marionesque gesture of donation (God without being) or the Heideggerian principle of event (the gift of being). It is not even a third kind (*genos*) beyond the altenatives of being and non-being. It is not a "kind" at all, but a radical singularity of which one might say—what is your name? (ON, p. 111). But *khora* cannot ever possess a proper or a common name. It is unnameable and unspeakable. And yet, both Derrida and Caputo keep repeating, it is the very impossibility of speaking about *khora* that is also the necessity of speaking about it!

But how can we do so? How can one say anything at all about *khora*? What we are seeking seems impossible. And yet, it is (in Derrida's words) something that "beyond all given philosophemes, has nevertheless left its trace in language" (Psy., 569). Plato, for starters, hazarded a guess at this nameless thing by calling it *khora*, with its attendant bevy of metaphors. And *khora*, unlike the words God or the Good, is a word-trace that "promises nothing" (PT., p. 37). In sharp contradistinction to the theological names deriving from the Good beyond being of Greek metaphysics or the Creator God of Judeo-Christian revelation, *khora* suggests an altogether alternative site—one that is "barren, radically nonhuman and atheological." So that if this "place" called *khora* can be said, like the God of negative theology, to indeed be "wholly other," it is so in a manner totally distinct from all theologies, apophatic or otherwise. Its desert is not a dark night of the soul waiting to be redeemed by light but a no-place that remains deserted. Just ashes and ashes, without ascensions into heaven. Abyss and abyss without elevation from the void. *Il y a la cendre*, to cite Caputo's paraphrase of Derrida.

So one is a little surprised then, is one not, to find Caputo suggesting that there is at bottom a certain undecidability between God and *khora*. Having persuasively demonstrated the radical difference between the two—as exemplified by Levinasian hyperbole on the one hand and Derridean deconstruction on the other—we now have Caputo asking: "what is the wholly other. . . . God or *khora*? What do I love when I love my God, God or *khora*? How are we to decide? Do we have to choose?" (PT., p. 37). I may be wrong but I suspect that Caputo is suggesting that we *don't*—since the issue remains radically undecidable? But I would like to disagree at this point and suggest that we *do* have to choose; and that a religious God is a nonsense unless it calls for such choice (what Kierkegaard called the leap of faith).

Moreover, Caputo would seem to allow as much himself when he claims that the antithesis between *khora* and God admits of no "passage" between the two. Whereas the one takes the high road towards the God/Good beyond being, the other sticks to the uncompromising and inconsolable emptiness of the abyss. Whereas Dionysius and other mystical-apophatic theologians praise and pray to God, invoking his kenotic goodness and hyperousiological generosity, *khora* is a very different kettle of fish. It does not command prayer or praise for it is neither good nor generous nor giving. It is radical "destinerrance" and those who end up in its desert always end up lost.

Fair enough. But if this be so, is Caputo justified in claiming that Derrida is at the same time on the side of the original desert fathers, the anhorites—or "an-khora-ites" as he rechristens them—with their lean and hungry looks? Can he legitimately nominate, even in jest, the advocate of deconstructive *khora* as "*Saint Jacques*, Derrida the Desert Father!"? For, unlike Derrida, the desert fathers *did* praise and dance and sing before their desert God. Anthony and Jerome, Simon and John Chysostomum, spent many months in their caves—to be sure—but they also walked out into the light from time to time and praised their Maker. To do otherwise would for them be to despair, or as Kierkegaard put it in *Fear and Trembling*, to take only the first step in the two-steps of faith: the step of infinite resignation which gives up creation without taking the second step of wanting it back again. (If Abraham had opted for endless "destinerrance" over religious faith, he would never have ventured his leap of faith and received Isaac *back*).

I am suggesting, in short, that Caputo cannot have it both ways. He cannot claim on the one hand that Derrida takes the path of a-theological desertification and then reclaim him as a saintly ankhorite father. Nor will it do to refuse the two alternatives altogether and declare the issue undecidable—God and/or/neither/nor *Khora*? That too is having it both ways. Not an option, I would submit, for the believer. (Though a perfectly consistent one for the deconstructionist).

By believer I mean, incidentally, not just a believer in God but also—why not?—a believer in *khora*. Perhaps *khora* is no less an interpretative leap in the dark than religious faith is? God and *khora* are conceivably two different names for the same thing—the same nameless, indescribable experience of the abyss. But the choice between names is not insignificant. Which direction you leap in surely matters? For while the former theistic option sees the experience in the empty desert as "a dark night of the soul" on the way towards the encounter with God, the latter sees it rather as a night without end, a place where prayer, promise, praise, or faith is *not* applicable. Not a place the desert fathers would want to hang around for very long, I suspect.

In the *khora* desert it is always inevitable that one loses one's way. Isn't that what the deconstructive commitment to "destinerrance" means? But in the ankhorite wilderness—traversed by the desert fathers and subsequent mystics like Eckhart, Teresa, Silesius, or St John of the Cross—the journey through desolation is made *in the fervent hope* that one will find a path to God, that the lost sheep will be found and brought home to the Father. (A prospect that must be anathema to all deconstructors, no?) There is a genuine difference between ankhorite fathers and deconstructive sons. A healthy difference to be sure; but one that can't be magicked away or turned into a soft-shoe-shuffle of undecidability. One cannot sit on double-edged fences for ever. (That's maybe unfair but Jack knows what I mean).

It boils down to this, as I see it: Deconstruction isn't just describing *khora* as one might describe a sunset or a storm at sea. It is describing it in the same way it describes *differance* or *pharmakon* or *supplement* or *archi-ecriture* etc. That is, it appears to express a marked preference for *khora*, and its allies, over its opponents. Not moral preference, granted, but in some minimal and irreducible sense, an evaluative preference nonetheless. As one reads Caputo one cannot help surmising that for him *khora* is—at bottom and when all our metaphysical and other illusions are stripped away—the *ways things are*. It is a better and deeper and more profound way of viewing things than its theological rivals, for example. It is, in the heel of the hunt, closer to the "reality" of things than all known non-*khora* alternatives. In that sense, yes, deconstruction does appear to take sides even when it is doing its most non-commital side-step of neither/nor/both/and. Deconstuction makes a preferential option for *khora*, while not denying of course (it would never be so intolerant) that non-*khoraites* can be nice guys too, people with the best of intentions, questioners who might even find their way back to the no-place of deconstruction, eventually.

But that is not the only disagreement I have with my two favorite *khoraites*—Jack and Jacques. I have a much deeper reservation about the nature of *khora* itself—if taken as the most anterior and irreducible site of sites. While I acknowledge that it is a place/no-place each of us must encounter, come to terms with, traverse sometime in our lives, I do not think it is the best place to spend our lives, or to encourage others to spend theirs indefinitely. (I am not talking here, I hasten to add, of Plato's purely cosmo-logical notion of *khora*; nor indeed of Kristeva's psycho-linguistic one: for neither of these, as I read them, see *khora* as an alternative to a theistic God[7]). No, I am speaking here of *khora*, as described by Caputo, in terms of an empty desert abyss, a no-place we experience in the fear-and-trembling moment of uncertainity and loss, a dark night of the soul waiting without response (or what Levinas terms the "mute, absolutely indeterminate men-ace" of the "there is"—the "horror" of "noctoral space." And Levinas leaves us in little doubt as to the a-theistic nature of this experience: "Rather than to a God, the notion of the *there is* leads us to the absence of God, the absence of any being . . . before the light comes").[8] Yes, I do acknowledge this experi-ence of *khora* as part and parcel of human existence. I do not deny that all of us have some experience of *khora/il y a* as the "horror" of the night with "no exits" which "does not answerable. . . ."[9] But I'm not sure I want to celebrate it as the best we can do. And I certainly wouldn't want to recommend it as an on-going *modus vivendi* for those who are suffering its darkness. If compelled, I'd personally opt for Levinas' move from the *Il y a* of irremissible existence to the *illeite* of ethical transcendence.

But what is *khora* in more familiar language? For most non-philosophers, *khora* is experienced as misery, terror, loss and desolation. *Khora* is Oedipus without eyes, Sisyphus in hades, Prometheus in chains, Ephighenia in waiting. *Khora* is the *tohu bohu* before creation; it is Job in agony, Jonah in the belly of the whale, Joseph at the bottom of the well, Jesus abandoned on the cross (crying out to the father) or descended into hell. It is Conrad's "heart of darkness," Hamlet's "flat stale and unprofitable" world, Monte Christo's prison cell, Primo Levi's camp. Or to put it in more contemporary idioms, it is Brian Keenan (the Irish teacher held hostage in Lebanon) locked in a hole in the ground, it is a Taiwanese or Turkish child trapped under rubble, a cornered East Timor prisoner, waiting, waiting, waiting . . . wishing for the relief of death to end the insomniac dark. Or more banally, more basically, more quotidianly—any one of us faced with the meaningless void of our existence and wondering why we should bother going on.

Now, given the fact that some of my best friends are existentialists and deconstructionists, I am the last person in the world to want to deny the *reality* of these kinds of experiences. They may well be the *most* "real" (at least in Lacan's sense) of all our human experiences, the most unspeakably traumatic "limit experiences" of something that excedes our understanding. The most sublime of horrors. But I'd find it hard to make a preferential option for them and suggest that others do likewise.

Well, I know Jack Caputo will throw his hands in the air and say, on reading this kind of list, "that is not what I meant at all! We know that the *khora* is unlivable; we know—with Eliot—that human kind cannot bear too much reality; we accept that people need to climb out of the *khora* cave into the light of everyday consolations and pastimes and distractions (call it the 'they world,' the 'natural attitude,' the 'metaphysics of presence,' or any number of religious beliefs in God as some saving, healing, loving, benevolent grace). All we are saying is—give *khora* a chance. Because even though it may not be livable it is what life is ultimately and ineluctably and at bottom about!" *Au fond, sans fond, il y a khora.* That's how I imagine Jack replying. (But he'll speak for himself in a moment, if he's still speaking to me. . . .)

Please don't get me wrong. I'm not suggesting we flee the shadow at the heart of existence. I'm not saying we shouldn't face up to the terrors and horrors and absurdities of the world and do so in fear in trembling. If we do not acknowledge the existence of ineffable emptiness and meaningless torment—how can we ever speak about it or go beyond it. As Camus rightly said, you must live the absurd in order to fight it. Agreed. But is that what Caputo is saying about *khora*? That we should confront it in order to struggle against it, go beyond it, put an end to it as soon as we can? I get the impression rather that for deconstructors like Caputo *khora* is really rather more fundamental and anterior and "really real" than God or the Good or Being and all that. Just as writing is more archi-ultimate than speech and textuality is more archi-ultimate than presence? If *khora* is indeed being lost in the desert—destinerrance—the undecidable, atheological absence of light and grace, I don't get the feeling that Jack is reassuring us that this is just temporary, that we may (with a few more prayers and tears) soon find our shepherd again, be saved by the Father, and redeemed into the Kingdom.

I may be wrong but I get the *opposite* impression reading *Prayers and Tears*: that to accept being lost in the desert of destinerrance, without looking for meaning or healing, is really more courageous, more steel-nerved and uncompromising than seeking to be found. Not that Jack doesn't have heaps of sympathy for those who can't hack it, who just can't take the cold of the desert night for too long, can't bear being scared witless by the horror of *toho bohu/il y a*. His heart goes out to those who need to put an end to the fear and trembling by taking a leap of faith and gettting their Isaac back, climbing down off the cross, opening the cell hatch, hankering for redemption and peace and calm. He bleeds for those who pray the black void of depression will soon fade, that the chalice will pass from them—even if it means adding a little prozac to their prayers at times. But he doesn't buy it. It's not for him, or JD and the other chevaliers of deconstruction. Higher than the knight of faith (or children of faith) is the knight of *khora* who braves the long day's journey into never-ending night. And never looks back. Nor forward.

But I read things somewhat differently. In my less heroic book, ankhorites went to the desert to find God, not *khora*. They didn't make a mystique of loss or a virtue of the void. And if it is indeed true that they traversed emptiness and destitution it was *faute de mieux*, an unavoidable detour on the way to grace. They'd have preferred (unless they were Levinasian *miserabilistes*) to have hit the land of milk and honey after the first dune. But since life isn't like that, they had to learn the hard way on their way to the kingdom. Losing life—yes—but in order to gain it.

What I'm basically saying is that I don't believe Jack Caputo is entirely neutral on the question of *khora*. If anything, I reckon he reckons it's the place (or no-place) to be if you really want to get to the heart of things. It's what is really out there (in here) once we go beyond alibis and illusions, salves and solaces, credoes and consolations, and open our eyes and ears.

I may be wrong of course. It's hard to be right about something as elusive as *khora*.[10] So by way of conclusion, let me return to Jack's extraordinary book, *The Prayers and Tears of Jacques Derrida*.

On p. 39 of *Prayers and Tears*, Jack Caputo does indeed admit prayer into the unholy of unholies—the *khora*; but it is a very specific kind of a-theistic, a-theological, deconstructive prayer; not at all like Dionysius' "Christian prayer, directed to the Trinity" (p. 39). This latter prayer—the kind invoked in the title of JC's book—is not one addressed to God "the saving name, the giver of all good gifts" (*ibid*). It does not seek to keep itself "safe from the abyss of *khora*" (*ibid*) by having recourse to something else beyond that formless anonymous "spacing" or "interval" within which all things find their place (*"Khora,"* ON, 125). Here prayer is no "desert guide" but an unconsoling, uncompromising and, as JC notes, "slightly sinful" mode of address—for it addresses an alterity in each and everything so terrifyingly sublime, so textually irreducible, that there is no exit (short of some quick backflip into theology/ideology/logocentrism—or some common sense of presence. An option for the fainthearted). This is why JC can agree with JD that *khora* has very little to do with a theistic divinity and everything to do with the "very spacing of de-construction" (ON, p. 80): something like a "surname for differance." (PT, p. 40)

For me, if I may repeat myself, the problem with JC's approach here— and I am not saying it is identical with JD's—is that it sets *deconstruction/differance/khora* up as an alternative to, even perhaps an adversary of, theology (apophatic or otherwise). Either *khora* or God. Either Dionysius or Derrida. (Or as he rephrases the alternative in a later chapter: either the "angelic doctor" from Aquino or the "devilish deconstructor" from the Rue d'Ulm p. 168–169). On the left side of the ring, Caputo marshals the idioms of the originary Father—fusion, presence, union, circularity, totality, economy, sameness. On the right, over and against them, he places the clearly preferred idioms of the "more maternal simulacrum" of *khora*—"aleatory gratuiteousness and anarchic abandon" (p. 169). If you say thanks to God the giver, concedes Caputo, you do *"not* say thanks" to *khora* (*ibid*). *"Il y a khora,"* he goes on to explain, "but she/it does not generously 'give' anything" and is not "the gesture of a donor subject" (*Khora,* 37–38/ON, 100). "Rather she/it is the spacing within which an unlimited number of events take place, in her/its place" (p. 169).

I have a problem with this kind of alternativism which risks turning theology (negative and positive) into a caricature and seems to assume that most canonized saints were either curia hacks or obsessional neurotics—suckers for ecclesiastical certainty and closure (as he implies of Thomas Aquinas after he had seen the light) (PT, p. 60–61). Not all mystical experience is "unitive" and fusional, as JC seems to imply in such passages. Certainly not the experiences of Teresa of Lisieux, Angelus Silesius, or Meister Eckhart. And not every notion of the Christian Trinitarian God—not to mention the Jewish Yahweh or Muslim Allah—is a paralyzing fetish of presence or hyper-essence. What of Eckhart's God beyond God? Silesius' rose without why? Cusanus' *Possest*. Or the wonderfully ludic notion of the three persons dancing around an empty space in respective acts of dispossession—*perichoresis* (translated by the Latins as *circumincessio*): an event of loving letting-be stunningly captured in Andrei Rublev's icon of the three angels? (The early Jack Caputo knew far more than most about these things).

This is all a far cry, is it not, from the metaphysical chestnuts of pure self-identical presence: *ens causa sui, ipsum esse subsistens, actus purus non habens aliquid de potentialitate*? Hoary chestnuts which we should all be grateful were cracked open, over various fires, by the likes of Nietzsche, Feueurbach, Marx, Sartre, and Derrida.

What I am trying to say, by way of conclusion, is that I think Caputo, and also at times Derrida, has a tendency to set up a somewhat precipitous and over-dramatic polarity between God (equated with fusion/union/essence/presence) and its deconstructive opposite (*khora/differance/ecriture/pharmakon*). While I can see the temptation to do this from a pedagogical point of view—we all need *some* black and white distinctions—it is rather surprising coming from the maestroes of deconstruction themselves. And surely something of a compromise of the celebrated deconstructive logic of both/and/neither/nor?

To avoid such polarizing gestures, I would suggest that there are many degrees of latitude and longtitude between the north pole of God (qua pure hyper-essence) and the south pole of *khora* (qua irreducible anonymous abyss). My shortlist above, ranging from Eckhart to *perichoresis*, mentions just a few of these possible "third-ways" beyond such polarity. Indeed I would suggest that we might go further still. Beyond two- and even three-fold approaches to a *four-fold* one including in its chiasmic interplay the following players: *khora*, God, being, and the Good. But that is for another day of dialogue and *disputatio* with my dear colleague and friend, Jack Caputo.

EPILOGUES

To be entirely fair to Jack, the arguments rehearsed above, do not perhaps tell the whole story of his approach to the *khora*/God relation. (Indeed how could it if this testimonial to Jack Caputo's wonderful book is to be more than servile paraphrase). In certain other passages of *Prayers and Tears*, it does appear that Caputo is offering a different take on this relation, but without acknowledging it as different (even incompatible). Whether it is a case of not noticing his own textual inconsistencies or of wanting to have it both ways, or simply being too dialectically subtle for the likes of me, none is really the issue. The important thing to note is that, at times, JC does acknowledge that *khora* may be an ally as much as an adversary of God. On one occasion, for instance, he even sees *khora* as a precondition of genuine theistic faith. *Khora*, he concedes here, is "a general condition of any 'belief'"; adding: "How could Derrida—for whom everything depends upon faith—rule out religious faith? Why would Derrida want to ban the name of God, a name he dearly loves" (p. 59). Caputo even appears, in this passage, to equate Derrida's version of *khora* with Kierkegaard's version of theistic faith: "Derrida does no more than follow Johannes de Silentio, Abraham's poet, from whose fear and trembling we learn that faith 'must never be a certainty' but a passion, the 'highest passion' that . . . still has the heart to push ahead (DM, 78/GD 80), which is the repetition forward and the marvel" (p. 59). But that is a change of note, is it not, from the more prevalent tune of either/or— either *khora or God*—rehearsed above?

A curious thing about Caputo's approach to *khora* and Derrida's is that the latter often seems more ready to make bridges (however provisional) between the engulfing *khora* and the saving God. It's as if Caputo, a crypto-theist, is desperately trying *not* to evangelize deconstruction by turning it into a crypto-theology. A case of the theist does protest too much? Whereas Derrida, a self-declared atheist, has far less difficulty throwing ropes across the ostensible gap between the ungodly *khora* and God. (Note that he has as little compunction about cutting these cords also!) While making sure never to identify God directly with *Khora*, Derrida seems prepared at times to go some considerable way in acknowledging unexpected analogies and overlaps between the two. Let me cite some startling passages from his famous "Post-Scriptum" to *Derrida and Negative Theology*, subtitled "Aporias, Ways and Voices."

I begin with his more than sympathetic commentary of the Christian mystic, Angelus Silesius: "'God' 'is' the name of this bottomless collapse, of this endless desertification of language" (p. 301)—a name which is, at the same time, interpreted by Silesius as "the divinity of God as gift" (p. 300), Derrida proceeds to relate this God of Silesius—a God whom he, Silesius, prays to give Himself to the prayer—to "some *khora* (interval, place, spacing)" (p. 301). Everything, says Derrida, "is played out here" (ibid). And to Silesius' equation of the "Place" (*Ort*) and the "word" (*Wort*)—*Der Ort und's Wort ist Eins*—Derrida adjoins this reflection: "It is not that in which is found a subject or an object. It is found in us . . . The here of eternity is situated there, already: already there, it situates this throwing or this throwing up . . . but first of all throwing that puts outside, that produces the outside and thus space . . ." (p. 301). Later in the same "Post-Scriptum," Derrida displays a deep fascination with Silesius' approach to God's giving in terms of *Gelassenheit* and *play*. (The verse of Silesius he is commenting reads: "God plays with creation/All that is play that the deity gives itself," ibid.)

But before we lapse into ecumenical euphoria, Derrida puts an end to equivocation by marking a clear and unbridgeable difference—an abyss in fact—between the reading of place as God and as khora. As this statement of Derrida's position is crucial I quote the passage in full: "*'Der Ort is das Wort* (1:205) indeed affirms the place as word of God.—Is this place created by God? Is it part of the play? Or else is it God himself? Or even what precedes, in order to make them possible, both God and his Play? In other words, it remains to be known if this nonsensible (invisible and inaudible) place is opened by God, by the name of God (which would again be some other thing, perhaps), or if it is 'older' than the time of creation, than time itself, than history, narrative, word, etc. It remains to be known (beyond knowing) if the place is opened by appeal (response, the event that calls for the response, revelation, history, etc.), or if it remains impassively foreign, like *Khora*, to everything that takes its place and replaces itself and plays within this place, including what is named God" (pp. 314).

Derrida leaves us in little doubt that a choice is called for here between two rival, incompatible, and mutually exclusive notions of place. "Do we have any choice? Why choose between the two? Is it possible?" he asks rhetorically. To which he proffers the following altogether non-rhetorical answer: "But it is true that these two 'places,' these two experiences of place, these two ways are no doubt of an absolute heterogeneity. One place excludes the other, one (sur)passes the other, one does without the other, one is, absolutely, *without* the other" (p. 315). And so we have the antithesis: "*on one side*, on one way, a profound and abyssal eternity, fundamental but accessible to the teleo-eschatological narrative and to a certain experience or historical (or historial) revelation; *on the other side*, on the other way, the nontemporality of an abyss without bottom or surface, an absolute impassibility (neither life nor death) that gives rise to everything that it is not. In fact, two abysses" (p. 315).

As I read him, Derrida is on the side of the latter—the nontemporal, bottomless, impassible abyss, that does the work of *khora* and *differance*. To be sure, Derrida does admit to a certain relation between these two "places" in terms of an "exemplarism" of conjunction-disjunction vis-à-vis the term "without"; but this highly complex notion cannot really distract from the fundamental opposition between the two senses of "place," nor can it mitigate or abrogate Derrida's fundamental choice (as I see it) for *khora* over God. A choice I respect, even admire, but do not share.

To repeat: despite numerous analogies, there is a radical difference, in the heel of hunt, between Derrida and Silesius. Silesius sees our experience of the place of play as "one abyss calling to the other" (as in Psalm 41)—the void within us crying out to the unfathomable deep of God. (Silesius: "The abyss of my spirit always invokes with cries/The abyss of God: say which may be deeper?") By contrast, Derrida construes the place as the "indestructible *Khora* . . . the very spacing of de-construction" (p. 318).

Where Silesius' God promises peace and healing, Derrida's *Khora* is "gulf and chaos" (p. 321). The choice is, at bottom, between theism and atheism. Or if one prefers Derrida's more recent terms, between messianism and messianicity. The two are as inextricably linked as siamese twins but they beat with different hearts. They may look exactly alike, but they think very different thoughts and signal very different options.

"My faith comes forth from the crucible of doubt," confessed Dostoyevsky, the crucible serving here the function of atheistic *khora*. But his faith does come forth; it surpasses and goes beyond the preconditioning crucible—rightly or wrongly, for better or worse. It does not remain within it. There is, after all, and in spite of what Jack Caputo sometimes seems to suggest, a fundamental choice to be made between *khora* and God. I know what Derrida chooses; I know what I choose. My question to Jack is, what do you choose?

NOTES

1. J. Caputo, "Dark Hearts" in *From Phenomenology to Thought, Errancy and Desire*, ed. (B. E. Babich, Kluwer, Netherlands, 1995), p. 267.

2. J. Caputo, PT.

3. J. Derrida, "Khora" in ON, pp. 89–127.

4. J. Derrida, Psy.

5. J. Derrida, "*Khora*" in ON, p. 124.

6. Plato, *Timaeus and Critias,* trans. H. Lee, (Penguin, 1965). In the *Timaeus* 48–53, Plato describes the *khora* as follows: "it is the receptacle and, as it were, the nurse of all becoming and change (49) . . . anything that is to receive in itself every kind of character must be devoid of all character. Manufacturers of scent contrive the same initial conditions when they make liquids which are to receive the scent as odourless as possible . . . In the same way that which is going to receive properly and uniformly all the likenesses of the intelligible and eternal things must itself be devoid of all character. Therefore we must not call the mother and receptable of visible and sensible things either earth or air or fire or water . . . but we shall not be wrong if we describe it as invisible and formless, all embracing, possessed in a most puzzling way of intelligibility, yet very hard to grasp (51) . . . (It is) space which is eternal and indestructible, which provides a position for everything that comes to be, and which is apprehended without the senses by a sort of spurious reasoning and so is hard to believe in—we look at it indeed in a kind of dream . . . (52)."

7. See Julia Kristeva's analysis of *khora* in *Revolution and Poetic Language*, excerpted in *The Kristeva Reader*, ed. Toril Moi, Blackwell, (London, 1986), pp. 93–98, 108–109, 115–117. Kristeva defines the indefinable *khora* in the following terms: ". . . the drives, which are 'energy' charges as well as 'psychical' marks,

articulate what we call a *chora:* a non-expressive totality formed by the drives and their stases in a motility that is as full of movement as it is regulated. We borrow the term *chora* from Plato's *Timaeus* to denote an essentially mobile and extremely provisional articulation constituted by movements and their ephemeral stases. We differentiate this uncertain and indeterminate *articulation* from a *disposition* that already depends on representation . . . the *chora,* as rupture and articulations rhythm, precedes evidence, verisimilitude, spatiality and temporality. Our discourse—all discourse—moves with and against the *chora* in the sense that it simultaneously depends upon and refuses it. Although the *chora* can be designated and regulated, it can never be definitely posited: as a result, one can situate the *chora* and, if necessary, lend it a topology, but one can never give it axiomatic form" (pp. 93–94). Blending Plato with Klein, Kristeva goes on to argue that it is this same "rhythmic space" of *khora,* devoid of thesis or position, which constitutes significance. Plato himself, she points out, "leads us to such a process when he calls this receptacle or *chora* nourishing and maternal, not yet unified in an ordered whole because deity is absent from it" (p. 94). And yet, though deprived of identity, unity, and divinity, the *chora* is "is subject to a regulating process which is different from that of symbolic law but nevertheless effectuates discontinuities by temporarily articulating them and then starting over, again and again" (p. 94). The *khora* thus emerges for Kristeva as a "pre-verbal semiotic space," before language, law, or cognition proper. As a psychosomatic modality of signifying, "anterior to sign and syntax," it is not something that can be assumed by a knowing, constituted subject but rather governs the very connections "between the body (in the process of constituting itself as a body proper), objects and the protagonists of family structure" (p. 95). Thus while the semiotic *khora*—as the place of unconscious, pre-cognitive, pre-verbal drives—is "on the path of destruction, aggressivity and death," it is also, insists Kristeva, the locus of a maternal "ordering principle." She explains the paradox thus: "This is to say that the semiotic *chora* is no more than the place where the subject is both generated and negated, the place where his unity succumbs before the process of charges and stases that produce him" (p. 95). And yet the very semiotic processes and relations that make up the space of *khora* are only, Kristeva admits, properly attended to in *"dream* logic" (here she agrees with Plato, *Timaeus,* 52a) or in the semotic rhythms of the literary *text:* "Indifferent to language, enigmatic and feminine, this space underlying the written is rhythmic, unfettered, irreducible to its intelligible verbal translation; it is musical, anterior to judgment . . ." (p. 97). For Kristeva—as for Plato, Klein, Derrida and Caputo—*khora* brushes against the limits of logic and language (what Lacan calls the symbolic order).

8. E. Levinas, "There is: existence without existents," first published in 1946 as a section of *De l'existence a l'existant* (Vrin, Paris) and reprinted in the *The Levinas Reader,* ed. S. Hand, Blackwell, (London, 1989), pp. 32–33. Elsewhere in this same passage, which first outlines his original and highly influential notion of the *there is/il y a,* Levinas writes: ". . . night and the silence of nothingness. This impersonal, anonymous, yet inextinguishable 'consummation' of being, which murmurs in the depths of nothingness itself we shall designate by the term *there is. . . .* The anyonymous current of being invades, submerges every subject, person or thing. . . We

could say that the night is the very experience of the *there is,* if the term experience were not inapplicable to a situation which involves the total exclusion of light" (p. 30). In terms reminiscent of Derrida's/Caputo's *khora,* Levinas goes on to explain the inextricable link between the *there is* and darkness: "When the forms of things are dissolved in the night, the darkness of the the night . . . invades like a presence. In the night, where we are riven to it, we are not dealing with anything. But this nothing is not that of pure nothingness. There is no longer *this* or *that;* there is not 'something'. . . . It is immediately there. There is no discourse. Nothing responds to us but this silence; the voice of this silence is understood and frightens us like the silence of those infinite spaces" (p. 30). But in so far as the *there is* is an impersonal form, like it rains, or it is warm, its anonymity serves to de-subjectivize and de-personalise the human self. "What we call the I," says Levinas, "is itself submerged by the night, invaded, depersonalized, stifled by it" (p. 31). Without actually invoking the aboriginal notion of *khora,* Levinas' *Il y a* bears many of its traces qua dark and undifferentiated "background of existence" (p. 32). But Levinas, like Derrida and Caputo after him, will add certain existential aspects to this pre-conditioning, anonymous, nocturnal space: "It makes things appear to us, in a night, like the monotonous presence that bears down on us in insomnia" (p. 32). And this bearing down takes the form not just of fear and trembling but of horror itself: "Horror is somehow a movement which will strip consciousness of its very 'subjectivity' . . . In horror . . . the subject is depersonalized" (p. 33). But this horror is exacerbated by the fact that the *there is* has no exits. It is more horrifying than death, indeed, for unlike death, it offers no escape. As the ludic event of the night, the *il y a* is, concludes Levinas, "like the density of the void, like a murmur of silence. . . . Darkness is the very play of existence which would play itself out even if there were nothing. It is to express just this paradoxical existence that we have introudced the term 'there is'" (p. 35). Levinas' notion of the *there is* was to exert a deep influence on subsequent thinkers, informing not only Blanchot's concept of "disaster" but also Derrida's and Caputo's reading of *khora.* Sean Hand offers this highly suggestive account of this enigmatic and elusive phenomenon: "'There is' is anonymous and impersonal being in general. . . . It exists prior even to nothingness, the rumbling within silence that one hears when putting a shell to one's ear, the horrifying silence confronting the vigilant insomniac who is and is not an 'I'" (Introduction to 'There Is,' *The Levinas Reader,* p. 29). The *il y a* recurs throughout Levinas' oeuvre—*Time and the Other, Totality and Infinity, Difficult Freedom*—receiving this final formulation in Levinas' last major publication, *Autrement qu'etre ou au-dela de l'essence* (Nijhoff, The Hague, 1974, p. 207): "Mais l'essence imperturbable, egale et indifferente a toute responsabilite que, desormais, elle englobe, vire comme, dans l'insomnie, de cette neutralite et de cette egalite, en monotonie, en anonymat, en insignifiance, en bourdonnement incessant que rien ne peut plus arreter et qui absorbe toute signification, jusqu'a celle dont ce remue-menage est une modalite. L'essence s'etirant indefiniment, sans retenue, sans interruption possible . . . sans repit, sans suspension possible—c'est l'*il y a* horrifiant derriere toute finalite propre du *moi* thematisant . . ."

9. E. Levinas, "There is," *op.cit.,* p. 34.

10. If hermeneutics always begins with an element of misreading or misunder-standing—as Gadamer reminds us—then there is, I suspect, both a certain creative mis-prism in Caputo's reading of Derrida on *khora*: as there is in Derrida's reading of Plato on *khora*; and in my reading of both of their readings. But the buck stops, momentarily at least, somewhere. Otherwise we could never begin or end.

ABYSSUS ABYSSUM INVOCAT:
A RESPONSE TO KEARNEY

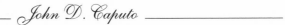

John D. Caputo

A year or so after *Against Ethics* appeared I received a letter from a former student who, having absorbed its last chapter on suicide and worms inching their way to silent graves was moved to asked me whether something had gone dreadfully wrong in my life! Not to worry, I said. I have always been fascinated—or hounded—by the abyss, an abyss, some abyss, from the *Abgrund* of the Godhead in Meister Eckhart, the abyss of Being in Heidegger, the *il y a* in Levinas, to Derrida's *khora*, abyss calling to abyss (Psy. 42:7), as the psalmist says, ceaselessly it seems, wherever I turned. Such flirtation with the abyss was trouble enough on its own but it was bound to buy me still more trouble from my readers, to expose my hide to the exquisite needling of the sort to which I am subjected by Kearney, Westphal, and Ayres. But this is important needling, because the work that the abyss does, or un-does, cannot be ducked. Abysses are tricky things, stretching as they do the all way from the *khora* in the *Timaeus* "up" to the mystical abyss of the Godhead beyond God, and they sometimes fall into a "possible confusion" with one another, as Levinas says. There are two tropics of negativity, Derrida said;[1] "at least," I would add. Consider that when you say "the rose is without why," you might mean that love or the gift is without why, which has all the makings of a lovely and benign abyss, or you might mean a Nietzschean play of forces, the great cosmic stupidity, which sounds downright nihilistic.

So the abyss, if there is one, repays reflection. But I do not think there is *one*, only one. The troubling thing about the abyss is precisely that this phenomenon lies at the outer limits of our experience, while our phenomenological powers function best with the medium sized things of quotidian life, in the temperate zones between the opposite polar regions. But the abyss lies at the outer limits, above or below, *au-delà de l'être* or *au dessous*, like the *agathon* or *khora*, or like God or *khora*, where there is, following Levinas, a possible confusion, or, following Derrida, a certain undecidability.

Like God or *khora*: that is the precise point of insertion for Richard Kearney's pointed blade. Richard Kearney, from whose brilliant "poetics of the possible" we have all so greatly profited, is worried about monsters. Good

friend that he is, he is worried about me, worried that I am left by this undecidability to twist slowly in the winds of indecision, one more despairing destinerrant deconstructionist wandering in the desert, a lost an-khor-ite *sans*
faith, an anchorite *sans* anchor, not a desert father but a stray son.

Richard Kearney does not want to be consumed by monsters. Who does?
But he tends to run together very disparate phenomena, like madness, terror,
il y a and *khora/différance*, which are hardly synonymous. They variously
point to an underlying stratum of anonymity that inhabits and disturbs our
world from within, but in very different ways. Richard tends to single out the
most extreme states of madness, misery, terror, torture, depression, and desolation, like the nightmare of a prisoner trapped in the ground or a child
crushed by rubble. But these phenomena would certainly need to be differentiated from *différance*, the play of differences in virtue of which we make
any distinctions or differentiations at all. *Différance*, while maddening enough
at times, does not constitute a state of madness, insanity, or terror, let alone of
torture or imprisonment, but rather of the inescapable "spacing," the play of
traces, within which we constitute or "forge" our beliefs and practices, some
of which are quite cheery, sane, and wholesome. *Différance* is that condition
in virtue of which whatever meaning we constitute is made possible, but also
impossible, that is, the quasi-transcendental condition which sees to it that a
meaning is a temporary unity that is forged from the flux of signifiers or traces
and that lasts just as long as the purpose it serves and the contexts endure in
which it can function. It is in virtue of *différance* that whatever we can do with
words can also come undone. That is at times awfully annoying, but it is hardly
madness, torture, desolation, or imprisonment.

Khora, Derrida says, is a "surname" for *différance*,[3] that is, *khora* is a figure found in the history of philosophy, in Plato's *Timaeus*, where the brute
"out of which" quality that simulates *différance* shows through the seams of
metaphysics, even here, in the founding moment of metaphysics, Plato himself. The *khora* thus constitutes a kind of counter-part to a Levinasian move,
when Levinas said that this very Jewish *tout autre* shows up occasionally in
philosophy, most notably in the *agathon*. So *khora* is a counter-image of what
is not beyond *ousia* but below it, a structure that falls below the level of
meaning and being, rather than exceeding them. Thus it is used by Derrida
to show how *différance* insinuates itself into everything. Whatever we say or
pray, think or believe, dream or desire, is inscribed in the shifting sands of
différance, that is, inscribed in *khora*. I emphasize Derrida's interest in the
mirror-image effect of the Platonic *agathon* and *khora*, in the way that the
beyond-being and below-being mirror each other. Now put that beside Levinas's observation that *illéité* (which is his way of appropriating the *agathon*)
is so far beyond the other one (*autrui*), so other than the other one (*autre
qu'autrui*), that it begins to fall into a "possible confusion" with *il y a*. By

putting these two mirror effects side by side, we see that there is a certain ambiguity or undecidability between the two. They share common characteristics, that is, neither belongs to the medium sized phenomena of daily life, neither has the determinacy, the form, the structure of a definite thing or being. That is why in the middle ages David of Dinant made the argument that God is prime matter, because God does not have and cannot be restricted by "form." Thomas Aquinas thought that was a particularly stupid thing to say and that David should have distinguished the way *ipsum esse subsistens* is beyond form from the way prime matter is below form. While Thomas was right to say that we can keep these *concepts* apart, I would say that David had hit upon a phenomenological point, that our *experiences* of the two are not necessarily so widely divided, for in both cases we experience a certain confusion (Levinas), a kind of bedazzlement (Marion), or what Derrida and I with him would call an "undecidability," which I think can only be resolved by *faith*.

But Richard has not discriminated the chiefly semiotic and quasi-transcendental function of *différance* as "spacing" from terror, torture, and desolation. Then, trading on that ambiguity, he says that Derrida and I have consigned us all to live in an unlivable desert space called *khora*, without hope or faith, wallowing without decision in the waters of undecidability. Kearney argues that Caputo and Derrida think that *khora*—conceived now as terror—is what is really real, what is really there, that every sense or meaning is a forgery, a fake, a simulacrum, an impostor, a fiction stretched over a void, and that all there is is the anonymous rustling of the *there is* that is eventually going to gobble us up or turn us to ash. *il y a là cendre*. He thinks that Caputo and Derrida have not been able to reassure us that *khora* is "temporary" and that we can "get beyond it," and that they have not shown us how we can be saved. They would rather be one of those hearty chevaliers, those knights, not of faith, but of nocturnal *khora* who go chin to chin with the abyss and try to stare it down. For the true anchorites (an-khora-ites), on the other hand, the desert was a medium through which they must pass on the way to redemption. You must first lose your self if you would save yourself according to the ancient economy. (Kearney wants to emphasize the anchoral economy, that you get something out of this, whereas Thomas Carlson wants to see if we can de-emphasize that and make the Neoplatonic God look more like *khora*.) Caputo and Derrida are knights of infinite resignation, whereas it is only the knight of faith that gets Isaac back.

But, I would say, Richard's argument falls wide of the mark on two counts. (1) He has consistently reduced undecidability to indecision, instead of recognizing that undecidability is precisely the condition of possibility of a decision. The opposite of undecidability is not a decision or decisiveness but rather "programmability." If you got rid of undecidability you would not get a

decision but a computer program. If a situation were not inhabited by undecidability then the decision could be made by a decision procedure, by a program or an algorithm that would process the components of the problem and
render the decision in a strictly rule-governed formalizable process. Undecidability means that human judgment and decision-making are required, which
means entering into an idiosyncratic situation that is not covered by the rules;
undecidability was first recognized by Aristotle in the *Nicomachean Ethics*,
where *phronesis* was precisely the acquired skill of figuring out what to do in
situations that are unique enough to fall below the radar of rules and univer-
sals. The emphasis on singularity in Kierkegaard and Heidegger, and in Derrida and Levinas, is it seems to me a radicalization of Aristotle's point, which
Gadamer also took up, which is why there are days when I am willing to
describe deconstruction as a form of "radical hermeneutics."

Hence when I say that as we approach the God who comes after metaphysics, we enter a region where we do not know whether it is "God or
khora," I am not leaving us twisting slowly in the winds of indecision. Rather,
I am describing the desert sphere in which any genuine decision or movement of faith is to be made, where God and *khora* bleed into each other and
create an element of ambiguity and undecidability *within which the movement of faith is made*, which shows up in mysticism as a dark night of the soul,
which I also mention in response to Carlson below, where the mystic does
not know if she believes in God. Without *khora*, we would be programmed to
seek God, divine automatons hard wired to the divine being, devoid of
responsibility, decision, judgment—and *faith*.

(2) Because Richard has misconstrued undecidability as indecision, he
thinks that the movement of decision, here faith in God, would somehow or
another extinguish *khora*, get us past it, put it behind us. That view goes along
with a "linear" interpretation of Levinas that I reject, that we can so decisively
surpass *il y a* that it goes away, that we can get on top of it or beyond it,
dominate it and drive it off for good, and then, resting from a hard day's work,
get a good night's sleep safe from its insomnia. I on the other hand think the
ghost of *il y a* is inextinguishable and irrepressible, that it disturbs our days
and haunts our nights, and that as such it is precisely the condition of possibility of the ethical decision. In other words, in rigorously Derridean fashion,
il y a is the very thing that makes ethical transcendence possible and impossible. It makes ethics possible, by confronting it with something to be over-
come, and impossible, by delimiting ethics as the ever haunting possibility of
the anonymous that never goes away, that refused to be banished, that returns
night after night. That is why ethics is a *beau risque*.[4]

Without *il y a* there is no *risque*, just the *beau*.

Without *khora* there is no *faith*, because then God would have plainly
and unambiguously revealed Godself, without any possible confusion.

Without *khora* there is triumphalism, dogmatism, the illusion that we have been granted a secret access to the Secret. That is the illusion that makes religion dangerous and that fires the fundamentalist religious hallucination. That is why religious people think that they have been hard-wired to the Almighty, that they know in some privileged way the Secret that has been communicated to *them*—because God prefers *them* to *others*, Jews to Egyptians, or Christians to Jews, or Muslims to Christians and Jews, Protestants to Catholics. Or whatever! It goes on and on.

Without *khora*, there is no "impossible," no poetics of the possible, no poetics of the possibility of the impossible, because there would be nothing to drive us to the impossible. Without *khora* we would know what we need to know, and we would not be pushed to the point of keeping *faith* alive just when faith seems incredible and impossible. After all, believing only what is highly credible is the mark of a mediocre fellow; rather than a *beau risque*, it always bets on the favorite horse, as Tom Carlson might want to say. Without *khora*, we would have every reason to think that we will succeed and we would not be forced into the impossible situation of hoping against hope, hoping when hope is impossible.

Without *khora*, the situation which evokes the impossible, which demands the impossible of us, which elicits faith, hope and charity would not obtain. *Khora* is the *felix culpa* of a passion for the impossible, the happy fault of a poetics of the possible, the heartless heart of an ethical and religious eschatology. *Khora* is the devil that justice demands we give his due.

NOTES

1. See Derrida's discussion of the two tropics of negativity in "Denials: How to Avoid Speaking," in *Derrida and Negative Theology*, eds. Howard Coward and Toby Foshay (Albany, NY: SUNY Press, 1992), pp. 100–108.

2. Jacques Derrida, *"Comme si c'était possible,* 'within such limits' . . . ," *Revue internationale de Philosophie*, No. 3 (1998): 497–529.

3. Derrida, ON, p. 126; for a commentary, see DN, pp. 96–105.

4. Emmanuel Levinas, *Autrement qu'être ou au-delà de l'essence* (The Hague: Nijhoff, 1974), p. 212; *Otherwise than Being or Beyond Essence*, trans. Alphonso Lingis (The Hague: Nijhoff, 1981), p. 167.

6 A READING OF JOHN D. CAPUTO'S "GOD AND ANONYMITY"

_____ LEWIS AYRES

> *From now on, therefore, we regard no one from a human point of view; even though we once regarded Christ from a human point of view, we regard him thus no longer. Therefore, if any one is in Christ, he is a new creation; the old has passed away, behold the new has come.*
>
> —*2 Cor. 5:16–17*

I would like to begin by saying how honored I am to have this chance to respond to the work of Professor Caputo.[1] His work represents one of the most interesting engagements with the work of Derrida in the English-speaking world.[2] That engagement is not one which involves only writing in the margins of Derrida himself, but is also an exploration of some of the foundational thinkers of the western tradition in the light of Derrida's work. My response here takes the form of a strong disagreement, but it is one whose direction and nature is in part rendered possible by the very work that it seeks to criticize, and thus it may perhaps serve as both critique and tribute.

The structure of my response to Professor Caputo's paper will be in two sections. First, I will try to draw out some of the key rhetorical strategies deployed in his argument, strategies that I suggest reveal a surprising debt to some aspects of modern thought. Second, I want to offer some remarks on the texture of faith and belief that raise questions about the legitimacy of Professor Caputo's division of minimalists and maximalists. As the last sentence will have revealed, my response to his work is that of a theologian not a philosopher—whether this will promote fruitful dialogue or just lead to mutual confusion we shall have to see!

129

Let's first consider the rhetorical strategies of Caputo's argument.[3] I want here to show how much of that argument might actually be presented in terms that he seems to have overtly repudiated. Despite his sincere denials, I suspect that a version of the search immediacy and "absolute presence" still haunts Caputo's pages in ways that a fully theological discourse should and must refuse. I want to allege, to put it most directly, that this variety of *post-modern* discourse is actually surprisingly *modern* in its direction.

To anyone who has spent time reading a few of the key texts within the broad field of postmodern thought this should, at one level, come as no surprise. Derrida himself makes no claim to have entered a new phase of thought, a new era of the post-modern; he claims only to have uncovered and highlighted the inescapable nature of western thought itself. Even where post-modern thinkers, such as Lyotard (and Derrida in some moments) advocate a particular programme for our future thinking, that programme occurs within, or as a strategy always *against* and parasitic upon modern or western forms of religious and philosophical thought.[4] However, if this is so, then one is entitled to ask how far some postmodernisms are dependent on an analysis of the history of western thought, on a sense of the moves that western thought has made, that is in essence a thoroughly modern story. This modern story may itself be controverted at key points—as, amongst others, many recent critics of Heidegger have shown (including Caputo himself).

I will come to some questions about the way history is represented or assumed to be by postmodern thought in the second section of my response—in this section, as I have said, I simply want to sketch two rhetorical strategies deployed by Caputo throughout his paper. The first strategy consists of the deployment of a particular contrast between, on the one hand, knowledge, formal naming or description, and on the other hand, the uncertainty of experience, the uncertainty which may be exposed by a "humble" "minimalist" phenomenology of anonymity. To put the same division in other terms, there is a rhetorical contrast between the chaos of existence examined humbly and the false ordering and structuring that is an attempt to construct more than there is—more than is "given."[5]

For Caputo, when Abraham is called he is unable to name the voice: indeed the significance of the reading of Abraham's story that Caputo uses *stems from* Abraham's refusal to name, his refusal to cover up the primary anonymity. To accept the trial and the call of the Voice is to accept the impossibility of naming : the very desire for naming "springs from an indentitarian impulse" (GAA, 12). These statements themselves begin to hint at the texture, at the feel of the opposition between a humble acceptance of the anonymous and the grasping constructive urge to name.[6] Caputo's reading of the story of Abraham is of course shaped by his immediately preceding discussion of the character of the "anonymous." In that section of his paper the "anonymous" is already the "nameless that absorbs every other name." The anonymous makes its impact when the exercise of reason, the processes of deduction, construction, and the collecting and the assembling functions of the memory are not working.

This location of a site for the appearance of the anonymous is complemented by a series of similes and metaphors: the anonymous is the great abyss, the endless dark space in which our small house with its feeble lights is situated; it is the haunting sense that always eludes our gaze. The theme of the anonymous eluding our gaze is key: Caputo insists at every turn (as readers of his work on Heidegger would expect) that the anonymous is that which makes *us* into objects. Abraham, for instance is addressed as object, there is no opportunity for looking back, no opportunity for the constructive operation of the eye.

Lastly, note the chaos and the violence of the anonymous. The anonymous is "fierce," "harsh" and "angry" (GAA, 11). Earlier we find "minimalists" are those aware that things at any moment may fall back into the chaos from which they came. In all of this we can, I want to allege, see a clear inter-penetrating set of oppositions at work. Most importantly, Caputo describes an opposition between the uncertainty and chaos of our deepest *experience* of existence vs. the false totalizing certainty of any attempts to describe, classify, and name the structure of our existence *as* structure. There is also a parallel but subtly different opposition in Caputo's rhetoric between the chaos of what actually is (not just at the level of our *experience* of reality) vs. the false and ephemeral stability, presence, and fixity of the constructions of reality for which we strive.

These rhetorical pairings are interwoven and interchangeable throughout Caputo's paper. Against this rhetorical background I want now to move on to consider the second and closely related rhetorical strategy of the paper, the contrast between Minimalists and Maximalists. I have to admit finding this contrast ironic: it is initially announced after Caputo has set out the problems of categorization, an irony he of course acknowledges. However, I suggest that, as one goes through the paper, this rhetorical contrast is not so much questioned or subverted as reinforced and turned to an increasing number of uses. However, the contrast itself: the minimalist is humble, willing only to talk of "what is," of what seems most clearly to resist or underlie the constructive metaphysical enterprise. The minimalist is, to offer a parallel, the one who will always stand up at a seminar and open any remarks with "I like to start from 'where people are.'"

The maximalist, on the other hand, sees things, especially those things that the minimalist sees simply "as they are," as only "imperfect forms" which need to be read as indications of some greater plenitude. Things "as they are" should be viewed as pointers, signifiers of the plenitude that is given. Maximalists distrust any limits and are driven always to construct visions of the infinite plenitude. They are the metaphysicians, the searchers for absolute presence, they are above all the neoplatonists (thus, for example, Marion's debt to phenomenology is countered by reference to his overriding "maximalist" neoplatonic interests). Caputo acknowledges that maximalists do not *think* they are talking of more than there actually is: but he does not really believe that this claim can be sustained. Maximalists believe in a "sort of" phenomenology but Caputo does not really believe they grasp the full necessity and significance of attending to things *only in so far as they are given.*

The *coup de grâce* to maximalism is administered when we discover that the best they can achieve is only a self-deceiving version of the minimalist project. This is so because ultimately, Caputo claims, that which a minimalist phenomenology of the anonymous may reveal is *indistinguishable* from the maximalist pseudo-phenomenology of the infinite. The experience of the infinite is indistinguishable from the experience of anonymity and aloneness, of our place as the small lit house in the infinite field of darkness: "nearly everyone who has been there . . . reports back of these limit states that they are indefinite, formless, nameless, unforseeable, unknowable . . ." (GAA, 6).[7]

The rhetorical presentation of the contrast between maximalists and minimalists thus seems to parallel directly the more general rhetorical strategies I outlined a few paragraphs ago. I think we may now go further and use the shape of these contrasts as evidence for placing (categorizing!) the direction of Professor Caputo's argument. As we explore Caputo's paper in terms of its rhetorical shape I think it becomes increasingly apparent that his argument may, rather paradoxically, be placed as distant cousin to a loose genealogy of modern thought which links together Romanticism, existentialism, some versions of neo-Kantian liberal theology and much of the post-seventeenth century discussion of the "mystical" and the "sublime." Professor Caputo is a cousin who does not travel home very often, but the family resemblances are still there. This might seem an extremely eclectic family, and indeed it is, but some common themes run between them. These features may initially be defined negatively: many members of this family attempt to avoid, controvert, or to find holes in the Kantian division between *noumena* and *phenomena* and in parallel divisions which preceded Kant. Members of this family are also trying to find ways round those Kantian arguments, especially those of the *First Critique*, which so clearly situate any thought of God.[8] In almost all cases, members of this family think that invocation of various sorts of 'experience' will provide a way forward. Intuition, mystical experience, limit experience, the sense of the sublime: the common link that runs between these lies, if nowhere else, in their *modern*-shaped refusals of an essentially modern dynamic. These refusals are essentially modern in their acceptance of the terms of the discussion, an acceptance of where and how any escape might be possible.

Of course one might say that the various varieties of postmodern thought are exactly that which tries to move *beyond* this project and as such there must surely be a distinction between them and the loose family to which I have alluded. I am not here trying to make any direct equation between Romanticism and Postmodern thought as a whole. Indeed I think a global equation of this sort is erroneous and bound to fail. However, I *do* want to allege that *this particular variety* of postmodern thought turns out to have a surprising set of family allegiances and a lineage that stretches back some centuries. This is so for two reasons.

Firstly, many postmodernisms have recently been criticized for their espousal of an ultimately chaotic, violent ontology—a critique perhaps raised in the English-speaking world particularly clearly by John Milbank.[9] I have already documented the "chaotic" nature of the anonymous in Caputo's paper—it is a portrayal he openly embraces. However, and again rather paradoxically, the relationship between the underlying chaotic ontology and the constructions of logocentric reason often parallels directly earlier relationships between the ordinary and the sublime or the mystical and the metaphysical. Thus the dynamics of postmodern chaos may be simply those of one version of modernity up-ended: the nameless intuitive or the sublime become the nameless chaos. Indeed, I think some of these links and yet reversals between some modernisms and some postmodernisms can be seen in the very course of Caputo's own work. In 1982 in *Heidegger and Aquinas*, he spoke (and in a surprisingly "maximalist" manner!) of the need for us to "learn to think of God not as the cause of the world but as that fullness of presence which is intimately present to the being of things." This presence is available to some as the "intensely Christian experience of being, a religious experience of God's presence." This "religious experience" is a mystical experience, "a simple immediacy and pristine contact of the soul with God," an experience beyond thought, "beyond the sphere of influence of the principle of sufficient reason."[10]

Caputo's most recent work has in many ways moved far from this earlier position, but some essential and perhaps surprising dynamics remain. Beyond thought, beyond any assumption of reason's sufficiency or controlling structuring focus we may now *experience* the always out of reach disturbing presence of the anonymous. The anonymous *may* be God, but we cannot know. Whatever the detailed twists and turns of Professor Caputo's thought, the deconstructive impulses of his earliest work, (primarily Heideggerian) and the Derridean impulses of his most recent work have much in common, and the link between them is, I want to allege, the seductive pull of certain very modern preoccupations with the immediacy of "true" experience as that which comes closest to the pre-cultural, to the infinite, perhaps even to the sublime Deity. To be fair I think that *some aspects of* Professor Caputo's *Radical Hermeneutics* of 1987 tend far more clearly towards a truly Derridean project, and that his work since has pursued a path latent in *Radical Hermeneutics*, but one which takes him much closer to an inverted version of his early Heideggerean themes.[11] So, through the progress of Caputo's work we see the relationship between "mystical" presence and the constructive totalizing reason slowly shift into the relationship between the chaos of what is and the constructive totalizing reason. However, in the case of Caputo we can go further than simply accuse him of adopting a general postmodern reversal (and thus acceptance) of this particular relationship. My second theme attempts to place Caputo much more squarely within a particular modern dynamic, and thus even raises questions about the Derridean nature of his current project as a whole.

The second way in which I think we are able to identify Professor Caputo's postmodernism as owing much to some modern dynamics, is by noting that his work seems increasingly to veer in the direction of what I sometimes term (rather pejoratively I admit) *soft*-postmodernism. By "soft-postmodernism" I mean to indicate a postmodernism with four features (features I take to be certainly necessary but perhaps not sufficient):[12]

1. Soft-postmodernisms, like all postmodernisms, repudiate foundationalism of virtually any sort.

2. Soft-postmodernisms, like all postmodernisms, do so on the ground that *all* discourses are subject to a deconstructive analysis which prevents their ever achieving any un-ironic move towards structure and presence.

3. However, soft-postmodernisms in particular use their deconstructive analyses to claim that an inescapable plurality of self-subverting expression, thought, or metaphysics stands over against a ground of chaotic, non-encompassable, primitive experience or presence which always resists our attempts to describe or symbolize. I might even go so far to say the degree to which chaos is invoked serves as an index against which we may judge the "hardness" or "softness" of this postmodern style.[13]

4. Soft-postmodern thinkers also have a tendency to prioritize ethical practice and non-foundationalist notions of justice above and beyond any particularly shaped constructive or phronetic tradition of reason about practice. Indeed soft-postmoderns often get generally unhappy

about the traditions of *phronesis per se,* seeing them as necessarily controlled by "elites" of various sorts.[14]

In sum then, soft-postmodernists are thinkers who want to appropriate some themes from postmodern thinkers, but who tend to do so in the name of certain very clearly modern liberal agendas, or while retaining certain modern liberal philosophical beliefs or assumptions. Placing Professor Caputo's work in this broad category might at first seem counter-intuitive, especially given his open acknowledgement of Derrida's influence. However, it is just that paradox that I want to raise to consciousness in this section of my response: how far is the influence of Derrida itself coopted into or subverted by other arguments and strategies that Caputo employs? This question is intended as reasonably open (although I have my suspicions).

I could, of course, have taken a very different path through his paper and work as a whole, a path which would have emphasized the influence of Derrida. In particular, Caputo is confusing about the language of experience: the chaos is at times that which is always objectifying us and hence that which is beyond experience. And yet so often the chaos is clearly *experienced as* that which objectifies—the dark space in which our little light burns. One path seems to open towards certain postmodern vistas, the other seems to point in very different directions. Hence, because of this ambiguity, the path I have taken is I think a defensible one, and the tension between these different strands is exactly that which makes his work so interestingly problematic as an exercise in postmodern thought.

The first section of my argument also enables us to see with clarity the contours of Professor Caputo's account of knowledge and faith. As for many "soft-postmodernists," faith is conceived in two ways. On the one hand, mistaken faith is an assertion of certainty over and against the apparent reality of what is, on the other, true faith is not so much an attitude of positive belief, but a minimalist trust which will enable action but which knows it does so only on the basis of ignorance. The division between types of faith is situated clearly and fairly obviously within the dualistic rhetorical strategy I have attempted to draw out from Caputo's paper. However, noting this account of faith and knowledge enables me to move on to my next section, and to consider the problems of the maximalist/minimalist division by offering, in outline, an alternative account of faith.

꙳

At one point Professor Caputo cites Thomas Aquinas on the nature of faith. Thomas is enlisted, at least momentarily, as a minimalist. For Caputo, Thomas knew that in this life we live in a world of faith, a world where "the signs [are] conflicting, the data confusing" (GAA, 4). Two points are being made in the passage where this citation of Thomas is to be found: on the one hand, Thomas is being used to help hint at the possibility of what I have already termed "true faith." On the other hand, Thomas is being cited to help rule out the possibility of any "clear sighted" phenomenology other than the minimalist version. Once again, *even if* one wishes to be a maximalist, this life permits only a realization of the minimalist project. I suggest that this attempt to enlist Thomas's support is both mistaken, and revealing. I suggest further that Thomas's account of faith *actually* provides an excellent point of departure for critiquing the very division of maximalist and minimalist positions so important for Caputo's argument.

In looking further at Thomas's account of faith I am particularly interested in the peculiar sort of certainty that faith is said by Thomas to possess. On the one hand faith is *more* certain than knowledge of things in the world because it concerns the *ueritas prima*, the first truth. On the other hand, faith is actually *less* certain than other more worldly sciences because we, as human, do not possess the principles on which theology operates.[15] Theology is a science concerned with God, and thus finds its principles in God's own knowledge or science. However, only God possesses the principles of God's self-knowledge, we approach them only through God's manifestation of them to us. Elsewhere I have tried to argue that understanding Thomas's account of the theological enterprise is dependent on understanding the tension inherent in the human striving to practice a science whose principles are not possessed.[16] "Tension" here indicates the struggle fallen humanity has in moving towards this science, but the struggle is most fundamentally founded in the fruitful potential of our created status, in which created nature (by definition not God) may share in the divine life through being perfected by grace.

One of the clearest indications of this theme is to be found in the first ten articles of the *Summa*, and especially in article six, which asks whether or not theology may be described as "wisdom." Ultimately, says Thomas, theology is wisdom in either of two ways. The practice of theology may be wisdom when a particular theologian is infused with the Spirit and thus has present the principles of the science, or theology may be counted wisdom in the sense that one becomes *in a sense* wise by learning to appreciate the exercise of a virtue that one does not oneself possess. Hence, it is only in this latter, derived sense that the theology one may acquire through study, however extensive, and be counted as wisdom.[17]

This subtle tension in the act of theology is also to be found in Thomas's account of the texture of faith itself. Learning the texture of faith as a mode of knowing comes through learning to participate in a discourse which shapes our understanding and perception *of reality itself*. There is of course a cognitive content to faith, a set of narratives and articulations of narratives (that is, articles of faith). However, it is through the discipline of learning to see and describe and narrate the world *within* those narratives and their articulations that one learns *how* to hold that cognitive content, and *how* to see the reality and substantiality of the world within which one lives and to which the creating and saving God is present.[18] Were we to pursue this theme further we could, for instance, explore the relationship between the quality of things as *intelligibilia*, as intelligible because of the link between mind and reality so important to Thomas, and their quality as *reuabilia*, their quality as vehicles of revelation. The parallels between the act of God as creating and the act of God as redeeming would here be essential, and we would see something of how Thomas's understanding of the role of reason and of metaphysics is only truly established in the light of revelation.[19]

On the one hand, then, faith itself then holds an ambiguous place between knowledge and opinion—reducible to neither of Caputo's categories. On the other hand, faith shapes one's account of and feel for the world, such that the idea of a "basic" phenomenology beyond figuration within any narrative, and as revealing the most fundamental nature of existence is simply a self-delusion. Such a phenomenology would not be "more basic," but either lacking a dimension of what is most fundamentally given, or deluding itself through accepting a different narrative of what is.

Something of the texture of faith as between knowledge and opinion, and as yet shaping our perceptions of reality, is apparent in Thomas's account of why the formation of structured articles of faith is not a false systematization of the scriptural plurality. His answer revolves around envisaging an article of faith as being necessary "wherever something is unseen for a distinct reason."[20] The different articles of faith are the different necessary nodes or pivots of differentiated knowledge through which God's activity in the created order is made known and which may in turn draw us towards the shape of God's mysterious action and presence. The practice of articulating and reflecting upon faith is thus also shaped by our gradual growth in understanding of the complex relationship between God's presence and the structures of our inescapable created material and temporal reality.[21]

These brief comments on the nature of faith enable and demand some further comments on the relationship between Thomas's ontology and his account of our speech about God. However, we need first to return for a second to Heidegger and to the ontological difference. In a brief but astute comment John Milbank links his treatment of the violent and chaotic ontology of some postmoderns to the earlier supposition made by Heidegger. Milbank agrees that Heidegger's sense that the ontological difference cannot be open to investigation: if beings are *constituted by* relationship to Being then we cannot survey the relationship *as if* the two poles were available to us. However, and this is the vital step in the argument, there is no necessary progress from this analysis of the relationship between Being and beings to asserting that beings continually fail in their attempt to represent Being, *or* to asserting a continual hiding of Being. Even given the basic intuition about the constitution of beings by relationship to Being, one might want rather to say that as much as a being is a particular existence and not being itself, it yet exhibits in its sheer contingency the inescapable mystery of Being.[22]

Conceiving of a dialogue between such a re-written Heidegger and Thomas now becomes interesting, especially given the work on Thomas's pseudo-Dionysian heritage and ontology that has been such a feature of Thomistic studies in the latter half of this century.[23] Both the ontology of Ps. Dioysius and the tradition of Augustine[24] insist strongly that there is no analogy of proportion between the creator and the creation, only a complex analogy of participation. Indeed, it is this ontology of participation that structures the possibility of our naming God as that which gives substance and being to what is. However, I do not want to argue in detail about the scope and significance of this earlier ontology and its possible difference from post-Socratic tradition; rather, I want to note the linkage between these ontological themes, the notion of faith I began to outline above, and the Incarnation.

Let us consider for a moment the Ps. Dionysian ontology of participation.[25] In Thomas's version (closely allied of course with a certain transformed Aristotelianism) it is subtly, but importantly inaccurate to speak as if that ontology were the one 'foundation' for our naming of God.[26] *All* of the various ways to God (including the famous five ways) may only be discovered in their true character by reference to God's one self-showing (*demonstratio*), the Incarnation. Attention to the presence of God in Christ is attention to the ability of the archetype of all things to exhibit "in sheer contingency the inescapable mystery of Being." This is so because the presence of God in Christ is the presence of the *Logos*, the Word through whom all things were made (John 1:3), "[who] reaches mightily from one end of the earth to the other, [ordering] all things well" (Wisd. 8:1), and the one who possess the principles of God's own knowledge or science.

Noting one aspect of Ps. Dionysius's own ontology will return us to the question of faith. So far I have sketched a view in which that ontology is the ground for our speaking of God, for our naming of God. I have hinted, I hope, that this may be so in a way which is not subject to Heidegger's critique, and may actually offer a different positive vision of Being's presence in beings. However, it is essential to note that in Ps. Dionysius this ontology is not only the basis for our naming of God, for our "cataphatic" theology, but also for the *"apophatic"* theology which is its natural and necessary counterpart.[27] Cataphatic theology is grounded in God's Creative gift to the creation. However, as Denys Turner has so clearly pointed out in his recent work, *The Darkness of God*, apophatic theology is best understood as having two stages. In the first stage we must learn the necessity of denying the ability of terms to describe God. In the second and culminating stage we must learn that God is beyond affirmation *or* denial: God is beyond the very process or ratio of distinction itself.

The discourse of the cataphatic, the apophatic and the *fully* apophatic functions not to lead us to an "experience" of the divine beyond our language and formulation, but rather it functions as a critique *within* language of the search for "mystical *experiences.*" Such a search is the ultimate delusion: firstly, because it falsely teaches that a state beyond the linguistic or the material, beyond the *created* is attainable; secondly, because it leads us to imagine that our denials at the first initially apophatic level actually give us some insight into the relationship between Being and beings (in Thomas we might explore something of this relationship by considering the differences between angelic intelligences and our own or between Christ's beatific vision and normal human knowledge of God). In this ontology the relationship between Being and beings is *not* open for inspection. The truly apophatic must always be a dynamic within language, and the presence of God is always within beings, always mediated (thus controverting many standard modern assumptions about the structure of "platonism" and especially Christian "platonism").[28] It is also the case that if one thinks that this theological perspective may be "recovered" by separating the ontology from the experiences which give rise to it, then one has misunderstood the structure of this discourse!

And yet how do we approach and grow in knowledge of that relationship and of that which gives it form? Well, at the very time recent scholarship has begun to draw out with increasing clarity this dynamic in the apophatic/cataphatic division, other complementary scholarship has begun to indicate with increasing clarity that Ps. Dionysius's thought is not exhausted by reference to its non-Christian neoplatonic debts (however important those may be), and that we need to see the symbolic world of these texts as one essentially liturgical in focus, and as one which owes much to previous Christian thought and practice. One's appreciation of the continual and unsurpassable dynamic of the cataphatic and the apophatic is intended to be shaped by continual liturgical representation and enactment of the story of God's action in history. The liturgy is the enactment of Being's presence in beings, an enactment that shapes the texture of faith. The eucharistic act and presence is that which reveals the given but hidden basis of all substantiality.[29]

Thus the reading of Thomas's notion of faith that I sketched and aspects of the Ps. Dionysian ontology are importantly compatible.[30] The very texture of our perception of our reality is shaped here by the practice of faith, a practice that finds its focus in the liturgical performance of God's action in history. The action in history is not of course celebrated as an action distinct from the lives of contemporary Christians, but rather as the narrative within which they find themselves—it is an enactment of the basic story and direction of all history. It is this enactment that shapes and enables the complex process of attention to reality that I have hinted at as the real challenge to Caputo's division of maximalist and minimalist. While things stand in complex relationship to their creator and retain their status as both *intelligibilia* and *reubilia* there is no possibility of a minimalist phenomenology which would not itself receive critique as failing in attention to the full reality of what is.

We can now draw the threads of this section of my paper together. We have seen so far that faith may be conceived as a practice whose texture enables a continual revisioning and refiguring of what is. Moreover, we have seen that this practice of faith may be conceived as functioning best *within* the context of an ontology of participation such that the discourse of faith is that which leads us to the presence of Being in beings *without* attempting to describe for observation the relationship between those poles. This ontology paradoxically saves us from seeking to do away with our createdness by asserting the very givenness and iconic character of reality. However, the last step in this sketch of an alternative is to notice the significance of the Incarnation.

Earlier, I indicated that for Thomas the many ways to God embedded in the structure of created existence find their *ratio*-nale in the universal "presence," the "being give-ness" of the logos. Further, we may say that it is the *incarnate* Logos which provides the center and focus of attention for the discourse of faith, and one central way in which it does so is by providing the basis for a reformation of our vision. We can see what I mean here most easily by turning to Augustine. For Augustine, the archetypal apostle for understanding the nature of Christian existence is Thomas.[31] It is Thomas who embodies the discourse of faith. Thomas begins by looking and by seeing, demanding that he will only believe when he can see the object of his belief. When he sees that he could actually put his hand in the side of Christ, Thomas does not yet directly *see* Christ as also God, but his *confession* that Christ is also God enables us to see that Thomas has embarked on a search for a new phenomenology of what is given. Thomas's task is now to come to "see" through faith (eventually through sight) Christ as human *and* as the presence of God. Note that it is the figure of the incarnate Christ who now functions as the epistemological and anthropological focus for the developing discourse of faith. Two things about this task are particularly noteworthy.

First it is a task in which much subtly and irony is expended on exploring the structures of this developing practice of "seeing." We learn to see through shaping our souls in a certain practice (learning to "see" God in the other)—a "seeing" which may only be achieved through an ironic lack of obsession with the eye. We learn to "see" also through attention to the eucharistic presence, the Eucharist being conceived as an act in which God's mysterious and universal presence is indicated—in this context we should consider his famous instruction to communicants, "receive what you are" (a statement which does not indicate a "low" view of the eucharistic elements but rather a "high" view of the body of Christ). Second, the practice of learning to "see" anew is one that may *only* reach completion in the vision of God. However, that final vision of God is *not* im-mediate in the sense of non-mediated: we "see" God through coming at last to see Christ crucified *as also* the presence of God. No "obstacles" are removed to enable immediate sight, rather the creation becomes icon.

Recently Philip Blond has argued that the current task for theologians wishing to engage with the phenomenological tradition is to explore the possibilities for a phenomenology of theological vision, and he does so in the hope of advocating a theological realism that will not simply offer "a purely ontic account of the real."[32] He indicates a possible dialogue with Merleau-Ponty who comes eventually in his *Le Visible et l'invisible* to maintain that the invisible is *given in* the visible, the separation of the two is a phenomenological sleight of hand which may be exposed and refused. To make these moves Merleau-Ponty does not renounce the reality of immanent bodies and the reality of individuated existence, but sees instead that the field of differentiated reality may also be a unity of existence. This presence of unity in diversity points always to a hidden but given-in-the-reality-of-things invisibility. Of course one need not perceive all of what is given in the nature of ontic existence, but to stop at a particular stage in one's phenomenology is to adopt a false minimalism, a minimalism that makes an always false claim to completeness. These perspectives only begin to hint at a theological construal of the real; much more needs to be done. This is especially so in so far as pursuing this path might lead one to a rather easy confusing of *esse commune* and the *esse* of God. Nevertheless these perspectives do hint at the possibilities for philosophical engagement with the legacy of phenomenology (although, of course, we are far from Husserl) that would find theological parallels deeply rooted in Christian traditions of thought.

Minimalism vs. maximalism, as it is presented in Professor Caputo's paper, is a contrast that will not stand for a number of reasons. Firstly, and most importantly, the contrast relies on the possibility of a humble basic observation of reality that may be accounted the only true phenomenology. However, this assumption is itself fundamentally problematic. Like many, if not all phenomenologies, "minimalism" relies on *a priori* assumptions of what is and what is not possible in the perception of reality and it cannot claim a simple humility. Secondly, many of those thinkers that Professor Caputo wishes to claim as maximalists have no intention of "getting round" or "removing" the obstacles in the path of the plenitude of givenness. Such a portrayal can only rest on an unsustainable sense of what the platonic and the neoplatonic tradition, especially in its Christian versions, aims towards.

Once we see that this contrast is itself unsustainable then the way is open to rethinking the questions with which Professor Caputo is concerned. Indeed, in the course of my challenge to his account I have tried to outline the structure of an alternative, more fully theological of religious discourse and its attitude to reality. Most fundamentally, this alternative not only may avoid the charge of onto-theology, it may in fact be the discourse which best preserves the mysteriously given but un-graspable relationship between Being and beings. Perhaps paradoxically I have tried to suggest that *within* the particular discourse of faith (but a faith neither "true" nor "mistaken" in Professor Caputo's terms), we may find a phenomenology that is also able to move at last beyond the modernist search for an unmediated basic human awareness of that which gives.

There is need for an important and necessary dialogue with the various facets of the postmodern insofar as we may be prompted by this dialogue to open up new (or old) paths back to the pre-modern and to develop new perspectives on which of the modern may best be retained, and what must be refused. However, in the perspective of this reader at least, while Professor Caputo's work has opened many possible avenues into that dialogue, his paper in this volume still rests upon a peculiarly modern pattern of argument that theology can and should resist at the outset. It is in learning the patterns of attention to the new creation, learning how to regard all in Christ, that we may best come to learn the subtlety to what is truly given and created.

NOTES

1. This paper is a response to Caputo's article "God and Anonymity: Prolegomena to an Ankhoral Religion," contained in this volume (hereafter cited as GAA).

2. Among English language theologians (as opposed to philosophers) other recent and significant sympathetic engagements are to be found in G. Ward, *Barth, Derrida and the Language of Theology* (Cambridge: Cambridge University Press, 1995) and K. Hart, *The Trespass of the Sign, Deconstruction, Theology and Philosophy* (Cambridge: Cambridge University Press, 1989). I would disagree with Ward over the way he relates Barth and Derrida, and with Hart over his portrayal of links between Derrida and "negative theology."

3. My understanding of "rhetorical strategy" owes much to K. Burke's *The Philosophy of Literary Form* (New York: Vintage Books, 1957).

4. Most famously in the last sentence of J.-F. Lyotard, *The Postmodern Condition: A Report on Knowledge*, trans. G. Bennington and B. Massumi (Manchester: Manchester University Press, 1984), p. 82: "The answer is: let us wage a war on totality; let us be witness to the unpresentable; let us activate the differences and save the honor of the name."

5. Although the theme is explored in very openly phenomenological terms in GAA, it appears in slightly different, far more Derridarean form in Caputo's RH, chaps. 6, 7 and 10, e.g., p. 269: ". . . whether or not one believes in God or mystics, one can still speak of something like a ground or fine point of the soul, a certain deep spot in the mind where the constructions of science go dim and the cunning of common sense and the agility of *phronesis* go limp . . . in the thin membranes of structures that we search across the flux, in the thin fabric we weave over it, there are certain spots where the surface wears through and acquires a transparency which exposes the flux beneath."

6. Caputo's discussion of the Abraham story should be treated as a commentary on Kierkegaard's, Levinas's and Derrida's re-telling and not as commentary on the Biblical text. This is so because Abraham clearly answers the "Voice," knowing it to be God and at the end of his journey knows that the appropriate attitude is one of worship (Gen. 22:1, 5). The Isaac story also takes place in the context of other stories that persistently speak of ways in which Abraham learns to name God and to wait upon God's faithfulness, especially Gen. 21, e.g., verses 1, 13 and 33. In the light of the second half of my paper the most fruitful theme to explore in this story is the linking between learning to name the Voice and learning to name the Voice without one's naming covering up its mystery.

7. Note also that Caputo is happy to equate "phenomenology" and "experience," GAA, 6.

8. For a recent analysis of the particular Kantian assumptions with which I am concerned see J. Milbank, *Between Purgation and Illumination: A Critique of the Theology of Right*, in K. Surin (ed.), *Christ, Ethics and Tragedy* (Cambridge: Cambridge University Press, 1989), pp. 161–196; for an example of the reading of "mystical" texts beyond the pre-occupation with "experience" see F. Bauerschimdt, "Julian of Norwich—Incorporated," *Modern Theology* 13 (1997), pp. 75–100. On the question of the modern discourse concerning religious "experience" see also M. Buckley, *At the Origins of Modern Atheism* (New Haven and London: Yale University Press, 1989).

9. J. Milbank, *Theology and Social Theory* (Oxford: Blackwels, 1990), p. 320ff.

10. J.D. Caputo, HA, p. 283, 247.

11. However, see above, no. 5.

12. G. Ward in his introductory survey "Postmodern Theology," in D. Ford (ed.), *The Modern Theologians* (Oxford and Cambridge, MA: Blackwels, 1997), pp. 585–601, divides theological responses to postmodernism into liberal and conservative postmodern theologies. My category of "soft-postmodernism" is a separate division not at all equivalent to his "liberal" category. The "soft" variety is, I think, found

far more commonly in the US, and has a complex relationship to both modern liberal as well as to postmodern movements.

13. And thus Professor Caputo's style of "soft postmodernism" might count as relatively "hard," over against the David Tracy of *Plurality and Ambiguity's* (which probably no longer adequately describes his position) strongly "soft" style. I offer this terminology somewhat mischeviously!

14. For Caputo's charge on these lines see his "Gadamers closet essentialism: a Derridarean critique," in D. Mchelfelder and R. Palmer, *Dialogue and Deconstruction: The Gadamer–Derrida debate* (Albany, NY: SUNY Press, 1987), pp. 258–264. The paper is interesting because the way it adds to a critique of Gadamer's conception of the unity of history an attack on traditions as *a priori* bad because of the way in which they marginalize and exclude minorities. While the former is a critique which asks some searching questions of Gadamer, the latter seems much less strong. *Even if* it were true that traditions necessarily marginalized and excluded in this way, Gadamer's analysis would remain unchallenged *both* because his attempted description of structures of knowledge might still be simply right, *and* because it might be the case that only learning appropriate moves within appropriate traditions could enable this tendency towards marginalization to be resisted.

15. ST. IiaIIae, q. 4, a. 5.

16. See my "On the Practice and Teaching of Christian Doctrine," *Gregorianum* 79 (1998), forthcoming.

17. ST. Ia, q. 1, a. 6.

18. My use of "figure" here is much indebted to the work of those such as Frei and Auerbach who have explored the nature of Christian figural existence outside the categories of a clearly "modern" hermeneutics which conceives mediation through the dual relationship between text and "meaning" and reader and "meaning." See e.g., D. Dawson, "Figural Reading and the Fashioning of Christian Identity" in Boyarin, Auerbach and Frei, *Modern Theology* 14 (1998), pp. 181–196. The overall scope of Frei's account of the demise of "hermeneutics" and the character of figural reading is to be found in Frei's "The Literal Reading of Biblical Narrative in the Christian Tradition: Does it stretch or will it break?," *Theology and Narrative* (Oxford and New York: Oxford University Press, 1995), pp. 117–152.

19. See for an example of a reading of Thomas on truth consonant with this sentence, B. Marshall "Aquinas as Postliberal Theologian," *The Thomist* 53 (1989), pp. 353–402. See also J. Milbank, "Only Theology Overcomes Metaphysics," *The World Made Strange: Theology, Language and Culture* (Oxford: Blackwels, 1997), pp. 36–57.

20. ST. IiaIIae, q. 1, a. 6.

21. See E. Rogers, Thomas Aquinas and Karl Barth: *Sacred Doctrine and the Natural Knowledge of God* (Notre Dame and London: Notre Dame University Press, 1995), chap. 1 for an excellent discussion of things as both *intelligibilia* and as *reuabilia*.

22. Milbank, *Theology and Social Theory*, p. 300.

23. A helpful survey of some modern trends of Aquinas is provided in the first half of W. Hankey, "Denys and Aquinas: Antimodern Cold and Postmodern Hot," in L. Ayres and G. Jones (eds.), *Studies in Christian Origins: Theology, Rhetoric, and Community* (London: Routledge, 1998), pp. 139–183. See also Hankey's earlier

"Making Theology Practical: Thomas Aquinas and the Nineteenth Century Religious Revival," *Dionysius* 9 (1985), pp. 85–127.

24. On this theme see my "Remember that you are Catholic": Augustine on the Unity of the Triune God," in R. Dodaro and G. Lawless (eds.), *Augustine and his Critics* (London and New York: Routledge, forthcoming), esp. my discussion of the general significance of such statements as that found at *serm.* 52, 23: "I do not say that these three things are in any way to be equated with the Holy Trinity, as if arranged according to an analogy, or according to a *ratio of comparison*. This I do not say."

25. I have not discussed this ontology in any detail here, for obvious reasons of space. However my understanding of it in Thomas's version owes much to R. Te Velde, *Participation and Substantiality in Thomas Aquinas* (Leiden: Brill, 1995).

26. My account here owes much to that of E. Rogers, *Thomas Aquinas and Karl Barth: Sacred Doctrine and the Natural Knowledge of God* (Notre Dame and London: Notre Dame University Press, 1995). For this paragraph see especially p. 64: ". . . demonstrations come in varying proportions to the word or *demonstratio Patris* as the first principle and cause in which their perfection preexists. Thus it is only by being taken up into sacred doctrine which depends upon the various identifying, miraculous and sacramental demonstrations in the life of Jesus, and which uses the *demonstratio Patris* as its own *medium demonstrationis* or formal rationale, that Aristotelian demonstrations can come to perfection."

27. My account of this theme is much indebted to D. Turner's, *The Darkness of God: Negativity in Christian Mysticism* (Cambridge: Cambridge University Press, 1995). Besides other recent scholarship in the same vein, I have found aspects of A. Golitzin's recent *Et Introibo Ad Altare Dei: The Mystagogy of Dionysius Areopagita, Analecta Vlatadon* 59 (Thessaloniki, 1994) particularly helpful in providing ways of exploring the theological context of Ps. Dionysius' thought. See also the introduction of A. Louth, *Denys the Areopagite* (London: Chapman, 1989).

28. See C. Pickstock, *After Writing: On the Liturgical Consummation of Philosophy* (Oxford and Cambridge, MA: Blackwell, 1997), Part I.

29. On the significance of liturgical practice in general, above and beyond particular consideration of Ps. Dionysius see C. Pickstock, *After Writing*, Her work in this area is closely related to that of such contemporary French scholars as J.-Y. Lacoste and J.F. Courtine.

30. I have indicated their compatibility without exploring in detail how far Thomas's account of naming God and his account of faith are actually Ps. Dionysian in shape. That must be the subject of another paper.

31. On this theme see my introductory presentation in "Augustine on God as Love and Love as God," *Pro Ecclesia* 5 (1996), pp. 470–487. On the question of vision more generally see my "The Discipline of Self-knowledge in Augustine's *De trinitate* Book X" L. Ayres (ed.), *The Passionate Intellect: Essays on the Transformation of Classical Traditions Presented to Professor Ian Kidd*, Rusch VII (Brunswick NJ: Transaction, 1995), pp. 261–296. On the place of Christology see my "Christology and faith in *De trinitate* Bk XIII: towards relocating Books VIII–XV," in V. Twomey and T. Finan (eds.), *Studies in Patristic Christology* (Dublin: Four Courts Press, 1998), pp. 95–121.

32. P. Blond, "Introduction" in P. Blond (ed.), *Post Secular Philosophy: Between Philosophy and Theology* (London and New York: Routledge, 1998), pp. 1–66, especially p. 21ff.; idem, "Prolegomena to Theological Perception," in D. Martin et al. (eds.), *Religion Modernity and Postmodernity* (Oxford and Cambridge, MA: Blackwell, 1998).

THE VIOLENCE OF ONTOLOGY:
A RESPONSE TO AYRES

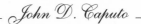
John D. Caputo

Lewis Ayres's paper belongs in the wake of Richard Kearney's imagination and makes a similar argument. I thank him for an articulate and bracing discussion of my work and I will respond first by establishing points of contact on which we can agree in the midst of sharp disagreements, then by a rejoinder rather like my response to Richard Kearney.

Ayres rightly points out that Derrida "makes no claim to have entered a new phase of thought" called "postmodernity." For one thing, Derrida distrusts easy periodizations (and for another, the word is Lyotard's not his). Instead, Derrida has repeatedly said that deconstruction represents a "new" Enlightenment, one that is enlightened about Enlightenment absolutes, twists free from transcendental subjects, pure reason, and absolute knowledge, not to mention the Eurocentric colonialization that accompanied the belief that the owl of Minerva has made its nest in Europe's tree.[1] Still deconstruction remains doggedly faithful to the Enlightenment's dream of "emancipation" (Lyotard's example of a "metanarrative"), of lifting from our shoulders the loadstone of authoritarian state power and authoritarian religion; it remains doggedly determined to break with the oppressive, top-down social structures of premodern times, with mythological conceptions of the "heavens" above and mythological biologies which identified humanity with male sperm, with a church that persecuted non-Christians and dangerously supplemented its armies and dogmas with its favorite metaphysical schemes which it ran together with the Word of God. On all these points, Derrida, and I with him, and I hope all of us, are *Aufklärer*.

Deconstruction thus is a continuation of the Enlightenment by another and less *Aufklärisch* means. My argument is that when the deconstructive project is carefully considered one *also* finds in it a deeply religious streak so that it has broken with still another Enlightenment dogma, viz., the clean cut between the light of pure reason and the darkness of faith. Deconstruction is driven by prayers and tears, by a messianic passion for justice, a messianic faith in a future to come. By its very structure as a "religion without religion" it runs new lines of communication between its eccentric late modernity (or postmodernity) and premodern masters like Augustine, especially the *Con-fessions* (*The City of God* is up to its ears in religious imperialism from which, glory be to God, we are still trying to twist free).

My first disagreement with Ayres comes with the way he, following Mil-bank, characterizes "modernity," viz., as a search for "an unmediated experi-ence" of things. As Heidegger has shown, modernity is the time when "subjects" scrutinize their "ideas" to see if they can serve as a bridge to "objects;" as such modernity is an age of "representations," of "pictures," where an "unmediated" relation to the world is given up as a project for medieval Neoplatonists who want to be One with the One in the One.[2] But not only is this not *modernity*, it is not *me*. By returning to the idea of the "factical" and "hermeneutical" situation of understanding, *everything* I have said from *Radical Hermeneutics* on is directed *against* "unmediated" experience. That is why I am fond of citing Derrida's quip that as soon as someone announces some-thing "unmediated" we are all visited by "the most massive mediatizing machines."[3] The whole point of the "speech and writing" debate for many years was to dispel the illusion that speech was some sort of pure transparent unmediated contact with the things themselves, without a trace of the trace.

Ayres does not fail to seize upon the irony that people like me, who make a good living out of making trouble for binary pairs, make new binary dis-tinctions—like mine, between "minimalists" and "maximalists"—at their own peril. So clearly I must treat this distinction, like all distinctions, as another Wittgensteinian ladder, provisional and strategic, and in the end undo them, which I explicitly do at the end of my piece, although that seems to slip Ayre's notice. Minimalists in this paper are hermeneuts, "radical" ones if you please—Ayres can't be against the idea of a "Radical *x*"—people who under-stand that they always and inescapably have to do with "interpretations," who dare not claim that this is the way things *are* but who claim that this is the best "take" they have today but who knows what tomorrow will bring. Accordingly, minimalism is the *opposite* of what Lewis Ayres says: it *never* claims to see things "as they are"—a phrase that does not appear in my paper—but only to have an "interpretation." Radical hermeneuts are poor existing individuals who are always subject to uncircumventable hermeneu-tic "conditions." That is why I wrote, "Minimalists think that what is given, what gives, does not quite give enough and that whatever is given requires a little supplementary interpretation." In Anglo-Americanese, there are no uninterpreted facts of the matter (not as far as I know). Maximalists—I was thinking of Jean-Luc Marion—on the other hand make the *most* of what is given and sometimes slip into speaking of something "unconditionally" given, a "givenness" made possible by a "reduction" of every subjective "condi-tion"—or "mediation." Thus "unmediated experiences" are what define max-imalists and so represent the *opposite* of the hermeneutic conditions and mediations that I am defending. The "unmediated" would be very un-hermeneutical, a Eucharistic hermeneutics to the contrary notwithstanding. But let there be no mistake: I do love the "unconditional" but precisely insofar as it is *never given* but always wept and prayed for, so that my "experience" of the unconditional is an impossible experience, an experience of the impossible. The impossible (Derrida's justice) or "unpresentable" (Lyotard's justice) does not exist, which is why I love it so much! But this impossible has nothing to do with an "unmediated" experience.

The upshot of my distinction is to force us to see that we have always to do with one faith or another, with contingent construals, historically enabled readings and particular understandings, whether in the search for God or the search for the Unified Theory of Everything. No individual or community, not as far as I can tell—either from what they say or how they behave—has been granted a privileged communication from Being, God, or Reason, of which the rest of us poor existing individuals have been deprived. We all pull on our pants one leg at a time. We do the best we can, while remembering that the impossible is what we love and desire. Minimalists insist that we proceed on foot by the feet of faith, like Cleophas and his unnamed friend on the way to Emmaus, while maximalists think we have some sort of mystical or metaphysical engine to power us about. Contrary to the way Ayres maps things out, it is "maximalists," particularly Neoplatonic ones, who sidle up to the idea of unmediated mystical or metaphysical experiences beyond speech, concepts, and time.

So I see myself wearing the white hat, siding with faith. I take myself to be following in the footsteps of Paul, as Keith Putt will argue on my behalf, defending faith against the *Neo*-Corinthians, be they from Cambridge or Paris, those who think that, if truth be told, God is a Christian Neoplatonist (or a neoplatonizing Neo-Thomist) and that Jesus's favorite way to pass an idle hour was debating the theory of emanation with Jewish peasants in dusty little Galilean towns. But Ayres complains that I have a fishy idea of faith. In fact— I am trying to make contact with Ayres—he will be surprised to know that I agree with most of what he, using St. Thomas as a point of departure, says about faith. I, too, take faith to have a cognitive content and to shape the way we see the world. Faith forms our understanding (*Verstehen*), our take (*Auslegung*) on things. I love Ayres's notion that faith constitutes "the texture of our perception of reality," a perception that is not solitary but woven by the historical world in which we find ourselves. (That by the way is a pretty good idea of "experience," a word that Ayres wants for some reason to surround and burn. Perhaps he is hearing "*Erlebnis*" instead of "*Erfahrung*"). I would only add that of course, faith, history, and interpretive communities do the same thing for other communities, of different faiths, with different practices and liturgies, whose historically woven perceptions are differently textured. These several faiths often enough conflict and there is no *Summa contra gentiles* to resolve the conflict. We are all *gentiles* and only maximalists would think you can attain the high ground from which to mount a *Summa* that is anything more than summary of an historical form of life.

I agree with Ayres when he distinguishes "seeing through faith" from "seeing through sight," which I would gloss as follows. Seeing through faith, is all we have, in *hoc statu vitae*, as Thomas put it, and this is known in hermeneutics as *"seeing as,"* viz., a fore-structured, preconditioned interpretative seeing which structurally and for principled reasons spelled out by Husserl and Heidegger takes things *as such and such*. Otherwise one won't see them at all. Whatever is received, we say in Thomistic hermeneutics, is received according to the mode of the receiver. There is no view from nowhere. "Seeing through sight," alas, is unavailable if, as Ayres and I agree, we are always already caught in language and communities of interpretation. I too have argued that the mystical claim to leave time and language behind for a pure unmediated experience is an illusion. Seeing through sight would constitute precisely the sort of unmediated experience of the world that I deny. We all need a faith, a way, which is our way to see and move about, our take on things, a way to give texture to our perceptions, a way to belong to our interpretive communities and practice its liturgies. But there is no way to say our way is The Way, no way I know of anyway. We are going to have to learn to live with the contingency of our inherited ways of seeing and taking-as and the way it conflicts with other ways. Such deconstructibility is not bad news, but the condition of messianic peace.

I believe in faith and in giving witness to our faith. I would say of faith what Augustine says of the senses of Scriptures: there should be as many faiths as possible, so long as all of them are true. But be on guard against the illusion that we have by faith—or by anything else, by science or mysticism, by phenomenology or Christian Neoplatonism, by metaphysics or overcoming metaphysics—been linked up with the Unmediated Truth. The occupational hazard of natural scientists—and this shows up in scientific realism—and of religious believers—and this shows up in fundamentalism—is to forget this. The faithful in particular sometimes suffer the illusion that they are escorted on the Wings of the Spirit from "witnessing" to their faith to the Truth *itself* and loosened from the condition of a believer. To have a faith is to be attached to "the way," which is of course *our* way, our faith, one more entry in the endless conflict of competing ways. "The Way" is the way nearly everyone describes their way.

As regards the anonymous, I again lay claim to the white hat: just as my idea of faith comes from I Cor. 1, my idea of the "anonymous" does not come from a dogmatic atheism, an unmediated intuition of the things themselves, or from embracing "an ultimately chaotic violent ontology," an idea that Ayres has picked up from Milbank. It comes from Genesis 1:1–2, from the creationist idea that the world has been formed, forged, and shaped from the chaos, and that it is a form of idolatry to attach too much substance to the contingent forms that things have assumed. That is why I love Peter Damian's argument that if God were so minded, God could even change the past; I do not think Peter's argument actually holds water (that is a problem with metaphysics!), but I love the direction in which it flows! One of the things I as a Radical Hermeneut have been pressing, to the great discomfort of both Radical Secularizing Deconstructionists and Radical Orthodoxists alike, is that the critique of the metaphysics of presence in deconstruction goes hand in hand with the biblical critique of idols, so that if deconstruction philosophizes with a hammer, it uses the hammer that Moses took to Aaron's gold calf. Levinas brilliantly transcribed the mytheme of the original chaos into a philosopheme by means of his quasi-phenomenology of the *il y a*. What the author of Genesis was talking about in his story also shows up in our "experience," in "the texture of our perceptions," as the de-texturability or deconstructibility of the texture or woven fabric of our perceptions.

So the anonymous, the *il y a*, Derrida's *khora*, and the *tohu wa bohu*, which can be very interestingly compared and must also be differentiated, all have this much in common: they are all ways to signify the contingency of things and the revisability, deconstructibility, and disruptibility of our constructions, the unravelability of the texture of our perceptions. This has a counterpart in Husserl's thesis of the annihilability of the world (*Ideas I*, §49), so we are *not* "so far from Husserl," to dispute with an aside one of Ayres's asides. Husserl, sober as a judge, was making an epistemological point about the contingency of the unity of the meanings that are constituted in experience (he was not leaping into an abyss or contemplating suicide). This indeterminate, somewhat like Aristotle's idea of *prote hyle*, does not signify *how things are in themselves* but what would happen if we lost our grips (*Auffassung*) on things and were unable to say a thing about them, which is why he spoke of "hyletic data," which also suggests something like *khora*! Now all of this is meant to say that our constructions are "constructed"—not that they are "false" or "illusions" or Apollonian veils over a the Dionysian thing in itself, which is the Schopenhauer-Nietzschean spin that Radical Orthodoxists like Ayres try to peddle about me and Derrida. The anonymous describes what we would be left with if we were lost for words, without a clue, without an interpretation, or to give it a Derridean twist, what would happen if *différance* gave out and we were unable to string (or weave) anything together. Far from giving us privileged access to "what actually is," far from describing the one "true" "unmediated" or "primitive experience or presence," or a "basic" experience of "the fundamental nature of existence," the subject matter of "the only true phenomenology," it would describe the condition of someone who was totally without access to anything, whose intentional lines had all snapped, for whom presence had just broken down. But suppose some mischievous fellow does come along and announce that this formless chaos *is* the *way things are*? That for me would just be one more interpretation to add to the endless conflict of interpretations. Thus Zarathustra spoke—his personal opinion. In fact, I saw this fellow coming, having *staged* his appearance with the "voice" of "Felix Sineculpa" in *Against Ethics*, and about him I have expressed the most severe and disapproving reservations.[4] Like Richard Kearney who thinks I am an indecisionist who, if forced to decide, would say that the *khora* is all in all, and like Merold Westphal, who mistakes this Nietzschean voice as *mine*, Lewis Ayres mistakenly thinks that I regard this to be the voice of being itself giving words to some Milbankian violent ontology that I am supposed to have embraced. I must, alas, protest—for all the reasons I have given Richard Kearney—and, doffing my white hat, scratch my head.

Allow me to conclude with a counter-complaint. I said, in responding to Kearney, that without *khora* we run the risk of triumphalism and dogmatism, the illusion that we have been granted access to the Secret, and that what makes religion dangerous is the idea that the Secret has been communicated to *us* but withheld from *them*. Now in the second "theological" half of his paper, Ayres speaks of seeing through or by way of the Eucharist—here we see an interesting convergence of Radical Orthodoxy and of Marion's Eucharistic hermeneutics—learning "to regard all in Christ" in order to see "what is truly given and created." That is one way, but it is not the way God reveals Godself at other times in other places—and, who knows, in other galaxies—to other people who are not Christian. Unless one claims that the Christian way is the One Privileged Way, the One True Faith, while all the other ways are forms of Mistaken Faith (so that Ayres's attribution of a fishy distinction between true and mistaken faith turns out to be a projection on his part). My concern is that, with no desert *khora* to pass through, it is in just that direction that this movement called Radical (Christian) Orthodoxy is rushing with a headlong rush, with all the violence of orthodoxy and ontology.

NOTES

1. I discussed the distinction between the old and the "new" Enlightenment in DN, pp. 50–60.

2. See Martin Heidegger, *The Principle of Reason*, trans. Reginald Lily (Bloomington: Indiana University Press, 1991), pp. 10–31.

3. Jacques Derrida, *The Truth in Painting*, trans. Geoff Bennington and Ian MacLeod (Chicago: University of Chicago Press, 1987), pp. 326–327.

4. See in AE what is said by all the pseudonyms except Felix, and then see RH, pp. 285–288.

7 POSTMODERNISM AND ETHICS: THE CASE OF CAPUTO

MEROLD WESTPHAL

Philosophically speaking, perhaps the most pressing question inherited by the nineteenth century from the eighteenth was this: How is theology possible after the Kantian critique of metaphysics? There was no shortage of "solutions." Some, beginning with Kant and Fichte, sought to ground theology in ethics. Others, beginning with Schleiermacher, sought to ground theology in feeling and experience. Others, beginning with Schelling, Schopenhauer, and the Schlegels, sought to make art into a new religion. And Hegel, of course, sought to make metaphysics once again (but differently) the foundation of theology.

It is possible to read these traditions in the light of the psalmist's lament, "If the foundations are destroyed, what can the righteous do?" (Psalms, 11:3). It would be better if we could have continued doing business as usual. But we can't, so we'll have to scurry about and find some new strategies for avoiding bankruptcy. For the most part, however, the nineteenth century followed Kant's lead when he pointed in a different direction. Speaking of the "positive advantage" of the critical philosophy by which speculative reason is "deprived of its pretensions to transcendent insight," he writes, "I have therefore found it necessary to deny *knowledge*, in order to make room for *faith*." Now that the spurious foundations are destroyed, the righteous are more fully free to flourish. They are actually better off!

Philosophically speaking, perhaps the most pressing question inherited by the twenty-first century from the twentieth is this: How is ethics possible after the (very Kantian) postmodern critique of metaphysics? After Nietzsche and the death of God, signaling a move beyond good and evil to the innocence of becoming? After Heidegger's critique of onto-theology? After Derrida's critique of logocentrism and the metaphysics of presence? After Lyotard's critique of metanarratives? After Foucault's genealogical linking of knowledge and power? After Rorty's insistence that our vocabularies are optional.

There has been no shortage of hand wringing, accompanied by claims that nihilism and cynicism are the necessary consequence (against the background of a choral ostinato setting of "If the foundations are destroyed, what can the righteous do?"). But already with Levinas we hear an echo of the Kantian "I have therefore found it necessary . . ." The *knowledge* he finds it necessary to deny he calls ontology, representation, thematization, intentionality, disclosure, adequation, and so forth. The *faith* for which he seeks to make room is, as in Kant's case, a kind of knowing, but not the kind to which philosophy is in the habit of giving its *imprimatur*. He calls it the ethical relation, the face to face, heteronomy before the claims of the Other, responsibility prior to any commitment, the trauma of being taken hostage for the widow, the orphan, and the stranger, and so forth.

Levinas clearly takes his own assault on theory to be in the service of ethics. What some see as the destroying of the foundations, he sees as pulling up the weeds to make it more difficult, if not impossible, for the righteous to flourish. Is it possible to extend this analysis more broadly to postmodern philosophy, to see its new critique of pure reason as friendly toward righteousness precisely by the way it is a scourge to self-righteousness?

Whether or not one is a Christian, the parable of the good Samaritan in Luke 10 has paradigmatic moral significance (just as Mother Theresa is a saint even to those who don't much believe in saints). Its setting is important. It is addressed to a lawyer, possibly a fresh Ph.D. in Torah studies, possibly a mature scholar with an impressive bibliography of books and essays on the good and the right. In any case, he is a theoretical expert on morality. It is as a rebuke to such a questioner that Jesus recites his mininarrative.

And why? Is he an anti-intellectual who opposes serious study of the law? I think rather that the answer is found in the perceived motive of the lawyer's question. "But wanting to justify himself, he asked Jesus . . ."

He has just given the twofold summary of the law (love the Lord your God and love your neighbor as yourself) that we elsewhere find on the lips of Jesus. His ethical WHAT is as good as it gets, since in the gospels you don't trump Jesus. The problem is with the HOW. The lawyer wants to be able to convert his moral knowledge into self-justification. By contrast, Jesus sees the same WHAT as setting an essentially unfinished task, as he makes clear in the words, Go and do likewise. The function of moral discourse (*logos*) on the one hand is legitimation; on the other hand it is a certain delegitimation. The lawyer's practice is delegitimized (judged, condemned, found wanting) because he has not yet learned to love the Other who is found across the barriers that give his society its structure. At the same time his theory is subjected to critique precisely because it has not allowed the Other to appear as Neighbor.

It is possible to make more explicit the "postmodern" dimensions of Jesus' critique of the lawyer's moral theory. He treats it as a totalizing theory, one which seeks to articulate the "whole duty of man" (Eccl. 12:13—I doubt the lawyer would have worried about gendered language) in such a way as to limit responsibility. There are many duties to be found in the law, but here is a complete list. No one, not even God, can ask any more of me than this. But, as postmodernists will insist, like every other totalizing project, this one succeeds only by exclusion. In Godelian fashion, its completeness is purchased at the price of inconsistency, the inconsistency of purporting to present the "whole duty of man" while eliminating certain responsibilities *a priori*.

The way in which Jesus opens up the closed system of the lawyer by inserting a pariah Samaritan, not merely as a neighbor to be loved but rather as a model of how neighbor love crosses boundaries of separation and hatred, ethnic in this case, makes it clear that we are not to enlarge the system a bit (so as to include Samaritans, perhaps) and then reclose it. The task of moral discourse is to pose infinite, not finite tasks. We can never even draw up a complete list of those for whom we are responsible, much less of what our responsibilities are.

By describing Jesus' parable as a mininarrative, I have deliberately evoked another postmodern theme, Lyotard's famous definition of the postmodern as "incredulity toward metanarratives." It is widely assumed that since Christianity is inescapably a metanarrative and postmodernism is incredulity toward all such stories, the two can only be implacably opposed. But it is not so clear that Christianity is a metanarrative in Lyotard's sense. Its story, that stretches from creation to the new Jerusalem is a grand narrative indeed, but a metanarrative is not simply a meganarrative. What makes the big stories of modernity, especially the philosophies of history of Hegel and Marx, into metanarratives is not just their size but especially their origin and function. Their origin is philosophy and their function is to legitimate the "new authorities" that constitute modernity: science and the state.[1] Modernity hires philosophers to tell it the kind of big stories that justify its practices.

On both counts, it can be argued, the grand Christian narrative is not a metanarrative. Its origin is obviously not philosophy as the purported voice of pure reason. Nor is its function that of a Lyotardian metanarrative. For example, when Jesus appeals to the big story, it is most often to a Final Judgment that functions as anything but a legitimation narrative. There is always the hint, sometimes not too subtle, that those who take themselves to be sheep will turn out to be goats, or even wolves. In the present instance, Jesus' moral discourse consists of a mininarrative whose purpose is not to validate contemporary practices but rather to call them into question along with the theories that justified them. So perhaps it is not entirely impossible to think of postmodernism as friendly toward righteousness precisely by the way it is a scourge to self-justifying self-righteousness. Perhaps, like Jesus, it finds moral philosophy to be too much the work of those too willing to justify themselves. Perhaps it wants to suggest that obligation exceeds the theories that purport to ground it while functioning to limit it.

I want to explore these possibilities in the context of a particular text. John D. Caputo is one of the most widely read American postmodern philosophers. His sympathetic readings of Derrida in books such as *Radical Hermeneutics* (1987), *Deconstruction in a Nutshell* (1997), and *The Prayers and Tears of Jacques Derrida* (1997) are essential reading for anyone wishing to have an informed opinion about deconstruction. He addresses the question of postmodern ethics in a book with the not entirely reassuring title, *Against Ethics* (1993). It opens with a defiant confession:

> I am against ethics.
> Here I stand. I cannot do otherwise.[2]

Ethics is the pope against which our Luther redivivus wishes to do battle. Unfortunately, it is all too common for statements like this to be "read" as follows. "What I (who have heard it reported that Caputo says he is against ethics) mean by ethics is morality, decency, a sense of right and wrong, a sense of duty, and so forth. Caputo himself tells us he is against all this. Doesn't this confirm that postmodernism is simply the enemy of the good and right, to be ignored where possible and denounced when necessary?"

Wouldn't it be better to find out what Caputo means by ethics and why he is against it? Especially since he immediately tells us that while he is against ethics, he is for obligation.

> Obligation happens. (AE, 6)

By ethics Caputo means moral philosophy, a meta-discourse about obligation which he identifies as "philosophy," "metaphysics," and "a certain *episteme*" (AE, 5–6, 12, 27, 31, 72).

Now Plato uses *episteme* to signify the top level of his divided line (or occasionally the top two levels). It stands for a tradition in which philosophy seeks, and often claims to find, the complete clarity and certainty that comes from being directly and fully present to its object. "My theory is the mirror image of the good and the right, the locus of the *adequatio* of the human understanding and moral reality. There are moral absolutes, and I am, at least cognitively speaking, their embodiment." Caputo is against moral philosophy whenever it does not decisively break with the *epistemic* claims of this tradition. "Deconstruction issues a warning that the road ahead is still under construction, that there is blasting and the danger of falling rock. Ethics, on the other hand, hands out maps which lead us to believe that the road is finished and there are super highways all along the way" (AE, 4).

But why is Caputonic (Caputian?) deconstruction against ethics, so conceived? It is not because ethics thinks, for example, that lying is wrong while Caputo thinks it is quite OK. Deconstruction's quarrel with ethics is not essentially about its first order substantive judgments but about the epistemic meta-claims it makes for those judgments. Of course, Caputo may have substantive disagreements with the ethics of Plato, or Aquinas, or Kant, or Mill. But one does not have to be a postmodernist to do so, to disagree, for example, with Kant's extreme view about lying. In any case, the substantive moral disagreement about which Caputo has been most vocal to date is not with the tradition but with another postmodern philosopher. A polemic against Heidegger's "originary ethics" reverberates throughout *Against Ethics* and is fully developed in *Demythologizing Heidegger*.[3]

So why the opposition to ethics? In part because Caputo finds traditional claims to correspondence (mirroring, adequation) unable to withstand postmodern critiques, deconstructive and otherwise. Both as a hermeneutics of finitude and as a hermeneutics of suspicion, he finds postmodern analyses (which are by no means utterly unique on either score) persuasive.[4] And he believes we do not have the right, even on behalf of the Good and the Right, to deceive ourselves about the level of our cognitive abilities and achievements.

But there is an even deeper reason, adumbrated above, for being suspicious of ethics. Like Levinas, Caputo finds it necessary to deny *episteme* for the sake of obligation. "Ethics contains obligation [read: is about obligation], but that is its undoing (deconstruction). Ethics harbors within itself what it cannot maintain . . . Ethics, one might say, cannot contain what it contains" (AE, 5).

Why is obligation the new wine that bursts the old bottles of moral philosophy? Because obligation is:

> . . . ugly, Jewish, Abrahamic. It lacks entirely the spirit of Greek beauty and autonomy . . . Obligation is the ugliness of discord and subjection, of being disrupted and disturbed by a call that comes from without. This dispossession and alienation will not do at all in ethics, which is philosophy. In philosophy, which is Greek, obligation must always be, in one way or another, something I do to myself, just as in philosophy, truth is something I have or am of myself . . . Philosophy runs autonomously, on the level of immanence, while obligation is constantly being shocked from without, transcendently. (AE, 12)

Caputo hammers away on this motif like Luther proclaiming justification by faith against papal indulgences. Obligation is a scandal for "metaphysics and its ethics" because it:

> . . . is not a rational utterance (*logos*) received on the other end as wholly intelligible . . . That would make it mine, me, a case of autonomy and auto-dictation. Obligation is not like a man talking to himself and offering himself counsel, which he judges to be the best advice he can get; it is instead a shock to the I, to my freedom and autonomy. (AE, 27)

When he talks like this Caputo sounds a lot like Kierkegaard and Levinas, and he cheerfully acknowledges his indebtedness to both.[5] But he also tells us repeatedly that he finds Levinas to be "too pious." It is the Nietzschean side of him that tells us this.

For in addition to the claim:

Obligation happens

we find the claim:

Obligation is a perspective. (AE, 190)

This statement comes as exposition of a brief essay by Felix Sineculpa, one of four pseudonyms whose eight essays (with commentary) comprise Chapter Eight. Felix articulates Nietzsche's innocence of becoming, the elimination of moral categories from the nature of things. He writes,

> Auschwitz is not Evil, not Absolute Evil . . . *Auschwitz is not a fact but a perspective. The condemnation of Auschwitz is made from the perspective of the lamb* . . . Is fire Evil because it burns the wood and turns it to ash? . . . Forces happen . . . Stronger forces dominate and overcome weaker forces . . . That, I would say, is the "law" of how things happen . . . There is no Evil here, just stronger and weaker forces. . . . (AE, 186–89; emphasis added)

It is in interpretive summary of Felix Sineculpa that Caputo writes, "The whole is innocent (*sine culpa*) . . . Obligation is a perspective" (AE, 190–91). We cannot simply attribute to Caputo the ideas of his pseudonyms, especially since they do not agree among themselves. What Caputo tells us is that the voice of Felix is the setting for the other voices, "indeed I would say the spectre by which the other authors are continuously menaced. Felix haunts the other authors like a ghost . . . and makes their words tremble. His cold vision is the fear and the trembling they confront . . . This fear and trembling is even more ominous than that of Abraham" (AE, 191).

It turns out that the other pseudonyms are not alone in being haunted by Felix's cold Nietzschean naturalism. For a long time Caputo himself has been spooked by Nietzsche, and indeed by a particular passage, which he once again calls to our attention. It comes from *On Truth and Lying in the Extramoral Sense*. Following Caputo's suggestion, I have substituted "obligation" where Nietzsche writes "knowing." In a universe of numberless solar systems:

> . . . there was a star upon which clever beasts invented obligation. That was the most arrogant and mendacious minute of "world history," but nevertheless it was only a minute. After nature had drawn a few breaths, the star cooled and congealed, and the clever beasts had to die. (AE, 16)

The implications of this passage are momentous. "You and I stand on the surface of the little star and shout, 'racism is unjust.' The cosmos yawns and takes another spin. There is no cosmic record of our complaint. The cosmos feels no sorrow and has no heart on which to record our complaint" (AE, 17).

Isn't this a dogmatic metaphysical claim, ill suited to the humble posture of a professed deconstructionist? Wouldn't one have to see the whole and see it quite clearly to know this? Nor is it easy to detect any undecidability in Caputo's announcement, "Obligation does not mean answering the call of Being, or of the History of Being, or of the History of Spirit, or the Voice of God" (AE, 5). Or again, "Obligations are strictly local events, sublunary affairs, between us. They are matters of flesh and blood, without cosmic import or support" (AE, 227). How does he know all this?

There are times when he remembers that he doesn't (e.g., AE, pp. 28, 31, 33, 85) and adopts an agnostic stance. Far more frequent throughout the text are passages with a decidedly dogmatic metaphysical ring to them like those just cited, serenely confident, epistemologically speaking, that Nietzsche was right (in a rather non-Nietzschean sense of "right"). If we ask the real Caputo to stand up, however, I believe we get neither a dogmatist nor a skeptic but a believer. A Nietzschean believer, to be sure, not a Kierkegaardian believer. Kierkegaard acknowledges that we have no Knowledge that would settle the ultimate questions; faith occurs in the context of objective uncertainty. But when it comes to the question whether "the cosmos yawns" in response to our moral outrage or "has [a] heart on which to record our complaint," he believes the latter just as clearly as Nietzsche believes the former.

Caputo sides with Nietzsche. Thus, in the midst of raising skeptical objections to ethics as *episteme*, he writes, "We have no star to guide us, no

messages from on high. Life is a disaster; the earth is adrift. Obligation is on
its own and will have to fend for itself. That is the faith of an incredulous infidel about salvific metanarratives . . . The Good, the *arche* and *principium*,
along with any overarching principle that assigns all things their place and
holds them mightily in its sway, has become unbelievable to me and has
earned my incredulity" (AE, 24, 31).

This text provides the context for saying, "Obligation is a perspective." It,
too, belong to Caputo's Credo. That Credo is not devoid of metanarrative, but
only of salvific metanarrative; for surely the Nietzschean story is a metanarrative of cosmic, if yawning proportions.[6] Nor does Caputo seem to be allergic to
"any overarching principle" as such; for surely the Nietzschean indifference
arches over all things and holds them as mightily in its sway as ever did the will
and word of Yahweh in biblical religion. What Caputo is allergic to, in his Nietzschean mode, is any claim that the ultimate cosmic power is good.

When he speaks in a dogmatic tone of voice, as believers inevitably do
much of the time, Caputo may seem to plead philosophical privilege, giving
the impression that the insights of deconstruction account for his preference
for Nietzschean over Kierkegaardian faith. But this linkage is spurious,
whether affirmed or only hinted at. For deconstruction is a theory of undecidability (AE, 5). As such it can remind us that faith is not sight (presence).
It can point to the difficulty and urgency of the choice between Nietzschean
and Kierkegaardian faith. But it cannot warrant the Nietzschean choice. Nor
can the overcoming of metaphysics be the basis for choosing between conflicting metaphysical claims as to whether the Good is built into the order of
things or not.

In confessing his Nietzschean Credo as such, as "the faith of an incredulous infidel," Caputo speaks most authentically; for he avows what he most
deeply believes and he disavows the implication that his beliefs have some
special philosophical privilege. Just how the moral interpretation of the universe excluded by this Nietzschean kerygma has "earned" his incredulity,
Caputo does not tell us.

We can now distinguish between two senses of the claim:

Obligation is a perspective,

a Nietzschean, ontological sense and a Derridean, epistemological sense. In
the Nietzschean sense the moral interpretation of the world is pure invention. When we say that Auschwitz or apartheid are evil, there is nothing of a
moral nature "out there" which such judgments express. They only express
the distress of the lambs who do not enjoy being devoured by wolves. In the
words of Felix Sineculpa, "There is no Evil here, just stronger and weaker
forces . . ." But in that case, while obligation may be invented and asserted, it
does not happen. The wolves are under no obligation, and neither are we.

When Caputo flirts with Nietzsche, he undermines the Levinasian side of his Credo. For if it is really the case that:

Obligation happens,

then surely we have good reason to abandon the "cold vision" Felix takes over from Friedrich.

N.B. To abandon Nietzsche's:

Obligation is a perspective

for Levinas'

Obligation happens

is not to comfort oneself with a salvific metanarrative. Obligation is one thing; forgiveness is another. Anyone who wants to pose as Luther should remember that law does not entail grace. Caputo does so when he contrasts the fear and trembling of Felix's cold vision with that of Abraham before Yahweh, who has been known to thunder, but never to yawn.

The Derridean sense of

Obligation is a perspective

is compatible with the notion that obligation really happens and is not sheer invention. It is the reminder that the Levinasian and Nietzschean visions are both interpretations. Neither derives from the sheer presence of the real to an intellect which merely mirrors what is given to it. We find ourselves face to face with an Other to whom we have an obligation prior to any commitment not because we first were face to face with Being and were able to see the Good in person, enabling us now to apply what we have seen in pure light to life in the shadowy cave where we encounter widows, orphans, and strangers. It is precisely to deny this model that Levinas insists the ontology is not fundamental.

For Derrida, the claim that obligation happens and, *a fortiori*, any general principles or particular judgments about what our obligations are, are interpretations and not intuitions. They do not come to us unmediated on a hotline from Being or from the Good or from God. As human seeings-as, they carry with them all the risk, contingency, and perspectival relativism that goes with interpretation. We are never in possession of a transcendental signified, a meaning so definitive and (thus) a truth so final they do not refer us beyond themselves to further interpretation. Only a thought capable of totality, that is, only an infinite thought would be able to be thus at rest.

But this does not mean that our judgments do not refer to anything or that our moral judgments are sheer invention. That is why Derrida, like Lyotard and Levinas, all of whom are "against ethics" in Caputo's sense, are also willing to speak about justice in ways that Nietzsche cannot.[7]

Caputo asks us to consider a child born with AIDS. According to his "cold truth," she "has no star to watch over her, no heavenly support . . . The claim of the child is finite and fragile. It is not absolutely commanding—not a Categorical Imperative that breaks through the world of appearances, nor the Form of the Good gradually being recalled, nor the traces of the Face of God showing up in the child's face" (AE, 38). These denials are required by Nietzsche's naturalism. The cries of the child are the bleating of a lamb hoping that wolves will have pity on her.

There are parallel but weaker denials required by Levinas, namely that it is not necessary first to have a private audience with the Categorical Imperative, or the Form of the Good, or the Face of God in order derivatively to recognize the legitimacy of the child's inconvenient claim upon us. Nothing about deconstruction compels us to adopt Nietzsche's stronger denials over Levinas' weaker ones. That is why deconstruction is compatible with the claim that:

> Obligation happens,

but only when not wedded to a cold, Nietzschean faith.

But it is equally true that nothing about deconstruction requires us to side (as I think Derrida himself does) with Levinas against Nietzsche. It is a theory of undecidability, something very much like what Kierkegaard's Climacus meant by objective uncertainty. Caputo reminds us that, "Undecidability does not detract from the urgency of decision; it simply underlines the difficulty" (AE, 5). It seems that the difficulty is too great for Caputo, that he remains undecided between his two faiths. "I move about," he tells us, "in the difference between piety and impiousness, between ethics and the innocence of becoming, keeping up a correspondence with Dionysus [Nietzsche] while staying in constant touch with my rabbi [Levinas]" (AE, 220). Here he seems to realize that he can't have it both ways, much as he would like to; but much as he is haunted by the child with AIDS, he remains equally haunted by a Nietzsche to whom he cannot say no. "I love Nietzsche and Ethics, to excess, really, but I lack the piety demanded by Ethics for its Good and its Infinity and its Categorical Imperatives, even as I cannot muster the lionhearted, macho courage required by Nietzsche's cold cosmic truthfulness" (AE, 233). Undecidability becomes indecision, though I suspect that like a good Humean skeptic, Caputo does not live by the lights of his theoretical paralysis.

All this is meta-ethics, which is appropriate given the concern that postmodernism undermines not just ethical theory but ethical responsibility. The question of the *possibility* of ethics in both senses, theory and practice, is a legitimate and pressing one. But what sort of substantive ethics do we find when Caputo temporarily sets aside the Nietzschean spectres that haunt him and simply reflects on the claim that obligation happens? What sort of obligations happen to us?

In books such as *Radical Hermeneutics* and *Demythologizing Heidegger*, Caputo sketches an ethic of compassion in the face of suffering. So it is not surprising that in his commentary on the essay of Johanna de Silentio, a non-Nietzschean pseudonym, he writes, "Obligation means the obligation to reduce and alleviate suffering, not to produce it, not to augment it . . ." (AE, 145). At the conclusion of his chapter on justice he writes that it consists of two things: "minimization of suffering" and "maximization of difference and letting many flowers bloom" (AE, 92). As with Richard Rorty, we find the familiar structure of liberal society here. The only legitimate limit to difference (read; different visions of the good) is the point at which a given vision, or rather its practice, imposes suffering. Any other restriction is itself the imposition of suffering. So it turns out that the two principles of justice reduce to one: minimize suffering.

Caputo points out that this is an anti-Nietzschean ethic. For Felix Sineculpa, "Suffering is everywhere a part of what happens, but it is not 'wrong' or 'against nature' . . . The joyful wisdom of Felix/Nietzsche is aimed [not at preventing suffering but] at preventing suffering from becoming the judge of life . . . Life is innocent, without guilt (*sine culpa*), the way the wolf is innocent, the way the waves that beat against the ship or the shore are innocent, however much destruction they do" (AE, 138). It is also anti-Heideggerian, for "Being shows no interest in damaged lives" (AE, 70; cf. 152, 160–62, 185). In other words, postmodernism is no monolith. This is a postmodern ethic at odds with those I like to call the (un)founding (un)fathers of postmodern philosophy.

What is distinctive about the presentation of this ethic of compassion in the face of suffering in *Against Ethics* is the way it is developed in terms of the category of flesh. "Flesh is the locus of obligation" (AE, 173; cf. 196, 216).

The description of this site is a simple phenomenology of flesh. Flesh is that by which we hunger and thirst. It is that by which we experience pain, agony, misery, suffering, disease, and death. It is our flesh that stinks and is disfigured. It is as flesh that we are exposed and vulnerable to hurt, humiliation, cruelty, and brutality (AE, 196–215).

Caputo calls this phenomenology a reduction to flesh, which is to say it is an anti-phenomenology, an alternative to the Husserlian reduction from the natural attitude to the realm of pure experience. Flesh is signified by the leper, by the *Pieta*, in which Michelangelo "makes stone sigh with sorrow," and by the statue Caputo wishes had been its follow-up, Polynices "dead and rotting, being sniffed by a dog" (AE, 212). By contrast, phenomenology takes it cue from *David*. Its bodies are too healthy, too "well clothed, well fed, and

well-housed," too active. They are subjects of intentionality rather than suf-
ferers of indignity. The concept that links the phenomenological ego to the
phenomenological body is that of agency. But flesh is *hyle*, not *morphe*, much
less *morphe morphing* (AE, 194–5, 203, 205, 209, 213).

This is why "flesh" is a different category from "body." It is true that Merleau-Ponty, the great phenomenologist of the body, pays some attention to an
injured and malfunctioning body. But in the case of "poor Schneider . . . it is
never mentioned by phenomenology that [his] motor peculiarities are a
source of misery and humiliation for Schneider . . . The humiliation . . . is neutralized by the phenomenological reduction, bleached out by a strictly Greco-
philosophical operation." The reason for this is that Merleau-Ponty's analysis
is "too epistemic." It is "still a form of the idealism against which he always
fought" (AE, 195, 201–210).

In other words, like Nietzsche and Heidegger, Husserl and Merleau-
Ponty are deaf to the cry of flesh. Even Foucault, a "great philosopher of
flesh" who powerfully describes the powers to which it is subject fails to
notice sufficiently that it is "no mere *hyle* but an active power that commands
respect, that elicits from me a certain 'regard' which I do not extend to anything else . . . Foucault does not analyze the power of the vulnerable body of
the Other to *prohibit* (I do not say to stop) violence, to issue a command
against violence" (AE, 213-14).

Well, that's about it. The anti-phenomenological reduction to flesh is
Caputo's ethics. Perhaps we can get a better feel for it by considering some
objections.

Objection One

This is clearly not a teleological ethic and most emphatically not a eudae-
monistic ethic. It does not respond to my question, How can I be happy?, by
telling me, "Surprise. The best way to be really happy is to be good and just."
It is a deontological ethic, as the just cited references to the commands that
emanate from flesh make clear. But these commands lack authority, since
they do not come from a source superior to those human desires (mine and
ours) which often enough increase suffering rather than reducing it. They do
not emanate from God, or the Good, or Reason, or Tradition, or Society, or
the People. They come from lepers, children, even animals (AE, 85, 145).

Reply One

Everything you say is true except that such commands lack authority, that
they are not superior to selfish desire. There are both epistemic and ethical
problems with your objection. Epistemically, the claim is that I must *first*

hear the fleshless voice of Authority and then, in obedience to that voice respond in compassion to flesh when I encounter it. It is, of course, relatively easy to know what Tradition, or Society, or the People expect of me. But, given the cruelty and humiliation these have so often sanctioned, it is not clear why they should be invested with a higher Authority than that of the suffering child. By contrast, it is not so easy to show that what I claim to be the voice of God, or the Good, or of Reason really is. Both the hermeneutics of finitude and the hermeneutics of suspicion render such claims deeply problematic. But why assume that we must have ascended on high so as to stand, to mix our metaphors, at once atop the divided line and in the sunshine outside the cave before obligation can happen to us?

An analogy with the philosophy of religion may be helpful here. Foundationalist evidentialism says we cannot speak of God until we have proved the existence and nature of God. But since this cannot be done, we must abandon God-talk. Reformed epistemology has replied by asking why we should make the first assumption. We cannot prove the existence of the external world or of other minds in non-circular, foundationalist ways. But we don't give up talking on those assumptions. Why should such severe entry requirements be imposed on God-talk?[8]

Similarly, in the case of ethics, the burden of proof shifts. Is it not arbitrary to assume that unless we are demonstrably in touch with Ultimacy, obligation cannot touch us. This invites a double disaster, the one that comes from declaring the task impossible and giving ourselves a permanent moral holiday, and the one that comes from claiming to have completed the task, thereby giving Absolute Authority to our moral judgments. We make ourselves into the Grand Inquisitor, or, as Bob Dylan and Joan Baez used to sing, "With God on our side, we'll start the next war."

There is also an ethical problem with assuming that I must first hear the voice of fleshless Authority before the cries of your suffering have any claim on me. When I say this I am saying that you are of no intrinsic value, that from my point of view you don't count. Of course, if it should prove necessary, in order for me to remain on good terms with God, or the Good, or Reason, or Tradition, or Society, or the People, I'm quite willing to do what they ask me. For while I have no respect for you, I do have a great respect (fear?) for (one or more of) them.

Objection Two

Physical suffering is surely of ethical import, but the focus on flesh is too narrow. One needn't be a dualist who treats the body as accidental rather than essential to our being to recognize that there are ethical concerns of a non-physical nature, mental cruelty, for example.

Reply Two

The focus on flesh is not meant to be restrictive. In the first place, the fundamental ethical problem is insensitivity, whether in the form of cruelty and oppression or of neglect and indifference, to the legitimate needs of the Other. From a psychological point of view, it may well be that the cry of the Other is more likely to melt our hearts of stone when it arises out of physical pain, even if it is the kind of pain that renders its victims mute. Flesh, in the literal sense, is a good place to begin.

But, in the second place, we should not interpret "flesh" in too literal a sense. In the brief phenomenological sketch given above, flesh is our vulnerability to cruelty and humiliation. Physical examples are given, but we need not read this as a restriction. Rather we can see hunger as a metaphor for all legitimate needs, including the needs of the soul, and physical violence as a metaphor for every expression of hatred. The point of the reduction to flesh as exposure to pain is to falsify, not to confirm, that desperate denial of childhood:

> Sticks and stones can break my bones,
> But ugly words can't hurt me.

Finally, there are many important questions about our obligations, even in relation to flesh in the literal sense, that are not addressed in Caputo's account. What Caputo gives us, stated in Kantian language which at every point is problematic from his perspective, is a *Grundlegung* that gives expression to the "fact of reason." It is not a *Metaphysics of Morals* that gives a detailed analysis of justice and virtue. In Levinasian language, less distant from his project, he give us an account of the ethical relation, of the face-to-face, of the one-for-the-Other. This is the point of departure for a life of moral responsibility, but it does not preclude the necessity of making justice concrete in "the rationality of an already derived order . . . by *comparing* in knowledge/thought 'incomparable and unique' persons." The demand for justice "is the obligation to compare unique and incomparable others; this is the moment of *knowledge* and, henceforth, of an objectivity beyond or on the hither side of the nakedness of the face."[9] Or, we might say, beyond the reduction to flesh, in order to indicate that nothing in Caputo's account precludes the legitimacy of this further reflection. What will be precluded in this derived order of rationality will be the cognitive ideals of "a certain *episteme*."[10]

Objection Three

This isn't really an ethical theory. The point of moral philosophy is *to present* substantive norms in the form of principles or rules or virtues, and so forth, *and to prove* them, to establish by argument that these are the obligations that happen to us. But Caputo doesn't do this. He presents no arguments to prove that the flesh of the Other should be of any concern to me.

Reply Three

The strong form of this objection has already been addressed. It is ethically dangerous to make ethical theory in this sense a *sine qua non* for obligation, and in any case, obligation shows precious little respect for such a philosophical ploy. It happens to us regardless of even the presence of reflective moral philosophy, and, *a fortiori*, of successful moral philosophy.

The weaker form of the objection, found in Kant for example, acknowledges that obligation does not await a go ahead from philosophy. Still, the point of ethical theory, after the fact of obligation, is to clarify and to justify our moral intuitions by converting their untutored form into the form of Knowledge (*episteme, scientia, Wissenschaft*).

I think it is safe to say that vis-à-vis these epistemic ideals, every form of postmodern philosophy is skeptical. We have already seen that Caputo begins *Against Ethics* by renouncing this task as impossible and as an invitation to dangerous self-deception. Beyond this skepticism, there is perhaps an unexpected link here with H. A. Prichard. Just as he once rejected the question, Why should I be moral? as an essentially immoral question,[11] so Caputo rules out of court the question, Why should the suffering of the Other be of any concern to me? Beyond doubts about the degree to which we can answer such a question, he has qualms about even asking it.

So what does he think the task of writing about ethics is? For even if he wouldn't want to describe his book as moral philosophy, given traditional connotations of that term, he has written a book about ethics and it does not consist in just the double claim a) that ethical theory as traditionally conceived is a fallacious fantasy, and b) that our moral intuitions are not grounded in anything cosmic or transcendent. Like traditional moral philosophy, his reduction to flesh is meant to guide our behavior.

How? By helping us hear the cries of wounded flesh. Rather than try to provide cosmic support for them, Caputo thinks "that such claims as afflicted flesh make [*sic*] upon us are frail and finite, and my supplementary poetic strategy is to lend these claims an ear, to provide them with an idiom, to magnify their voice, to let them ring like bells across the surface of our lives and to discourage cruelty. After that, I do not know what else to do" (AE, 209). This is why he often describes his project as a poetics of obligation, signifying a task more rhetorical than logical. "The best anyone can do is to make the claim of the child [the one born with AIDS, before whose anguish the cosmos yawns] look as strong as possible, to let its appeal

. . . ring out as loudly as possible, to sound the alarm of disasters as loud as we can, and to make indifference look as bad as possible, as bad as it is" (AE, 38).[12]

Two observations, in conclusion, about this concept of "moral philosophy." The primacy it gives to rhetoric over logic may make philosophers nervous, since it offers them no monopoly on serious moral discourse. For a poetics of obligation, it may well be that novelists, journalists, who knows, perhaps even poets, will be as good or better at giving voice to vulnerable and violated flesh than those of us who are philosophically trained. Maybe Rorty will put us all out of business after all.

But there is plenty of work to go around, and I think that Caputo's work, along with that of Levinas, Derrida, Foucault, and Lyotard shows that philosophers need not abandon philosophy in order to have something distinctive to say about how we should live. What Caputo suggests is that they will do so more successfully if they model themselves, as philosophers, less on the scientist or geometer and more on the journalist, the novelist, the filmmaker,[13] and so on, beginning, perhaps, with the kind of examples we use.

Finally, suppose one thinks, as I do, that the cosmos does not yawn, that "the Lord, who made heaven and earth . . . will neither slumber nor sleep" (Psalms, 121:2 and 4) but in a wakefulness that precludes moral holidays, commands us day and night to love our neighbor as we love ourselves. Would that give one reason to disparage Caputo's notion of moral philosophy as poetics? I think not. The reality of God is anything but a guarantee that we can achieve the clarity, certainty, consistency, and completeness of "a certain *episteme*." The believer *as such* might be led to think that the hermeneutics of finitude gives us reason to doubt the possibility of such "modern" projects and that the hermeneutics of suspicion gives us reason to find them morally dangerous.

A certain amendment might well suggest itself, however. If the philosopher can be seen as a kind of poet, why not also think of the philosopher as a kind of witness, one who bears witness, who gives testimony. One need not claim prophetic privilege or apostolic authority to try to give a voice to suffering flesh by giving voice to the God who became flesh and suffered for those who cause suffering (people like me and Slobodan Milosevic).[14] Caputo himself calls for a "new [*sic*] theology, one where God *suffers*" (AE, 58). What the poet and the witness have in common is that they speak out of their own experience without first converting themselves into the essentially impersonal producers and examiners of arguments (the scientist, the geometer, the logician).

But doesn't metaphysics precede ethics for the believer? Yes, in the *ordo essendi*, but not necessarily in the *ordo cognoscendi*. I think it is more obvious to most people most of the time that the child born with AIDS deserves our compassion than that there is a God who commands us to love our neighbor. Why not just recognize, without requiring any theological preamble, that in our awareness of that child, obligation happens? Then we can notice that while we might have felt compassion in a Nietzschean world, obligation couldn't have happened. It could only have seemed to happen. So, just to the degree that I am convinced that obligation has happened, I have good reason to think in non-Nietzschean ways about the real. This isn't quite a moral argument for the existence of God, but perhaps it is a step in that direction.[15]

NOTES

1. Jean-François Lyotard, *The Postmodern Condition*, trans. Geoff Bennington and Brian Massumi (Minneapolis: University of Minnesota Press, 1984), p. 30.

2. John D. Caputo, AE, p. 1. Subsequent references will be given in the text.

3. John D. Caputo, DH.

4. An earlier draft of this paper was presented to the Society of Christian Philosophers at the Pacific Division of the APA. I am indebted to Phil Quinn of Notre Dame and Robin Wang of Loyola Marymount for their helpful commentaries. One part of Phil's response was entitled "Where We Should Be Bored." He called attention to places where Annette Baier, Bernard Williams, Stephen Toulmin, Roderick Chisolm, and Martha Nussbaum have made claims with a recognizable similarity to points made by Caputo. But rather than being bored when I find philosophers of very different styles, canons, and vocabularies saying the "same" thing in different ways, I get excited, both because I think they may be onto something important and because I see opportunities for dialogue and conversation across all too rigid boundaries. Novelty is not a necessary condition of insight. See Nancey Murphy, *Anglo-American Postmodernity* (Boulder: Westview Press, 1997).

5. Levinas in particular emphasizes the way in which responsibility for the other does not arise out of knowledge, as episteme, and that welcoming the Other is not applied knowledge. In her commentary Robin Wang made the helpful comparison with a famous passage from *Meng Tzu* (the *Book of Mencius*), 2A:6, in which Mencius claims that "No man is devoid of a heart sensitive to the suffering of others" and asks us to think of seeing a young child about to fall into a well. The benevolence shown in the attempt to rescue the child arises from a "heart of compassion." British moral sense philosophy is also relevant here, especially when it is not too quickly assimilated to moral intuitionism and its emphasis on feelings, sentiments, and affections is preserved. In none of these contexts is the trans-cognitive character of obligation and responsibility the basis for moral relativism.

6. Caputo does not employ the distinction made above between meganarratives and metanarratives, strictly speaking. I here use the term in this inclusive sense.

7. See especially Jacques Derrida, "Force of Law: The 'Mystical Foundation of Authority,'" in *Deconstruction and the Possibility of Justice*, ed. Drucilla Cornell et al. (New York: Routledge, 1992).

8. See, for example, *Faith and Rationality: Reason and Belief in God*, ed. Alvin Plantinga and Nicholas Wolterstorff (Notre Dame: University of Notre Dame Press, 1983), especially the essays by the editors.

9. Emmanuel Levinas, *Entre nous: on think-of-the-other*, trans. Michael B. Smith and Barbara Harshav (New York: Columbia University Press, 1998), pp. 165–67. Cf. 195, 202, and 204–205.

10. Given the method of reflective equilibrium, I see nothing in the Rawlsian project of *A Theory of Justice* that is excluded by Caputo's argument. But it is easy to forget what one has given up by adopting this method and to think that the result has an "elevated epistemic status" (I borrow this phrase from Phil Quinn) that it cannot have. *Against Ethics* is a sustained warning against the twin temptations of exaggerating the degree to which our moral beliefs are cognitively justified and our moral practices morally justified. Deconstruction has critical bite on both fronts (without monopoly—see note 4 above).

11. H. A. Prichard, "Does Moral Philosophy Rest on a Mistake?" in *Readings in Ethical Theory*, ed. Wilfrid Sellars and John Hospers (New York: Appleton-Century-Crofts, 1952).

12. Quinn questions whether the "as bad as it is" belongs "in a discourse patterned on Rorty." But that depends on whether Rorty's perspectivism is Nietzschean or Derridean, as distinguished above. What is clearer, I think, is that the "as bad as it is" requires a break with Nietzsche, for whom it could only mean "as bad as it seems to the lambs."

13. I quite agree with Quinn that no philosophical text "even comes close to *Shoah*, or even to *Shindler's List*, in making the Holocaust look as bad as possible."

14. The ethnic cleansing of Kosovo is going on as I write.

15. I wish to thank Sage Publications for permission to incorporate into this essay a few paragraphs from an earlier review of *Against Ethics* which appeared in *Philosophy and Social Criticism*, 23/4 (1997).

"O FELIX CULPA," THIS FOXY FELLOW FELIX: A RESPONSE TO WESTPHAL

John D. Caputo

I have always been grateful for the light and good humor that Merold Westphal sheds on philosophical argument and now I find myself grateful for the illumination he sheds on me, I who am a question unto myself, as St. Augustine says. At the end of this excellent study he puts his finger on exactly what is at stake in *Against Ethics*. Earlier on, he had pointed out that by leaving "obligation" in place, *Against Ethics* leaves substantive ethical judgments in place—"racism is unjust"—having reorganized them chiefly in terms of minimizing suffering and evil, even as it has shown the door to "the epistemic metaclaims it [ethics] makes for those judgments." These judgments, I am arguing, are on their own, and the search for an epistemic or metaphysical back-up for them is in vain, even as it can be in certain circumstances obscene. Just how many and what sorts of "arguments" do you require before you concede the horror of rape or murder? That means that a treatise on obligation should take the form of a "poetics," not a noetics, an attempt to magnify the voice of wounded flesh, to lend it an ear, and to discourage cruelty. Westphal astutely points out that this is not to abandon philosophy for poetry but to give philosophy a different twist, to let it emerge more closely interwoven with poetry, narrative, and rhetoric than hitherto—rather than delivering it all wrapped up in geometry or the physical sciences in the manner of the Enlightenment or contemporary analytic ethics. On this point, he and Cleo McNelly Kearns see eye to eye. This approach to obligation also has, I might add, something of an Aristotelian pedigree, inasmuch as it sets out in search of a kind of "ethical" attunement (*Stimmung*), of well-tuned feelings that take pleasure in the pleasure of the friend, and let us add, the stranger, and feel pain at their pain, rather than the approaches to ethics that emphasize rules and first reaching cognitive clarity about what the good is in order then to do it.

But despite this sensitive reading of *Against Ethics*, I am, alas, forced to disagree with Westphal on a point very similar to the one that I made against Kearney and Ayres, who were reading *Prayers and Tears*. Westphal mistakes the *status* I assign to Nietzsche and to his poetic stand-in, Felix Sineculpa, who is a *dramatis persona* for Zarathustra, who is in turn a *dramatis persona* for Nietzsche (I suppose). Felix has a liturgical name, or an anti-liturgical one. Just as Zarathustra came to preach the good news of the religion of the earth, Sineculpa preaches the innocence of becoming. But if Sineculpa is right, that would undermine the hymn in the Holy Saturday vigil that sings of Adam's sin as a happy fault (*O felix culpa*)—for there would then be no fault which merited so great a redeemer and we would then not need Christ. But if there is no fault, there is no obligation, and neither a noetics nor a poetics of obligation, and the argument (or the "insistence") of *Against Ethics*, that "obligation happens," with or without the support or the objections of the philosophers, falls on its face. So when Merold Westphal decides that I *prefer* Nietzsche to Kierkegaard, that though I mostly hold an agnostic position, I occasionally let my Nietzschean *belief* slip out, which means I prefer the innocence of becoming to the *me voici* of Abraham, he has, I think, been beguiled by this foxy fellow Felix. That also brings Westphal's position close to Kearney's kettle argument: that I am an indecisionist ("he remains undecided between his two faiths") who decides for *khora* or at least exhibts khoral tendencies, whereas I, a mere supplementary clerk of obligation, am simply trying to underline the underlying undecidability in which the movement of faith, here faith in obligation, transpires.

For me the very appearance of "Felix" (and the other pseudonyms) is a Kierkegaardian ploy. If *Radical Hermeneutics* took its key from *Repetition*, my *Against Ethics* is meant as a kind of postmodern rewrite of *Fear and Trembling*. (Unlike Kierkegaard, however, I had neither the wit nor the money to publish them on the same day.) The undecidability is formulated by framing a string of discourses on obligation within the opening and concluding discourses of Felix, each voice disrupting and disturbing the other. Now I would like to say of Felix what Kierkegaard says of his pseudonyms: I have not the least first person relation to Felix; I am no more identified with him than Shakespeare is with Richard III. But Merold Westphal will not believe that, for he knows that Felix is a voice I hear, a specter who disturbs my sleep, a "haunting possibility" that invades my thoughts and dislodges what Lyotard rightly calls the "piety" of Levinas, and that this disturbing dream has been going on for some time now. That is true. But Felix/Nietzsche is a specter not a "dogma" for me (no more than he was, I would think, for Nietzsche himself), an *irreducible perspective* that unsettles my assurances. I do not give him dogmatic authority; I just can't shut him up. When this Nietzschean voice says "the cosmos feels no sorrow," (AE, 17), I am not saying that he has achieved the metaphysical standpoint from which he can decide what the cosmos does or does not feel, but rather that he introduces a disturbing hypothesis here that we cannot simply shout out of court on the grounds that this would make life quite monstrous. I am not signing on to any Nietzschean metaphysics or metanarratives or to a violent Nietzschean ontology. I am always saying that I have no head for that, that I am a simple supplementary clerk, pleading a certain non-knowing, an epistemic agnosticism, which also stokes the fires of the passion of a certain non-knowing. But I have to be careful that my epoche does not have the ring of a negation or Merold Westphal will make me pay for it. Indeed, it was with Merold's admonitions in mind that I said in the "Introduction" to *More Radical Hermeneutics: On Not Knowing Who We Are:*[1]

> We have not been given privileged access to The Secret, to some big capitalized know-it-all Secret, not as far we know. (If we have, it has been kept secret from me.)

So the disturbing voice of Felix has the function for me of serving as a specter, of seeing to it that when "obligation happens" it happens within a horizon that includes the haunting possibility that there is no obligation, that obligation is just the bleating of the wounded lamb, even as it includes the more edifying Levinasian possibility that it is the trace that God leaves behind on the face of the stranger. Indeed it is only if these two possibilities remain alive side by side that faith is *faith*. For what grief Felix causes the cause of obligation in *Against Ethics* is repaid in kind by the feminine voices who are summoned to *unsettle Felix*, and so dislodge any dogmatic authority Felix might feel he enjoys. They rejoin him point by point, the result of which is supposed to be to show that if we heed the voice of obligation we take what Levinas calls a *beau risque*, a fine or lovely risk,[2] and they clearly sign on to the idea of witnessing to a truth that we do but do not demonstrate, which is what Augustine called *facere veritatem*, which is the important sentiment with which Merold Westphal concludes his paper and with which I agree entirely. A lovely risk and a testimony is also what Derrida would call a decision in the midst of undecidability, as I argued against Kearney. Ethics for me comes down to a "faith" in obligation, with no knock-down argument that Nietzsche is wrong, and nothing to guarantee that Levinas is right, which is "the faith of an incredulous infidel." By this I did not mean one who believes Nietzsche while not believing Yeshoua, but one who is not one, who is disturbed by both a believer and a non-believer within. Specifcally, it was a Lyotardian incredulity about metanarratives that I had in mind with that phrase and I don't think that if you understand what Lyotard means by a metanarrative you want to say that Christianity is one, which is the point Kierkegaard was always making against Hegel. Metanarratives, which have to do with the broad sweep of the movement of millions, do not take account of every hair on our head, or of the least among us, as Johannes Climacus took pains to point out.

Finally I would repeat what I said in *Against Ethics*, and I said again to Kearney and Ayres, that all of this talk of abyss and undecidability is not in the service of dogmatic atheism or of a thinly disguised affirmation of a violent ontology, but rather comes precisely by way of preparation for faith.[3] But it does this in such a way as to make it plain that the movement of faith does not extinguish what Levinas calls the *il y a* or Derrida calls the *khora* or, for that matter, what the opening chapter of *Ecclessiastes* calls vanity. That is why I said against Kearney that *khora* is the *felix culpa* of faith, for without *khora* we would never be pushed to the point of faith but we would continue to suffer the illusion that we are in full control. We would never get past what is possible, the sphere of our own powers and possibilities, never come to understand that things begin *by* the impossible. So I am not beguiled by Felix Sineculpa, the silver tongued devil, the foxy fellow. Despite my love of the logic of the *sans* (*sine*), my heart is with the *felix culpa*.

NOTES

1. John D. Caputo, MRH, p. 1.

2. Emmanuel Levinas, *Autrement qu'être ou au-delà de l'essence* (The Hague: Nijhoff, 1974), p. 212; *Otherwise than Being or Beyond Essence*, trans. Alphonso Lingis (The Hague: Nijhoff, 1981), p. 167.

3. See AE, p. 286n6. I now wish, instead of confining that remark to a footnote, I had put it on the dust jacket, and repeated it every ten pages in the text.

8   SQUARING THE HERMENEUTIC CIRCLE: CAPUTO AS READER OF FOUCAULT

THOMAS R. FLYNN

"For hermeneutics in the broadest sense means for me coping with flux, tracing out a pattern in a world in slippage."

—*Caputo,* Radical Hermeneutics

In his several highly original and arresting books on radical hermeneutics, ethics, and the philosophy of religion, John Caputo rarely mentions Michel Foucault. In view of the dominant place given Jacques Derrida in his later works, one wonders why Derrida's contemporary and rival sun in the Parisian firmament received such scant notice. Could it be that Foucault is taken to be a post-, if not an anti-hermeneutical thinker, as the title of one widely read book suggests[1] and so is considered deserving of little notice in hermeneutical circles . . . until now? For when Caputo does devote an insightful essay to Foucault in a volume he co-edits on the topic in the early 90s, it is to enlist him in "a kind of" hermeneutic camp. So it is to that unique locus that I turn as I consider several aspects of Caputo's "radical" hermeneutics that do indeed resonate with Foucauldian themes, while pointing out some serious difficulties that Foucault raises against hermeneutics in general and suggesting a line of inquiry underscored in Foucault's last works that opens the way to "a kind of hermeneutics," though perhaps not the kind that Caputo is proposing.

TRACING A PATTERN IN A WORLD IN SLIPPAGE

Both Caputo and Foucault are rewriting the history of philosophy or, as Foucault would say, of "thought," in the late modern era. Yet each is doing so in his own way: Caputo *ab intra*, Foucault *ab extra*. Taking a line from Kierkegaard that Derrida pursues via Heidegger, Caputo "opens up" the philosophical discourse of the past by tugging at its loose ends, unraveling its apparently tightly woven arguments in a gesture that reveals its internal weaknesses, tensions, and aporetic character. The goal is not to reconcile these inconsistencies in some higher viewpoint à la Hegel, but to settle for indeterminacy, free play, and inconclusiveness. Caputo's project is skeptical, practical, "aesthetic" in a broad sense, and subversive of the metaphysical tradition from Plato to the early Heidegger. And yet, contrary to Foucault, the (almost) enemy of Enlightenment, Caputo affirms the Heideggerian "openness to mystery" as a positive value at work in his radical hermeneutics.[2] *Omnia exeunt in mysteria* (everything ends up in mystery), it seems; at least, Caputo's hermeneutics does not exclude such a culmination or "exit" in principle.

Though its effect may be similar, Foucault's tack is quite different. In each of the three aspects or phases of his research, namely, the archaeological, the genealogical, and the problematizing, but especially in its archaeological dimension, his aim is to write a "history" of thought (*la pensée*) and especially of what goes by the honorific of "science" in the Western world by uncovering the rules and practices unconsciously employed to make sense of the world during a chosen period, working *as if from outside* that epoch and in contrast with it. His method is comparative, his vision diacritical.

Philosophical orthodoxy faces both writers with the Archimedean challenge to legitimize their critical stances by appeal to some *tertium quid*, some warrant that would justify the comparisons made and the implicit criticisms mounted. The matter is perhaps more pressing for Foucault than for Caputo, at least at first blush, because it is commonly conceded that, by "arguing" from within the hermeneutic circle, one is exempt from foundationalist demands to begin at the absolute beginning rather than in the midst of things. Caputo claims this exemption when he suggests that Heidegger, unlike Derrida, Kierkegaard and, by implication, himself, might be "another faint-hearted friend of the flux" (RH, 59) and when he goes on to employ the "Socratic analogy" in dealing with Derrida.[3] In fact, he seconds Foucault's critique of modern thought for being schizoid in its simultaneous appeal to a double self: one situated in the flux of the world, the other fully self-identical and transcendental, because it is aimed at the foundationalist fallacy of an uninterpreted givenness of consciousness to itself (see RH, 57).

Foucault seems more vulnerable than Caputo to the legitimacy question since he is not willing (if he were even able) to employ the hermeneutical exemption. At least, he claims not to do so. And yet he too seeks to render the Archimedean objection innocuous by simply denying its premise, namely, that one must stand on an unquestionable ground (Descartes's *fundamentum inconcusum*) in order to assess other epistemic models. When challenged to acknowledge that his own categorial structures are subject to transformation and displacement like the ones he is analyzing, Foucault simply agrees. But he then questions the need for a transcendental *locus standi* and denies that his own liability to epistemological displacement disqualifies his descriptions and assessments.[4]

Foucault mounts his critique *ab extra* in at least two respects. First, archaeology avoids the deep meanings and intentions of hermeneutics by addressing a level of analysis "between" words and things. No doubt the existence of such a level is disputed, but its claims to "externality" seem quite clear. Secondly and more importantly, he tries to *distance himself* from his own society by questioning its fundamental sureties and necessities such as authorship of texts, normalizing rationality, received historical, causal sequences, universal rules, and the like. He insists that it is possible to undertake an ethnography of one's own society. His project in *The Order of Things* is to do just that.[5] So, despite a similar disregard for origins and foundational discourse, archaeology differs from hermeneutics by holding its own "tradition" (its takens-for-granted and its very preunderstanding) at a critical remove rather than immersing itself deeply into the flux of the present. In other words, Foucault is "outside" or "foreign" but not unsituated (transcendental). The very fact that "interpretation" emerges in the nineteenth century as the method proper to the social sciences, for example, demands an archaeological account.

But this "ethnography"—this study of one's own society to which one has rendered oneself "foreign" by the basic beliefs one holds in suspense—resists appeal to a transcendental viewpoint from which to pursue its project. Such a viewpoint and the desire that engenders it are likewise grist for this skeptical mill. Foucault's skeptical cat is let out of its Kantian bag. As Nietzsche and other hermeneuts would insist, "it's interpretation all the way down." But Foucault would claim further that there is no need for such a downward movement: what you see is what you get ("almost," as Caputo would caution). Such is Foucault's much discussed "happy positivism" (see AK, 234).

So it seems that Foucault, at least as archaeologist, does not appeal to the hermeneutic circle or employ the method of *Verstehen* that Dilthey and Weber made almost synonymous with the "human sciences." In fact, it is now common knowledge that both these sciences and the concept of "Man" itself come under direct and probing attack in *The Order of Things*, which may well be why the names "Foucault" and "hermeneutics" seldom appear in the same sentence.[6] So let us turn to this work with its tables and angular metaphors to determine Foucault's difficulty with hermeneutics as commonly conceived.

An Archaeology of Hermeneutics

It has been claimed that the hermeneutic circle is at least as old as Plato's *Meno*.[7] It surfaces in one of Caputo's favorite authors, the bishop who questions God hermeneutically: "And how shall I find Thee, if I remember Thee not?"[8] In the nineteenth century modern hermeneutics emerges from Biblical exegesis to become an explicit method of cultural interpretation and finally as the vehicle of understanding proper to "texts" in general and the social sciences in particular. Hermeneutics is a phenomenon closely tied both to commentary and, as the distinctive method of the social sciences, to what Foucault calls the "anthropological quadrilateral," the skeleton of the modern episteme. Consequently, its fortune seems tied to the future of that quadrilateral itself, which Foucault believes is on the verge of disappearing.

In his archaeological attempt to bring to light the rules that condition sense-making in the nineteenth century (what he calls the modern "episteme"), Foucault uncovers four basic conceptual pairs, namely, the positivities and finitude, the empirical and the transcendental, the modern *Cogito* and the unthought, and the retreat and return of the origin, that he characteristically arranges in spatial fashion as segments of the "anthropological quadrilateral." While it is unnecessary to parse this abstract structure in detail, it is relevant to our discussion that the strategic effect of the model is to locate the "Man" of contemporary humanism and "anthropology" at the intersection of its diagonals. And the quadrilateral establishes "a philosophical foundation for the possibility of knowledge," based not on representation, as in the previous century, but on man's mode of being (OT, 335). The "problem of Man" thus becomes the question *of* the human sciences and not simply one *for* the human sciences and inversely. Foucault's prescription in *The Order of Things* is to dismantle this quadrilateral or, better, to exhibit the possibility of its immanent collapse in the face of what we might call the emergence of a "postmodern" or better, "counter-modern" episteme. This would call for a crisis, an archaeological event, as profound as the one which displaced the Classical episteme toward the end of the eighteenth century, which he traced with an astounding display of *Wissenschaft* in that work.

Hermeneutics and phenomenology, Foucault argues, are two methods that rise and fall with the career of this quadrilateral, conceived as the set of rules and relations that "define for us man's mode of being" (OT, 335). Consider the example of that segment which he terms "the empirical and the transcendental," that is, the influential Kantian view of the human being as a member of two realms, Nature and Freedom. Apropos of phenomenology and its historical compatibility with philosophical Marxism in the third quarter of the twentieth century, he remarks: "Their recent rapprochement is not of the order of tardy reconciliation: at the level of archaeological confirmation they were both necessary—and necessary to one another—from the moment that anthropological postulate was constituted, that is, from the moment when man appeared as an empirico-transcendental doublet" (OT, 321–322). We noted that Caputo also recognizes this doublet, another name for the metaphysically schizoid condition of modern "Man" (see RH, 57–58). But Foucault sees in the impending eclipse of Man both a *displacement* of Kantian transcendence (OT, 323) and an attempt to recapture some epistemic balance by cantilevering a newly revived theme of the *Cogito* with the widespread acknowledgment of the *nonthought* (the factical, the other-than-thought, the unconscious, and, as he will sometimes say, Desire). Philosopher of minuscule but decisive breaks, hiatus and incongruities, Foucault argues that the "and" which is essential to each conceptual segment of the modern episteme (namely, retreat *and* return, thought *and* unthought, empirical *and* transcendental, the order of positivity *and* the order of foundations)—this gap denotes a "distance creating a vacuum within the Same, . . . the hiatus that disperses and regroups it at the two ends of itself." These two ends he denominates "identity," separated from itself by a distance that constitutes it, and "repetition," a Kierkegaardian theme favored by Caputo. "It is this profound spatiality," Foucault explains, "that makes it possible for modern thought still to conceive time—to know it as succession, to promise it to itself as fulfilment, origin, or return" (OT, 340).[9] This hiatus is likewise the source of the "tragic category" that Caputo considers essential to Foucault's characterization of the human being (but perhaps specifically of "modern Man").

Foucault sees the Kantian division of the empirical and the transcendental along with the doctrine of the two viewpoints (of Nature and Freedom) to resolve the antinomies generated by traditional metaphysics as constituting an anthropological configuration of modern philosophy that consists in "doubling over dogmatism, in dividing it into two different levels, each lending support to and limiting the other: the precritical analysis of what man is in his essence becomes the analytic of everything that can, in general, be presented to man's experience" (OT, 341). But he believes this confuses "the circularity of dogmatism folded over upon itself in order to find a basis for itself within itself with the agility and anxiety of a radically philosophical thought" (OT, 341). Echoing Cato the Elder on Carthage, not to mention Heidegger on the history of Western philosophy, Foucault insists that "there is no other way [to recall philosophic thought to the possibilities of its earliest dawning] than to destroy the anthropological 'quadrilateral' in its very foundations" (OT, 341–342).[10]

He distinguishes two contemporary attempts at such dismantling. The first is the search for a "purified ontology or a radical thought of being." This is explicitly Nietzschean in character, by his account, but arguably it is early Heideggerian as well. The other dismantling enterprise attempts "to question afresh the limits of thought and to renew contact in this way with the project for a general critique of reason" that rejects "not only psychologism and historicism [as did the first approach], but all concrete forms of the anthropological prejudice" (OT, 342). The first is a kind of preparatory move that "marks the threshold beyond which contemporary philosophy can begin to think again." We may view both Foucault's archaeological and his genealogical investigations as exercises in this next phase of "thinking," namely, *a general critique of reason*. So any attempt to read Foucault as a hermeneuticist must respect the force of this project of a general critique of reason itself, including, as we have just seen, *hermeneutic* reason. In any case, if there is to be a Foucauldian "hermeneutics," it must be one that escapes "the anthropological prejudice."

How does this affect hermeneutics as the method of interpretation proper to the social sciences? Foucault's criticism of Sartrean existentialism in the 1960s may cast some light on this question. Sartre had spoken of a "hermeneutics" of our practices as integral to his "existential psychoanalysis" introduced in *Being and Nothingness*.[11] Subsequently, he defended the method of *Verstehen* in his *Search for a Method*.[12] In an interview given in 1966, Foucault contrasted the existentialist humanism with what replaced it among the next generation of philosophers, what he called "system" (DE, 1:513). For an account of system as Foucault understands it, we can look to *The Order of Things* and his critique of the human sciences.

He observes two parallel shifts within the human sciences throughout the nineteenth century. One occurs from biological to economic to linguistic models whereas the other moves from function, conflict, and signification in each of these models respectively to a corresponding emphasis on norm, rule, and system. Within the linguistic model he marks the shift from signification to system and cites the work of Georges Dumézil to exemplify that change (see OT, 360). Though he does not mention it explicitly in this context, it is clear that for Foucault the linguistic model is the locus of hermeneutics and the transition from signification to system corresponds to the displacement of hermeneutics by structural analysis. In fact, in his inaugural lecture at the Collège de France, Foucault credited Dumézil with having introduced him to the method of comparative structures.[13]

The role of the concept of system as complement to signification is to show that the latter is *derived* from system and is never primary. System is always unconscious in its operation. "The signification/system pair," Foucault explains, "is what ensures both the representability of language (as text or structure analyzed by philology and linguistics) and the near but withdrawn presence of the origin (as it is manifested by man's mode of being by means of the analytic of finitude)" (OT, 362). The result is that the human sciences "are constantly demystifying themselves" in the form of an unveiling.

This constant uncovering might suggest that the human sciences are hermeneutic, not in the sense of *Verstehen* as Dilthey, Weber, Aron and others have insisted, but in the sense of an "interpretation" or "reading between the lines" as in the "hermeneutics of suspicion" that Paul Ricoeur made famous. This may well characterize hermeneutics as the method proper to the human sciences, but it serves equally to separate it from an archaeology of those same sciences. To the extent that both hermeneutics and "analysis" broadly taken to include not only psychoanalysis but archaeology as the analysis of epistemes and genealogy as the analysis of power relations—to the extent that each relies on the "unveiling of a pregiven dimension of experience, both approaches are alike. But to the extent that hermeneutics directs its attention to the "pre" conscious domain rather than the unconscious, that it is heavily psychological in its orientation, and that it examines the content rather than the form of such awareness, hermeneutics, unlike archaeology, is an incurably "modern" phenomenon and is tied to the anthropological quadrilateral at its center. Such hermeneutics is the vehicle of the sciences of "Man" *par excellence*.

Foucault describes the situation as follows. After pointing out the confrontation in modern thought between historicism and what he calls the "analytic of finitude" (which resembles Heidegger's *Daseinsanalyse* and pertains to the positivity-finitude segment mentioned earlier), he observes that the historicist perspective "always implies a certain philosophy . . . of living comprehension . . . , of interhuman communication . . . , and of hermeneutics (as the re-apprehension through the manifest meaning of the discourse of another meaning at once secondary and primary that is more hidden but also more fundamental)." The analytic of finitude, on the contrary, "never ceases to use, as a weapon against historicism, that part of itself that historicism has neglected," namely, the relation of the human being to the being [viz., time] which, by designating finitude, renders the positivities [of the human sciences] possible in their concrete mode of being" (OT, 337).

Interpreting Foucault as Interpreter

Caputo begins his only essay on Foucault with the thesis that "Foucault's thought is best construed as a hermeneutics of who we are."[14] Given the popularity of the Dreyfus and Rabinow study entitled "Michel Foucault: Beyond Structuralism and Hermeneutics," this is a challenging claim. But in view of Caputo's suggestive concept of "cold" or "radical hermeneutics," it is neither implausible nor surprising. Still, the question remains: Is it justifiable? Is the master of the anthropological quadrilateral caught in a hermeneutic circle of his own? Is the one who decried those who could not formalize without anthropologizing (OT, 342) (a shot at transcendental phenomenology) himself giving us a "theory of man" nonetheless? The answer turns not only on whether one can "formalize" without anthropologizing—the structuralists did so on principle—but on whether one can practice hermeneutics in any meaningful sense without anthropologizing as well and, if so, whether this is how Foucault's thought is "best construed."

Though he wisely relies on the concept of madness which plays so important a role in Foucault's thought, Caputo jeopardizes his case for a hermeneutic construal of Foucault's *oeuvre* (a term the latter disliked) by focusing heavily on a text that Foucault did not want translated, *Mental Illness and Psychology*.[15] The early "existentialist" Foucault doubtless weighs the scale in Caputo's favor but may leave the "structuralist" Foucault of the anthropological studies unaffected. In fact, one could turn against Caputo the criticism he levels against Dreyfus and Rabinow of failing to recognize a continuing hermeneutical dimension to Foucault's thought, namely, that they rely too heavily on *The Order of Things* from which they derive their concept of hermeneutics (see FCI, 247 n. 44).

Noting that Foucault's interest in madness lies not in its "psychological" basis but in its "truth," Caputo concludes: "He is not addressing its physiology or its therapeutics but its 'hermeneutics' and the way in which psychological science conceals, represses, forgets, and silences the truth of madness" (FCI, 236). In this initial observation, Caputo cautiously places "hermeneutics" in scare quotes. But those precautionary marks drop from the page as he progresses. He writes: "[Foucault's] interest is hermeneutic: he wants to hear what one says who has been driven *in extremis.*" Moving to the abridged version of Foucault's larger thesis for the State doctorate, *Madness and Civilization*, Caupto reads Foucault's account of the silencing of "unreason" in the age of Reason in terms of "the tragic category," which he interprets as "the great motionless structure" that Foucault sees underlying the dispute between reason and unreason in the sixteenth century. In other words, he takes Foucault to be characterizing the deep structure of human being as *tragically* split, irreparably divided into contrary spheres—a condition that did not obtain in previous centuries. This certainly renders tragic the schizoid condition of modern "Man."

But the problem of madness (*la folie*) and unreason (*la déraison*) is more complex than Caputo would lead us to believe. Unreason is a creature of the Age of Reason, its counter-concept, whereas madness (*la folie*) is as old as civilization itself. The function of the mad in various societies changed with that society itself, but their banishment to the realm of silence and otherness, Foucault argues, began with the Age of Reason. Although Foucault at times does seem to employ the terms interchangeably, once unreason is registered as such, he is quite explicit in distinguishing them. For example, he observes:

> In the classical period, the awareness of madness and the awareness of unreason had not separated from one another. . . . But in the anxiety of the second half of the eighteenth century, the fear of madness grew at the same time as the dread of unreason.
>
> It is after this period [the end of the eighteenth century] that the time of unreason and the time of madness received two opposing vectors: one being unconditioned return and absolute submersion; the other, on the contrary, developing according to the chronicle of a history.[16]

In an important note, Foucault adds:

> Psychoanalysis, which has tried to confront madness and unreason again, has found itself faced with this problem of time; fixation, death-wish, collective unconsciousness, archetype define more or less happily this heterogeneity of two temporal structures: that which is proper to the experience of Unreason and to the knowledge it envelops; that which is proper to the knowledge of madness, and to the science it authorizes. (MC, 297 n. 9; FD, 383 n. 3)

In other words, Foucault's concern is to reveal the *transformation* and *displacement* at work in the "history" of madness in the West. His project, arguably, even in his dissertation, is archaeological, as he implies on at least one occasion[17] and one could even say "genealogical in its anticipation of an argument which appears in his subsequent *Discipline and Punish*.[18]

But, again, is it hermeneutics? Does it deal with people's explicit or implicit intentions? In the famous maxim of classical hermeneutics, does it seek "to understand the text better than the author understands it himself"?[19] In the final analysis, is the method focused on consciousness and experience or on structure and system?

The common view, the one propounded by Dreyfus and Rabinow, is that Foucault abandoned the "existentialist" interest of his early work for the structuralist and subsequent *post*structuralist interest of his major writings. (They qualify this view by designating his position "interpretive analytics" which is neither structuralist nor hermeneutical.) Foucault himself seems to confirm this view in his Introduction to the English translation of Georges Canguilhem's *The Normal and the Pathological*.[20] There he traces two lines of thought that have divided French intellectual life since the 1930s: one pursuing experience, meaning (*sens*), rationality and the subject, the other focusing on knowledge (*savoir*), rationality, and the concept. On one side stood Sartre and Merleau-Ponty, on the other Jean Cavaillès, Bachelard, Canguilhem and, presumably, Foucault himself. This opposition between meaning (*sens*) and concept or, as we have seen earlier, between experience and system, indicates Foucault's larger view of hermeneutics. Insofar as it is a philosophy of experience, of consciousness and of *sens*, hermeneutics lies clearly on the far side of the Foucauldian divide. The shift to concept and system marks a deliberate countermove, one "beyond" hermeneutics and phenomenology.

Admittedly, Caputo emphasizes the tragic category and speaks of a "tragic hermeneutics" operative throughout Foucault's work. The early writings, he argues, are "keyed" to Nietzsche's *The Birth of Tragedy* rather than to his *The Genealogy of Morals*, as most commentators, including Foucault himself, have claimed. I believe Caputo is on to something that most readers of Foucault's work have overlooked. There is a "tragic" (one might even say, "existentialist") aspect to the entire Foucauldian corpus. Elsewhere I have spoken of the "Greek" character of the torsos he produced and of his life so painfully cut short.[21] And what I had in mind was obviously Greek "tragedy." And yet, tragic or happy, the question remains: not whether we can "read" Foucault's life hermeneutically but whether he is "reading" the object of his studies—say, discursive practices, power relations, problematizations, games of truth (to select a few in roughly chronological order)—in a hermenetucial manner. In other words, is *he* practicing hermeneutics?

By now one is probably tempted to dismiss this question as a mere *lis de verbis*, a terminological dispute. And there are a number of distinct, if overlapping, uses of the term "hermeneutics" to which one might appeal in this regard. But even if one takes it to mean "the unmasking and ferreting out of a repressed truth that tells the truth of man," as Caputo insists it does for Dreyfus and Rabinow, it is unlikely that Foucault is practicing hermeneutics even in this generous sense for at least two reasons. First, I do not recall his ever having claimed to have uncovered the "truth of man" (which is not to deny that he ever employed that expression), though it is clear that he thought he had discovered the "truth of MAN," in the anthropological sense. One can take that as the aim of the quadrilateral. Second and more importantly, the epistemes (grids of intelligibility and regulators of discursive practices), though unconscious, are never repressed as are libidinal thoughts by the Freudian censor. What his archaeology offers us is not a variation on an old, hermeneutical game, but an entirely new game, one that seems to leave hermeneutics on the sideline.

Objecting to the claim by Dreyfus and Rabinow that the later Foucault, at least, gave up the hermeneutical concept of repressed truth in the name of which man is to be liberated, Caputo appeals to a version of the plank of Carneades to save Foucault from drowning in a sea of skeptical relativism. This has become a standard response to skeptical arguments and is repeated by such critics as Harbermas, Nancy Fraser, and others, including Dreyfus and Rabinow themselves at the conclusion of their book. In Caputo's version it comes down to the question: "If madness is just produced in various ways, if nothing is repressed, lost or silenced, why worry about what historical form the historical constitution of madness takes? If nothing is repressed, then nothing is to be liberated" (FCI, 248). He believes that, in fact, Foucault sustains a "hermeneutic impulse that is so clearly evident in his early writings" in his later works as well. It is merely a case of "seeing that Foucault has moved beyond a certain hermeneutics, but not another hermeneutics more radically conceived" (FCI, 248).

I shall offer a Foucauldian response to this type of objection in my concluding section, though one can imagine from what I have said about Foucault's reaction to the Archimedean challenge what that response will be. But let us first examine Caputo's reconstruction of the "other hermeneutics more radically conceived" that he finds at work in the later Foucault.

A Hermeneutics without Comfort

To begin with, Caputo conveys a fine sense of Foucault's resistence to any normative concept of who we should be, a conviction he obviously shares:

> [Foucault] wants to keep the question [of who we are] open, and above all, to block the administrators and professionals and managers of all sorts from answering this question, thereby closing us in on some constituted identity or another that represents a strictly historical, that is, contingent constraint. (FCI, 250)

He reads this "refusal of an identifying truth" as a form of his sought-after radical hermeneutics, namely, a "hermeneutic of refusal." Quoting heavily from Foucault's "Afterword" to the first edition of the Dreyfus and Rabinow volume, Caputo stresses Foucault's aim "to promote new forms of subjectivity through the refusal of this kind of individuality that has been imposed on us for several centuries" (quoted in FCI, 253).

What Caputo is seeking in Foucault's writings is the concept of "a residue, an irreducibility, a fragment that cannot be incorporated" in any dialectical totalization (FCI, 253). Curiously, if found, this would resemble the Sartrean concept of an "irrecuperable" individual that resists totalities even as it totalizes.[22] And not surprising, except perhaps to Foucault himself,[23] Caputo finds it in "a purely negative, always historical capacity for being-otherwise, which is what Foucault means by freedom" (FCI, 253).

But this freedom is *tragic* (again, like Sartre's "futile passion" to achieve conscious self-identity). As Caputo explains: "The tragic always means the split, the rupture of human being" (FDI, 241). And it is Foucault's hermeneutic task, he argues, to unveil this underlying and unassimilable freedom, this "tragic Freedom," as the existentialists would say, not only in the tension of reason and unreason, madness and norm, but throughout his archaeologies and genealogies. What give Foucault's remarks in subsequent works their critical bite, Caputo insists, is not the movement "beyond" hermeneutics but his adoption of the previously mentioned "hermeneutics of refusal":

> Foucault wants to defend the impossibility of reducing us to truth, to shelter the irreducibility and uncontractability of being-human, its refusal of identity and identification, its refusal of an identifying truth. (FCI, 251)

Which leads him to conclude: "Foucault thus has an entirely negative idea of the individual" and to liken it to the "apophatic" discourse with which negative theologians speak of God.[24] "Against the positive production of individuals in keeping with some normative standard," he argues, "Foucault holds out for the negative freedom of the individual to be different" (FCI, 252).

Caputo appreciates the "situational" character of Foucault's inquiries, what Foucault calls famously a "history of the present." Such "histories" derive their critical punch first of all, though Caputo fails to mention this, from the sheer fact of showing the *contingency* of our most established necessities, the possibility of changing our received and well-sanctioned norms and practices. "Things *can* be otherwise" is the first critical lesson of his analysis. "But why should we bother to change?" ask Habermas, Dreyfus, Rabinow, Fraser and others, whom Caputo wishes to answer by introducing the notion of repressed freedom in Foucault's works. The agonistic relation of power-freedom is well analyzed as is the correlative concept of resistance by which freedom shows its presence and distinguishes power from physical force. Again, it is worth noting that Caputo cites Bernauer's characterization of such freedom as "transcendence," linking it with the latter's guiding motif of Foucault's "negative theology." But Caputo reads Foucault's project more modestly, settling for "*re*scendence," that is, for freedom as a "stepping back" (FCI, 255).

But I do not think that Caputo's caution is necessary. For it seems clear to me that Bernauer is using "transcendence" in a perfectly "this worldly," indeed, existentialist sense. Just as Sartre characterizes the power of human reality to "transcend" its facticity toward possibility,"[25] so Foucauldian freedom, on Bernauer's cogent reading, "transcends" or "moves beyond" the fixed norms and established practices of our society and era. It is in this sense that what he calls Foucauldian "spirituality" "bears witness to the capacity for an ecstatic transcendence of any history that asserts its necessity."[26]

Approaching the end of his essay, Caputo repeats his general thesis: the early Foucault was a hermeneut, seeking to uncover the positive secret of who we are in support of a Dionysian vision of "tragic unreason" as our secret truth. If, in his last works, Foucault abandoned a positive idea of who we are, Caputo insists:

> He has not given up the idea that *something* is being repressed, something much looser, more unspecifiable and indefinite, something negative and unidentifiable. It is no longer an *identity* we need to recover (a secret tragic identity) but a *difference*. It is no longer a positive ideal which needs to be restored but simply a certain capacity to resist the identities that are imposed upon us just in order to free our capacity to invent such new identities for ourselves as circumstances allow. In short, the movement has not been beyond hermeneutics-and-repression but beyond a hermeneutics of identity (as positive tragic hermeneutics) to a hermeneutics of difference (a negative hermeneutics of refusal). (FCI, 256)

Had Caputo examined the unlikely (for his thesis) *Archaeology of Knowledge*, he would have been delighted to discover the following epitome: "[Archaeology] establishes that we are difference, that our reason is the difference of discourses, our history the difference of times, our selves the difference of masks. That difference, far from being the forgotten and recovered origin, is this dispersion that we are and make" (AK, 131). But the problem—one might even say the recurrent "metaphysical" problem—is whether this "we are difference" is employing the (inevitable?) "is" of identity. Are Foucault (and Caputo, by implication) claiming that this is who we truly are? That we are the kind of beings that, Sartre's famous phrase, "are what we are not and are not what we are"? If so, then it would seem that Foucault is allied to a metaphysical view and not merely to a hermeneutics of identity, whether tragic or not.

At this point Caputo appeals to the cataphatic/apophatic distinction of the mystical and negative theologians.[27] The "difference" that we "are," on this apophatic account, is more a warning than a predicate, an "instruction for use," if you will, rather than a qualitative denomination of the subject. To say "we are difference," in effect, is to advise us always to look again and elsewhere when we think we have settled the identification of a subject. As Foucault said of those who worried about his classification as philosopher or historian: "Leave it to our bureaucrats and our police to see that our papers are in order" (AK, 17).

Yet granted the difficulty to pin Foucault down as well as his insistence on singularity and refusal, these could more plausibly be attributed to his *nominalism*, both epistemic and ontological, and not to any "negative hermeneutics of refusal." In other words, there is reason enough for the elusive nature of Fouculdian discourse in that discourse itself without introducing the "apophatic." And yet Caputo's appeal to mystery and the ineffable is potentially quite fruitful, as we shall see. So we are left to ask: What is at stake finally in this debate between Dreyfus-Rabinow and Caputo?

I suspect it is the question of "Man" and of the humanism that it engenders and serves to justify. Both sides agree that Foucault has rejected "a whole series of humanisms of truth—*homo psychologicus, homo economicus, homo religiosus*, including his own earlier contribution to this scheme, *homo tragicus*" (FCI, 257). But has he rejected even the *anti-humanist humanism* of Caputo's "cold truth" that we *are* an abyss of possibilities? The concluding section of Caputo's essay suggests he has and that this lacuna must be filled. To do so, Caputo thinks it necessary to discuss sin as "the Other within" (which, curiously, is Sartre's description of epistemic "authority"), healing gestures and forgiveness as "active forgetting." What we discover at the end—and what moves Caputo "beyond Foucault," as he titles this section of his essay—is a kind of religious, one could even say "Christian," humanism—one inspired not only by the God of Abraham, Isaac, and Jacob, but equally by Augustine, Pascal, and Kierkegaard. Not the god of the philosophers, to be sure, but the god of the *counter*-philosophers, the nonacademic, nonprofessional "living God" Who speaks to us from the abyss—from "outside," as Foucault might say, alluding to Bataille: what we might call "The God beyond the death-of-God." This is why Caputo's radical hermeneutics is open to mystery whereas that of Foucault is merely open.

THE HERMENEUTICS OF REFUSAL OR THE REFUSAL OF HERMENEUTICS?

Let me briefly introduce support for Caputo's position from another quarter, the "existential" Marxism of Fredric Jameson. In his *The Political Unconscious*, published four years before *Foucault and the Critique of Insitutions*, Jameson remarks:

> Deleuze and Guattari's proposal for an anti-interpretive method (which they call schizoanalysis) can equally well be grasped as a new hermeneutic in its own right. It is striking and noteworthy that most of the antiinterpretive positions enumerated . . . above have felt the need to project new "methods" of this kind: thus, the archeology of knowledge, but also, more recently, the "political technology of the body" (Foucault), "grammatology" and deconstruction (Derrida),

"symbol exchange" (Baudrillard), libidinal economy (Lyotard) and "sémanalyse" (Julia Kristeva).[28]

In sum, poststructuralist theories should be understood as alternative hermeneutics. As David Shumway remarks apropos of this list of authors: "The fact is that by any of a number of definitions of the word, these self-proclaimed anti-interpretive projects are shot through with interpretation."[29] And so it would seem that Foucault is committed to hermeneutics willy-nilly.

Or is he? If we deny the dogmatic principle that *everyone* is an interpreter because that is the nature of *Dasein*—the human condition, Man or whatever—then it becomes an empirical question whether Foucault in fact "interprets" the actions of others in terms of their stated intentions and/or their deep meaning. And it would seem that this is excluded by the destruction of the anthropological quadrilateral. In other words, it appears that Foucault believes in the end of hermeneutics along with the end of "Man" as ingredient in the "event" whose proximity he sees on the horizon of the collapse of the modern episteme (see OT, 387).

One could retort that, whatever the strictures of the archaeological method with its quadrilaterals, triangles, and the rest, the "genealogical" Foucault is four-square committed to hermeneutics by his *inversion* of received views of historical causality (regarding the rise of the modern prison, for example) and his corresponding *reading* of the power-relations at work in our most self-congratulatory avowals of prison reform. A version of the hermeneutic of suspicion with a vengeance, so it would seem—the *pudenda origo* of Nietzschean "hermeneutics."

But before we stamp "QED" on this account, let us examine the matter more closely. Foucault claims to be a philosopher of surfaces, not of depths, which is one reason why he can insist that "Power" does not exist. What seems hermeneutic in the genealogies of the carceral society or Victorian sexuality is not appeal to some deeper, repressed reality (for if Power does not exist neither does "Freedom"), but a set of relations and directions on how to deal with situations whose now evident contingency may have rendered intolerable. Just as Marx insists that humankind only raise the kinds of problems it can solve, Foucault seems to be claiming that a state of affairs becomes truly intolerable only when it is possible to effect its change. And this, of course, is part of the "critical" significance of his "histories," whether archaeological or genealogical. Again, his nominalism removes his genealogies as it did his archaelogies from the reified categories of libido, will-to-power, and socioeconomic class—referents of the paradigmatic hermeneutics of suspicion. And again, as we have come to suspect from Foucault, his "method" is not a new move in an old game (hermeneutics) but an entirely new game to which he gives the names "archaeology," "genealogy," and "problematization."[30]

While it may be true that Foucault, like everyone, "reads" or "interprets" other's actions and intentions in the course of his broad historical investigation (how could he fail to do so?), this does not make him a philosophic hermeneut except in some banal and uninteresting sense. The question remains: Is hermeneutics consistent with and *integral* to his system/ method? And my *pen*ultimate answer is that it decidedly is not, at least not after the advent of his archaeologies and his explicit concern with questions of methodology.

CIRCLES WITHOUT CENTER: A FINAL TURN

I offered my previous conclusion as penultimate.[31] For, if we read Foucault in a "retro" hermeneutical way (as he often read himself, namely, in reverse, claiming that his current interest, whether power, subjectivation, or truth, was what he had always been interested in)—such a reading lends a kind of *post factum* support to Caputo's claim. It could be that Foucault's latent reading of his own works opens a new path for applying the hermeneutical hypothesis that has been our topic all along.

What I have in mind is the rather abrupt movement of the category of *experience* to the forefront of Foucault's investigation. Thus, in one of his last works, he observes:

> [W]hat I have tried to maintain for many years is the effort to isolate some of the elements that might be useful for a history of truth. Not a history that would be concerned with what might be true in the fields of learning, but an analysis of the "games of truth," the games of truth and error through which being is historically constituted as *experience*; that is, as something that can and must be thought. What are the games of truth by which man proposes to think his own nature when he perceives himself to be mad; when he considers himself to be ill, when he conceives of himself as living, speaking, laboring being; when he judges and punishes himself as a criminal? What were the games of truth by which human beings came to see themselves as desiring individuals?[32]

Elsewhere I have pursued the concept of experience in Foucault.[33] But it bears mention at the conclusion of this essay, for it turns the Foucauldian kaleidoscope another notch, enabling us to reconsider his major works under the aspect of experience. Correspondingly, it renders the traditional concept of hermeneutics with its "fore" structure potentially relevant once more. And the problematic now shifts with this kaleidoscopic reconfiguration: Can we employ the hermeneutical apparatus without appealing to either a *unifying* subject or a *unified* meaning? Are hermeneutic circles possible without subjective centers? Or can the circle revolve around (?) a centerless "point" without swirling into a black hole (Caputo's abyss)? Or if it swirls and swirls—Yeats's "gyre"—do we simply accommodate ourselves to the risk?

This, I gather, is the kind of neo-Stoic resoluteness that some would counsel in the face of a "fragmenting" hermeneutics. But neither Foucault nor Caputo will hear of it. Foucault, whose torso of a life and work bares something of the Hellenic tragic about it, was seeking meaning, if not comfort, in an aesthetics of existence. Given the severed nature of that life and view, it would be unfair to assess it as a whole or even as a final recommendation. What we have is his last, not his definitive, word on the subject. His work like the life that led or, some would say, that followed it, simply ended; it did not conclude.

Caputo has been blessed with added years and additional reflection. He has been allotted the gift and the challenge to navigate this perilous passage. Thus far he has avoided being drawn into the Whirlpool by keeping his eye on the Rock, while evading shipwreck via increasingly deft maneuvers. In his final section we catch a glimpse of this salvific vision in Caputo's concluding appeal to the "healing gestures" of compassion, commonality, and forgiveness. Could it be that Foucault's aesthetic of existence was incapable of preserving the balance that Caputo found elsewhere, plunging the former headlong into the swirl? In any case, the wily messenger of the gods may harbor yet another perspective on the Foucauldian life and work—one that Caputo may have been among the first to sound, if not yet fully to fathom.

NOTES

1. Hubert Dreyfus and Paul Rabinow, *Michel Foucault: Beyond Structuralism and Hermeneutics* with an Afterword by Michel Foucault, 2nd ed. (Chicago: University of Chicago Press, 1983), hereafter cited BSH.

2. John Caputo, RH, p. 267.

3. "[I]t will do no good to propose revolutionary schemes which are then formulated in terms of the ruling discourse. For they thereby are already assimilated and declawed. The task of deconstruction is to keep the ruling discourse in question, to expose its vulnerability, and the tensions by which it is torn" (*RH* 195).

He describes Derridian deconstruction approvingly as providing "not . . . criteria but conditions for a fair game" and adds that "the sense of the play in which all things are caught up has nothing to do with irrationalism." On the contrary, he avows, "I do not see how a sensible view of reason can be developed apart from a recognition of this play" (RH, 197).

4. See Michel Foucault, *The Archaeology of Knowledge*, trans. A.M. Sheridan Smith, and *The Discourse on Language*, trans. Rupert Swyer (New York: Harper Colophon Books, 1972), 205–206, hereafter cited as AK. Asked about his own *locus*

standi, he admits that in order to think what he calls "the unthought before thought, the system prior to every system" he was "already constrained by a system behind the system, which [he] did not know and which would withdraw to the extent that [he] discovered it or it made itself known" (Michel Foucault, *Dits et écrits*, ed. Daniel Defert and François Ewald with the collaboration of Jacques Legrange, 4 vols. [Paris: Gallimard, 1994], 1:515, hereafter cited as DE with volume and page number) I elaborate these claims in my *Sartre, Foucault and Historical Reason*, vol. 1 *Toward an Existentialist Theory of History* (Chicago: University of Chicago Press, 1997), 250–253.

5. Michel Foucault, *The Order of Things: An Archaeology of the Human Sciences*, trans. Alan Sheridan (New York: Pantheon, 1970), 377, hereafter cited as OT; see also Michel Foucault, *Foucault Live*, ed. Sylvère Lotringer (New York: Semiotext(e), 1989), 29.

6. A notable exception, aside from the title of the Dreyfus-Rabinow volume, which merely proves the point, is Salvatore Natoli's *Ermeneutica e genealogia: Filosofia e metodo in Nietzsche, Heidegger, Foucault* (Milano: Feltrinelli, 1988). Given the more recent interest in the Heideggerian strains of Foucault's thought, one could expect a corresponding search for his "hermeneutical" proclivities as well.

7. See, for example, Gerald L. Bruns, *Hermeneutics Ancient and Modern* (New Haven: Yale University Press, 1992).

8. St. Augustine, *Confessions*, trans. Edward Bouverie Pusey (Chicago: Encyclopedia Britannica, 1952), X, 26.

9. And yet this profound spatiality, when transformed into archaeological reasoning, leaves in doubt the temporally prior "fore-structure" of understanding.

10. Of course, it is questionable whether "we" can do anything about this destruction other than await and recognize its coming. The contingency of epistemes may increase our hope, but this scarcely warrants our counter-activity. And this raises one of the aporiae of Foucauldian archaeology: how autonomous are the structures that govern our cultural practices? Can they not change incrementally, at least under the pressure of innumerable instances the way a natural language develops until a threshold occurs that "changes its fundamental character" and another language appears? Or is the analogy closer to a Cartesian structure à la Chomsky or to what Umberto Eco terms "ontological structuralism"? In other words, how *"a priori"* is the "historical *a priori*"?

11. Jean-Paul Sartre, *Being and Nothingness*, trans. Hazel E. Barnes (New York: Philosophical Library, 1956), 569.

12. Jean-Paul Sartre, *Search for a Method*, trans. Hazel E. Barnes (New York: Random House Vintage Books, 1968), 153 ff.

13. AK, 235. In fact, he is glowing in his praise of Dumézil in the Introduction to the first edition of his *Folie et déraison*, an encomium conspicuously absent from the second edition when Foucault's "structuralism" is under fire. In fairness it must be acknowledged that the latter Preface is a brief, grudging critique of the need for prefaces at all, so there are other obvious reasons for the omission of Dumézil's name. On the other hand, his name is not to be found in the lengthy preface to the English translation of the abridged edition of the same work.

14. John Caputo, "On Not Knowing Who We Are: Madness, Hermeneutics, and the Night of Truth in Foucault," in *Foucault and the Critique of Institutions*, John Caputo and Mark Yount, eds. (University Park, PA: Pennsylvania State University Press, 1993), 233–262; hereafter cited as FCI.

15. Michel Foucault, *Mental Illness and Psychology*, trans. Alan Sheridan (Berkeley: University of California Press, 1987).

16. Michel Foucault, *Madness and Civilization: A History of Insanity in the Age of Reason*, trans. Richard Howard (New York: Random House Vintage Books, 1973), 212, the author's abridgement of *Histoire de la folie à l'âge classique*, 2d ed. (Paris: Gallimard, 1972), 383, hereafter cited MC and FD respectively.

17. "But what is for us merely an undifferentiated sensibility must have been, for those living in the classsical age, a clearly articulated perception. It is this mode of perception that we must investigate in order to discover the form of sensibility to madness in an epoch we are accustomed to define by the privileges of Reason. . . . Obscurely, these themes are present during the construction of the cities of confinement and their organization. They give a meaning to this ritual, and explain in part the mode in which madness was perceived and experienced by the classical age" (MC, 45–46; FD, 67). At this early stage in his career, he is, in effect, undertaking an inchoate "archaeology" of Classical perception of madness.

18. Consider, for example, his description of how consciousness of madness was transformed over the eighteenth century in a process that was gradual and more political then philanthropic in character (see MC, 223–234; FD, 417–418). Similarly, his account of the birth of the Asylum anticipates arguments mounted to explain the birth of the prison in the nineteenth century (see MC, 245; FD, 503).

19. "The task [of hermeneutics] is to be formulated as follows: 'To understand the text at first as well as and then even better than its author'" (Friedrich Schleiermacher, *Hermeneutik*, ed. Heinz Kimmerle [Heidelberg: Carl Winter, 1974], 84; *Hermeneutics: The Handwritten Manuscripts*, trans. James Duke and Jack Forstman [Missoula, Mont.: Scholars Press, 1977], 112).

20. Georges Canguilhem, *On the Normal and the Pathological*, trans. Carolyn Fawcett (Boston: D. Reidel, 1978), ix–xx. In a slightly modified later version of the same essay, Foucault adds Alexandre Koyré to the formalist side and admits that an analogous opposition could be traced to nineteenth-century thought (see DE, 4:763).

21. Thomas R. Flynn, "Foucault as Parrhesiast: His Last Course at the Collège de France," in James Bernauer and David Rasmussen eds., *The Final Foucault* (Cambridge, MA: MIT Press, 1988), 102–118.

22. This is a recurrent theme in Sartrean existentialism: "I am always more than myself." It finds dramatic expression as the final word of the existential hero of *Dirty Hands* who is about to be executed because he will not subscribe to the opportunistic back-and-forth of the Party line: "*Irrécouperable!*" (Jean-Paul Sartre, *Les Mains sales* [Paris: Gallimard, 1948]; translated by Stuart Gilbert as "unsalvageable!" in *Dirty Hands* in *No Exit and Three Other Plays* [New York: Random House Vintage Books, 1948], 248).

23. When faced with the suggestion that his ethics of self creation resembles Sartrean existentialism, Foucault seems to bristle in denial, allowing that, if to anyone's,

his view is closer to Nietzsche's than to that of Sartre (see Foucault's Afterword (1983) to BSH 237).

24. James Bernauer is the first to draw this parallel in his careful study of the entire Foucauldian corpus. See his *Foucault's Force of Flight: Toward an Ethics for Thought* (Atlantic Highlands: Humanities Press International, 1990) and "The Prisons of Man: An Introduction to Foucault's Negative Theology," *International Philosophical Quarterly* 27:4 (December 1987), 365–381.

25. See *Being and Nothingness*, especially 56–57, on facticity and transcendence (freedom) as necessary conditions for "bad faith."

26. Bernauer, *Forces*, 180–181.

27. "Foucault opposes all 'cataphatic discourse about individuals, discourse that tries to say what the individual is or should be, and he does so in the name of a kind of 'apophatic discourse, of preserving a purely apophatic freedom." As he explains, "Foucault wants to keep open the negative space of what the individual is *not*. Of what we *cannot* say the individual is, to preserve the space of a certain negativity that refuses all positivity, all identification . . ." (FCI, 251).

28. Fredric Jameson, *The Political Unconscious: Narrative as a Socially Symbolic Act* (Ithaca, NY: Cornell University Press, 1981), 23 n.7.

29. David R. Shumway, "Jamison/Hermeneutics/Postmodernism," in Douglas Kellner, ed. *Postmodernism/Jameson/Critique* (Washington, DC: Maisonneuve Press, 1989), 183; hereafter cited as PJC.

30. This is probably what Geoffrey Bennington has in mind when he insisted apropos of Derrida: "Deconstruction is not a form of hermeneutics, however supposedly radical, for just this reason: hermeneutics always proposes a convergent movement towards a unitary meaning (however much it may wish to respect ambiguity on the way), the word of God: deconstruction discerns a dispersive perspective in which there is no (one) meaning" (Geoffrey Bennington, chapter 50, "Derrida," in Simon Critchley and William R. Schroeder, eds., *A Companion to Continental Philosophy* (Malden, MA: Blackwell, 1998), 552.

31. I borrow this title from the work of a colleague of many years ago, Enrico Garzilli's *Circles without Center: Paths to the Discovery and Creation of Self in Modern Literature* (Cambridge, MA: Harvard University Press, 1972).

32. Michel Foucault, *The Use of Pleasure, The History of Sexuality* Vol. 2, trans. Robert Hurley (New York: Pantheon Books, 1985), 5–6, emphasis added.

33. See my *Sartre, Foucault and Historical Reason*, vol. 2 *A Poststructuralist Mapping of History* forthcoming, and Bernauer, *Force*, 103 and 215 n. 83.

HOUNDING HERMENEUTICS:
A RESPONSE TO FLYNN

John D. Caputo

The reason I do not mention Foucault often is that I have always found it difficult to draw nourishment from Foucault. The essay that Thomas Flynn has so perspicaciously analyzed is my one attempt to do so. I have sometimes quipped that if this is *not* what Foucault is saying then I give up and will stop trying to be nourished by him and leave Foucault to nourish the Foucauldians. Now while I have moved past the Heideggerian "openness to the mystery" thematized in *Radical Hermeneutics*, which Tom Flynn has singled out for attention in this essay, I remain very much attached to the project of this essay on Foucault, so much so that I have recently made it the lead essay of *More Radical Hermeneutics* (Bloomington: Indiana University Press, 2000) and used its title as my subtitle: *On Not Knowing Who We Are*. So I read Tom Flynn's essay with the most intense interest—to see if I should give it up (as I am often advised on this and other matters).

Flynn's delineation of Foucault's critique of hermeneutics forces me to say just what it is that I mean by "hermeneutics," even more radically conceived, since, like Foucault, I think that hermeneutics from Schleiermacher to Gadamer tenders us various forms of "essentialism." After abandoning its nineteenth century goals of getting the author's intentions right, or getting the spirit of the age right, hermeneutics had recourse, in Gadamer and Ricoeur, to Hegel: either by way of reconciling conflicting interpretations in a higher unity (Ricoeur) or by way of a metaphysics of inherited truth, transmitted by the "classic" (Gadamer). I stand with Foucault's happy positivism, and with his nominalism, which sees these received understandings as constructions "all the way down," with the acute proviso added by Flynn that there is no down, no depth, and what you see is what you get. That is why I have pretty much abandoned the Heideggerianism "openness to the Mystery," which comes out in my exchange with Bill Richardson, and why anything I say about negative theology now should be read in conjunction with Derrida, not Heidegger, for whom *Geheimnis* turns on the *Heim*, the hidden home of Being's mystery. Nowadays I speak not of the mystery but of the mess we are in, of the confused and diffused play of meanings, and emphasize the exile and the homeless not the home. I have found it easier to make this argument in terms of what Derrida calls the infinite grammato-logical superficiality of *différance*, which is an anonymous, pre-subjective quasi-structure, rather than archeologies and genealogies. While having a constitutional preference for the way Derrida conducts his business, it seems to me that Foucault and Derrida—who also thinks that hermeneutics is a big mistake of trying to "arrest" the play of meaning—are headed in pretty much the same direction, viz., the displacement of subjectivism and humanism, not in the name of chaos, violence, or the inhuman, but in the name of the right to be different. That is why I have also not allowed myself to be drawn into the war between Derrideans and Foucauldians that Searle for one has tried to incite.

But if I have moved past this late Heideggerian openness to the mystery, which is one of the decisive differences between Foucault and the standpoint of *Radical Hermeneutics*, then why not make more use of Foucault and less of "hermeneutics"? If, like Foucault, I too reject the normativity of authorial intention, or the ideal of getting to understand the text better than its author (classical hermeneutics), and if I also reject the hermeneutical circle of truth, of occupying *ab intra* a pre-understanding of some transmitted content that is deeply true and that has us before we have it (post-Heideggerian hermeneu-tics), and if I too consort with pre-subjective and anonymous quasi-structures like *différance*, then why, for heaven's sake, speak of hermeneutics at all, hermeneutics of any kind, radical, moderate, or conservative? After we have let Derrida or Foucault hound hermeneutics half to death, what life is left in the poor fellow? Why not give up hermeneutics for dead? That is what Flynn is forcing out of me.

What remains is what I would call the *necessity or inescapability of inter-pretation*, the unavoidable need to construe the shadows, to continue read-ing precisely in the face of the unreadability of the text, of the secret that sees to it that we will never be done with literature.[1] Interpretations are needed, as many as possible, St. Augustine says, come what may, since we have no access to the things themselves and are not hard-wired to Being, God, or the Good, but we must still make it through each day. It is both urgently neces-sary to reach a decision yet impossible to nail things down once and for all. For even after we have pointed to the pre-subjective structures that pre-structure our beliefs and practices, deconstructively or genealogically, facti-cal life is still waiting for us at the door, holding our hat and gloves. That is what I mean by radical hermeneutics. To put it in a more upbeat way, since I do not want to make interpretation sound like a prison sentence, let us speak of an affirmative invitation to interpret, of the joy of interpretation, as a way of preparing for the incoming (*invention*) of something unforeseeable (*tout autre*), for which we cannot really prepare, which is my form of a "felicitous positivism," a happier hermeneutics, so long as we do not forget that this comes along with unavoidable risk.

But does this persistent attachment to at least a kind of hermeneutics not implicate me in some version of the "anthropological quadrilateral" that goes to the heart of Foucault's critique of hermeneutics, as Flynn rightly demands to know? I do not consort with anthropologizing if that means allowing the well-being of everything else to be sacrificed to the well-being of human beings, whereas I have signed on to the *tout autre est tout autre*, and I would like to think that there are other others than human others. Nor if it means suffering the illusion of the autonomous subject that is not pre-structured from the start by forces—discursive practices, power relations and problematizations—that it did not see coming and over which it has no disposition. I am simply trying to describe the fix we find ourselves in, we who can hardly say "we," who have our doubts about the privileges attached to *anthropos*, *just because* of these pre-subjective structures unearthed in our several archeologies and genealogies. We do not know who we are—*that* is who we are. Here we are, with no guidebook to show the way (The Way), where we never quite are what we are, just as Sartre said. But that, I would contend, is not to succumb to the anthropological prejudice; that's just life. That's a fact. Not an uninterpreted fact of the matter, to be sure, but the fact of factical life that presses hard upon us all through the day, the facticity of having to get through the day, and the night.

Tom Flynn, acute reader of Sartre that he is, also asks whether I am sailing close to the shores of a *metaphysics of difference*. We *are* difference, we are what we are not, Foucault would be saying on my account, somewhat in the manner of a Sartrean ontology of freedom. I am inclined to say that it is rather a *pragmatics* of difference, a *refusal* of identification in the concrete, offering practical resistance that takes the form of concretely situated historical analyses that expose the historical contingency of the various ways we have been constituted. But as I do not read Foucault as offering any positive metaphysical back-up for these analyses neither do I think that such is needed, for they stand on the legs of their own historical persuasiveness. Writing a history is as powerful a way to deconstruct something as one could desire, for a history shows that something that is trying to pass itself off as having dropped from heaven has been historically constituted, which is how, by the way, I try to get Derrida and Foucault on the same track. So my Foucault does not need a metaphysics of freedom; he just has to write a good history of how we tend to be taken in by various contingencies trying to pass themselves off as necessities. Whence the apophatic strategy: we do not know who we are and every time someone tries to tell us who we are, we can write a history that exposes the contingency of the construction of that identity. The histories keep the future open, while the metaphysics wall us in. Foucault's nominalism and what I call a negative hermeneutics of refusal are of a piece.

So when Tom Flynn says that "Caputo's radical hermeneutic is open to mystery whereas that of Foucault is merely open," I can use a moving target defense. I have since given up on "openness to the mystery" as a loaded Heideggerianism and a latent essentialism. I prefer the idea of openness to the *tout autre*, which can certainly be taken as the kind of unqualified openness suggested by the phrase "merely open." Still, being "merely open," requires qualification since Foucault is not open to regimes of power that denounce and persecute gays and lesbians, that imprison and sedate the mentally different, that rigorously discipline bodies, etc. That ethical and political concern is part of the reason I am sticking with the word hermeneutics. A radical hermeneutics of refusal implies an ethics of refusal, an ethics sans ethics, an ethics *against* ethics in the positive normative and normalizing sense, since it is also worried that there is something unethical about that sort of ethics.

If "hermeneutics" means to interpret human practices in terms of the intentions that lie behind them, as Tom Flynn says (pp. 13, 22), which is hermeneutics in the straightforward or traditional sense and certainly not what I mean by radical hermeneutics, then I completely agree with him that Foucault's archeology or genealogy—like Derrida's deconstruction—should never be confused with hermeneutics, since their point is to expose the nonintentional structures that pre-structure such practices and intentions. Nor am I suggesting that the tragic hermeneutics persists after Foucault's early work, as Tom Flynn sometimes suggests I am saying but for which—and this is very interesting to me—he himself thinks there may in fact be some basis. I am pointing to the fix we find ourselves in *after* such an exposition of all the de-anthropologizing pre-structuring analyses have been made and we still find it necessary to get out of bed each morning. That is what I mean by the *radical* hermeneutical situation, a fix that I am claiming is very much on Foucault's mind and why I think that the cool prose of his analyses is astir with a certain ethical passion. For "life"—or "experience," as Tom Flynn says—is always waiting at the door, and at this point it seems to me Tom Flynn seems to come around to my argument.

When Tom Flynn picks up on Foucault's resuscitation of the category of "experience" as the field that is constituted by the "games of truth and error" that Foucault said he was always analyzing, it is like the angel showing up at the crucial moment at the sacrifice of Isaac. Flynn very generously stays his sword and gives me a way out, since everybody agrees that hermeneutics takes "experience" as its concern. Foucault's archeologies, genealogies, and problematizations seem to me to be motivated by an attempt to open up the field of "experience" just as Tom Flynn describes it. But I would add that these analyses have an *ethical* cutting edge and constitute an ethics of refusal, an ethics that is "against ethics" in the sense in which I argue we should all be against ethics. So by the "apophatic" I do not mean to get us all misty eyed about mystical abysses, but simply to refuse the sort of ethics that are enforced by the bureaucrats and police. I am perfectly happy just to call it a happy nominalism, as Tom Flynn recommends, but I am insisting that nominalism has an ethical-hermeneutical punch. For what else is Foucault about in describing all the things that have been prescribed for us in modernity if not the endless search to open up new and unheard of ways of flourishing, ways that are at present *indescribable* (whence the "apophatic" spin) and *imprescribable* (the coming of the *tout autre*)? That is why I cling so hard-headedly to this talk of the "hermeneutics of refusal," which refuses normativities and normalizations meant to hem us in, now or in the future. Otherwise I do not see what point these analyses have. If I am wrong about Foucault's ethics *sans* ethics, then I will give up and leave Foucault to the Foucauldians.

That is also why I think that Foucault admits of a certain "therapeutic" graft, which seizes upon the point that the prison, the hospital, and the confessional are *also* so many scenes of suffering that require healing, compassion, and responsibility, not simply archeological, genealogical, or problematizing analysis. If nominalism has a certain biblical resonance in the biblical critique of idols (which is one of the first and most radical theories of "contingency"), whereas essentialism is the love of *ousia*, a trademark of Hellenism, then nominalism also has in my view a prophetic streak, which is the argument Dooley makes on behalf of Rorty. Nominalism proceeds from a view that all things made can be made *new* (or at least *different*). That is why I think that there are prayers and tears to be found in Foucault, too, if we have the ears to hear, all the while respecting the fact that Foucault quite rightly passes for an atheist. I am delighted that the final word in Tom Flynn's rigorous reading of my text is the suggestion that this might indeed constitute another way to read Foucault.

NOTE

1. Derrida, ON, pp. 29–30.

9   IN PRAISE OF PROPHESY: CAPUTO ON RORTY

_____ Mark Dooley

I was not at all surprised when I learned recently that Richard Rorty's maternal grandfather was the "Social Gospel" theologian, Walter Rauschenbusch. The latter's searing denunciations of those politicians and bureaucrats "who have cloaked their extortion with the gospel of Christ,"[1] not only remind one of Kierkegaard's equally deprecating remark to the effect that the so-called "blessed chain of witnesses to the Truth" have made a profit from the crucifixion, but also of the deeply committed social theologies of Paul Tillich and Hans Kung, not to mention the unsettling voices of the many liberation theologians who have courageously taken the side of the poor and the weak in the face of ridicule, excommunication, and sometimes even death.

Neither was I surprised to learn that many of Rorty's relatives "helped write and administer New Deal legislation."[2] For, on my interpretation, Rorty's work stands as a monumental testament to the lives of those writers, thinkers, and activists, many of whom he associated with during his formative years, who dedicated themselves tirelessly to the eradication of social injustice through the New Deal and other progressive initiatives. To many of his critics this positive characterization of Rorty will undoubtedly seem like an exercise in hagiography. But it is not. When I began to take a serious interest in Rorty, I reacted with the same level of indignation as expressed by these critics to particular features of his vision. I too felt as though Rorty was not sufficiently sensitive to tackle the pressing demands of contemporary life. His apparent insouciance on matters of immense philosophical and political importance amounted, I believed, to intellectual irresponsibility. People like Terry Eagleton, John Searle, and Stanley Hauerwas, still believe this to be the case. But after some years of careful and patient reading, I have come to think of Rorty as one of the most able and responsible intellectuals writing today. I now consider his work as a noble embodiment of the Social Gospel of

201

his grandfather, the philosophy of his intellectual hero John Dewey, and the politics of people like Martin Luther King jnr. and Bill Bradley. As such, I consider those characterizations of Rorty as a relativist, or as someone whose views have potentially dangerous consequences, as being utterly unfounded and misbegotten. They will only appear relativistic and dangerous to those who wish to perpetuate the established order, and to those like Alasdair Mac-Intyre who have long since eschewed democracy, but not, as I will argue, to those who agree with Rorty that "hope for social justice is the only basis for a worthwhile human life."[3]

On my reading, Rorty is a philosopher of justice and hope, one for whom the love of social solidarity and progress are most worthy and venerable ideals. His dream is of a "barely imaginable cosmopolitan society of the future,"[4] one in which inequality and indigence will have been entirely eradicated. For him, "the most distinctive and praiseworthy human capacity is our ability to trust and cooperate with other people, and in particular to work together so as to improve the future."[5] It is this insatiable longing for a future time in which social, racial, class, and ethnic divisions will have been surmounted, which highlights the deeply prophetic strain in Rorty's work. It is this strain which allies him most closely with the social gospel theologians like Tillich and Rauschenbush, with the *prophetic* pragmatism of Cornel West, and with the *prophetic* postmodernism of Jacques Derrida. Like these figures, Rorty sees his role as one which aims at clearing "the road for prophets and poets" so as "to make intellectual life a bit simpler and safer for those who have visions of new communities."[6]

Such visionaries are not in the business of predicting how things will eventually unfold, but are, to steal a phrase from Derrida, "prophets without prophesy"[7]—prophets, that is, who see history not as a process which will one day culminate in the coming of a particular kingdom or state of affairs, but as a fully contingent process with no underlying teleological impetus, no *terminus ad quem*. The only goal for such prophets is a world in which there "is constant vigilance against the predictable attempts by the rich and the strong against the poor and the weak," a world in which the realization of social justice is prized above all else. They yearn for a time when hope for a wonderfully changed future, a future which is truly "global, cosmopolitan, democratic, egalitarian, classless, and casteless"[8] will have replaced a longing for eternity.

The prophets Rorty favors, thus, are those who abjure from predicting what is going to happen, why, and when. They deny having any superior insight into the mind of God or History. Consequently, they refuse to be seduced by those who tell us that one day, under certain conditions, we shall reap heavenly rewards, or by those who proclaim the imminent coming of our preferred utopia. They are men and women who believe that because the future is formless and opaque we should seize the opportunity to make it unrecognizably different from the past. While they do not sing hymns to destiny, they do, however, recite "the poetry of social hope."[9] No theme has been more pervasive throughout the work of Richard Rorty than than that of social hope. He is mesmerized by poets of hope such as Vaclav Havel, individuals who, because of their own experience of the utterly aleatoric nature of events (e.g., Havel's dramatic and unbelievable accession to power in 1990), have substituted "groundless hope for theoretical insight."[10] Hope according to this line of thought is not prognostication. It is hope for a time which is out of mind, for a time which will render our current social and political experiments either quaint or simply obsolete. It is the type of hope instanced in the prophetic calls for justice in both the New Testament and in the *Communist Manifesto*. For Rorty, "both documents are expressions of the same hope: that some day we shall be willing and able to treat the needs of all human beings with the respect and consideration with which we treat the needs of those closest to us, those whom we love."[11] But we should take care while trying to draw inspiration from both texts, to skim lightly over those passages which, because their authors believed themselves to have cracked either sacred or historical codes, forecast the imminent arrival of redemption or salvation, of apocalypse or doom. Rather, we should seek out those passages which were written in a spirit of hope for a better world to come. "We should read both," urges Rorty, "as inspirational documents, appeals to what Lincoln called 'the better angels of our nature', rather than as accurate accounts of human history or of human destiny."[12] If we do so, then there is still an important place for both Christianity and socialism in our contemporary situation. For those who are convinced that Rorty is out to exorcise the ghost of religion (a point I shall return to below), the following quotation should encourage them to reconsider:

> If one treats "Christianity" as the name of one such appeal [to "the better angels of our nature"], rather than as a claim to knowledge, then the word still names a powerful force working for human decency and human equality. "Socialism," similarly considered, is the name of the same force—an updated, more precise name. "Christian Socialism" is pleonastic: nowadays you cannot hope for the fraternity which the gospels preach without hoping that democratic governments will redistribute money and opportunity in a way that the market never will. There is no way to take the New Testament seriously as a moral imperative, rather than as a prophecy [founded on theoretical insight rather than on social hope], without taking the need for such redistribution seriously.[13]

One writer who agrees with my characterization of Rorty as one of the most responsible, intriguing, and courageous intellectuals writing today, is John D. Caputo. Caputo has been a long time admirer of Rorty's courage in taking on the analytic establishment in philosophy circles in the United States, and of his willingness to listen and learn from other traditions. He has also praised Rorty's defense of the weak and the marginalized, and has supported his trenchant opposition to the Republicans or anyone else who stands in the way of social and political reform. But Caputo stops short of agreeing with me when I argue that Rorty is, like Derrida, a "prophet without prophesy," a prophet of social hope. In so doing, he joins ranks with Simon Critchley,[14] someone for whom Rorty is too parochial or too nationalistic to be counted among those who have groundless hope in, what Derrida calls, a time which is always to come or which is forever out of joint. This particular take on Rorty leaves me, I have to say, somewhat perplexed. It does so because on nearly every page of his published work Rorty has, as noted above, specified why he thinks our highest aspirations should take the form of trying to build a multi-cultural global utopia animated by a will to see the absolute eradication of social injustice and inequality of opportunity. Hence, the charge of parochialism is, I believe, quite inapposite. While I think Caputo is correct to assume that there are significant differences between his Derridean position and that advanced by Rorty, I am nevertheless convinced that such differences are minor when compared to the common ground which both authors share especially at a political level. For the remainder of this essay, therefore, I want to critically engage with Caputo's reading of Rorty in his "Parisian Hermeneutics and Yankee Hermeneutics" in *More Radical Hermeneutics*.[15] In so doing, I will endeavor to persuade Caputo of Rorty's prophetic credentials as a way of narrowing the divide between deconstruction and pragmatism as practiced by both men. For I am fully convinced that if intellectuals such as Caputo and Rorty could begin to see what they have in common, rather than what divides them, the so-called "Cultural Left" might become more effective in political terms than it is today.

On Circumventing the Quasi-Transcendental

I want to split up my analysis of Caputo's reading of Rorty into two parts. Firstly, I wish to respond to the claims he advances under the subtitle of "Is Derrida a *Quasi*-Transcendental Philosopher (or, It Takes One to Know One)" (p. 95). My comments in this section will focus primarily on the *philosophical* differences which separate Derrida and Caputo on the one hand, and Rorty on the other. I will then go on to argue that these philosophical differences notwithstanding, Rorty's politics are every bit as prophetic as Derrida's. This will take the form of a critical analysis of Caputo's final section of "Parisian Hermeneutics and Yankee Hermeneutics," entitled "Why Deconstruction is *Not* America."

In his chapter from *More Radical Hermeneutics*, "Parisian Hermeneutics and Yankee Hermeneutics," Caputo argues that Rorty's take on Derrida suffers from a lack of understanding regarding the nature of what has become known as the "*quasi*-transcendental." The "*quasi*-transcendental" refers to that side of Derrida which argues, as Caputo informs his reader, that "economies produce their effects by a kind of 'spacing,' by producing marks or traces which make nominal unities called 'words' or concepts or meaning—or beauty, rhythm, symmetry or asymmetry, or whatever one needs—not merely and not primarily in virtue of the intrinsic 'substance' of the 'signifier' but in terms of the 'differential' relationship—the 'space'—between the signifiers."[16] This theory derives from Saussure's contention that signs do not correspond to any natural signified, but attain their value in and through their relationship with other signs. Derrida appropriates this Saussurian insight and gives it a universal flavor by arguing that the identity of a person or a thing is not determined by its rank in the great order of being, the *ordo essendi*, but by virtue of its relationship to other persons or things.

Such a view is common to most antiessentialists including Rorty. Being as thorough an anti-dualist as one is likely to get, Rorty is entirely in agreement with Derrida and Caputo regarding the view that identity is never pure and unmediated, but is always contaminated and incised by difference. As he says, "{e}verything that can serve as the term of a relation can be dissolved into another set of relations, and so on, for ever. There are, so to speak, relations all the way down, all the way up, and all the way out in every direction: you never reach something which is not just one more nexus of relations."[17] That, says Caputo, is yet one more way to make a *quasi*-transcendental point; Rorty, in other words, is saying much the same thing about language and meaning as Derrida, *albeit* in a less Parisian and more Yankee vernacular. There is little substantial difference, that is, between saying, as Derrida does, that "every referent, all reality has the structure of a differential trace, and that no one can refer to this 'real' except in an interpretative experience," (18) and, as Rorty does, "that *all* inquiry is interpretation, that *all* thought consists in recontextualization, that we have never done anything else and never will."[19] There is only, on Caputo's reading, an *idiomatic* or *semantic* difference.

Rorty is being disingenuous, thus, when he criticizes Derrida for being *too* philosophical and gratuitously transcendental. For when the former says that everything can be recontextualized, that interpretation goes all the way down, he is being no less philosophical or transcendental than Derrida. Of course, his transcendentalism does not take the form of universal *a priori* claims about conditions of possibility; as a good "psychological nominalist," Rorty does not believe that we can tap into some form of pre-linguistic experience, or that there are language-independent realities "out there" in the world which may be accessed in their raw state by the human mind. But he does make strong claims about language, about the way it functions and what that means for the way we relate to the world. While he may have given up on strong foundationalism, he still retains some degree of transcendentalism. As Caputo argues:

> What Derrida calls "iterability" is a feature of any mark, and he is not bashful about that claim, no more than Rorty is bashful about saying things like "anything can be anything if you put it in the right context." But is that not exactly what Derrida means by a *quasi-transcendental*? Does Rorty not make a second order claim about anything that anybody is going to say? . . . I do not see why Rorty thinks he is so much cleaner of the stain of philosophy than Derrida.[20]

Like Derrida, Rorty "does have an idea of what language 'must be.'"[21]

Unlike Caputo, however, I do not believe that Rorty is being in any way disingenuous or hypocritical when he accuses Derrida of sounding *too* transcendental. For, *pace* Caputo, I do not contend that Rorty does have an idea of what language *is* or *must be*; he does not, that is, inflate his claim that "anything can be anything if you put it in the right context" into a *transcendental* claim about "how things get said and can always *and in principle* come unsaid." While Caputo says somewhat the same about Derrida when he admits that the latter's theory about language is only a *partial* or *quasi*-theory, a theory which is "tentative" and hypothetical at best,[22] he does not tease out the full implications of this point. He continues, that is, to speak of Derrida's take on language in transcendental terms, to speak of it as if it were *"the* Truth" about language, as if Derrida had somehow managed to twist free of his socio-linguistic moorings and obtained a handle on how language works from a language-free viewpoint.

Rorty, on the other hand, refrains from saying that his particular "theory about what is going on in language," is the truth about language. There is, I want to argue, much more at stake here than merely a semantic confusion between a Yankee and a Parisian. For Rorty consistently abjures from the temptation to say that his views on language, truth, representation, meaning, and correspondence, are an accurate and objective depiction of how things *really* are. While Derrida confesses time and again that anything he says is an "effect of the differential play of language," and not the play itself, he nevertheless continues to talk about "the play," as if the play of signifiers functioned by itself in the absence of any particular speaker. Rorty, we might say, is "cleaner of the stain of philosophy than Derrida" precisely because he does not beef up his beliefs about language, or anything else for that matter, into transcendental or *quasi*-transcendental claims about the conditions of possibility of getting something said and unsaid. If Derrida and Caputo propose theories and *quasi*-theories, Rorty can only offer redescriptions of our situation for which he claims no objective status.

In order to shed more light on these issues, allow me to examine in somewhat more detail Rorty's general philosophical position. Above all else, Rorty will be remembered for the way in which he challenged the presumptions of philosophers, theologians, and scientists, to have access to the world or reality in a way which the rest of humanity does not. While those in the *agora* continually confuse appearance with reality, the priests, philosophers and sages, have ways of penetrating through illusion in an effort to grasp truth. Like Derrida, Rorty considers such age-old attempts to dismantle the veil of appearance so as to confront the world as it is in itself, as something which we can now afford to give up. We can afford to do so because such attempts have proved to be impediments to social progress. The belief, in other words, that some humans (philosophers, scientists, and natural theologians) have the capacity to identify standards and goals which non-human forces decree we humans should realize and adhere to, renders us incapable of dreaming up new social initiatives so as to fulfil our ever-changing human needs and interests. As long as it is presumed that some of us have the wherewithal to transcend our acculturation and socialization so as to take up a view from nowhere, we will, on Rorty's telling, continue to fan the flames of religious, racial, cultural, and social division.

As stated at the outset, Rorty's principal objective is to persuade his reader that "the most distinctive and praiseworthy human capacity" is not to know things as they are in themselves, but "is our ability to trust and to cooperate with other people, and in particular to work together so as to improve the future." [23] As a philosopher of solidarity and fraternity, he endeavors to dream up ways of dissolving age-old prejudices which have their source in the dualistic account of human nature bequeathed to us by the Greeks. He strives, that is, to rid us of the belief that we differ from all other species by virtue of having something extra in our constitution which the animals lack. While we do indeed differ from animals, this difference is not due to the presence within us of something divine or nonhuman. Rather, it is due merely to a greater degree of complexity and sophistication. In saying this, Rorty is seeking to undermine the hierarchical structures around which we have traditionally ordered our societies and lives. Such structures privilege those who are perceived to be in possession to a greater degree than others, what Rorty calls, "the extra added ingredient which makes us truly human." [24]

In order to slough off this metaphysical inheritance, an inheritance which provided an intellectual backup for prejudice and subordination, Rorty urges that we simply drop the "appearance and reality" distinction. He urges us to drop it in favor of the "distinction between the more useful and the less useful."[25] In so doing, we will not make the mistake of saying that the Greek way of looking at the world was inaccurate or wrong, for that presupposes that we have a way of determining which description of the world is the correct description or which matches reality—thus once more invoking the appearance-reality distinction. What we can say, however, is that such a description of our situation is less useful *to us*, by virtue of the fact that it has become an impediment to building a society which privileges universal fraternity above inequality. This suggests that we have different purposes and projects than our forebears, purposes and projects which demand a more useful vocabulary or description.

The alternative description which Rorty purveys takes its point of departure from Darwin rather than from the Greeks. On this account, the aim of inquiry is not to represent reality accurately, but to develop ways of coping with, and using the environment which fulfil to the optimum degree our needs and interests. One set of tools which we developed in our endeavor to control the environment is language. Words, like any other tool, help us to achieve certain tasks more efficaciously and efficiently. Usually when we find that a tool is no longer adequate to our current tasks we tend to discard it. The same holds true for words: when we find that a word or a group of words is no longer sufficient for coping with our demands we generally drop it from our vocabulary and replace it with a more useful alternative. Language, thus, is not a medium standing between us and the world "outside," not a clear and distinct picture of reality, but a set of tools that help us to make our way around the environment with as much ease as we can.

For Rorty, this Darwinian view is *more useful* than the metaphysical alternative because it helps us to avoid the pitfalls of representationalism; that is, it furnishes us with a way of discarding the notion that we have some special ingredient, such as "reason" or "knowledge," which allows us to escape from our "human peculiarities and perspectives"[26] so as to observe the world as it is in itself, thus allowing us to check our words against what they are said to represent. If language is considered as a set of tools which help us to cope with the environment, tools which may be replaced by other tools when our purposes change, then language does not represent at all. This is also in keeping with Rorty's psychological nominalism—i.e., the suggestion that there is no pre-linguistic experience, no way "to step outside of language . . . and to grasp reality unmediated by a linguistic description."[27]

On this pragmatist account, there can be no knowledge by acquaintance, no knowledge which manages to take hold of an object in any pure sense. All we can know about any object is "what is stated in sentences describing it."[28] This assumes that beliefs about the world are not mental pictures of reality, but are what contemporary analytic philosophers call, "sentential attitudes," or, the affirmation or denial of certain sentences by us language-using organisms. We affirm or deny certain sentences depending on what our particular purposes are at a given time; to say that someone believes what I believe is simply to say, therefore, that he or she will agree with me, and behave in ways which accord with my own behavior, when I affirm the veracity of certain sentences. In short, to share a belief with someone is to have the same *purposes* as that individual. It is to assume that the descriptions of the environment purveyed by him or her are more appropriate given one's needs and interests than any other currently available. Consequently, we do not measure the efficacy of our beliefs by comparing them with what they are said to represent. A *good* belief or description is, rather, one which is capable of accomplishing a task better than any of the available alternatives. But, to repeat, as our purposes change so too will our descriptions and beliefs. Different purposes require different tools.

To argue that "there is no such thing as the way the thing is in itself, under no description, apart from any use to which human beings might want to put it,"[29] is to say that there is no point of view more exalted than *our own*. It is to argue that trying to see things under the aspect of eternity, or from a privileged (i.e., descriptive-free) standpoint, is futile simply because there is no way that the human can become nonhuman, no way that we can shed our language in an effort to determine whether or not our descriptions are accurate and true (in the sense of being perfect images of what is really "out there"). As Rorty says, "there is no independent test of the accuracy of correspondence."[30] This goes for those who claim divine favor as well as for those who claim to have the privileged insight into reality which science assumes. Such a redescription of ourselves helps us to replace what was a useful tool for our ancestors' purposes—i.e., the belief that human life was hierarchically ordered by virtue of there being, to a greater or lesser extent depending on the individual in question, "an extra added ingredient which makes us truly human"—with a tool which is more in keeping with our current purposes of trying to realize a truly egalitarian and classless society. For once you substitute the belief that there is a nonhuman reality against which you can check the objective status of your beliefs and judgments, with the belief that what we call "objective" is the outcome of free and open discussion between human beings who are not subservient to anything bigger or more powerful than themselves, then the traditional ways of "justifying both subordination and conformity" are rendered highly dubious. While the former description proved useful to an inegalitarian society, one which perpetuated "the social division between contemplators and doers, between a leisure class and a productive class,"[31] the pragmatist's preferred description changes the emphasis from the eternal to the future, from *stasis* to ever increasing freedom and growth. While one tries to live up to a predetermined standard, the other endeavors to "come up with a way of bringing people into some degree of comity, and of increasing human happiness, which looks more promising than any other which has so far been proposed."[32]

It would, therefore, be highly inconsistent of Rorty, given all that he says about trying to rid ourselves of the dualistic frame of mind recommended by the metaphysical tradition, to declare that his redescription of ourselves and our situation is how things *really* are, or how things *objectively* stand. He cannot say, that is, that Darwin got reality right while Plato did not. All he can afford to say is that looking at things from a Darwinian angle is *a more useful strategy* given our current purposes. There is no way, in other words, that Rorty can claim to have reached an ideal cognitive situation if he is to avoid contradicting himself. Consequently, he can claim neither transcendental or *quasi*-transcendental status for any of his claims. Neither can he claim that Derrida's *quasi*-transcendental position is erroneous. But he can legitimately say that the redescription which is advanced by Derrida is not as useful for *our* current purposes as the one he is proposing. The issue of which is better cannot be determined by reference to some neutral court of appeal which stands over and above all descriptions of the environment. Rather, the only way we have of choosing between alternative descriptions is by invidiously comparing them, or by juxtaposing their respective advantages in an effort to ascertain which will solve our current problems more expeditiously and efficiently. Hence, Rorty will always abjure from making claims about language which make it seem as though he has discovered the real truth about the way language works.

In accusing Rorty of saying what Derrida says except in a different vernacular, Caputo overlooks this vital point. But the ineluctable fact of the matter is that Rorty never says that his take on the way language functions is closer to the truth about language than Russell's, Heidegger's, Frege's, or Husserl's. As he says:

> . . . you should notice that it would be inconsistent with my own antiessentialism to try to convince you that the Darwinian way of thinking about language—and, by extension, the Deweyan, pragmatist way of thinking of truth—is the objectively true way. All I am entitled to say is that it is a useful way, useful for particular purposes. All I can claim to have done here is to offer you a redescription of the relation between human beings and the rest of the universe. Like every other redescription, this one has to be judged on the basis of its utility for a purpose.[33]

To be fully antiessentialist, in other words, you have to be prepared to accept that one day your preferred description might be jettisoned in favor of a better description, where "better" signifies "more useful." Indeed, you will *hope* that someday your description will be surpassed.

It is easy to understand why Rorty suggests, therefore, that Derrida's theory of language, his *quasi*-transcendental position, is *less useful* than the Darwinian-pragmatist account. For by exalting language in this way you tend, as Rorty argues, "to think of language as something more than just a set of tools," you tend, that is, to capitalize "Language," to treat it "as if it were a quasi-agent, a brooding presence, something that stands over and against human beings."[34] Talk of "the play of language" gives rise to the belief that language is a type of anonymous force analogous to Hegelian "*Geist*" or "History"—a force which appears to have a mind and an agenda of its own. But in making such claims about language you are implicitly suggesting that you have somehow broken through appearance to reality, that you have assumed a position which allows you to determine the precise nature of language's relation to the environment. You are, so to speak, sneaking the old dualism in through the back door, and, in so doing, you are in danger of losing the many advantages gained by replacing the appearance-reality distinction with the distinction between the more useful and the less useful. Once again, Rorty is not saying that "language *really* is *just* strings of marks and noises which organisms use as tools for getting what they want." For this "description of language is no more the real truth about language than Heidegger's description of it as 'the house of Being' or Derrida's as 'the play of signifying references.'" "Each of these," Rorty continues, "is only one more useful truth about language—one more of what Wittgenstein called 'reminders for a particular purpose.'"[35] None of them can claim to have "finally gotten language right, to have represented it accurately or as it really is," but only to have offered yet one more redescription.

Rorty, consequently, is not in the same boat as Derrida, for he is not prepared to purvey an "idea of what language 'must be.'"[36] While Derrida's nominalism shares many of the same features as Rorty's pragmatism, there is one significant point of divergence: Derrida does not follow Rorty in saying that his take on language is just one more reminder for a particular purpose. As such, I think Caputo is right when he says that this "goes to the heart of the difference between Rorty and Derrida. . . ."[37] But unlike Caputo, who concludes that Rorty is being no less philosophical than Derrida in what he says about language, I want to maintain that Rorty certainly is being less philosophical *stricto sensu*, when one defines philosophy in metaphysical terms. Caputo complains that after "denying that language and the world are separated by an abyss which philosophy must find a way to cross, after rejecting the idea that language is some sort of I-know-not-what medium which mediates between us and the world, either by representing the world accurately or bringing the world to expression,"[38] Rorty nevertheless proceeds to urge that "instead of all this theory-building, we should just content ourselves with the fact that vocabularies . . . are 'tools' we use which vary with our purposes. . . ."[39] In so doing, argues Caputo, "he restarts the argument and perpetuates the conversation by substituting an alternate and competing philosophical theory about language."[40] This interpretation of what Rorty is up to, to repeat, overlooks the fact that while the latter is content to call himself a philosopher, he does not claim any objective status for his philosophical take on things. His Darwinian-pragmatic theory of language is put forward as a more useful theory in that it helps us to abandon a certain description of our situation, one which has come to be an impediment to the realization of our social hopes. So it is true that Rorty does offer a *philosophical* redescription of ourselves, a redescription which suits our current purposes. But this is no more the truth about who we really are than any other which has so far been imagined. It is simply more useful *for us now*.

It is also true, as Caputo argues, that "Rorty is contesting ideas that have never crossed the mind of non-philosophers by introducing another idea that has never entered the head of people who spend their day in the natural attitude"[41]—such as the idea that "all vocabularies are contingent." Rorty, as I have stated above, has never denied that he is a philosopher, and has never sought to have himself described as anything other. He would surely agree with Caputo's contention that those who have never been exposed to philosophy are not likely to ask the sort of questions about language that both he and Derrida are used to asking. But I do not know why this means, as Caputo charges, that "he is still implicated in a certain kind of philosophizing in a stronger sense then he is willing to concede."[42] For, to reiterate, he does not accord any foundational status to any of his philosophical statements, but only a pragmatic status.

Moreover, Rorty has consistently tried to change our definition of philosophy by arguing that all theory, including his own, only works if and only if it makes a difference to practice. So the type of philosophy which Rorty favors is that which "encourages people to have a self-image in which their real or imagined citizenship in a democratic republic is central." "This kind of philosophy," he continues, "clears philosophy out of the way in order to let the imagination play upon the possibilities of a utopian future."[43] This is why any "philosophical" claims which Rorty makes about language, contingency of vocabularies etc., are always placed in the context of yet another useful description for our current purposes. They are never inflated into full-blown, or even *quasi*-transcendental theories. Philosophy, according to this line of thought, "is always parasitic on, and always a reaction to, developments elsewhere in culture and society."[44] Hence, the function of philosophers is not to stand over their theories as if they were delivered by a divine mid-wife. Rather, it is to come up with "better" descriptions of ourselves, where "better" means leading to a fairer and more just future.

Consequently, the philosopher will do all that he or she can to render his or her theories more accessible to those stuck in the so-called natural attitude. Indeed, such philosophers will not see the world divided into those in the natural attitude and those who have achieved the status of a transcendental ego. They will strive to make their redescriptions of our situation more plausible to all men and women so that the differences that currently separate them will one day disappear. Rorty's redescription does not claim to have risen above language so as to have, as Caputo says, "gotten beneath it." For it never pretends to be anything more than a way of thinking about language which, if adopted, might bring us closer to the ideal of a truly egalitarian society:

> . . . giving up on Plato and Kant is not the same as giving up on philosophy. For we can give better descriptions of what Plato and Kant were doing than these men were able to give of themselves. We can describe them as responding to the need to replace a human self-image which had been made obsolete by social and cultural change with a new self-image, a self-image better adapted to the results of those changes. We can add that philosophy cannot possibly end until social and cultural change ends. For such changes gradually render large-scale descriptions of ourselves and our situation obsolete. They create the need for a new language in which to formulate new descriptions.[45]

In other words, Rorty wants to change the definition of philosophy from that which defines it as a quasi-science which investigates and discloses conditions of possibility, to one which defines the philosopher as someone who tries to find ways of bringing diverse groups into greater harmony with one another.

To think of the philosopher in this way is to afford him no more privilege than any other group with similar aims. For now his job, like that of the good journalist, critic, social novelist, and principled politician, is to persuade those who are still skeptical that freedom and tolerance are more essential virtues than those which we have heretofore privileged. Having renounced his credentials as a link between the human and the nonhuman, the philosopher now considers himself as an arbiter between cultures, or as one who thinks that the goal of mankind is not to reach eternity, but to build a world in which fraternity and solidarity between all peoples is prized above all else. In such a world, the philosopher would not pride himself on his rational faculties or his wisdom, but on his imagination.

The big difference, thus, between Caputo and Derrida, on the one hand, and Rorty on the other, is that the latter admits that his "philosophical" take on things is only a more useful description of our situation, useful for our current purposes, and is no closer to the way things really are than any other description. Both Caputo and Derrida never make such an admission. Rorty does not, as Caputo argues, have a "competing and appealing non-foundationalist, non-metaphysical but still philosophical line . . . with which to outwit other philosophical lines, a line that is nicely situated in the locale of what Derrida calls the quasi-transcendental."[46] Rorty is not in the business of trying to outwit at all. His anti-essentialism will not allow him to condemn any competing philosophical viewpoint for being wrong or out of touch. No such viewpoint can be judged against an ideal standard which transcends our human needs and interests. All we can say, once more, is that such and such a viewpoint is better than its competitors because it helps us to realize *our* particular aims more efficiently than any other tried so far. So Rorty is in no position to claim that he and Derrida are right and Aquinas or Augustine wrong. All he can afford to say is that if you privilege the goal of universal democratic fraternity above all else, then you are more likely to find the tools of deconstruction and pragmatism more useful than the tools of scholastic metaphysics. But if you feel the quite legitimate human need to get in touch with something more than human, then Plato, Aristotle, Aquinas, Augustine, and Kant are more likely candidates to help you satisfy such urges. With this move I believe Rorty does indeed manage to circumvent the *quasi*-transcendental.

THE VOICE OF PROPHESY

Let us now see how all this cashes out in political terms. I began this essay by stressing that Rorty's objective is to "clear the road for prophets and poets," so as "to make intellectual life a bit simpler and safer for those who have visions of new communities."[47] We have learned from Jack Caputo's writings over the past fifteen years or so, that Derrida is one such prophet, that his eye is always cast towards the future. As I also mentioned at the outset, Derrida is not your common or garden variety of prophet, not one who is in the business of predicting the end of days, but rather a prophet *without prophesy*. For him, the present order is but a contingently configured formation which is no less subject to the vagaries and vicissitudes of time and chance as the lilies of the field and the birds of the air. What Derrida loves is the unpredictability of events, their uncontrollability. So he is a prophet of hope rather than of doom. It is this central motif in Derrida's work which Caputo has picked up on and made much of. In so doing, he has helped us to reappraise Derrida, to see him more as an apostle of Kierkegaard and Levinas, and less as the twentieth century's incarnation of the bad side of Nietzsche.

My own belief is that Rorty is another such prophet without prophesy. I do not consider his passion and hope for what is to come as being any less intense than Derrida's. As argued above, the common theme stretching throughout Rorty's work since *Philosophy and the Mirror of Nature*, is that of social hope. Rorty's hope is for a time when fraternity and solidarity are achieved on a global scale, when caste and class collapse beneath the weight of every individual's right to be treated, first and foremost, as a member of the type of cosmopolitan utopia envisaged in the Christian scriptures, a utopia in which social justice is privileged above all else. As he instructs:

> Moral development in the individual, and moral progress in the human species as a whole, is a matter of remarking human beings so as to enlarge the variety of the relationships which constitute those selves. The ideal limit of this process of enlargement is the self envisaged in the Christian and Buddhist accounts of sainthood—an ideal self to whom the hunger and suffering of *any* human being (and even, perhaps, that of any other animal) is intensely painful.[48]

Having given up on the appearance-reality distinction, Rorty substitutes the desire for eternal salvation with hope for a human future in which the social divisions perpetuated by belief in post mortem rewards are surmounted. If you think, as Rorty does, that the noblest virtue the human being possesses is his or her ability to cooperate with *all* others so as to strengthen our sense of solidarity and fraternity, then you will not regret exchanging the Platonic description of our situation for one which emphasizes the relativity of descriptions to purposes. That is, if you yearn for a time when artificial boundaries between people no longer matter, you will not mourn the passing of a vocabulary which privileged the contemplators (those with more of the special added ingredient which makes us truly human) over the doers (those with less of the special added ingredient, or those in the lower echelons of the order of being). The reason why Rorty's "less useful and more useful" distinction is better than the Greek distinctions, is because it helps us to turn our eyes towards an open-ended future, a future in which ever new and more imaginative descriptions of ourselves are tried out and tested. Of course, there will never come a time when we hit upon a description that comes closest to the way we *really* are, for there is no limit to the amount of descriptions we can dream up. But we can hope that future descriptions of ourselves and our world will approximate more and more to the ideal self envisaged by Christian and Buddhist accounts of sainthood.

Caputo, however, does not fully appreciate this side of Rorty. He does not think, in other words, that Rorty's social hope is as prophetic as Derrida's. While Derrida dreams of a "democracy to come," a democracy which no particular structure or existing framework can be said to exemplify, "Rorty's tendencies are more protective of the existing frame of reference, more attached to the American way, and hence they run the risk of being unguarded about the shortcomings of American democracy."[49] I find such a reading of Rorty totally at odds with the latter's unbounded hope for what an open-ended future may throw up, as well as with his belief that no identity—national or personal—is closer to the essence or nature of humanity than any other. Caputo thinks that the reason why Rorty is less passionate than Derrida about "the democracy to come," is because when Derrida talks in such "messianic" terms he "tends to sound uncomfortably preternatural or even *religious*, a category to which Rorty has an even greater allergy than 'transcendental.'" Caputo goes on to argue that "Rorty approves of some sort of 'civil religion,' like that of William James and Dewey, which means a living faith in democracy, but he has no time for religion in any stronger sense, and it makes him downright nervous when Derrida starts sounding like a Jewish prophet—or like Levinas."[50]

Let me address each of these concerns in turn. Firstly, as I have argued in other contexts, it is a mistake to think that Rorty favors some sort of American parochialism or provincialism, or that he represents some form of crypto-nationalist who considers the nation-state as the acme of political progress. How could someone who is so attentive to the fragility and contingency of vocabularies and to the ineluctability of time and chance, as well as someone whose track record as an ardent anti-essentialist and anti-foundationalist is unblemished, be any less committed to keeping the established order or the existing framework open to change than Derrida or Caputo? It would surely be out of kilter with his nominalism for Rorty to argue that the American way of life, or any other presently existing way of life for that matter, is closer to an ideal state of affairs or to human nature than any other. All he is entitled to say in this regard is that the concrete advantages of one particular description of ourselves outweigh those of the presently available alternative descriptions, given *our current purposes*. From a pragmatist's point of view, the sole way of determining which communities are better than others is to ask which are more likely to afford as many of their citizens as possible the wherewithal to maximize their chances of greater happiness, freedom, and fraternity. So when Rorty talks of "achieving our country," he ought to be interpreted as saying, if he is to be consistent, that of the presently available alternatives our description of ourselves is more likely to bring us into a greater degree of solidarity and fraternity than any hitherto dreamed up.

When Rorty speaks of "our country" or "America," therefore, he does not have any topographical configuration in mind. Rather, he is referring to a frame of mind which considers freedom and equality as the highest goals of humanity; he is referring to a description of ourselves which is not predicated upon the appearance-reality distinction, but on the "more useful, less useful" distinction. He has in mind something like the America of the Founding Fathers, one in which the metaphysical picture of the Old World, would be replaced by a description of ourselves which enabled us to realize "that trust, social cooperation and social hope are where our humanity begins and ends."[51] As Rorty observes in an essay entitled, "Back to Class Politics":

> The whole point of America was that it was going to be the world's first classless society. It was going to be a place where janitors, executives, professors, nurses, and sales clerks would look each other in the eye and respect each other as fellow citizens. It was going to be a place where their kids all went to the same schools, and where they got the same treatment from the police and the courts.[52]

So on this reading, "America" does not stand for the America of the here and now, but the form of life (*qua* description) dreamed up by those who yearned to see the day when metaphysics and orthodox monotheism would be replaced by a will to see the Kingdom of God realized here on earth in the form of social justice for all. "America," in this context, connotes both a repudiation of the metaphysics of presence and an experimental frame of mind. It is "shorthand for a new conception of what it is to be human."[53] "Achieving America," thus, suggests achieving a casteless and classless society which looks to the future rather than to eternity.

Caputo will rejoin, no doubt, that—as he puts it in "Parisian Hermeneutics and Yankee Hermeneutics"—". . . I am worried, and I am sure Derrida would be worried, that Rorty is just too unguarded about this name 'United States of America,' too 'complacent' about 'our country'—those are the spooks that scare Derrida—that Rorty ought to be a more ironic and cautious nominalist about this name and even about the older name democracy. His love of 'our country' ought to be paleonymical, the love of an old name which may or may not need to be replaced down the road, a road that Rorty should agree is unforeseeable."[54] But this is exactly what Rorty *does* think. As argued above, Rorty is, like Derrida, a prophet without prophesy, one whose hope is not "that the future will conform to a plan, will fulfil an immanent teleology, but rather that the future will astonish and exhilarate."[55] No description of ourselves or our world is more essential than any other because, for all the reasons purveyed above, no such description is any closer to reality than any other. So identity is something we make up as we go along. While we cannot take leave of our socio-cultural skins, we can nevertheless make them more malleable by continually expanding and adding to our presently available self-descriptions.

For Rorty, there is no end to enquiry, no point at which the human species will settle down having convinced itself that it has come up with one *true* description of the way things really are. What metaphysicians usually call "truth," Rorty calls a more justified set of practices given our current needs and interests, a set of practices which will one day, when the needs and interests of future generations change, become obsolete. Hence, we must always use the adjective "true" in a *cautious*—as distinct from an *absolute* or *objective*—sense. This, says Rorty, is "the voice of prophesy." In a remarkable passage which makes the differences between Derrida and Rorty at a political level appear somewhat factitious, the latter addresses the type of concern expressed by Caputo head on:

> So I think of the cautionary use of "true," the use in which it swings free of present practices of justification, as the voice of prophesy. This voice says, Some day the world will be changed, and then this proposition may turn out to be true. That romantic hope for another world which is yet to come is at the heart of the anti-Platonist's quest for spiritual perfection. I am tempted to follow Derrida in thinking of such hope as marking the fundamental difference between the Jews and the Greeks. . . . I think of romantic (or, for Derrida, Judaic) hope as saying, Some day all of these truth candidates . . . may be obsolete; for a much better world is to come—one in which we shall have wonderful new truth candidates. . . . I am obsessed by the possibility of the disclosure of new worlds. My deep wish for everything to be wonderfully, utterly changed keeps me from saying that truth is idealized rational acceptability. After all, you can only idealize what you have already got. But maybe there is something you cannot even dream of.[56]

Rorty, no less than Caputo and Derrida, is "obsessed by the possibility of the disclosure of new worlds." As such, he does not afford any special favor or privilege to the world *as it is now*. Indeed, he hopes that one day everything will be utterly and beautifully changed, that our current self-descriptions will give way to redescriptions that render them defunct. If, as Caputo tells us time and again, Derrida's passion is not for "the possible," or for what is foreseeable and programmable, predictable and calculable, but for what shatters the horizon of expectation, for "the *impossible*," then it may be assumed, given his predilection for the Jewish voice of prophesy, that Rorty is no less committed to dreaming this impossible dream. I simply cannot agree with the contention that "when Derrida starts sounding like a Jewish prophet" Rorty becomes "downright nervous."[57] For it is precisely this strain in Derrida's thought which appeals to Rorty above all else.

All cultures are, according to Rorty, "engaged in a project the outcome of which is unpredictable."[58] Like Derrida, he urges that we give up the tendency to think of history as having a teleological momentum, or as having a predetermined goal towards which we are getting ever closer. This is why it is wrong to compare Rorty's position with that of Francis Fukuyama, whose celebration of "the end of history" Derrida rightly derides.[59] For Rorty, a genuine romantic hero is someone like Vaclav Havel, someone who "seems to go all the way in substituting groundless hope for theoretical insight,"[60] someone for whom the teleological theory of history promulgated by the likes of Lenin and Kojeve, is best forgotten. For there is no telling where we are going to end up, no predicting the direction future generations will take. As prophets of social hope, "we are not so much fearing to lose our identity as *hoping* to lose it." We are not committed, that is, to what Rorty calls "a culture of endurance,"[61] a culture which continually confirms "its own identity by systematic processes of exclusion."[62] Rather, we are committed to a "culture of permanent revolution" or a "culture of experimentation"[63]—a culture, in other words, which is constantly on the lookout for "toeholes" in its moral and political fabric, gaps and apertures which open up new horizons of possibility and new candidates for belief. Consequently, we passionately hope that our society can "become a different society," one which is willing "to enlarge its imagination and merge with other groups, other human possibilities, so as to form the barely imaginable, cosmopolitan society of the future."

For Rorty, thus, cultures do not have distinct essences. They are, rather, sets of shared practices that can be interwoven with other sets to enlarge the scope of both sets. The faculty which helps most in the attempt to break down traditional ethnic, tribal, religious, and political boundaries, is not reason but *imagination*. If, like Rorty, you romantically long and hope for a time when the type of universal fraternity suggested in the "Christian and Buddhist accounts of sainthood" becomes a reality, you will not regret the passing of a particular culture. For you will want to minimize as many differences which presently separate people as you can. This does not mean, of course, that you will actively seek the demise of cultures. But it does mean that you will try to persuade people that an ideal self is one "to whom the hunger and suffering of *any* human being (and even, perhaps, that of any animal) is intensely painful,"[64] irrespective of his or her ethnicity. Such a culture of permanent revolution will continually look for ways to enlarge its horizon; it will actively imagine ways to transform its moral identity or its current self-description. Solidarity, according to this view, is "not discovered by reflection but created." It is always something to be achieved, something *to come*. For, as argued, there is no true description of ourselves out there waiting for us to stumble upon it, but only more useful descriptions yet to be imagined.

One particularly powerful description of ourselves for the purposes of engendering greater solidarity amongst diverse groups is "potential fellow-sufferers." Rorty considers such a redescription of our moral identity as "making it more difficult to marginalize people different from ourselves by thinking 'They do not feel it as *we* would,' or 'There must always be suffering, so why not let *them* suffer?'" To imagine people thus, demands that we increase "our sensitivity to the particular details of the pain and humiliation of other, unfamiliar sorts of people."[65] This is achieved not by attempting to "effect large theoretical syntheses of the 'spirit' or the 'essence' of distinct cultures," but by people who "in the course of the next few centuries, unravel each culture into a multiplicity of fine component threads and then weave these threads together with equally fine threads drawn from other cultures."[66] For Rorty, the person who is best set to undertake the task of stitching cultures together in this way is, what he calls, the "agent of love" or the "specialist in particularity."[67] Such individuals—the ethnographer, the muck-raking journalist, the socially concerned novelist, and the responsible historian—force us to take notice of the pain and suffering of other unfamiliar groups of people in a much more vivid, detailed, and striking way, than we have hitherto. Their work appeals to imagination and sympathy, to feeling and empathy, as distinct from reason and theory. They endeavor to realize imaginative identification with individuals whom we have heretofore regarded as being alien, foreign, different, or untouchable, thus making it more difficult to see *them* as being distinct from *us*. To redescribe ourselves in the light of the findings of the agent of love, is to reappraise the story we have traditionally told about ourselves; it is to broaden one's narrative so as to accommodate the novel and the new. It is to become a specialist in detail.

The reason why Rorty urges that we come to think of imagination rather than reason as the most eminent moral faculty, is because the former is short on detail. Moral theory, in other words, tends to describe human beings in distinctly abstract terms (rational agent, etc.), or in terms which tend to favor universality above particularity. But can ethnic, religious, and tribal differences be surmounted by ignoring particularity? Rorty believes, rightly in my estimation, that it cannot. For, as he argues, "{i}f you told most white Americans before the American Civil War that the blacks were rational agents in Kant's sense, they would not get your point. They would insist that these creatures are *black* and that that it is a good enough reason to treat them very differently."[68] However, after Harriet Beecher Stowe's *Uncle Tom's Cabin*, captured the imagination of these same white Americans, the belief that blacks were devoid of the "special added ingredient" which makes us truly

human, became a little less plausible. As such, the agent of love is better
equipped, as Rorty says in his debate with Lyotard, to remind us "of our cus-
tomary imperialist hypocrisy,"[69] for she forces us to imaginatively redescribe
ourselves in an effort to accommodate those for whom we have spilled sentimental tears. In a passage which so reminiscent of Caputo in *Against Ethics*,
Rorty spells out the consequences of privileging imagination and particularity above theory and universality:

> In a moral world based on what {Milan} Kundera calls "the wisdom
> of the novel" moral comparisons and judgments would be made
> with the help of proper names rather than general terms or general
> principles. A society which took its moral vocabulary from novels
> rather than from ontico-theological or ontico-moral treatises would
> not ask itself questions about human nature, the point of human
> existence, or the meaning of human life. Rather, it would ask itself
> what we can do so as to get along with each other, how we can
> arrange things so as to be comfortable with one another, how insti-
> tutions can be changed so that everyone's right to be understood has
> a better chance of being gratified.[70]

"Social protest," on this view, "is not a matter of what you call 'diagnosis
regarding the state of the psyche' but rather of calling attention to the effects
of injustice on the victims."[71]

So when Caputo cautions Rorty to balance the "lofty vision of the founding 'fathers,'" by "singing songs to today's *immigrants*,"[72] I can only rejoin that
Rorty's poetry of social hope has never been written for anyone but those same
immigrants. Rorty, like Derrida, looks to a world in which we have ceased
"interfering with our children's marriage plans because of national origin, religion, race, or wealth of the intended partner, or because the marriage will be
homosexual rather than heterosexual."[73] He looks to a time when the works of
the agents of love and connoisseurs of particularity will have "replaced the ser-
mon and the treatise as the principal vehicles of moral change and progress."[74]
For these "works of brilliant bricolage,"[75] as argued above, serve to sew unfamiliar groups together "with a thousand little stitches," thus invoking "a thousand little commonalites between their members. . . ."[76] The ideal result will be
a barely imaginable culture which "will find the cultures of *contemporary
America* and contemporary India as suitable for benign neglect as we find
those of Harappa or of Cartage."[77] (*my emphasis*)

This is Rorty's romantic-Jewish hope, a hope for a much better world to
come, one which will have redescribed and enlarged its moral identity to
such a degree that traditional "systematic processes of exclusion" will have
been surmounted. In this culture of constant revolution, a culture in which

humanity is considered an ongoing adventure, the outcome of which is totally unpredictable, there would be no tears shed for the loss of "our country," "our nation," or "our identity." For all these are just shorthand for "the way we are now." But for those who speak in praise of prophesy, there is an abiding hope that a much better way can be imagined, or that a new world may be disclosed, a world which transcends *our* wildest dreams. Accordingly, we ought to interpret Rorty's call to "achieve our country," as a call to let go of cultures of endurance which still cling to philosophies of presence and Greek dualisms, and to cultivate a frame of mind which thinks of the self as an experiment in the making, or a constant process of enlargement like that envisioned in the Christian and Buddhist accounts of sainthood, or indeed in Derrida's notion of a "democracy to come."

Caputo will certainly object to this latter comparison; he is likely to argue that when Rorty uses "we" it "smacks of the assimilative commonality and community"[78] which Derrida has taught us rightly to distrust. But I think Rorty is much more circumspect in this regard than either Derrida or Caputo appreciate. For, as noted above, he does not think that cultures have deep essences, or that there is any ideal standard against which to judge them. The "we" of any culture is but a loosely constituted web of beliefs and practices which can be rewoven with other webs at many levels and for many reasons. Indeed, if there is to be genuine moral and political progress, Rorty argues, "[t]he only 'we' we need is a local and temporary one,"[79] what Derrida and Caputo call the "we" who cannot say "we." The agents of love continually confront us with the possibility of breaking down traditional biases which make it seem as though there is an unbridgeable gap separating "us"—"the paradigmatic human beings"—from "such dubious cases of humanity as foreigners, infidels, untouchables, women, homosexuals, half-breeds, and deformed or crippled people."[80]

As a philosopher of universal solidarity and fraternity, Rorty is as distrustful as Derrida of any system or structure which claims to be anything more than a highly miscegenated, malleable, and provisional formation, one which is constantly trying to enlarge its range of sympathies and to be ever more responsive "to the needs of a larger and larger variety of people and things."[81] His hope is that we will never cease to imagine ourselves differently, that we will forever strive to come up with novel and original descriptions of ourselves which get us ever closer to the type of harmony dreamed of in the Christian scriptures and in Derrida's "messianic hope for justice." This is why, when in discussion with Habermas on the relative merits of the pragmatic approach to political questions, Rorty appeals to Derrida's later work— the work around which Caputo has so beautifully and eloquently weaved his most evocative texts. Both Caputo and Rorty consider "the messianic hope for justice" to be Derrida's most important notion. Indeed, Rorty goes so far as to argue that with this appeal to justice beyond law, Derrida has signalled the culmination of "European Emersonianism":

> Derrida nowadays puts a great deal of emphasis on what he calls "the only deconstructable notion," namely, the messianic hope for justice. If you think of Derrida as the culmination of European Emersonianism, you will think of him as saying something like this: "If we stop thinking of truth as the name of the thing that gives human life its meaning, and stop agreeing with Plato that the search for truth is the central human activity, then we can replace the search for truth with the messianic hope of justice."[82]

Could it be, therefore, that Rorty possesses the same type of religious sensitivity as Derrida when it comes to matters political? Let me conclude by saying why I believe this to be the case.

I cited above Caputo's contention that "Rorty approves of some sort of 'civil religion,' like that of William James and Dewey, which means a living faith in democracy, but he has no time for religion in any stronger sense, and it makes him downright nervous when Derrida starts sounding like a Jewish prophet. . . ."[83] I have tried to show why I believe the latter part of this statement does not chime with Rorty's panegyrics on behalf of Derrida's romantic cum Jewish "hope for another world which is yet to come."[84] If one now accepts that Rorty's overriding passion is for such Derridean justice, then it is not incorrect to assume that Rorty is as religious as Derrida, if, that is, one defines "religion" in the same terms as Caputo when he says: ". . . deconstruction is set in motion by an overarching aspiration, which on a certain analysis can be called a religious or prophetic aspiration, what would have been called in the plodding language of the tradition . . . a movement of 'transcendence.'" "Deconstruction, as a movement of transcendence," he continues, "means excess, the exceeding of the stable borders of what is presently available."[85] Such a "religion without religion" eschews dogmatism, fundamentalism, sectarianism; "{i}t repeats the passion for the messianic promise and messianic expectation, *sans* the concrete messianisms of the positive religions that wage endless war and spill the blood of the other. . . ."[86]

Caputo, following Derrida, wants to save the religious disposition from religious fanaticism; he wants to save faith, *qua* groundless hope, from those who claim to have direct knowledge of the Divine, or from those who believe themselves to be in possession of the "Truth." Such religion without religion takes justice for the outcasts and the marginalized as the principal religious category. If defined in this way, little separates Rorty's civic religion from that espoused by Derrida and Caputo. For Rorty is not, as Caputo maintains, anti-religion; after having dispensed with the appearance-reality distinction, he is not in a position to say that the religious description of the world and our-selves is the right or the wrong description. He cannot, in other words, con-demn religion on the basis that there is no evidence for its claims. All he can afford to say is that it is useful for particular purposes and not for others. So, to be consistent with his pragmatist position outlined above, Rorty cannot allow himself to scoff at, or deride religion. He can, however, recommend that religious fundamentalism be privatized because it is less useful for polit-ical purposes than the discourse of social democratic politics. That is, the dis-course of religious fundamentalism is less likely to work "as a basis for social organization" than "the idea of fraternity and equality."[87]

Rorty follows Dewey in defining the "religious," as distinct from "religion," as "a faith in the future possibilities of mortal humans, a faith which is hard to distinguish from love for, and hope for, the human community."[88] It is entirely plausible according to Rorty, thus, to be religious without having any strong commitment to any concrete religion as such. On Rorty's terms, you are being eminently religious when, like Derrida, you passionately hope for a world which is yet to come, or when you have groundless/messianic hope for justice, or for the future possibilities of the human community. Such is what he terms a "religion of love" or, as suggested, a "civic religion." Rorty's religion of love endeavors to sever the "traditional link between the religious impulse, the impulse to stand in awe of something greater than oneself,"[89] from the attempt to acquire knowledge of the will of God. It looks to a formless future full of sur-prise and unpredictability in the hope that it might present us with possibilities which we, from our limited perspective, consider impossible. It is a religion which has at its core the theologies of the "Social Gospel" and "the most social-istic of the papal encyclicals." For each of these has, according to Rorty, privi-leged the prophetic or the messianic over the formal and concrete messianisms, thus enabling "the struggle for social justice to transcend the con-troversies between theists and atheists." According to the knights of social jus-tice, "we should read the New Testament as saying that how we treat each other on earth matters a great deal more than the outcome of debate concern-ing the existence or nature of another world."[90] We should, that is, have as our primary religious ideal the form of fraternity which the Christian and Buddhist accounts of sainthood recommend.

In dreaming of the democracy to come, therefore, both Derrida and Rorty hope it will take the form of such a barely imaginable classless and casteless world, a world in which hospitality will be given as freely to the widow, the orphan, and the stranger, as it is to our own. Such hospitality, says Rorty, is "the redeemed form of God."[91] It amounts to what John Dominick Crossan calls, when talking about the social ideals of the historical Jesus, "radical egalitarianism."[92] It is a hope that one day the Kingdom of God may be realized here on earth. On this reading, Rorty's religion of love, his civic religion of social hope, is no more or less religious or prophetic than Derrida's religion without religion. While both eschew the literalness of the Scriptures, the belief in divine favor and retribution, as well as the "efficacy of the sacraments," they nevertheless remain inspired by the religious impulse. To paraphrase Derrida, the constancy of God in their lives is called by other names, and they both believe, to quote Rorty, "that the sort of 'aggressive atheism' on which Nietzsche prided himself is unnecessarily intolerant."[93] When Derrida says that he "rightly passes for an atheist," or that he does not know whether he believes in God or not, he is echoing Rorty's belief that "{a}ll of us, I think, fluctuate . . . between God as a perhaps obsolete name for a possible human future, and God as an external guarantor of some such future."[94] Both have what Dorothy Allison calls, "a kind of atheist's religion"[95] (for Rorty a most felicitous phrase and one which he cites approvingly) or a religiousness which is forged from, as Rorty nicely puts it, the "fuzzy overlap of faith, hope and love."[96]

I hope that these reflections may convince Jack Caputo that Richard Rorty is perhaps more of a kindred spirit than he has heretofore believed him to be. For I long for a day when men of such admirable character will stand shoulder to shoulder in an effort to revive the Left from the apathy and lethargy to which it appears to have succumbed. Both of these prophets continually remind us that what matters more than truth is justice, and that justice is only justice when it calls attention to the plight the poor. Such is their religion without religion. But their's are lonely voices in a world which is witnessing the alarming reemergence of conservative forces on both sides of the Atlantic. Surely now is the time for these voices of prophesy to start singing from the same hymn sheet. If they do so, it might just be possible to transform the political landscape in a way which Rorty's fictional writer of the following passage has in mind, a passage which Caputo could very well have written:

> Here, in the late twenty-first century, as talk of fraternity and unselfishness has replaced talk of rights, . . . political discourse has come to be dominated by quotations from Scripture and literature, rather than from political theorists and social scientists. Fraternity, like friendship, was not a concept that either philosophers or lawyers knew how to handle. They could formulate principles of justice, equality and liberty, and invoke these principles when weighing hard moral or legal issues. But how to formulate a "principle of fraternity"? Fraternity is an inclination of the heart, one that produces a sense of shame at having much when others have little. It is not the sort of thing that anybody can have a theory about or that people can be argued into having.[97]

NOTES

1. Walter Rauschenbusch, *Prayers of Social Awakening* (Boston: Pilgrim Press, 1909), p. 101. Cited in Richard Rorty, *Achieving Our Country: Leftist Thought in Twentieth-Century America* (Cambridge: Harvard University Press, 1998), p. 59.

2. Ibid., p. 60.

3. Richard Rorty, "Failed Prophecies, Glorious Hopes" in *Philosophy and Social Hope* (London: Penguin Books, 1999), p. 204.

4. Richard Rorty, "The Notion of Rationality" in Josef Niznik and John T. Sanders eds. *Debating the State of Philosophy* (Westport: Praeger, 1996), p. 85.

5. Rorty, *Philosophy and Social Hope*, p. xiii.

6. Richard Rorty, *Truth and Progress: Philosophical Papers III* (Cambridge: Cambridge University Press, 1998), pp. 214–215.

7. See "The Becoming Possible of the Impossible: An Interview with Jacques Derrida" this volume.

8. Rorty, *Philosophy and Social Hope*, p. xii.

9. Rorty, "The End of Leninism, Havel, and Social Hope" in *Truth and Progress*, p. 243.

10. Ibid., p. 236.

11. Rorty, "Failed Prophecies, Glorious Hopes," pp. 203–204.

12. Ibid., p. 205.

13. Ibid.

14. I have argued at some length against Critchley's interpretation of Rorty in my "Private Irony vs. Social Hope: Derrida, Rorty, and the Political" in *Cultural Values* Vol. 3 No. 3, July 1999 (Oxford: Blackwell), pp. 263–290, and in "The Civic Religion of Social Hope: A Response to Simon Critchley," *Philosophy and Social Criticism*, vol. 27 no. 5, pp. 35–58.

15. John D. Caputo, "Parisian Hermeneutics and Yankee Hermeneutics" in MRH, pp. 84–124.

16. Ibid., p. 96.

17. "A World Without Substances or Essences" in *Philosophy and Social Hope*, pp. 53–54.

18. Jacques Derrida "Afterword: Toward and Ethic of Discussion" in *Limited INC* (Evanston: Northwestern University Press, 1988), p. 148.

19. Richard Rorty, "Inquiry as Recontextualization: An Anti-Dualist Account of Interpretation" in *Objectivity, Relativism, and Truth: Philosophical Papers Vol. I* (Cambridge: Cambridge University Press, 1991), p. 102.

20. "Parisian Hermeneutics," pp. 96–97.

21. Ibid., p. 96.

22. Ibid.

23. *Philosophy and Social Hope*, p. xiii.

24. Rorty, "Pragmatism, Pluralism, and Postmodernism" in *Philosophy and Social Hope*, p. 266.

25. Rorty, "Relativism: Finding and Making" in *Philosophy and Social Hope*, p. xxii.

26. *Objectivity, Relativism, and Truth*, p. 13.

27. "A World without Substances or Essences," p. 48.

28. Ibid., p. 54.

29. Rorty, "Pragmatism and Post-Nietzschean Philosophy" in *Essays on Heidegger and Others" Philosophical Papers, Vol. II* (Cambridge: Cambridge University Press, 1991), p. 4.

30. *Objectivity, Relativism, and Truth*, p. 6.

31. Rorty, "Truth without Correspondence to Reality" in *Philosophy and Social Hope*, p. 29.

32. Rorty, "Pragmatism, Pluralism, and Postmodernism," p. 273.

33. Rorty, "A World without Substances or Essences," pp. 65–66.

34. Rorty, "Pragmatism and Post-Nietzschean Philosophy," p. 3.

35. Ibid., p. 4.

36. Caputo, "Parisian Hermeneutics," p. 96.

37. Ibid.

38. Ibid., p. 107.

39. Ibid.

40. Ibid.

41. Ibid.

42. Ibid., p. 109.

43. Rorty, "Globalization, the Politics of Identity and Social Hope" in *Philosophy and Social Hope*, pp. 238–239.

44. Rorty, "Philosophy and the Future" in Herman J. Saatkamp ed. *Rorty and Pragmatism* (Nashville: Vanderbilt University Press, 1995), p. 199.

45. Ibid., p. 198.

46. Caputo, "Parisian Hermeneutics," p. 111.

47. Rorty, "Feminism and Pragmatism" in *Truth and Progress*, p. 215.

48. Rorty, "Ethics without Principles" in *Philosophy and Social Hope*, p. 79.

49. Caputo, "Parisian Hermeneutics," p. 121.

50. Ibid., p. 112.

51. Rorty, *Philosophy and Social Hope*, p. xv.

52. Rorty, "Back to Class Politics," in *Philosophy and Social Hope*, p. 259.

53. Rorty, *Achieving Our Country*, p. 18.

54. Caputo, "Parisian Hermeneutics," p. 124.

55. Rorty, "Truth without Correspondence to Reality," p. 28.

56. Rorty, *Debating the State of Philosophy*, pp. 50–51.

57. Caputo, "Parisian Hermeneutics," p. 112.

58. Rorty, *Debating the State of Philosophy*, p. 85.

59. See Jacques Derrida, SoM.

60. Rorty, "The End of Leninism, Havel, and Social Hope" in *Truth and Progress*, p. 236.

61. Rorty in Anindita Niyogi Balslev, *Cultural Otherness: Correspondence with Richard Rorty* (Atlanta: Scholars Press, 1999), p. 42. This volume takes the form of a highly informative set of exchanges between Balslev and Rorty. It is from the latter's correspondence that I am quoting.

62. Rorty, *Debating the State of Philosophy*, p. 85.

63. Rorty in Balslev, *Cultural Otherness*, p. 43.

64. Rorty, "Ethics Without Principles," p. 79.

65. Richard Rorty, *Contingency, Irony, and Solidarity* (Cambridge: Cambridge University Press, 1989), p. xvi.

66. Rorty, "Rationality and Cultural Difference" in *Truth and Progress*, p. 201.

67. See Rorty, "On Ethnocentrism: A Reply to Clifford Geertz" in *Objectivity, Relativism, and Truth*.

68. Rorty, *Debating the State of Philosophy*, p. 49.

69. Rorty, "Cosmopolitanism without Emancipation: A Response to Jean-Francois Lyotard" in *Objectivity, Relativism, and Truth*, p. 219.

70. "Philosophers, Novelists, and Inter-Cultural Comparisons," p. 118.

71. Rorty in Balselv, *Cultural Otherness*, p. 45.

72. Caputo, "Parisian Hermeneutics," p. 124.

73. Rorty, "Ethics Without Principles," p. 86.

74. Rorty, *Contingency, Irony, and Solidarity*, p. xvi.

75. Rorty in Balslev, *Cultural Otherness*, p. 69.

76. Rorty, "Ethics Without Principles," p. 87.

77. Rorty, "Rationality and Cultural Difference," p. 201.

78. Caputo, "Parisian Hermeneutics," p. 121.

79. Rorty, "Cosmopolitanism Without Emancipation," p. 214.

80. Ibid., p. 204.

81. Rorty, "Ethics Without Principles," p. 81.

82. Rorty, *Debating the State of Philosophy*, p. 27.

83. Caputo, "Parisian Hermeneutics," p. 112.

84. Rorty, *Debating the State of Philosophy*, p. 50.

85. John D. Caputo, PT, p. xix.

86. Ibid., p. xxi.

87. Rorty, "Pragmatism as Romantic Polytheism" in Morris Dickstein ed. *The Revival of Pragmatism* (Durham: Duke University Press, 1998), p. 32.

88. Rorty "Religious Faith, Intellectual Responsibility, and Romance" in Charley D. Hardwick and Donald A. Crosby eds. *Pragmatism, Neo-Pragmatism, and Religion: Conversations with Richard Rorty* (New York: Peter Lang, 1997), p. 15.

89. Rorty, *Achieving Our Country*, p. 18.

90. Rorty, "Failed Prophecies, Glorious Hopes," p. 206.

91. Rorty, "Religious Faith, Intellectual Responsibility, and Romance," p. 17.

92. John Dominick Crossan, *Jesus: A Revolutionary Biography* (San Francisco: Harper Collins, 1995).

93. Rorty, "Pragmatism as Romantic Polytheism," p. 25.

94. Rorty, "Religious Faith, Intellectual Responsibility, and Romance," p. 16.

95. Ibid.

96. Ibid.

97. Rorty, "Looking Backwards from the Year 2096" in *Philosophy and Social Hope*, p. 248.

ACHIEVING THE IMPOSSIBLE—
RORTY'S RELIGION:
A RESPONSE TO DOOLEY

John D. Caputo

I agree with my dear friend Mark Dooley, whose great generosity and Herculean efforts have made this volume possible, that Richard Rorty is the most interesting American philosopher of the day, the one voice in American philosophy whom someone other than academic insiders read and listen to, and the most important American thinker to read Derrida and take him seriously. That is why I said in the "Introduction" to *More Radical Hermeneutics*[1] that:

> . . . the work of Richard Rorty's pragmatic and upbeat, democratic and, as I call it, "Yankee" hermeneutics, plays an important role in what follows. For Rorty has given up on the classical metaphysical idea of philosophy as a kind of super-science that cuts through the soft surface of appearances and hits the hard rock of Reality, even as he has given up on the modern and transcendental idea of philosophy as . . . a higher meta-scientific tribunal before which the several sciences present their disparate findings for adjudication. So Rorty is to be included in my catalogue of the masters of non-knowing . . . a hero for those of us who think that we get the best results by disavowing any claims to any secret *savoir absolue*.

Add to that my admiration for Rorty's command of the idiom of American English and you would think Mark Dooley would be a happy man. But Dooley wants me to put my money where my mouth is, to walk the walk and not just talk the talk about having an "American voice." My man in Dublin wants me to get behind this American or rather stand shoulder to shoulder with him and work for our common cause. Dooley is a hard bargainer, and I can see I will have to do a good deal more before I can put a smile on his face. He has made a rigorous argument that has put Rorty in a slightly different light for me, enlisting Rorty *too* in this religion without religion and making of him, if you can believe it, a believer in the impossible. Where will it stop?

Mark Dooley and I are agreed that Rorty and Derrida have similar projects: a non-foundationalist view of knowledge even and a deep commitment to a leftist democratic politics. I have tried to fine-tune Rorty's non-foundationalism in a Derridean direction, by saying that we always need *some* account of why we cannot have a *Final* account of how things are, otherwise non-foundationalism is just a caprice of someone having a bad day. Such an account is what Derrida calls a "quasi-transcendental," which Rorty thinks is just another philosophical gimmick. As regards politics, I have suggested that we ought to put a little more space between ourselves and "our country" or "America" (or "France," or "Ireland," etc.) than Rorty is willing to do. But Dooley tells me to leave well enough alone; if anything, it is Derrida who has a thing or two to learn from Rorty. Dooley has written a stimulating essay which has given me some pause, so let us take each point in turn.

We need to avoid the suggestion that non-foundationalism is just a personality quirk of people with contrarian personalities and a dislike for absolutes, like preferring chocolate to vanilla. We need to support the idea that if someone contradicted Derrida or Rorty the latter would have a good response to make (as they always do). That means they have "good reasons" for saying that we have no access to some Pure Reason or an Ideal Meta-language in which to conclusively adjudicate competing claims. If challenged, Derrida can always point to the differential play of traces and the constitution of provisional unities of meaning through the endless process of iterability, even as Rorty can talk about endless recontextualization in virtue of which the same marks can mean different things in different contexts where they are put to different purposes. If marks were *not* indefinitely iterable or recontextualizable, Derrida and Rorty would be wrong and we would have to concede either that there are some overarching ahistorical assertions out there or find a better way of explaining why we doubt it. Otherwise, as I said in *More Radical Hermeneutics*, "the whole thing is crazy, and Derrida is just running off at the mouth."[2] That, of course, is exactly what Derrida's worst critics say he is doing and both Mark Dooley and I spend a good deal of time rebutting them. The means that Derrida has chosen to explain himself in what he calls a "quasi-transcendental," a term that he introduced by way of a joke that Rodolphe Gasché made into something deadly serious.[3] A quasi-transcendental explains why you cannot have hard or full-blown transcendentals, and why Derrida is happy enough to be called a "philosopher," which is exactly what his worst critics deny. Rorty on the other hand says that a "quasi-transcendental" is an "unnecessarily highfaluting"[4]—a good Yankee word—way to put it and that Derrida should confine his attention to making fun of words like that, and not indulge in inventing new ones that invite further ridicule. "Philosophy," says Rorty, is a category whose main use is to allow librarians to knock off at five o'clock instead of hanging around after hours wondering where to put books written by Rorty and

Derrida, Heidegger and Wittgenstein. When I argued that Rorty is being a little too disingenuous, that his notion of endless pragmatic recontextualizability constitutes a perfectly recognizable philosophical critter of just the sort that Derrida is calling in his Parisian idiom a "quasi-transcendental," that the difference is one of idiom, Mark Dooley decided to let me have it!

For Dooley insists that Derrida has gone too far in a philosophical direction and Rorty's idea of philosophy as a catalogue librarian's term is just right. Dooley says that I treat Derrida's claims as context-free claims about the Truth of Language and that I and/or Derrida have hypostasized and capitalized Language and treated it as a quasi-agent. Now, for the life of me, if I ever said that, and if Mark Dooley can show me where, I will renounce it and all its pomps. In the meantime, allow me to cite what I really did say in full:[5]

> You might even say he [Derrida] has a certain "theory," or kind of theory, although that is a strong word implying mastery and a totalizing overview and Derrida avoids it, usually preferring to speak of his "hypothesis," which is very tentative, about which he is not sure, which he hesitates to bring up before this very intimidating audience, etc. He has at least a *quasi*-theory about what is going on in language . . . , which goes under the name of the quasi-transcendental.

Rorty, on the other hand, comes off better than Derrida for Dooley because he is just "redescribing" our situation, "and he can claim neither transcendental nor quasi-transcendental status for any of his claims." Dooley wants to argue that Derrida's talk about quasi-transcendentals is not as *useful* as Rorty's talk about tools. Now I entirely agree with Mark Dooley that you will get further arguing in terms of a "set of tools" at the American Philosophical Association even as you will get further arguing about "quasi-transcendentals" at the École des Hautes Études en Sciences Sociales. Things that are more useful in EHESS are useless at the APA, and conversely. I who have let Parisian ways of speaking bleed into my Yankee English have learned that the hard way! But that in no way implicates me in thinking, or in thinking that Derrida thinks, that he has hit upon the one true objective over-arching Idea of Language. Furthermore, it in no way exonerates Rorty from coming up with answers when he gets to the Q&A period and people from the floor challenge what he is saying, in which case he will present his quasi-theory that vocabularies are sets of tools whose worth is determined by pragmatic purposes, which is his Yankee way of saying what Derrida is saying back in Paris when he speaks of a quasi-transcendental.

Dooley says that Rorty "does not claim any objective status for his philosophical take on things"—if by "objective" Dooley means "transcendental," I agree—but only that is "a more useful theory." But then let me ask Mark Dooley in turn, *why*? Why is it a *more* useful theory than its competitor theories? How can that *comparative judgment* be made? Why not say it is more useful to think of vocabularies as bunches of bananas, or as alien beings from another planet who have taken up residence in our brain stems? *Because*—here comes a philosophical reason; *Attention*! there's a philosopher in the building—vocabularies are "sets of tools" whose meaning and reference shift with shifting contexts and the shifting purposes to which they are put. Rorty puts an ironic distance between himself and people speaking in the natural attitude, steps back and offers a second order account of what they are doing when they open their mouths or turn on their word processors.[6] That account is a philosophical reason, a critter of the same type, with the same thrust and epistemic status as a quasi-transcendental. Now, of course, you *could* construe a first-order context in which it would be more useful to think of vocabularies as a bunch of bananas, in an allegory, say, or some secret code, or you might even, if you spent too much time by yourself in the woods, say that language is the house of Being, just as Derrida can find a context in which "green is or" makes sense. But *that* would be so because of the *second order claim* that vocabularies are sets of tools, which Rorty hopes sticks, or that marks are indefinitely iterable, which Derrida hopes sticks.

Mark Dooley says that Rorty's "anti-essentialism will not allow him to condemn any competing philosophical viewpoint for being wrong or out of touch." But surely *anti*-essentialist sounds at least mildly disapproving if not outright condemnatory of essentialism, which is a competing philosophical viewpoint. What does it mean to say that his anti-essentialist view is a "more useful theory" if this does not make it preferable to the "competing philosophical viewpoints" like essentialism, which must be less useful? Why does Rorty side with *anti*-essentialism? *Because* vocabularies are sets of tools whose meaning and reference are determined by use and context. Dooley is trying to slip Rorty's second order account of vocabularies under the rug of their first order use, but I think we can all see a rather large bump in that rug. In the first order natural attitude, philosophical ideas are not entertained at all, nobody ever heard of "anti-essentialist," and if anybody slumped over a bar looked up from his drink and said in a slur "vocabularies" are "sets of tools," he would empty the room. In the second order, quasi-transcendental attitude, philosophical arguments are made that we have no access to essences or hard transcendentals and that philosophy has other work to do, viz., to keep what we say about the present provisional enough to keep the future open, to keep hope alive, as Jesse Jackson says—and Rorty and Derrida, Dooley and Caputo all agree.

That brings us to politics. My argument in *Prayers and Tears* is that deconstruction embodies a kind of *prophetic politics*, a radical messianic expectation for a democracy to come. About that Mark Dooley and I are very much agreed, as we also are that the common key to understanding both Derrida and Rorty is to see that they both insist upon the tentative and provisional character of our constructions in order to keep the future open for reconstruction, and they both do so in terms of a radical democratic vision. In *More Radical Hermeneutics* I point out that Rorty has even revised his view, advanced in *Contingency, Irony and Solidarity*, that deconstruction lacks public and political significance, for he now writes:[7]

> When Derrida talks about deconstruction as prophetic of the "the democracy to come," he seems to me to be expressing the same utopian social hope as was felt by these earlier dreamers [Dewey, Mill]."

But Dooley wants to push me further, to wring from me the concession that Rorty too belongs to this prophetic religion without religion. He makes a surprisingly strong case.

For Rorty clearly thinks that Derrida has gone too far, this time not in a *philosophical* direction, but in a *religious* one. Now I have always taken Rorty to entertain a deeply *naturalistic, empiricist, secularist, humanistic, and reductionist distrust of religion* which he regards as superstitious, and that he dreams of the day when the word "God" will drop out of our vocabulary. But it is on exactly that point that Mark Dooley does a vigorous job of trying to change my mind.[8] Rorty says that Derrida and Levinas are too inclined to "offer a quasi-religious form of spiritual pathos," that talking about "the infinite, and the unrepresentable are merely nuisances," and that thinking of the "impossibility . . . of justice" is a temptation to "Gothicize," and to treat democratic politics as "ineffectual, because unable to cope with preternatural forces."[9] Talking about the *tout autre*, Rorty says, is "gawky, awkward, and unenlightening."[10] He thinks that the best thing you can do with religious ideas like that is to secularize them as swiftly and completely as possible, beat these religious swords into democratic ploughshares as fast as you can, and get on with organizing labor unions. "God" undergoes a straight, irreversible translation into democratic politics. Derrida's and Levinas's *tout autre* are "Gothic tales" full of spooks, a new theology, where we are all haunted by infinite alterity, all of which he calls not "prophetic" but rather "pointless hype."[11]

So I would ask my good friend Mark Dooley, whenever Rorty does point out the political good that religious ideas can do, is he not advocating a direct and outright *reduction* of religion into secular politics (civil religion), rather than a theory of *undecidability*?

Dooley argues, very impressively, that Rorty too is prophetic without prophesy. I would agree, and he has convinced me. But I fear to take the

next step, as Dooley daringly does toward the end of his piece, when he says
that "little separates Rorty's civil religion" from Derrida's religion without
religion. I would say that there is no spectral logic of undecidability in
Rorty's *sans*, as in Derrida, and that Rorty would *not* say, as Derrida says in
the interview that Mark Dooley himself conducted, that he does not know if
really he is an atheist. I would think that for Rorty, religion is to be translated
into politics, irreversibly and with no remainder, with no awe for something
more than human or greater than the human (which is how Sartre defined
humanism), and then we can be done with the Gothic spooks once and for
all. Except on weekends and in private for those who have a taste for spooky
things. But Derrida is interested in the way we are continually spooked by
the ghost of Marx and by the specter of the justice to come that is astir in the
religions of the Book, which is not a private matter but goes to the heart of
the political order. Rorty, like Marx, has chased away one ghost too many.

But Mark Dooley is a tough man and he will not let up. For he also wants
to give me a hard time about my claim that Derrida's notion of the democracy
to come is more messianic and open-ended than Rorty's, which is bound by
Rorty's favorite concrete messianism, American democracy. Rorty takes Derrida to be a revolutionary who wants to throw the existing order to the wolves
while waiting for some deep shift to occur in things by a mystical-religious
(Gothic) force. But Derrida, I argue, is a "piece-mealist," looking for inter-
ventions here, there, and everywhere, while keeping the future radically *open*,
so that what is *to come* may not *be called* or even *be* "democracy."[12] Rorty
draws the line in the sand at this point and says that with democracy, the West
has undergone its last conceptual revolution and the rest is fine tuning, imple-
menting, and *actualizing—"achieving"—an ideal* that has already been put in
place once and for all by the Declaration of Independence in Philadelphia.
Rorty advocates a democratic reformism, the ongoing fine tuning of the present democratic paradigm, *despite* his anti-essentialism, following a logic of
actualization or achieving the pre-set horizon of "our country," America. Derrida, on the other hand, simply regards what is presently called "democracy"
as the least bad empirical instance of the "democracy to come," in which
phrase the "to come" is more important than the "democracy." I do not identify Rorty's left-wing politics with Fukuyama's right-wing politics, but I am saying that they both make use of the same logic of asymptotic gradualism, of the
"regulative ideal" of democracy which Derrida has quite effectively criticized.

Now if in the phrase "democracy to come," "to come" is more important
than the "democracy," it also follows that *a fortiori* the "democracy" is much
more important than "America!" Let it be said that I thought I made it plain
in *More Radical Hermeneutics* that I agree with Rorty that there is a context
in which it is more useful to speak about "America" and loving our country,
and that is how I concluded my discussion:[13]

To be sure, Rorty's advocacy of "national pride" is centered on rallying us around the flag of the old and—I would like to think—timeless liberal idea of social justice . . . I agree that "we intellectuals" have to join hands with the unions and the labor movement to accomplish this. He insists that this is just not going to happen as long as "we intellectuals" sit around at conferences on postmodernism thinking up meaner and meaner things to say about the "system."

I fully agree with Rorty that in the present post-Reagan era in the United States, the only effective way to change the political scene for the better is to get the old and the new left together, to get a politically useless academic left together with labor unions, whose members distrust academics down to their bones just because of the academic distrust of nationalism, the effect of which has been to turn the country over to the right wing.

Rorty has hit upon an important political aporia facing the left in the United States. To that extent Mark Dooley and I are agreed that Rorty is right to talk about loving America. But I don't think Mark Dooley is helping us much when he defends Rorty by saying that by "America" Rorty means "freedom and equality" and "the highest goals of humanity," that "America" is "shorthand" for "what it is to be human." For that is *precisely* the unguardedness that Derrida warns against under the name of "exemplarism," and it is structurally akin to Victor Hugo saying that "France" means "humanity," to Husserl saying that "Europe" actually means "Reason," or to saying "man" when you mean "humanity" or "fraternity" when you mean friendship. That is the stuff of Eurocentrism and colonialism and of all the centrisms. I am worried that there is something unguarded in Rorty's discourse, and so is Rorty.[14]

I am grateful to Dooley for coming with texts in which Rorty seems to push past the dichotomy of the American Ideal and its current achievement or actualization, like the passage from "The Notion of Rationality," which I had not read. There Rorty says that the hope for "everything to be wonderfully, utterly changed" keeps him from speaking of "idealized rational acceptability"—which would include speaking of an "idealized America" and of "achieving" that ideal—and then adds that "you can only idealize what you have already got. But maybe there is something you cannot even dream of." At that point, I would say, Dooley has hit the mark and shown that Rorty has moved past the idea of Achieving the American Ideal and has begun to dream of what cannot be dreamt, which is to dream the impossible. That would force the exemplarist position about the American Ideal in *Achieving our Country* beyond itself. If Dooley is right, then my recommendation for a second edition of this book is a new title: *Achieving the Impossible*.

While Dooley has given me pause about Rorty the Prophet, my remaining question has to do with undecidability. What is truly interesting to me about Derrida is the fluctuation between justice, God, and the impossible, the notion that there is some irresoluble structure of hope and expectation that will not allow itself to be resolved into one determinate form or historical shape, religious, philosophical, or political. I am not surprised to hear Rorty say that the name of God can be put to work in the name of hope for social justice, or to hear him speak of an atheist's religion, but I am inclined to take such remarks in the sense of a reductionistic Deweyan naturalism, viz., that we can and should translate the name of God into a democratic political aspiration, and that translation is a one-way street. The question that is provoked by Mark Dooley's splendid paper is this: does the translation go *both ways?* Is Rorty open to the idea that the love of justice also constitutes a way to love God, even if we do not know that it is God we love? I would say not, but if I do, my dear friend Mark Dooley will never let me hear the end of it.

NOTES

1. John D. Caputo, MRH, p. 7.

2. John D. Caputo, MRH, p. 99.

3. Jacques Derrida, *Glas*, pp. 151a–162a. See Rodolphe Gasché, *The Tain of the Mirror* (Cambridge: Harvard University Press, 1986).

4. *Deconstruction and Pragmatism: Simon Critchley, Jacques Derrida, Ernesto Laclau and Richard Rorty*, ed. Chantal Mouffe (London: Routledge, 1996), p. 16.

5. John D. Caputo, MRH, p. 96.

6. John D. Caputo, MRH, pp. 107–109

7. *Deconstruction and Pragmatism*, p. 13–14; cf. MRH, p. 277n33.

8. Rorty recently reviewed Garry Will's *Papal Sin* with great glee. See Richard Rorty, "Acting Fallible," review of Garry Wills, *Papal Sin: Structures of Deceit* (New York: Doubleday, 2000), in *New York Times Sunday Book Review*, June 11, 2000, p. 10

9. Richard Rorty, *Achieving our Country: Leftist Thought in Twentieth Century America* (Cambridge: Harvard University Press, 1998), pp. 96–97.

10. *Deconstruction and Pragmatism*, p. 41.

11. *Deconstruction and Pragmatism*, p. 42.

12. See "Politics and Friendship: An Interview with Jacques Derrida," trans. Robert Harvey, in *The Althusserian Legacy*, ed. E. Ann Kaplan and Michael Spinker (London: Verso Books, 1993), pp. 18–231; see pp. 197, 199, 213.

13. John D. Caputo, MRH, p. 124.

14. *Deconstruction and Pragmatism*, p. 75.

10 FAITH, HOPE, AND LOVE: RADICAL HERMENEUTICS AS A PAULINE PHILOSOPHY OF RELIGION

_____ B. KEITH PUTT

> But now abide faith, hope, love, these three; but the greatest of
> these is love.
>
> —St. Paul

> So faith is linked . . . with trust, and trust is inseparable from love:
> have faith and trust in God's love for you, which is at least as great
> as his love for the lilies of the field. For God is love and what God
> gives is best, because God's will, God's heart, is good through and
> thorough. The kingdom of God: viens!
>
> —John D. Caputo

One should not be surprised that John Caputo has changed his mind about certain things throughout the history of his thought, for after all he constantly reminds us that being and reason are mobile and mutable, both caught in the play of a certain kinetics that never ceases to flow in an interminable flux. Since he, himself, holds no privileged position outside this process, his life and thought are not exempt from existential motility. An example of his alterable philosophy is the developing perspective he takes on Jacques Derrida, a thinker of no small importance for his radical hermeneutics. In an article published in 1985 on the issue of Heidegger's critique of Derrida, he characterizes Derrida's deconstruction as an example of "Kierkegaardian aestheticism";[1] however, most recently in _The Prayers and Tears of Jacques Derrida: Religion Without Religion_, wherein he proves beyond reasonable doubt that Derrida is indeed a man of faith and an occupant of Kierkegaard's religious stage of existence, he identifies the earlier interpretation as the "reassuring illusion" of those who have "'visibly and carefully avoided reading' Derrida"![2] Of course, in a 1990 article, he acknowledges his misinterpretation of Derrida but insists that the same confusion has "beset some of North America's finest minds!"[3]

Notwithstanding such a significant *Kehre* with reference to Derridean deconstruction, Caputo's philosophy has not been void of certain tenacious consistencies that serve to forge his philosophy into something of a quasi-system. One such consistency, indeed perhaps the legislating consistency, has been his insistence on the importance of religion as a necessary topic for philosophy, conceivably even as a *sine qua non* for philosophy, a non-original origin for philosophical speculation. Caputo has always manifested personally and professionally an implicit obligation to deal with religion, with what he considers to be the mystery that lies inherent in the flux. As a matter of fact, his earlier misinterpretation of deconstruction stemmed from his failure to realize that Derrida actually does allow for an "openness to the Mystery," one of Caputo's synonyms for religion. From his earliest works on mysticism, Aquinas, and Heidegger up to his most recent work-in-progress on anonymity and God, Caputo has focused his radical hermeneutics on advocating the continued relevance of religion by granting it a "permanent residence permit"[4] within postmodern culture, and, in doing so, he has become one of the most important advocates for developing Continental philosophies of religion.

The contemporary direction of his philosophy of religion was initially mapped out in 1987 in the final section of *Radical Hermeneutics* entitled "The Hermeneutic Project," which reveals a definite Kantian cartography. The three chapters of this section correspond to Kant's three primary questions: What can I know? What ought I to do? For what may I hope?[5] These questions identify the most prominent topics for Caputo's radical hermeneutics, those *topoi* or places along the way that he wishes to use as landmarks for finding his headings as he moves through the flux. Consequently, epistemology, ethics, and hope are issues repeated in various unpublished papers, published articles, and books that compose the Caputoan corpus of the past decade and that come to a creative synthesis in his most recent *magnum opus*, *Prayers and Tears*.

Although there is no denying the Kantian provenance for the three guiding topics, when one examines the rubrics under which Caputo has prosecuted them during the last ten years, one may discover another possible source for his postmodern radical hermeneutics of religion. For him, epistemology eventually becomes the question of faith, ethics becomes the question of love, and hope becomes the question of a certain teleological openness to the unprogrammable future.[6] If one reverses the order of the second and third topics, one discovers a familiar trinity—faith, hope, and love—and one is, thereby, confronted with the possibility that Caputo's philosophy of religion is not only Kantian but also Pauline, specifically bearing the marks of St. Paul's taxonomy of Christian virtues found in I Corinthians 13. Now I realize that such a genealogy for the three foci of Caputo's philosophy of religion may provoke some apprehension, given that he is on record as having a negative view of certain aspects of Paul's theology. He states categorically that he wishes to promote a de-Paulinized Christian religion, a wish that ensues from his agreement with Nietzsche's negative assessment of Paul's apparent soteriology of *ressentiment* and retribution, a soteriology predicated upon a penal economy of sin, guilt, and debt. Caputo interprets Paul as undermining Jesus's own poetics of the Kingdom of God as a reality of giving, forgiving, and forgetting, of canceling debts not demanding that they be repaid, of responding in grace to wounded flesh not requiring the *quid pro quo* of a deserved "pound of flesh."[7] Consequently, to read Caputo as if he were a second Timothy, another follower of the missionary from Tarsus might appear to be indefensible.

Yet, a broader reading of Caputo reveals that his response to Paul is irreducible to his agreement with the Nietzschean critique, for his radical hermeneutics is profoundly and positively affected by other Pauline perspectives. For example, in *Demythologizing Heidegger* and *Against Ethics*, he references Paul's use of *"ta me onta"* (the things that are not) in I Corinthians 1 as an appropriate jewgreek designation for the disenfranchised and alienated people of the world.[8] In *Radical Hermeneutics*, *Deconstruction in a Nutshell*, and *Prayers and Tears*, he extensively uses Paul's image of the "glass darkly," found in I Corinthians 13, as an expression of undecidablility.[9] In *Prayers and Tears*, he also paraphrases Paul's quotation in I Corinthians 2 of the prophet Isaiah's prediction that the eye has not seen nor ear heard what is yet to come.[10] Finally, the Pauline *piece de resistance* in Caputo's thought is a little phrase filtered through Kierkegaard, a phrase whose uses are too numerous to cite, that is, Paul's exhortation in Philippians 2 that Christians are to work out their own salvation with "fear and trembling."

Given the above examples of how Paul's texts have influenced Caputo's thought, I do not think it too implausible to examine the evolution of his radical hermeneutics according to the Pauline rubrics of faith, hope, and love. In the remainder of this paper, I will briefly treat each of these themes in the Caputoan order of faith, love, and hope, examining how they have come to expression over the past decade primarily through his major works *Radical Hermeneutics*, *Against Ethics*, and *Prayers and Tears*.

By Faith and Not by Sight

Caputo maintains a certain cynicism toward metaphysical polarities, wary of them primarily because, in their bifurcated clarity, there seems to lurk an artificiality. He frequently engages, like the good Derridean he is, in the twofold strategy of reversal and displacement. One finds an example of this in his response to the traditional distinction between faith and reason. Ostensibly, he adopts a Kantian approach and desires to critique reason in order to make room for faith, to reverse the pecking order so to speak; however, it soon becomes apparent in his philosophy that he actually adopts a more dialectical perspective, not in the Hegelian sense of effecting an *Aufhebung* wherein each is absorbed into the other but in the sense of recognizing a certain miscegenation between the two. He interprets the tension between faith and reason as a decidedly modernist prejudice, arguing that one does not always find the two as antagonists. Instead of the two competing against each other, one might understand them as complementary, as bound together in some epistemological Gordian knot. Of course, Caputo's perspective on this modernist polarity reveals the tension in his own personal intellectual journey between the medieval synthesis of Aquinas and the ironic nominalism of Kierkegaard. Although both are influential on his displacement of the faith/reason dichotomy, he actually ends up closer to St. Thomas than to St. Søren.

Now he does adopt a Kierkegaardian bias when he attacks reason's arrogant claim to systematic totalization. Like a postmodern Climacus, he attempts to reveal that reason cannot explain every aspect of existence and that thought always takes place within the limiting constraints of history, culture, and language. Here a bit of Heidegger comes into the mix—which according to Caputo is just another form of Kierkegaard—with the embarrassing question of why reason cannot give reasons for itself. There do seem to be mysteries to life, an *ohne warum* implicit in things like rose blooms or putative encounters in the moment with the Absolute Paradox.[11] There do seem to be more things in heaven and earth than reason can even dream about. This possibility is the specter that continually haunts reason, the spirit that every System wishes to exorcize, which is, of course, in itself inconsistent since by definition a system should cast out nothing but subsume everything within itself. In other words, every rational system should be a digestive system that absorbs all experience with no resulting detritus. Yet, Caputo "knows" that such a system can never be constructed, that real human beings caught within the ongoing kinetics of the flux live in shacks off to the side of those vast rational edifices just nibbling away on philosophical table scraps.

So Caputo *is* a good Kierkegaardian; however, he ends up a better Thomist, for finally he confesses that it is ultimately not a question of either/or but of both/and. Interestingly enough, it is precisely here with St. Thomas, the angelic doctor, that a certain atheistic Jewish *bricoleur* begins to putter around in Caputo's thought. Jacques Derrida contends that one need not choose between faith and reason, for indeed one cannot avoid either. One does not need to critique reason to make room for faith, because faith is already inherent in every instance of reason. One cannot avoid it. One cannot not believe—*Je ne sais pas. Il faut croire.* It is necessary to believe. Like some deconstructive Augustinian, Derrida structures an epistemology exemplifying the traditional *credo ut intelligam*—I believe in order to understand. Caputo could not agree more. Faith is, according to a certain Kantian repetition, a way of thinking past what one can know. It is a certain kind of uncertainty, a *non savoir* and a *sans savoir,* or according to a certain Kierkegaardian repetition, *la passion du non-savoir*, the passion of non-knowing, of desiring to think what thought itself cannot think.[12] It is also a movement *sans voir*, a type of blindness. As a blind person must trust in his guide, or in the end of his cane, or even in the eyes of his dog, so, too, every person in some way proceeds ahead only by trust, only by believing in the other person, only by assuming the veracity of the other's testimony. Or, as St. Paul would express it, everyone walks by faith and not by sight (II Corinthians 5:7).

Walking by faith and not by sight, however, does not mean for Caputo that one stumbles aimlessly through an abyss, groping around in some nihilistic chaos. On the contrary, faith enables a person to progress, to move ahead in the flux. In other words, although faith is *sans voir* (without seeing), it is not necessarily *sans yeux* (without eyes), for indeed in *Radical Hermeneutics*, Caputo writes passionately about the "eyes of faith," about how one makes her way through the darkness, "seeing" with eyes acclimated to the penumbra of God's absence, watching for those places where the flux thins a bit and something (Someone?) mysterious breaks through (*Durchbruch*).[13] With the eyes of faith, the believer does not just grope in the darkness but actually comes to grips with the flux, yet not in the sense of *Begriff*, of comprehending the flux through the static, well-focused clear ideas of rational systems. Speculative reason, like some arrogant optometrist, always wants to prescribe dogmatic spectacles to improve faith's vision. Propositional orthodoxy, for example, is just such an attempt to supply transparent lenses through which the full presence of the divine and the radiant splendor of absolute truth may be seen. Yet, Caputo rejects the idea that the light of reason can disperse all of the darkness. No, on the contrary, when faith looks at the flux, it always looks through a glass darkly.[14]

These ideas about faith continue consistently through his subsequent works. In *Against Ethics*, a work that primarily avoids the question of faith, bracketing it for the sake of a radical quasi-phenomenological investigation into obligation, Caputo repeats that faith is an ontic affair, a factical *Lebensform*.[15] The person of faith has not been raptured out of the shadows of the flux nor "infused" with clear and distinct ideas about the world and/or God. Instead, she has been immersed even more genuinely into the play of reality and gazes into its ambiguity seeing evidence that, perhaps, "Someone looks back at [her] from the abyss."[16] In *Prayers and Tears*, a work that removes faith from the *epoché* of *Against Ethics* and confirms the religious prejudices lying explicitly in Derridean thought, Caputo once again employs Pauline semantics and insists on faith's seeing only through the dim mirror. In this work, he calls for a new *sans*, not only faith as *sans voir et sans savoir* but now faith as a *foi sans foi*, a faith without faith, a *fides qua* that avoids a total contamination by the various dogmatic prescriptions of a *fides quae*.[17] Such a faith interprets the "glass darkly" as an example of undecidability, which leads not to the paralysis of despair but to the *kinetics* of a leap of faith, a moving on in the flux, of saying yes and "putting its hand to the plow . . ."[18] The believer, then, confesses her faith only through her life and her testimony, through which she promises that she is telling the truth when she says what she faithfully loves when she loves her God.[19]

Finally, in *Prayers and Tears*, Caputo has brought the ten years of interpreting faith to its logical conclusion by identifying through Derrida's notion of a religion without religion a faith that cannot be deconstructed, because it is a *foi sans foi* that is simultaneously a *foi sans voir, sans savoir, sans vision, sans verité, et sans révelation*.[20] This faith may never be a determinate faith with exclusionary dogma, since particular systems of belief may always be deconstructed given that they are historico-linguistic effects. In a section appropriately entitled "The Eyes of Faith," Caputo admits that "life is a tissue of faith . . ."[21] Faith is a tissue, a weaving of life that gives it texture, a textuality that fabricates various patterns in the flux. The patterns may be deconstructed, since they have themselves been constructed, but the weaving, the weaving must be accepted . . . on faith. How does Caputo know that? *Il ne sait pas. Il faut croire.*

FAITH WORKING THROUGH LOVE

Caputo claims in *Radical Hermeneutics* that "humility and compassion are the first 'virtues' which the flux breeds . . ."[22] Humility addresses the Kantian question of knowing and expresses the primary pathos of faith, since what Caputo calls for in his critique of reason and his panegyric on faith without faith is a more humble acceptance of the fix in which human beings find themselves. He would agree with T.S. Eliot that the wisdom of humility is the only wisdom that perdures.[23] Compassion broaches the other side of faith, the affection that should accompany the realization that the flux is not merely the open-ended play of patterns and competing interpretations of life but that it frequently becomes the theater of suffering, of other human beings whose flesh and spirits bear the wounds of disease, oppression, loneliness, and exclusion. Consequently, Kant's second question comes to the fore: What ought I to do in these situations? Caputo finds this question philosophically unavoidable but, more importantly, religiously significant. He insists in *Radical Hermeneutics* that the notion of suffering provokes a genealogy of religion, that perhaps the rudimentary motivation for looking through the eyes of faith hoping to discover God is the passion to find some loving power in the midst of the flux taking the side of victimized human beings and offering the potentiality of a healing response. For Caputo, therefore, religion must include an affirmation of the worth of the other and a protest against the suffering of the other.[24] Genuine faith will promote genuine compassion, since faith without works of love is useless.[25]

In *Radical Hermeneutics*, Caputo interprets compassion as an ethics of dissemination and of *Gelassenheit*. The former, like faith, admits the humility of living with uncertainty and denies that one may ever occupy a privileged position outside of the inter-textuality of life from which one can establish as a *fundamentum inconcussum* the legislating principles for proper behavior. Quite often, these metaphysical foundations become the very power clusters that alienate, oppress, and depersonalize human beings. Caputo claims that only by disseminating power across multiple perspectives and only by appropriating various ethical interpretations, may one genuinely allow compassion to break through. Instead of standing on deceptively stationary ethical grounds, one must accept the cold hermeneutics of the flux and be willing to shiver a bit in uncertainty, to experience the *ébranler* or "fear and trembling" that characterize facticity. Yet, such dissemination is conjointly a willingness to let the other be as other, a "letting-be" or *Gelassenheit*, which in its initial expression in the thought of the great mystic Meister Eckhart means loving the other.[26] The religious embodiment of these two ethical approaches is the compassionate response to the face of the other in the face of the other's suffering. Consequently, Caputo integrates religion and ethics as a synthesis of faith and love.

Against Ethics serves as the consummate exposition of Caputo's ethics of dissemination/*Gelassenheit*. In this brilliant, quasi-Kierkegaardian treatment of postmodern ethical problemata, Caputo fleshes out his earlier statements on compassion toward the face of suffering by broaching the issue of obligation toward suffering flesh. He insists that obligations just happen, perhaps *ohne warum*; there is—*es gibt, il y a*—obligation. Individuals simply find themselves addressed by the others who experience disasters, by the widows and orphans, by the *les juifs* who are disenfranchised, excluded, expelled, excommunicated, executed, excised, X'ed out by the powers that be. Instead of waiting until rational principles can be discovered, verified, and then used as reasons to act or of waiting until the call of Being, God, or Conscience can be heard and voice-printed for verification, individuals should embrace the *ébranler* of uncertainty, commit to the "cold faith"[27] that there is no escaping the play of the flux, and respond to the accusation of obligation with a *me voici*—here I am.[28] Response happens for no other reason than because the wounded flesh of the other voices the call of obligation.

Although *Against Ethics* does not read much like a religious text, it does indeed contribute to radical hermeneutics as a philosophy of religion in two ways. First, Caputo intends his stance against ethics to be a de-Hellenizing approach, a move away from a Greek, Parmenidean rational stability toward a more Hebraic, Abrahamic fear and trembling. The Kierkegaardian spirit of this move raises the interconnection of obligation (*ob-ligare*—being bound toward the other) and religion (*re-ligare*—being bound back, perhaps, toward God).[29] Second, Caputo embodies his Hebraic stance against ethics in the kerygma of Jesus of Nazareth, whom he calls a poet of obligation. Jesus's poetics demands an existence of expenditure without reserve or return, a mad economy of investing in the lives of others by responding therapeutically to their cries for healing, by forgiving and forgetting without any desire for reimbursement.[30] Such a willingness to show compassion by responding in love to singular individuals is what Jesus calls justice in the Kingdom of God. He reprises the prophetic theme that God desires, not sacrifices and rituals, but obedience to the demands of obligation, to love mercy, to do justice, and to walk humbly. Love and justice, then, are synonyms in Jesus's kerygmatics of the kingdom.[31]

In *Prayers and Tears*, Caputo reprises all of the issues discussed above and does so in a more overt radical hermeneutics of religion, one might even say in a radical philosophical theology, since one of the fundamental themes in the book is Derrida's Augustinian question, "What do I love when I love my God?"[32] Twice in the text he connects *Gelassenheit* with love, specifically love for the other, the *tout autre*, the only kind of love that deconstruction knows.[33] In the "Edifying Divertissement No. 4" entitled "Deconstruction and the Kingdom of God," he once again discusses Jesus's poetics of obligation and contends that the Kingdom of God is a kingdom of love and forgiveness, a genuine concern for every *tout autre* especially "the least of God's children."[34] Caputo boldly professes that Derrida's aspiration to deconstruct the Law in the name of undeconstructible justice exemplifies Jesus's second great commandment from Leviathins 19:18: "Love your neighbor as yourself."[35] On four occasions in the text, he references the defining Augustinian non-principle of his religio-ethical hermeneutics: *dilige, and quod vis fac*— love, and do what you will. One also finds this same principle used multiple times in *Radical Hermeneutics* and in *Against Ethics*, where it is actually the title of a chapter section.[36]

Finally and, perhaps, most importantly for my thesis, one finds Caputo directly accepting a Pauline hypothesis of the extravagance of Christian love. In a scathing indictment of Hegel's misunderstanding of Christian *agape*, Caputo briefly recounts Paul's various responses to the tension between

Christianity and the Law and in that discussion claims that Paul's "best and most brilliant argument was that love is the *pleroma* of the Law . . ." Granted, Caputo accuses Paul of misusing that idea for anti-Semitic purposes (an accusation that is, to say the least, questionable); however, he enthusiastically approves of Paul's interpreting love as an extravagance, an *au-dela*, a "beyond" all of the rational, sane, and parsimonious principles of legal structures.[37] Here even Caputo must admit that no great gulf exists between Paul's construal of agapic immoderation and Jesus's poetics of the Kingdom of God as a mad economics of expenditure without reserve or return. Consequently, Caputo, who insists on a duty without debt (*devoir sans devoir*) might find little to fault in Paul's economics of the kingdom expressed so succinctly in Romans 13:8: "Owe nothing to anyone except to love one another."[38] Or, as Paul might have written, had he spoken postmodern French instead of *koin'* Greek: "*Il faut aimer*"—it is necessary to love.

HOPE THAT IS SEEN IS NOT HOPE

Recently Caputo has foraged around in deconstruction searching for nutshells, meaty little kernels that in some way summarize the "essence" of Derrida's philosophy. One such nutshell is the idea of the messianic, an idea that lies at the "heart" of Derrida's religion without religion, that is, his *foi sans foi*, his non-dogmatic doubling of dogma.[39] Borrowing the notion from Walter Benjamin and filtering it through his own Jewish tradition, Derrida has promoted the epistemological, ethical, and religious significance of maintaining an openness for what is not yet, for that which is "to come," the *à-venir*. Epistemologically, the "to come" is a cipher for undecidability, the Derridean idea that one cannot pre-program the future, that decisions must be made without absolute fore-structures anticipating exactly what will ensue. Ethically, the "to come" prepares one to accept *l'invention de l'autre*, the in-coming of the other as other—*tout autre est tout autre*. In this sense, a messianic ethics awaits the coming of justice. Religiously, the "to come" impassions a passion for the impossible, a radical openness to the secret, a perpetual interrogation of what Caputo calls the "question of all questions": *quid ergo amo, cum deum meum amo?*—what do I love when I love my God?[40] The messianic inculcates all of these considerations and provokes the deconstructionist to cry *Viens! Viens! Oui, oui.*

Caputo's quasi-Pauline trinity of Christian virtues comes to completion with the messianic, for it does, indeed, convey the significance of hope in his philosophy of religion. Interestingly enough, this theme, unlike faith and love, is not so easily traced through his work in a teleological direction but must be engaged archeologically. Only in *Prayers and Tears* does the topic of hope come to explicit expression, which then, in turn, allows one to trace its function back through Caputo's earlier works. Of course, one has to read *Prayers and Tears* in order to discover the significance of hope; one cannot merely consult the index, for the word never appears there. In my own informal indexing, however, I have discovered over fifteen references to hope in the text. Caputo utilizes the word constantly as he explains how the messianic broaches the question of futurity, how it provokes the passion for the aleatoric impossibility of the "to come."[41] For example, early in the text, he refers to the messianic as a structurally "open-ended hope" for the incoming of the *tout autre*.[42] Later, when he articulates exactly what the messianic—the messianic as a "religion within the limits of reason alone"— means, he says that it is:

> . . . oriented by the hope of what has no present substance, and is itself the substance, the stuff and the testimony, of things that appear not, of what is utterly heterogeneous with the present or current state of things.

He, then, follows this quote with explicit references to Paul's image of the "glass darkly" and to the biblical characterization of faith in Hebrews 11 as "the real stuff of what is not real yet but only hoped for . . ."[43] Obviously, for Caputo hope and faith correlate precisely at the point where each expresses the necessity for individuals to anticipate the future (*Viens! Viens!*) affirmatively (*oui, oui*) while recognizing the structural blindness of that anticipation and affirmation. Moreover, hope correlates with love, since the messianic *non-savoir*, in some manner, always yearns for the justice that is to come. So, Kant's third question applies. For what do I hope? *Je ne sais pas. Il faut espérer.* I do not know. It is necessary to hope, to "'keep hope alive.'"[44]

Once one understands messianic hope as the affirmative repetition of *oui, oui*, as the passion for the impossible, and as the *l'invention de l'autre*, one discovers that hope has been a consistent, albeit not explicitly-named, theme throughout Caputo's philosophy of religion. First, the *"oui, oui"* is another name for repetition, for the *kinetics* of moving forward through the flux with faith and hope.[45] If that is true, then all of the involved discussions on repetition in parts one and two of *Radical Hermeneutics* may be read as an extended preface to a Caputoan theory of hope. Second, if "passion for the impossible" names an aspiration toward the secret of the promised future as *non-savoir*, then it functions as a translation of "openness to the mystery," which, of course, is the title of the concluding chapter to *Radical Hermeneutics* where the religious is explained as responding to the suffering other with the hope that there is a loving presence in the flux. Third, if *l'invention de l'autre* refers to the anticipation of a justice to come, to the willingness to accept the alterity and singularity of the *tout autre,* and to the duty without debt of responding to the call of obligation with a *me voici,* then obviously the ethical analyses in *Radical Hermeneutics* and *Against Ethics* have lying inchoate within them a certain interpretation of hope.

Conclusion

I am convinced that one may discover a consistent philosophy of religion in Caputo's thought that is both radically Pauline and radically hermeneutical. It is radically Pauline because it depends significantly, if not intentionally, on Paul's three Christian virtues of faith, hope, and love. Had time permitted, I could have adduced even more evidence supporting this thesis. For example, I have written little about the profoundly prominent place the topic of gift has in Caputo's understanding of religion as something more than an economics of reciprocity and retribution. For him, the Kingdom of God is a kingdom of gift, of faith, love, and hope as gifts.[46] Yet, Paul claims precisely the same in I Corinthians 13, since in that chapter he identifies faith, hope, and love as the greatest of all the *charismata,* God's spiritual gifts to the church.

I also want to emphasize that Caputo's philosophy of religion is radically hermeneutical, because I do not want to be misunderstood as claiming that faith, hope, and love function as metaphysical principles that offer to suspend the flux and supply an ahistorical, non-perspectival, absolute position outside of existence from which the total truth and certainty of religion may be identified. On the contrary, these gifted virtues and virtuous gifts only offer possible ways of construing the flux, of forging more humble *ad hoc* responses to the uncertainty of factical experience, that is, of interpreting the flux with a warm-hearted, cold hermeneutics that acknowledges the difficulty of life. Caputo might possibly refer to faith, hope, and love as formal indications that trace out the possibility and impossibility of comprehending the flux. Under the circumstances, I actually prefer to utilize a synonym for "formal indication," the well-used term "quasi-transcen*dental.*" I accent the final two syllables purposely, since in a couple of texts Caputo makes a "dental" examination of two of the three virtues. In one passage, he defines faith as a "certain resolve to hold on by one's teeth . . ."[47] In another, he agrees with Meister Eckhart's theology of extravagant love, calling it "a principle of caritas with some teeth in it . . ."[48] I do so wish I could cite you a Caputo text in which he connects teeth and hope. Alas, I cannot; however, if you allow me the license to play with the messianic and use a little French idiom, I would contend that, for Caputo, hope means being alert to the in-coming of the impossible, to maintaining a "heads-up" vigilance toward the *tout autre,* that is, of "staying on one's toes," or, as the French say *sur les dents,* "on the teeth!"

Caputo's quasi-transcendental Pauline hermeneutics of religion is a philosophy of religion *sans religion, sans voir, sans avoir, sans savoir, sans vision, sans verité, et sans révelation*. It is a *foi sans foi, mais avec foi, avec espoir, et avec amor*. Throughout the past ten years of his radical hermeneutics of religion, Caputo has been proclaiming this prophetic message, insisting on three things: *Il faut croire; Il faut espérer;* and *Il faut aimer*. I conclude, therefore, by saying of Caputo what he says of Derrida:[49]

> He has faith in something incoming, hope for a justice to come, love for the gift of the expenditure without reserve.

NOTES

1. John D. Caputo, "From the Primordiality of Absence to the Absence of Primordiality: Heidegger's Critique of Derrida," in *Hermeneutics and Deconstruction*, ed. Hugh Silverman (Albany, NY: SUNY Press, 1985), p. 199.

2. John D. Caputo, PT, p. 211. Cf. also John D. Caputo, "Beyond Aestheticism: Derrida's Responsible Anarchy," *Research in Phenomenology*, 18 (1988), p. 65.

3. John D. Caputo, "Hermeneutics and Faith: A Reply to Prof. Olthuis," *Christian Scholar Review*, 20 (December 1990), p. 166.

4. I borrow this phrase from Zygmunt Bauman's article "Postmodern Religion?" in *Religion, Modernity and Postmodernity*, ed. Paul Heelas (Oxford: Blackwell Publishers, 1998), p. 55.

5. John D. Caputo, RH, pp. 209, 214.

6. I recognize that Caputo does not actually discuss faith until the final chapter of *Radical Hermeneutics* and that the chapter on epistemology, in which he critiques reason's institutionalization into possibly oppressive constellations of power, serves as a propaedeutic to his postmodern theory of ethics as well as his theory of religion. Still, I maintain that his desire for a postmetaphysical rationality finally comes to expression as an apologia for a post-secular understanding of faith.

7. PT, pp. 216, 222.

8. John D. Caputo, AE, pp. 55, 237; John D. Caputo, DH, p. 7.

9. RH, p. 281; PT, pp. 60, 63, 314; John D. Caputo, DN, p. 159.

10. PT, p. 149.

11. Cf. John D. Caputo, "The Rose is Without Why: An Interpretation of the Later Heidegger," *Philosophy Today*, 15:3–15 (Spring 1971). Caputo's beautiful dedication of his first book to his wife communicates the most imposing *ohne warum* of them all: "To Kathy, who knows that love is without why" (ME).

12. PT, pp. 311, 101. Kierkegaard refers to this desire to discover something that cannot be thought as both a paradox and a passion (*Philosophical Fragments/Johannes Climacus. Kierkegaard's Writings, VII*, ed. and trans. Howard V. and Edna H. Hong [Princeton: Princeton University Press, 1985], p. 37).

13. RH, p. 279. Caputo argues that God's absence is not an absolute disappearance of the deity but is the "twilight space, of flickering images, a space in which the

withdrawal leaves its trace behind, like a fissure in a surface left behind by something, *je ne sais quoi*, which has passed through it and disappeared. Faith is defined by this withdrawal . . ." ("Bedeviling the Tradition: On Deconstruction and Catholicism," in *(Dis)Continuity and (De)Construction: Reflections on the Meaning of the Past in Crisis Situations*, ed. J.B.M. Wissink [Kampen: Pharos, 1995], p. 23).

14. RH, p. 281.

15. Caputo acknowledges that *Against Ethics* appears to be rather impious; however he assures his readers that he does not intend to undermine faith, but to engage in a laconic quasi-transcendental deduction of the parameters of faith. He promises that in the future he will take up the question of faith in more depth (AE, p. 286, note 6). It is a promise that he kept.

16. AE, p. 245. Caputo takes Heidegger to task for separating faith and questioning (cf. Martin Heidegger, *An Introduction to Metaphysics*, trans. Ralph Manheim [New Haven: Yale Univeristy Press, 1959], pp. 6–7), since faith without the passion of honest questioning would not be faith but knowledge. The believer has no transparent perspective on the flux but engages it interrogatively by asking what she loves when she loves her God (PT, p. xxii).

17. PT, p. 61.

18. Ibid., p. 64.

19. Ibid., p.157.

20. DN, p. 166. Caputo's progressive appreciation for the significance of religion in Derrida's thought may be recognized from the following two quotes from 1990 and 1997: "I do not think that Derrida is an antagonist of religion . . ." ("Derrida and the Study of Religion," *Religious Studies Review* 16 (January 1990), p. 25) and "Deconstruction *is* . . . a messianic religion within the limits of reason alone . . ." [emphasis added] (PT, p. 150).

21. PT, p. 312.

22. RH, p. 259.

23. T. S. Elliot, *Four Quartets*, "East Coker" (New York: Harcourt Brace Jovanovich, 1971), p. 27.

24. RH, p. 280.

25. Such is my Caputoan gloss on James 2:20.

26. RH, p. 267.

27. AE, p.24.

28. Ibid., p. 34.

29. Ibid., p. 18.

30. Ibid., pp. 146–150. For one of the most beautiful of Caputo's many discourses on the antithesis between forgiveness and retribution see his "On Not knowing Who We Are: Foucault and the Night of Truth," in *Foucault and the Critique of Institutions*, eds. John Caputo and Mark Yount (University Park: Pennsylvania State University Press, 1993), pp. 261–262.

31. For a more complete explication of Caputo's understanding of Jesus's revelation of the kingdom see his "The Good News About Alterity: Derrida and Theology," *Faith and Philosophy* 10 (1993): 453–470 and "Reason, History and a Little Madness: Towards a Hermeneutics of the Kingdom," *Proceedings of the American Catholic Philosophical Association* 68 (1994): 27–44. A briefer discussion may be

found in "Instants, Secrets, and Singularities: Dealing Death in Kierkegaard and Derrida," in *Kierkegaard in Post/Modernity*, eds. Martin J. Matuštík and Merold Westphal (Bloomington: Indiana University Press, 1995), pp. 232–237.

32. PT, p. xxii.

33. Ibid., pp. 49, 248.

34. Ibid., pp. 222–229.

35. Ibid., p. 249. For an exceptional commentary on Derrida's audacious pronouncement of the undeconstructibility of justice, see Caputo's "Hyperbolic Justice: Deconstruction, Myth, and Politics," *Research in Phenomenology* 21 (1991): 3–20. This article appears in an edited form as Chapter 10 of DH, pp. 186–208. For a Caputoan gloss on Jesus's second commandment as it relates to subjectivity and an economy of gift see *Nutshell*, pp. 148–149.

36. PT, pp. 49, 177, 229, 308; RH, pp. 187, 265, 267, 293; AE, pp. 41, 92, 121. Caputo confesses that "[d]econstruction is love, the love of something unforeseeable, unforegraspable, something to come, absolutely, something undeconstructible and impossible, something nameless" (DN, p. 173).

37. PT, p. 236.

38. Ibid., p. 221.

39. Ibid., p. 141.

40. Ibid., p. 286.

41. Caputo indicates that the idea of impossibility does not function in Derrida's thought as "a simple logical contradiction, like x and not-x, but [as] the tension, the paralysis, the aporia, of having to push against and beyond the limits of the horizon, *passage à frontières*" (DN, p. 133).

42. PT, p. 41. The "open-ended hope" for the *à-venir* of the *tout autre* takes place in the present; however, this present "is always to be pried open with hope and expectation, for the present is most certainly not the messianic time" (John D. Caputo, "The End of Ethics." Forthcoming in the Blackwell Guide to Ethics, p. 11).

43. PT, p. 149.

44. Ibid., p. 151.

45. Ibid., p. 64; cf. also p. 272.

46. Ibid., p. 229.

47. Ibid., p. 12.

48. RH, p. 265; cf. also "Mysticism and Transgression: Derrida and Meister Eckhart," *Continental Philosophy, II* (1989), p. 38.

49. PT, p. 329.

HOLDING ON BY OUR TEETH:
A RESPONSE TO PUTT

————————— *John D. Caputo* —————————

After having been criticized as a faithless and unbelieving rascal by Ayres, Kearney and Westphal, it is delightful to be accused of being a follower of St. Paul by Keith Putt. Everyone should have a reader like Keith Putt, who has read everything and remembered everything, including a couple of early pieces I did years ago on Derrida that, to be honest, I would thank him to forget. He has adroitly singled out the last three chapters of *Radical Hemeneutics*, as the precise point where everything changes and I shift into the gear in which I am still motoring along today. His creative reformulation of these chapters, which sketch the route I subsequently pursued, cannot be improved upon. I did not see it coming but what Keith Putt says is completely true: Kant's three questions have been transmuted into St. Paul's three virtues: epistemology gives way to faith, ethics gives way to love, and hope becomes an openness to the unprogrammable future. Putt takes no little delight in pointing out that I have landed myself in a Pauline camp and ended up singing a hymn to Paul's "taxonomy of Christian virtues" (I Corinthians 13:13). Putt is right and I will not try to twist free from the claim (accusation/congratulation) he makes in this sensitive and detailed reading. In fact I will strengthen it by revealing a secret. When I was, many years ago, a member of a Roman Catholic religious order (the Brothers of the Christian Schools, founded by Jean-Baptiste de la Salle, whose "normalizing" teaching methods Foucault singles out for abuse in *Discipline and Punish*), I freely chose the name "Brother Paul," and Paul is the name we gave our second son (I had left the Christian Brothers by that time!) So there was a time in my life that if someone said, "Paul!," I would have said *me voici*. I answer to the name of Paul, and so does our son. There is no escaping Paul in my life, and no desire to, even if, as happens in the best of families, I sometimes give him—which one? St. Paul? my son? or myself?—a piece of my mind.

My reservations about St. Paul to which Putt discreetly refers have to do with his "economy of salvation," the economy of sin and debt whose accounts are balanced by means of Christ's sacrificial death. God sent Jesus into the world to take the hit for the rest of us because somebody had to pay God back for what sin has cost Him (the masculine pronouns are appropriate here; this is a male economy). I much prefer to understand the crucifixion as a prophetic death, as did many early followers of "the Way," in which a just man is unjustly executed for calling for justice, and to think in terms of God's relationship to humanity in terms of giving, gifts, and of forgiveness instead of debts to be paid. I prefer the figure of the father in the parable of the prodigal son to Paul's sacrificial economy, where the offended father forgives his errant son the first chance he gets and instead of letting him be crucified throws him a party. For a father, or let us say a parent, is the giver of gifts, not a keeper of accounts. Now even though Paul's version became canonical, I prefer to think that the palms go to another view astir in the early Christian communities where forgiveness is in fact closer to what Jesus was up to and the sacrificial economy was much more Paul's idea than anyone else's. Paul's extraordinary and powerful religious imagination overran the early Christian communities, including the ones populated by people who actually knew Jesus in the flesh, as Paul, of course, did not. Instead, Paul invoked special divine revelations about what Jesus said, with the result that Paul reinstated a lot of ideas that were meant to be disturbed by Jesus's teaching of *metanoia* and unconditional forgiveness. That this line of New Testament scholarship is also congruent with Derrida's *The Gift of Death* I will not point out.[1]

Keith Putt, a wise steward and prudent defender of the classical faith, and I, an impudent supplementary clerk of unorthodox troublemakers, have been arguing with each other about this for as long as we have known each other, in the course of which he has instructed me about the theological idea of a suffering God, for which I am deeply grateful. So it is a deft move on Putt's part to point out that, all this disagreement with Paul notwithstanding, I am up to my ears in Paul. I concede it. Paul was a stunning religious genius who seemed to provoke a riot wherever he visited (which is one of the things I like about him). Had he visited Cambridge, he would have started another riot and would never have been given an honorary degree. His *Letter to the Romans* is, in my view, the single greatest work of religious imagination the West knows, a dark, brooding, almost Nietzschean vision of a world which does not make sense without the love of God to lean on.[2] Paul issues a fundamental challenge to the "autonomy" of philosophy which deludes itself into thinking that we can make sense of things with pure reason or what Paul called the "law" (*Nomos*), allowing for the fact that the *Torah*, translated as the "teaching," was reduced to the object of a polemical attack by Paul. His scolding of the Corinthians is a scolding of *us* for trafficking in the foolishness of onto-theo-logy. "For it is written," Paul says, "'I will deconstruct the wisdom of the wise-aleck ontotheologicians,'" (I Corinthians 1:19, loosely translated!). Without Paul, we would have no Augustine or Luther (Nietzsche is smiling), no Kierkegaard or *Being and Time* (the analytic philosophers are smiling). I love Paul's view of this tormented, self-conflicted, passionate, weepy, wounded being of whom he says "I do not understand my own actions. For I do not do what I want, but I do the very thing I hate . . . I can will what is right, but I cannot do it. For I do not do the good I want, but the evil I do not want is what I do." (Romans 7:15–19). Anyone who has ever been on a diet knows how true that is! So much for the pure self-identical autonomous transcendental subject (who would never be overweight!) that philosophers have been trying to peddle from Plato to Husserl! Paul is a principal source of the great and subversive counter-tradition—of the mystics contesting scholasticism, Pascal contesting Rationalism, Luther contesting the Roman church, Kierkegaard contesting Hegel, and I would say the deconstructionist troubling of metaphysics, that has always surfaced whenever we are overrun by the illusion of rational autonomy.

Putt has carefully documented in particular the several ways in which, certainly without having planned this in advance, I have been gradually repeating Paul's teaching on faith, hope, and love. This is an important argument particularly because it was no part of my intention but it worked its way into my text. That suggests that somebody who has read St. Paul and also a certain streak of continental philosophy stretching from Kierkegaard to Derrida will likely end up having recourse to Pauline tropes, structures, ideas, and passions. That is further testimony to the argument a lot of us have been making that philosophy does well to let its guard down and expose itself to the other, by which I do not mean (only) poetry, but the Scriptures, the biblical tradition, both Jewish and Christian, which is a little too other for most philosophers. In Derrida, this repetition of biblical religion takes the form of the pure messianic, detached from the concrete historical messianisms, but as Putt points out in the end, I do not think it is possible to maintain such pure desert abstraction. I accept Putt's point that just as we can always locate the desert desire of deconstruction as marked by the time and place in which it is forged, it is also true that what I have been doing is unmistakably marked by its Christian origins. That is precisely what makes Derrida nervous about all this interest on the part of *les Catholiques* (speaking very broadly, of course) in deconstruction.

To Putt's very careful argument, which I embrace happily and without reserve (almost), I would only add a little addendum. The theologians call these three virtues, rather chauvinistically, in my opinion, the "theological virtues"— Putt calls them Pauline, and I prefer that—which they distinguish from the "cardinal" virtues, practical wisdom, justice, fortitude, and courage, the ones picked out by the Greek philosophers. So this is a distinction between lists drawn up by religion, by Paul, and by the philosophers, Plato and Aristotle. The four "cardinal" virtues, from *cardo*, hinge, the four hinges upon which the legs of a table stand firm, describe a more or less self-standing, independent autonomous four square rational being, one of Plato's and Aristotle's leisurely gentlemen who go to all the best schools and make themselves beautiful. But Paul's virtues are for the unhinged, *ta me onta*, the nothings and nobodies who have recourse to the surpassing love of God to make it through the day, or, as Tom Carlson might prefer, these are the virtues of the unhorsed. As opposed to the perfectly reasonable idea of staying with the things that are within the scope of our possibilities, our *Seinskönnen*, Paul's virtues, I would say, have the virtue of dealing with *the* impossible, which is when we most have need of faith, hope and love. For faith is really faith just when we are faced with the unbelievable; the more reasonable and credible things are the less faith we need. Again, hope is hope, Paul says, when it is hope against hope, when it looks hopeless, so that hope is structured by a certain despair, just as faith is structured by the incredible, in the "teeth" of which hope persists. And love is love when we are faced with the unlovable, above all with the enemy, which is impossible, for it is no great challenge to love those who fall all over us in admiration. The dynamics of *the* impossible, the dental dynamics, as Putt would put it, describe quite precisely what is going on in Paul's list of virtues, for these are the virtues of this conflicted being who has come unhinged and has to hold on by his teeth—and by what comes forth from the mouth of God.

To all this agreement with Keith Putt, I would add, in a parting gesture that I cannot forgo, one more case of the logic of the impossible that Paul leaves out: it is just when we are confronted with the *unforgivable* that forgiveness is most at work, whereas forgiving someone who has paid all off his debts and has satisfied the demands of a sacrificial economy seems to me the mark of what Johannes Climacus called a "mediocre fellow."

NOTES

1. For a review of some alternate early Christologies, see Edward Schillebeeckx, *Jesus: An Experiment in Christology*, trans. Hubert Hoskins (New York: Crossroads, 1985), pp. 404–438.

2. See A. N. Wilson's excellent take on the Letter to the Romans in *Paul: The Mind of the Apostle* (New York: Norton, 1997), pp. 192–198.

11 CAPUTO'S EXAMPLE

"Like a horse in the desert . . ."
—*Isaiah 63:13*

If in the earlier twentieth century, Martin Heidegger's epoch-making philosophy tends in the direction of a demythologizing reduction that would articulate and elaborate the ontological and existential grounds to which such ontic, existentiell fields as religion would have to be traced back, one of the more significant trends in later twentieth-century, post-Heideggerian thinking can be seen to trouble and disrupt just such a subordination or subjugation of the religious to the philosophical—by bringing to light the significant debts of philosophy itself to the very religious thought and experience it would claim to ground or contain.[1] As if responding anew, then, to some still open possibility or promise, a number of thinkers are seeking today to elucidate and elaborate those crucial intersections between philosophy and religion where the one could not simply be subordinated to the other—thanks to a mutual indebtedness wherein each might prove both greater and smaller than the other. At precisely these ambiguous intersections, a new philosophic discourse might be seen to emerge, neither reductive nor apologetic, whose sense is captured well by the logic of "religion without religion."

In this direction, one could not cite a more exemplary work than John D. Caputo's *Prayers and Tears of Jacques Derrida: Religion without Religion*, the most thorough treatment to date of the relation between religion and Derrida's deconstructive philosophy.[2] Caputo's *Prayers and Tears*—and this is where his work might stand as a model—does not seek to approach religion philosophically so as to reduce the religious to something other than itself; nor does it seek simply to make theological arguments by philosophical means. Rather, moving always in at least two directions at once, Caputo opens our eyes both to the religious dimensions of a certain philosophy (Derrida's primarily, but others as well) and to the philosophic implications of certain religious traditions and categories (primarily the prophetic and messianic, but again, many others as well, from the apophatic and apocalyptic to the sacrificial, circumcisionist, and confessional). By moving always in at least two directions, Caputo's reading of Derrida troubles any clear, stable distinction between a "founding" philosophic discourse and a "founded" religious field, and it thus solicits those crucial points at which any priority between the philosophic and the religious proves undecidable. It is the exploration of just such undecidability, I think, that makes Caputo's work exemplary for philosophic and religious thought today, and it is in the very logic of "exemplarism" that Caputo is able to find such undecidability.

By insisting in his reading of deconstruction on points of undecidability between the philosophic and the religious—or between purportedly "founding" and "founded" modes of discourse—Caputo gives scandal both to the secularizing devotees and to the faithful, especially Christian, foes of Jacques Derrida, most all of whom would all too quickly and all too comfortably agree that Derrida's thought—or deconstruction more broadly—is, in its presumed atheism, nihilism, relativism, subjectivism, etc., a simple poison for religion. Reading the Derridean poison as gift, Caputo can argue that Derrida's obsession with figures of paradox and aporia signals more deeply, and more accurately, a "passion for the impossible"—that is, a passion that suffers the "incoming of the *tout autre*, the excess or breach that exceeds and shocks our expectations" (PT, 22), a passion that is finally taken best as a form of radical faith. Because open to the wholly new, and in this sense incurably blind, such faith would be a faith "without dogma" (PT, 57) and without the closure or violence of dogma, a faith "without faith" or "without the assurances of faith" (PT, 62); it would be an unfounded and uncertain faith that, in its very lack of determinacy, proves to be "messianic." That is, its most basic trait would be its passionate hope or desire for an ever imminent future, for the coming of an undefined "justice" that remains always yet to come, a justice that remains ever insecure because it remains, as distinct from law, beyond all programmatic calculation. According to a logic and temporality of the irreducibly unforeseeable and incalculable, then, such a faith would exceed every established horizon of possibility and expectation, and in that excess it would devastate every self-satisfied rule of "the same"—every rule, that is, of orthodox dogma and its violence.

In this focus on the religious significance of "the impossible," Caputo argues that the unsettling, disruptive force of the incomprehensible and ineffable in Derrida—which many have read in relation to the traditions of "negative theology"[3]—is finally more "prophetic" than "mystical," more Jewish than Christian. Emphasizing a certain "Jewish alliance" that would bind Derrida—beyond both simple continuity and straightforward rupture—to his "Jewish heritage" (PT, xxiv), Caputo wants to argue that "as long as we center everything on Derrida and 'negative theology'—a 'European, Greek, and Christian term'" (*Sauf*, 39/ON, 47)—important as this issue is, the question of Derrida's religion, of the heart of "my religion," of his prayers and tears, remains somewhat out of focus. For it is important to see that Derrida's religion is more prophetic than apophatic, more in touch with Jewish prophets than with Christian Neoplatonists, more messianic and more eschatological than mystical" (PT, xxiv). Invoking here a whole chain of distinctions that will frame his argument, Caputo sets the ground for his central effort to draw out an otherwise hidden or misunderstood Derrida.

Indeed, this concern to move discussion away from the Christian, Neoplatonic and mystical toward the Jewish, prophetic, and messianic is a concern to underscore the ethical and political dimensions of deconstruction that would have been ignored or misunderstood by so many critics of Derrida. Caputo wants to argue that "the non-knowing, the 'without-knowing' [. . .] of deconstruction has more to do with bearing an ethico-political witness to justice than with the *docta ignorantia*" (PT, xxiv). The prophetic and messianic Jew, on this reading, would be more acutely attuned to ethical and political urgency than would be the apophatic and mystical Christian—and Caputo's intuition on just this point would motivate and guide the work's central effort to "recast" the entire question of religion in Derrida "away from negative theology to the prophets, away from Greco-Christian texts to Jewish and biblical ones, and more generally away from 'theology' to 'religion'" (PT, 28). The move from the theological to the religious, from the Greco-Christian to the more Jewish and biblical, from the apophatic to the prophetic, from the mystical to the messianic, is for Caputo a move in the direction of a more promising ethics and politics. This move, however, does not simply abandon the apophatic and mystical; it attempts rather to open and expand their unsettling power.

While Caputo—following a certain line in Derrida—would suspect the Neoplatonic and Christian theological traditions to involve a "hyper-essentialism" or a "high ousiology" whose discourse finally proves all too secure and all too knowing in its ostensible claims to "apophasis" and "unknowing," the "messianic hope" of Derrida's more Jewish and more religious faith would signal for Caputo a more "generalized" apophatics and a more radical unknowing. This generalization is intended to *open* negative theology to its own most powerful and promising dimensions, to *save* negative theology from its own tendency toward closure. "So to the *theologia negativa*, one could add an *anthropologia negativa*, an *ethica negativa, politica negativa*, where of the humanity, or of the ethics, or the politics, or the democracy to come we cannot say a thing, except that they want to twist free from the regimes of presence, from the historically restricted concepts of humanity, ethics, and democracy under which we presently labor. [. . .] The effect of this *ignorantia* is to keep the possibility of the impossible open, to keep the future open, to have a future, which means something to come . . ." (PT, 56). Touching our conception not only of God but also of humanity and its ethical and political potential, the force of the negative here must, at bottom, resist the closure that can bring stasis and satisfaction with "the same," it must keep us *open* to the truly new, the incoming of the truly other in a future that cannot be defined by the present.

Assuming, then, the force of an ethico-political affirmation, obsessed with the urgency of a never-satisfied demand for better justice and a democracy still to come, Caputo's generalized apophatics is shaped primarily by his notion of a messianic hope or expectation whose basic structure requires a future that remains irreducibly open and indeterminate. As with the gift that exceeds all calculation, as with a faith whose leap is never assured, such an openness and indeterminacy alone might save a true coming of the new, and such a coming of the new, always yet to be, always a question of possibility and promise, can alone give the very meaning of futurity:

> The *à-venir*, the "dream" of a democracy to come, is not the vision of a democracy in the future present, not the gradual realization of an already envisaged ideal. The *à-venir* is not foreseen but "blind," and does not have a positive content but remains "absolutely undetermined" (SdM, 111/SoM, 65), the object of a faith, not a plan. [. . .] The *à-venir* of which deconstruction "dreams" is rather a completely open-ended, negative, undetermined structure—the heart of what I am calling here a generalized apophaticism—that goes along with a non-essentialism, a nominalism, and a generalized *ignorantia* about what is coming, that cultivates the possible not *as possible*, but as *the* im-possible. For the future present, insofar as it is already pre-envisioned, belongs to the regime of the same, of a "future modality of the living present" (SdM, 110/SoM, 64–65), which is not the absolutely undetermined surprise that Derrida calls the "messianic hope." (PT, 56)

The structure of this indeterminate futurity, which recalls very powerfully the Being-toward-death that haunts so much of Derrida's writing on paradox and aporia, is to be understood, for Caputo, primarily in terms of the messianic hope or faith that is not to be confused with the determinate content of any positive, historical messian*isms*.[4] In this distinction from the content of all determinate messian*isms*, the structure of the messianic "itself" would finally amount to "a non-dogmatic doublet of dogma [. . .], a structural possibility of religion without religion, the structural possibility of the religious unencumbered by the dangerous baggage of particular, determinate religions and their determinate faiths" (PT, 195).[5] In short, the truly open future of promise and possibility is for Caputo a messianic future that resists the closure of all dogmatic messianisms—and as such it signals a structural possibility of religion whereby the religious as possibility might be thought beyond or outside of the closure and violence toward which actual, determinate religions so often tend.

Both in its subtitle and in its main argument, then, *Prayers and Tears* interprets Derrida's faith without dogma—his "messianic hope," which, in its distinction from all determinate messianisms, would issue only in relation to the radically "open-ended," "negative," and "undetermined" structure of a never present future—as the kind of "religion without religion" that Derrida articulates in *The Gift of Death*. Such a thinking would seek in various ways to "repeat" "without religion" the very "possibility of religion,"[6] thereby yielding a kind of discourse "concerning the possibility and essence of the religious that does not amount to an article of [determinate, orthodox] faith" (GD, 49)—but that nonetheless remains faithful to faith, and hence proves neither simply reductive nor apologetic in its aim.

Operative variously in thinkers from Kant, Hegel, and Kierkegaard through Levinas, Ricoeur, and Marion, such a discourse on religion "without religion" might move in two distinct directions which both could be read finally to signal the deep instability of just such distinction itself; as exemplified in the approaches taken by Jan Patocka and Heidegger to the relation between philosophy and Christianity (as discussed in GD), these two directions would be as follows: the first "reontologizes the historic themes of Christianity and attributes to revelation or to the *mysterium tremendum* the ontological content that Heidegger attempts to remove from it" (GD, 23), while the second repeats "on an ontological level Christian themes and texts that have been 'de-Christianized'" (GD, 23).[7] Whether tending in the one direction or the other, both approaches, on Derrida's reading, could be taken to signal the operation of a "non-dogmatic doublet" of dogma that would attempt to articulate the possibility and significance of revelation without having to establish its actuality as event.[8]

Now, as Derrida repeatedly insists—and Caputo will elaborate and exploit this point very powerfully—the pivotal distinction here between religion and its possibility, or between religion's actuality and essence, or between undetermined structure and determinate content, is a distinction that always remains unstable because it cannot avoid the reciprocal indebtedness—and hence the undecidability—between ostensibly "founding" and ostensibly "founded" modes of discourse. Derrida finds a privileged instance of this instability, precisely, in Heidegger's attempted distinction between "revelation" (*Offenbarung*) understood as singular, determinate, historical event and "revealability" (*Offenbarkeit*) understood as a more universal, indeterminate structure or condition of possibility:

> In its most abstract form, then, the aporia within which we are struggling would perhaps be the following: is revealability (*Offenbarkeit*) more originary than revelation (*Offenbarung*), and hence independent of all religion? Independent in the structures of its experience and in the analytics relating to them? [. . .] Or rather, inversely, would the event of revelation have consisted in revealing revealability itself . . . ?[9]

While Heidegger would claim that the light of revealability in some general, indeterminate sense logically or ontologically precedes and makes possible the light of any single, determinate revelation, Derrida wants to argue that one could not ultimately decide on the definitive priority of one light over the other—and such an undecidability would unsettle Heidegger's own "fundamental" ontology itself: while seeking to repeat at the de-Christianized and thus more fundamental level of ontology those ontic themes that issue from the determinate Christian traditions, Heidegger's supposedly "founding" discourse would in fact prove to be substantially shaped by—and thus indebted to—the supposedly "founded" discourse of those very Christian themes (such, for example, as the Pauline eschatology that can be traced behind Heidegger's account of temporality).

According to this logic of reciprocal indebtedness or "double inclusion" (a logic one could trace as well in countless other thinkers) the distinction between founding and founded, between the indeterminate form or structure and the determinate content, between possibility and event, would become at a certain point undecidable:[10] one could never be quite sure which discourse is an example of which, which a translation of which. As Caputo puts it, the logic of "exemplarism" in Derrida gives way to an "endless translatability and substitutability" where "we do not know what is an example of what, where things become unnervingly open-ended" (PT, 13). While Derrida elaborates such an undecidability in relation to multiple terms and contexts, for Caputo the irreducible—and unnerving—open-endedness toward which the logic of exemplarism points makes the "messianic" a particularly good example of how that logic works.

The Derridean analysis of the messianic remains undecided between two alternatives that echo the alternatives Derrida delineates in Heidegger between revelation and revealability. *Either* "the religions" (especially those of "the Book")[11] "are but specific examples of [the] general structure of messianicity" on the ground of which "there have been revelations, a history which one calls Judaism or Christianity and so on"[12]—and in this case, one would have to carry out "a Heideggerian gesture" that would "go back from these religions to the fundamental ontological conditions of possibilities of religions . . ." (DN, 23, quoted in PT, 136). *Or else* "the events of revelation, the biblical traditions, the Jewish, Christian, and Islamic traditions, have been absolute events, irreducible events which have unveiled this messianicity" (DN, 23, quoted in PT, 136)—and in this case "singular events would have unveiled or revealed these universal possibilities and it is only on that condition that we can describe messianicity" (DN, 24, quoted in PT, 137).[13] As Caputo glosses, the alternative seems to be this: "*Either*: the messianic fits into a Heideggerian-Bultmannian schema of a demythologizing fundamental ontology in which one would strip away the existentiell particularities of the particular historical religions in order to unearth the universal, existential structures, the existentialia that represent the condition of possibility of ontico-existentiell messianisms. *Or*: the historical messianisms have a kind of absolute anteriority without which the messianic would be completely unknown" (PT, 137). The question, of course, concerns how the alternatives are to be understood in relation to one another, or, above all, what sense the distinction between founding and founded might have.

To reconcile the alternatives, Caputo notes, one might be tempted to invoke the traditional language of *ratio essendi* and *ratio cognoscendi*, in which case the messianic could be taken to constitute an essentially a priori ontological ground that itself comes to be known only in and through the actually existent messianisms. This approach would seem to clear up any ambiguity between founding and founded by giving ultimate priority to the ontological ground of all existent messianisms while acknowledging the relative priority of those messianisms within the order of knowing. "The problem," however, as Caputo quickly points out, "is that the whole discussion is framed with an assured set of distinctions—between fact and essence, example and exemplar, real and ideal, particular and universal—which it is the whole point of deconstruction to disturb" (137–138). In taking the deconstructive path, Caputo will want, with Derrida, to emphasize the undecidability or oscillation between these alternatives—an undecidability or oscillation that finally proves irreducible.

Just as the Heideggerian distinction between revelation and revealability cannot remain stable, since one can never decide which would be an example of which, or which brings which to light, so Derrida's own discourse on the messianic will both draw from the cultures of the determinate messianisms and, at the same time, elucidate a more general, more indeterminate, more desert-like structure or condition that would exceed any particular messianism (see PT, 137)—and it will do so without giving priority to one over the other as essence over existence, universal over particular, ideal over real, etc. At this point, Caputo indicates, the task is "to describe the *status* of this undeterminability, this indeterminable messianic, without specific content, which cannot be a true or conventional or garden variety universal" (PT, 139).

To move in that direction in his deconstructive manner, Caputo invokes very fruitfully the young Heidegger's "formal indication," which allows Caputo to maintain an undecidability between founding and founded fields of discourse in such a way as to signal the power of such undecidability itself for any thinking attuned to the complex interplay between philosophy and the concrete factical life embodied in the religious[14]—an interplay rendering untenable the simple subordination of one to the other:

> Unlike the traditional concept or category that purports to seize or comprehend its object, the "formal indication" is but a projective sketch that traces out in advance certain salient features of an entity or region of entities. Instead of a conceptual mastery of its material that reduces the individual to an instance of the general, the formal indication is related to the factical region as the imperfect to the perfect, as a schema or anticipatory sketch to the idiomatic fullness of concrete life (PT, 139).

By turning to the formal indication that the young Heidegger employed in his "own attempt to extract existential structures from the experience of 'factical life' in the early Christian communities" (PT, 139), Caputo can open philosophy to the "trauma" of its sources, and through that traumatic opening, the security of philosophy's generalizations and abstractions would be shaken—precisely because exposed to the urgency of concrete factical life. Such an approach would recognize the sense in which "philosophy requires the trauma of revisiting its sources, and a new humility about its own conceptuality, which needs both to be reforged on the basis of its exposure to factical existence and to be distrusted in terms of the extent of its reach, a reach which is never transcendental but at best 'quasi-transcendental'" (PT, 139). While "transcendental conditions" would "nail things down, pin them in place, inscribe them firmly within rigorously demarcated horizons," the more humble "quasi-transcendental conditions" of a traumatized philosophy would rather "allow [things] to slip loose, to twist free from their surrounding horizons, to leak and run off, to exceed or overflow their margins" (PT, 12–13). The trauma of revisiting philosophy's sources reshapes philosophy itself by shaking the claims of the transcendental to establish conditions of possibility in a set and one-sided manner; unsettling the clear distinction between founding and founded discourse, resisting philosophy's claim to predetermine clear a priori grounds for the religious, such a traumatic revisiting allows—or indeed, forces—the margins of the philosophic and the religious to blur somewhat, or to leak into one another, thereby signaling the senses in each might both draw on and exceed the other.

Significantly, the trauma involved here is not simply destructive, nor is the uncertainty or ambiguity it yields a simple relativism or nihilism. Rather, much to the contrary, Caputo's use of the formal indication in his reading of Derrida wants to highlight the sense in which Derrida's "quasi-transcendental" messianic involves an ethical urgency that was in fact lacking in the formal indication of Heidegger. On Caputo's reading, "the messianic in general" would itself operate as "a formal indication of the concrete messianisms that are to be found in the religions of the Book. But a formal indication, on Heidegger's accounting, has the status of an empty schema which lacks existential *engagement* whereas Derrida's 'messianic' is the very structure of urgency and engagement" (PT, 141)—and it is so precisely to the degree that it constantly unsettles the fixity of the determinate messianisms (whose secure closure always verges on violence) even as it draws on, or remains bound to, them. This tension and interplay signal perhaps the deepest logic of the messianic itself as a figure of the deconstructive passion for the impossible:

> The messianic, I am arguing all along, is deconstruction's passion and deconstruction is impassioned by the impossible. That is why, I think, in accord with a fundamental gesture of deconstruction, that there cannot be a clean-cut and well-maintained border between the two messianic spaces. [. . .] Derrida's desert-like and arid, an-khôral, atheological messianic enjoys a great deal of the life of the historical messianisms, of their historical hope, of their religious affirmation of something freeing that is to come, a great deal of the energy of *engagement*. The *whole idea* of "abstracting" from the concrete messiahs is to intensify the urgency of the messianic. (PT, 141–42)

Indeed, such abstraction, which unsettles the fixed content of any given messianism, is part and parcel of the messianic itself as that which in its very definition remains open to the *coming* of the new; such abstraction is essential to the messianic's definitive openness. It is in this light, then, that Derrida will speak of the *ascesis* that "strips the messianic hope of all biblical forms, and even all determinable figures of the wait or expectation; it thus denudes itself in view of responding to that which must be absolute hospitality, the 'yes' to the *arrivant(e)*, the 'come' to the future that cannot be anticipated . . ." (SoM, 168). Such an ascetic denuding or abstraction, such an aphairesis, would be vital to the defining temporality of the messianic logic that moves within all messianisms, whose future *must* remain beyond the expectation or anticipation that can turn the open and incalculable future into a future present that is subject to the calculation of a closed program.

To put this in somewhat different terms: Derrida's messianic *hope* is not a well-grounded optimism but indeed a groundless affirmation tied necessarily to a certain *despair*, for "without this latter despair and if one could *count* on what is coming, hope would be but the calculation of a program. One would have the prospect but one would no longer wait for anything or anyone. Law without justice" (SoM, 169). The ascetic denuding of all determinate messianisms (which too often seem to see too clearly what is coming) would be necessary to that openness and uncertainty which alone save the possibility of a justice that promises more and other than the mechanical implementation of law. Justice demands a hope that passes beyond the hope of any given messianism, a less certain and more indeterminate hope. At the same time, however, again, the very logic of such messianic openness, uncertainty, and indeterminacy might first be given only in and through the concrete messianisms whose content at the same time risks the dogmatic closure that would annul the messianic. The attempt to maintain a tension and undecidability between the one and the other is an attempt to save the messianic itself in all its ethical promise, and it is precisely this undecidability and its ethical promise that are central to Caputo's reading of Derrida.

Caputo is at his most forceful, I think, when explicating and exploiting precisely those senses in which, as Derrida suggests, one can never finally decide which of these two modes of discourse is founding and which founded: would any given determinate religious faith be an example of the religious in its broadest and most desert-like formal sense—and thus intelligible, or indeed possible, only on the basis of the latter? Or, on the contrary, would the religious in its broadest, formal sense become intelligible or possible only on the prior basis of such determinate faith? Would the historical messianisms first bring to light any sense of the messianic "in general," or would the formal structure of the messianic itself first make possible the very historical appearance and sense of any given messianism? Deconstruction itself falls for Caputo in just this space of undecidability, for "deconstruction is a certain negative propheticism, a negative or apophatic messianic, whose most vivid and perfect illustration or exemplification (or repetition) is to be found in the biblical, prophetic notion of justice, so long as we add the little proviso that throws everything into undecidability" (PT, 196).

Caputo locates Derrida's distinctively messianic faith, then, in the interspace of this undecidability. Just as a formalizing, desertifying philosophical discourse of the messianic would disrupt the determinate closure of the religious faith or dogma it indicates, so the determinacy of singular religious traditions and events would both feed and resist the universalizing tendency of such philosophic discourse. Each checking the other, each both informing and resisting the other, the "messianic" and the "messianisms" remain in the irreducible tension of undecidability—and just that tension and undecidability give the radical openness of expectation in terms of which messianic faith itself might operate, for such a faith answers to the groundless, indeterminate hope of an unforeseeable future—the hope for a justice that, because always yet to come, because unforeseeable according to law or programmatic calculation, no actual orthodoxy could ever pre-determine, accommodate, or master. Under this privileged figure of the messianic, the promise of the unforeseeable in Derrida would draw on particular messianisms while ever also disrupting them—repeating their own inner logic of openness to the future in order thus to resist the closure through which orthodoxy can exercise its violence. While drawing on determinate messianisms, Derrida would always also exercise a certain asceticism or abstraction, an aphairesis or apophasis, in any case "a certain *epoche*[15] of the content of any particular messianism, a 'desertification' and 'abstraction,' in order to think 'the messianic in general, as a thinking of the other and of the event to come,' where 'the formal structure of promise exceeds' or 'precedes' the particular promises made in particular, concrete covenants" (PT, 128).

In this way, the unsettling logic of "the messianic" proves exemplary for the analysis of all the various figures of the impossible in Derrida. Treating successively the apophatic, the apocalyptic, the messianic, the gift, circumcision, and confession, Caputo highlights in Derrida the insistent disruption of the actual or established by that which remains radically open and yet to come—thanks to the possibility of "the impossible" that no actuality ever masters. According to this messianic logic of (im)possibility, Caputo can finally include deconstruction itself among the "religions without religion"—and to very powerful effect, for such an inclusion "closes deconstruction off from mindless charges of nihilism and subjectivism" even as it "closes religion off from mindless fundamentalism" (PT, 279). In short, Caputo opens us to the religious resonance of deconstructive philosophy and to certain deconstructive currents in religion—and by doing so he demonstrates in exemplary fashion how it is that the intersection between philosophy and religion might be approached without simply subjugating one to the other. The "very idea of the quasi-transcendental," Caputo insists, "means that, regarding the idea of deconstruction and prophetic religion, we do not know which is an example or repetition of which. This is what undecidability (un)means" (PT, 196).

Now, at the heart of Caputo's exemplary work is the logic of exemplarism itself and the undecidability that such exemplarism would imply. One can also note, however, that Caputo's treatment of exemplarism and its undecidability, concerned as it is to read deconstruction in the direction of a certain ethical and political urgency, is at the same time founded on a some insistent distinctions and important decisions. The primary distinction falls between a Jewish notion of the prophetic and messianic and a Christian understanding of the apophatic and mystical; the primary decision, following from this distinction, would favor the Jewish, prophetic and messianic over the Christian, apophatic and mystical in treating the interplay between deconstruction and religion. The decision, of course, is motivated by Caputo's perception of a tendency toward closure in the Christian and mystical contexts that would be checked or undone by the openness of the Jewish and messianic. While not ignoring the significance of the apophatic to deconstructive thought (and vice versa), Caputo will nevertheless insist repeatedly, out of his concern for justice, that Derrida's religion is more Jewish, prophetic and messianic than it is Christian, apophatic and mystical, that it is more religious than theological, more biblical than metaphysical, etc. On Caputo's own understanding, "the main work" of PT itself is "to follow that more Jewish and religious turn" in Derrida (PT, 28). But does this set of clear distinctions—and the set of decisions bound to them—actually hold up in the way or to the degree that Caputo's argument can seem to suggest?

Caputo's enthusiasm over a distinctively Jewish and messianic Derrida— a Derrida that he very rightly and brilliantly elucidates for us—leads to an oddly weighted reading of "negative theology" and its relation to Derridean thinking, a reading that, by associating negative theology too closely and fully with Hellenistic philosophy, over-emphasizes the potential tendency of such theology toward a metaphysic of presence. The following passage from the opening pages of PT conveys his position well:

> As a hyperousiology, negative theology drops anchor, hits bottom, lodges itself securely in pure presence and the transcendental signified, every bit as much as positive onto-theo-logy, and in a certain sense more so. Its difference from kataphatic or onto-theology, from "metaphysics," lies in claiming to touch bottom not by means of representational thinking, of concepts and discursive reasoning, but by leaving all such representational paraphernalia and parerga in the vestibule and entering into a wordless, imageless, timeless inner sanctum of the temple [. . .]. Far from providing a deconstruction of the metaphysics of presence, negative theology crowns the representations of metaphysics with the jewel of pure presence, and effects in a still higher way [. . .] the triumph of presence over representation. [. . .] To that extent, deconstruction is its nemesis. But that does not have the effect of leveling or razing negative theology, but rather of liberating negative theology from the Greek metaphysics of presence in which it is enmeshed and forcing it to come up with a better story about itself than the hyperousiological one that it has inherited not from the Bible but from Neoplatonism. (PT, 11)

Caputo's core argument here is that negative or apophatic theology constitutes only the reverse side of a positive or kataphatic theology that would itself be "onto-theological"—which would mean that negative theology still remains inscribed within the logic of onto-theological metaphysics, presenting only a more subtle, inverted expression of it. Trapped in its metaphysical closure, which always threatens violence, negative theology would need deconstruction to "save" that theology from such closure and violence. If we follow Caputo at this point, the Greco-Christian traditions of negative theological discourse—grounded ultimately in a claim to full and secure presence, or something "correct in itself" (PT, 344), and overly inclined toward the violence of such security and rectitude—would need to be checked by the unsettling force of more Jewish and more biblical traditions, to whose sense of justice deconstruction would keep us vigilant.

This reading of negative theology, however, is probably not as generous as it could be. To begin, Caputo's initial equation between kataphatic theology with "onto-theology"/"metaphysics" is questionable to the degree that a founding figure like the Pseudo-Dionysius in fact associates the "positive," or "kataphatic" naming of God not primarily with Greek metaphysics but indeed with the names that he takes to be revealed in scripture. Because he believes his God to surpass speech, mind, and being itself, Dionysius insists in the *Divine Names* that "we must not dare to resort to words or conceptions concerning that hidden divinity which transcends being, apart from what the sacred scriptures have divinely revealed (*para ta theôdôs hémin ek tôn hierôn logiôn ekpephasmena*)."[16] Kataphatic theology is, in Dionysius' own thinking and writing at any rate, tied at least as intimately to the biblical *logia* as to those of Greek metaphysics.

Furthermore, just as the equation of kataphatic theology with onto-theology is questionable, so might one resist the understanding of "negative theology" as a mere reversal of the positive. As I've indicated, Caputo takes the negative movement of Christian apophatic theologies to offer only the simple reverse of a positive or kataphatic theology, which itself he has equated with onto-theological metaphysics; the negative, on this reading, would constitute but a higher, if disguised and inverted form of the positive, another if more subtle discourse of an all too Greek presence and its seeming security. The weakness of this reading is that it does not acknowledge the sense in which a theological tradition like that of Dionysius in fact insists, with some complexity, that negation is finally no more adequate than affirmation; both are equally insufficient, and neither ever "drops anchor" or "touches bottom." The Dionysian texts and traditions themselves, even without deconstruction's help, can yield a more complex picture, they can tell a better story about themselves, within which a redoubled negation or a hyper-negation (associated especially with the mystical) would, as distinct from any double negation of the Hegelian sort, oscillate endlessly *between* the kataphatic and the apophatic in a movement not wholly unlike that of Derridean (or Caputoan, or Taylorian) *différance*.[17] Such an oscillation, I would emphasize, goes hand in hand with a movement of desire and expectation whose logic is not entirely foreign to that of the messianic passion that Caputo discerns in deconstruction's religion without religion—all of which leads me to ask the following, in the spirit of broadening Caputo's promising model of religion without religion.

Could one not read the irreducible tension and undecidability between the determinate, concrete messianisms and the indeterminate, desertifying structure of the messianic in Caputo's approach to religion without religion as a repetition, translation, or example of the oscillation between the kataphatic and the apophatic modes of theological discourse in a mystical thinking and writing like that of Dionysius and his heirs? In both cases, one might argue, the determinate content of the first would be necessary to any articulation of the second, even as the unsettling indeterminacy, the formal and desert-like aridity, of the second would constantly trouble and undo the stability and content of the first (as well as its own).

On this reading, the notion of a divine causality "beyond being" in Dionysian contexts could in fact prove just as radically indeterminate and unsettling as that which Caputo wants to set in contrast to it: the (Platonic) "*khôra*," which (somewhat strangely[18]) would constitute a "second name" of the "religion without religion" that Caputo discerns in the very Jewish and messianic Derrida, a second name for that "postmodern faith and hope," that "postmodern reason and universality," which, thanks to the "most extreme abstraction" from the "concrete messianisms," becomes the "the heart of a justice and a democracy to come in a heartless world" (PT, 156). For Caputo, *khôra* would signal "the placeless place of absolute spacing, which is more 'without being' than any Platonic or Christian Neoplatonic *epekeina tes ousias*, older than any 'Greco-Abrahamic' synthesis of Yahweh with the *ousia* of the unmoved mover" (PT, 156)—but in his own language surrounding *khôra*, I think, we can still hear a powerful resonance of the divine cause beyond being as Dionysius articulates it.

Indeed, just as Caputo will insist that the Derridean *khôra* "is neither Being nor Nothing, God nor Man, Nature nor History, Matter nor Spirit, but a 'place of infinite resistance, of an infinitely impassible remainder: a *tout autre* without face" (*Foi*, 31); just as he will understand it as a "tropic of negativity" in which "there is there (*il y a là*) something that is said, very apophatically, to be *neither* being nor non-being, neither sensible nor intelligible, that is not analogous to either, and is unable to be hinted at by metaphors" (PT, 35); just as he will assert with Derrida that "*Khôra* is neither present nor absent, active nor passive, the Good nor evil, living nor nonliving (*Timaeus*, 50c)" (PT, 35–36)—so will Dionysius himself insist throughout his writings, and notably in the ultimate lines of his foundational treatise on mystical theology, that the "cause of all," which is "not in any place" (MT, 1040D), cannot be spoken of and [. . .] cannot be grasped by understanding. [. . .] It is not immovable, moving, or at rest. It has no power, it is not power, nor is it light. It does not live nor is it life. It is not substance nor is it eternity or time. It cannot be grasped by the understanding since it is neither knowledge nor truth. [. . .] It is neither one nor oneness, divinity nor goodness. [. . .] It is not sonship or fatherhood and it is nothing known to us or to any other being. It falls neither within the predicate of nonbeing nor of being. Existing beings do not know it as it actually is and it does not know them as they are. There is no speaking of it, nor name nor knowledge of it. Darkness and light, error and truth—it is none of these. It is beyond assertion and denial. We make assertions and denials of what is next to it, but never of it . . . (MT, 1048A–B)

Given these literal resonances, why not press further an inquiry into their conceptual force? Here, at any rate, I think that one would be hard pressed to argue without further qualification that Dionysius reaches "bottom," that he attains the transcendental signified, or that he secures a full presence as such; one would be hard-pressed to insist that the desert of the *khôra* is somehow *more* arid or abstracted, and thus less secure and more unsettling, than this cause beyond all speech and knowledge, being and non-being, light and darkness, truth and error, presence and absence, assertion and denial—this cause in approaching which, being "neither oneself nor another" (MT, 1001A), one would be dispossessed, in an ascetic and desertifying movement that is not simply or wholly foreign to the messianic. Caputo will himself recognize at points that "there is an interesting fluctuation or undecidability between the two tropics of negativity, between the discourse about *khôra* and the kenotic, self-emptying desertification of apophatic theology" (PT, 37)—but having recognized that undecidability, he does not finally maintain or develop it as he might. Rather, he finally decides that the God of Dionysian tradition is ultimately the God of a high ousiology—but why decide in this direction rather than another? Why become so decisive just here? Is the Yahweh with whom Caputo concludes his work really any more indeterminate, undecidable or unsettling than the divine, causal nothing in Dionysius? If anything, he would seem the reverse—and thus more distant from *khôra* than the Dionysian God.

On the one hand noting and powerfully explicating the fluctuation or undecidability between the negativity of the faceless *khôra* (from which he moves somewhat strangely to the face of Yahweh) and the kenotic desertification of apophatic theology, Caputo finally wants to decide between the negativity of *khôra* and that of Dionysian theology—or more generally, between those empty deserts and those overfull oceans which at least some of the mystics have been able to see in their indiscretion. To do this, however, he needs to assert of Dionysius what seems to me not entirely on target—that Dionysius finally follows "the high road of a high ousiology, the assured path provided by the *hyperousios*, the well-rounded circular path of *aletheia*" (PT, 38), in short, that "Dionysius does not get lost in the desert" (PT, 38). To uphold these assertions, one must downplay precisely those passages just cited—and those running throughout the Dionysian corpus—which insist that the divine cause, like *khôra*, is neither being nor non-being, neither error nor truth, neither perceptible nor intelligible, neither presence nor absence, neither activity nor passivity, neither living nor nonliving, neither assertion nor denial, etc. Remaining beyond all metaphor and analogy, beyond all assertion and denial, opening a discourse that, like Aristotle's prayer, is neither true nor false, the Dionysian God can be read to give way to an endless oscillation *between* assertion and denial, position and erasure, thesis and negation—and in that endless oscillation lives and moves a desire or expectation that knows no end, a profoundly eschatological desire whose primary "type" for Dionysius is Moses, who did, after all, spend some time in the desert (MT, 1001A).

Prayers and Tears is very effective in showing the apophatic force of the messianic, but it is less successful in keeping open the messianic expectation that lives in many of the apophatic mystics, and at this point I'm not sure Caputo remains faithful to the logic of exemplarism that he himself so brilliantly deploys. Just as I'm not convinced that the distinction between desert and ocean, between *khôra* and the Dionysian cause, can finally be maintained as Caputo tries to maintain it, so I am not convinced that the expectation of the messianic—in all of its ethical and political urgency—is wholly foreign to the desire that drives many of the mystical theologians, not only in their thinking and writing but also in their spiritual practice and liturgical life.

Hoping, then, to suggest that there might be more (or less!) to the apophatic mystics than Caputo at times allows, I would close by noting a striking resemblance between the messianic desire in Caputo's Derridean example and the mystical desire of the apophatic traditions in which Dionysius appears. "There is in Derrida," Caputo concludes,

> what one might call a certain overreaching, trespassing aspiration, what I have been calling here, all along, a dream, or a desire, a restlessness, a passion for the impossible, a panting for something to come. This passion is not a determinable wish or will for a definable goal or foreseeable objective, however hard any such goal may be to attain. [. . .] Over and beyond, beneath and before any such determinate purpose, there is in Derrida, in deconstruction, a longing and sighing, a weeping and praying, a dream and a desire, for something non-determinable, un-foreseeable, beyond the actual and the

possible, beyond the horizon of possibility, beyond the scope of what we can possibly imagine. (PT, 333)

From just such a perspective, I think, one could very fruitfully read the mystical desire of Dionysius—or, what resembles it so deeply, the desirous straining of endless *epektasis* or expectation in Dionysius' predecessor, Gregory of Nyssa (c. 332–395). In both these figures and their heirs, the desire for a God who cannot be thought or named, the expectation that drives a soul to seek knowledge of the unknowable and to name the unnameable, is a desire or expectation—embodied not only in theological discourse but also in the ascetic practice and liturgical community—that feeds on the possibility of the impossible; according to just this logic of the possibility of impossibility, as articulated in Gregory's *Life of Moses*, the true vision of God is this: "never to be satisfied in the desire to see him. But one must always, by looking at what he can see, rekindle his desire to see more. Thus, no limit would interrupt growth in the ascent to God, since no limit to the Good can be found nor is the increasing of desire for the Good brought to an end because it is satisfied."[19] The desire exemplified in Moses is, precisely, a "desire for *what is still to come*" (LM, II.242), a desire that always reaches forward, ever open, never satisfied—or satisfied only in its own deferral and disappointment, a desire tied intimately, therefore, like Derridean hope, to a certain despair.[20] In Gregory and his heirs one never drops anchor or reaches bottom, and divine presence does not secure satisfaction; rather, one is driven by an eschatological desire or expectation, an endless *epektasis* according to which the satisfaction of desire for God is given only in the denial of desire, or in despair, where the apophatic unknowing of God does not yield a higher security, a circular satisfaction, or fulfilled stasis, but rather a life of infinite striving that always hopes, beyond hope, for a greater virtue that is never known or achieved.

Now, I am hoping that Gregory especially might help me to nudge Caputo a bit here not only because Gregory is a genius of apophatic expectation (which he is), but also because Gregory—like Caputo—appreciates the sense in which a desire for the always imminent future is related not only to effort but also to incalculable chance, to the kind of chance, perhaps, whose passionate hope— and, equally, whose bottomless despair—anyone glimpses who has ever spent an afternoon at the horse races. Yes, the horse races. You see, I suspect that Caputo is a thinker who might enjoy a good horse race—and in any case, I know that Gregory did, since he writes in the very first line of his masterpiece on expectation, the *Life of Moses*, the following: "At horse races, the spectators intent on victory shout to their favorites in the contest, even though the horses are eager to run" (LM, I.1). What might we read in such a passionate and excessive shout, a shout that adds eagerness to eagerness?

We might read, I think, a hope or intention that exceeds all effort, a desire that passes beyond what is already or ever actual—in short, an openness to incalculable chance. And in all of this, I think, one could, by the right light anyway, glimpse a shadow or a ghost, a translation or repetition, an example of that hopeful desire—and of that despair—expressed by the one who says to the very face of the Messiah: when will you come? It is Caputo's example that helps me to glimpse this possibility, and it is this very sense of possibility that seems to me so promising in the discourse emerging today somewhere between philosophy and religion.[21]

NOTES

1. The debts and correspondences of Heideggerian thought to the religious field have long been a central concern of Caputo's—from ME and HA to DH. Two other recent books also elucidate very effectively the significant religious background to Heidegger's philosophy: Theodore Kisiel, *The Genesis of Heidegger's Being and Time* (Berkeley: University of California Press, 1993); John Van Buren, *The Young Heidegger: Rumor of the Hidden King* (Bloomington: Indiana University Press, 1994). For two fine recent articles on Heidegger's relation to theology, see Françoise Dastur, "Heidegger et la Théologie," in *Revue philosophique de Louvain*, vol. 92, nos. 2–3, May–August 1994; and Jean-François Courtine, "Les Traces et le Passage du Dieu dans les *Beiträge zur Philosophie* de Martin Heidegger," in *Archivio di filosofia*, nos. 1–3, 1994.

2. John D. Caputo, PT.

3. See especially Kevin Hart's *Trespass of the Sign: Deconstruction, Philosophy and Theology* (Cambridge: Cambridge University Press, 1989), or, more recently, my own *Indiscretion: Finitude and the Naming of God* (Chicago: University of Chicago Press, 1999).

4. It is worth noting that for Caputo the primary Derridean figure of the impossible/aporetic is *justice* taken in this messianic sense, which, significantly, he privileges over other, perhaps equally valid (or invalid) figures—such as death. The impossible *"as such"* does not necessarily justify such a privilege. As Derrida will indicate, for example, "the ultimate aporia is the impossibility of the aporia *as such*. The reservoir of this statement seems to me incalculable. This statement is made with and reckons with the incalculable itself. Death, as the possibility if the impossible *as such*, is a figure of the aporia in which 'death' and death can replace—and this is a metonymy that carries the name beyond the name and beyond the name of the name—all that is possible only as impossible, if there is such a thing: love, the gift, the other, testimony, and so forth," in *Aporias*, p. 79.

5. Here and elsewhere, Caputo can tend to desire a purity and a peace where one might expect rather to find one violence traded for another, one sacrifice made to save another. To say that "Derrida's distinction between the concrete messianisms and the messianic in general" amounts to "a distinction between war and peace" (PT, 195) seems too clear-cut.

6. Jacques Derrida, GD, p. 49.

7. I treat these passages and themes at greater length in "The Binds that Tie the Ethical and the Religious: Philosophy of Religion after Derrida," in *Svensk Teologisk Kvartalskrift*, no. 74 (1998).

8. This seems much like the aim in Jean-Luc Marion's recent phenomenology, which reaches a summit in the phenomenological treatment of revelation as possibility. See *Etant donné: Essai d'une phénoménologie de la donation*, esp. § 24 (Paris: Presses Universitaires de France, 1997).

9. Jacques Derrida, "Faith and Knowledge: the Two Sources of 'Religion' at the Limits of Reason Alone," in Jacques Derrida and Gianni Vattimo, eds., *Religion* (Stanford: Stanford University Press, 1998), p. 16.

10. This has been a key question, of course, in relation to the work of Marion, whose thinking involves both theological and phenomenological dimensions between which the distinction may be less clear-cut than Marion himself would have it. On Marion's distinction between the theological and the phenomenological, see *Etant donné* or, in English, "Metaphysics and Phenomenology: A Relief for Theology," trans. Thomas A. Carlson, *Critical Inquiry*, vol. 20, no. 4 (Summer, 1994). For my argument that the phenomenological and theological in Marion may draw on one another in ways that Marion wants to downplay, see *Indiscretion*, ch. 6.

11. It is worth remembering that the discussion of religion from this Derridean-Caputoan perspective does fall very squarely within the Judeo-Christian-Islamic context—leaving quite open the question concerning the pertinence or promise of *this* approach to the religious for those countless other traditions that one might include among the religions. My guess is that the central operations of exemplarism and undecidability will in fact yield very fruitful results in the analysis of traditions for which the Book and its specific messianisms remain foreign.

12. Jacques Derrida, DN, p. 23, quoted in PT, 136.

13. Derrida here addresses in the context of the Villanova roundtable discussion that distinction—and undecidability—so crucial to *Specters of Marx*: "How to relate, but also how to dissociate the two messianic spaces we are talking about here under the same name? If the messianic appeal belongs properly to a universal structure, to that irreducible movement of the historical opening to the future, therefore to experience itself and to its language (expectation, promise, commitment to the event of what is coming, imminence, urgency, demand for salvation and for justice beyond law, pledge given to the other inasmuch as he or she is not present, presently present or living, and so forth), how is one to *think* it *with* the figures of Abrahamic messianism? Does it figure abstract desertification or originary condition? Was not Abrahamic messianism but an exemplary pre-figuration, the pre-name [*prénom*] given against the background of the possibility that we are attempting to name here? But then why keep the name, or at least the adjective (we prefer to say *messianic* rather than *messianism*, so as to designate a structure of experience rather than a religion), there where no figure of the *arrivant*, even as he or she is heralded, should be pre-determined, pre-figured, or even pre-named? Of these two deserts, which one, first of all, will have signaled toward the other?" in SoM, pp. 167–168.

14. For an illuminating treatment of the sources and senses of "formal indication" in the young Heidegger, see especially Kisiel's *Genesis of Heidegger's Being and Time*.

15. Derrida himself, of course, has signaled the interesting proximity between theological apophasis and the phenomenological *epoché*: ". . . transcendental phenomenology, as it passes through the suspension of all *doxa*, of every positing of existence, of every thesis, inhabits the same element as negative theology. One would be a good propaedeutic for the other," in "Post-Scriptum: Aporias, Ways, and Voices," trans. John Leavey, in H. Coward and T. Foshay, eds., *Derrida and Negative Theology* (Albany, NY: State University of New York Press, 1992), p. 308.

16. *Divine Names*, 588A, in *Pseudo-Dionysius: The Complete Works*, trans. Colm Luibheid (New York: Paulist Press, 1987). All citations to Dionysius will henceforth appear parenthetically as follows (according to the Migne pagination): DN=*Divine Names*; MT=*Mystical Theology*.

17. For my discussion of Dionysius' hyper-negation, see *Indiscretion*, ch. 5.

18. Caputo's reliance on the Derridean analysis of *khôra* strikes me as strange not in itself but in light of his later appeals to a Yahweh whose face and personality would, in Caputo's eyes, render him a better figure of the divine than the faceless and impersonal Good (*to agathon*) of Greco-Christian traditions (see especially PT, 334–337). Caputo's criticism of the *agathon*, along with the broader attack on apophatic theology as the mere reverse of an onto-theological, kataphatic discourse grows, I think, out of his general suspicion and aversion toward a Hellenism that he believes to infect the Christian mystical traditions. Sensing in that Hellenism a corrupting and dangerous diversion from the intuitions and insights of Jewish biblical traditions, Caputo really gives hell to the Hellenes—but the enthusiasm of his attacks can lead to this strangeness just noted, which has two dimensions. First, the deep antagonism that Caputo establishes between a Greco-Christian conception of the Good and a Jewish understanding of Yahweh really shortchanges the rich and complex understandings of the Good within the Christian traditions, understandings that emphasize, in fact, the relational, interpersonal, and liturgical aspects of the Christian life; in its Christian versions at any rate, the Good may have a bit more personality than Caputo grants. Second, and perhaps more strangely, in his emphasis on the antagonism between the Greco-Christian Good and Yahweh, Caputo seems to forget that he himself reaches and frames his discussion of Yahweh only in relation to his own powerful discussion of the Derridean *khôra*, which does after all go back to Plato and not the Bible, and which surely proves *at least* as impersonal as the Good whose perceived personal deficiency Caputo attacks in favor of Yahweh.

All of this leads to a double question. First, why assume so readily that the metaphysics of presence is such a wholly Greek invention that would be foreign to the biblical contexts themselves? Can one not trace in the biblical writings an understanding of God as supreme source of all life, movement, and being—indeed as supreme origin and end of all that is? Is this biblical understanding of God so wholly distant from the onto-theological conception of God as highest cause who serves also as ground of all being? Second, conversely, why accept so readily that the apophatic theologians of Dionysian tradition are, because indebted to Neoplatonism, therefore also so very distant from the biblical? One could argue, I think, both that Dionysius is more biblical and that the Bible is more metaphysical than Caputo's position wants to allow.

19. Gregory of Nyssa, *Life of Moses*, trans. Abraham J. Malherbe (New York: Paulist Press, 1978), II.239. Hereafter cited parenthetically (according to book and paragraph number) as LM.

20. "The heavenly voice now grants the petitioner's request and does not deny this additional grace. Yet again He leads him to despair in that He affirms that what the petitioner seeks cannot be contained by human life" (LM, II.220). Gregory uses "despair" (*apelpismós*) to signal precisely that desirous relation to God in which the soul never attains God.

21. A good example of such discourse can be seen emerging in the recently formed Society for Continental Philosophy and Theology, which organized a roundtable discussion of *Prayers and Tears* where I presented an earlier version of this essay (Denver, October 11, 1998). I want to express here my gratitude to all of the participants in this new society for their collegial spirit and commitment to open, critical discussion. I note especially the other roundtable members, Adriaan Peperzak, Philip Buckley, and Cleo Kearns; and the organizers, Bruce Benson, Norman Wirzba, Merold Westphal, and John Caputo.

ON BEING LEFT WITHOUT A PRAYER:
A RESPONSE TO CARLSON

John D. Caputo

> "... horse and rider he has thrown into the sea."
> —Exodus 15:1

Thomas Carlson, one of the new stars in the firmament of continental philosophy of religion,[1] has identified the nerve of *Prayers and Tears*. This book is framed by an Introduction, "A Passion for the Impossible," and a Conclusion, "A Passion for God," that are meant to signal the endless translatability of "God" and "the impossible," the substitutability of the one for the other, which I have called, following Derrida, the problem of "exemplarism." If we *knew* which was the translation of which, which the exemplar and which the instantiation, there would be no problem of undecidability. If we knew whether the passion for God boils down to a passion for justice, or our passion for justice is but a form of a passion for God, then we would know what is what. But we do not, resulting not in chaos, but in a mutual exposure of religion and deconstruction, as passions of a comparable kind, which are joined at the point that I call "religion without religion." This phrase, used by Derrida to describe Kierkegaard and Levinas and others, I attribute to deconstruction itself, and that Derrida does not decline it when it is put point blank to him by Dooley.[2] Carlson's formulation of this argument is remarkably powerful and insightful formulation of what is going on in this book.

Tom Carlson then goes on to see if he can nudge me away from some of the things I say about negative or mystical theology, which I called a "high ousiology." By that I meant that throughout the darkest nights of negative theology, throughout all its profound renunciation of concepts, judgments and argumentation—"God is neither this nor that"[3]—there persists a still more profound movement of unity with God. The negations of apophatic theology are part of a larger or deeper economy, a way of negating every name of God (*deus est innominabile*) in the name of saving God's name, for God is everything save the names we give to God. Carlson wants to weaken the links I have made between mystical theology and Hellenistic metaphysics. Now I am happy to be nudged and instructed by Tom Carlson on several points. I accept Carlson's point that in Christian Neoplatonism kataphatic theology is not Greek but biblical, because it is the Scriptures that teach us to name God in personal terms, as loving and merciful, for God is love, while it is the Neoplatonist side of these thinkers that lead them to talk of a divine abyss or desert behind or older than the divine persons. That indeed is part of the trouble that Meister Eckhart, who belongs to the Neoplatonic tradition fathered by Gregory and Pseudo-Dionysius, bought for himself with his Franciscan inquisitors (a diversionary tactic mean to distract attention from William of Ockham!). I tried once to balance this Christian and Neoplatonic components in this equation, at least as regards Meister Eckhart.[4] I am also happy to embrace Carlson's point about the structure of *epectasis*, of insatiable desire beyond desire, happy to be nudged in the direction of Gregory of Nyssa, about whom Carlson offers a suggestive and persuasive account, which would build an important bridge to the structure of messianic expectation.

The main point, however, as I see it, concerns being "lost," and this—if this does not seem too ornery—it seems to me, is still standing. I think *Prayers and Tears* is right on track about being lost. Mystical theology as such, that is, mystical writers in their *first* or dominant voice, precisely insofar as they write from out of an experience of divine things, *pati divina*, are not "lost," however long, wide and deep the string of renunciations they profess. Now I do not claim that mystical theology is the "flip side" of onto-theology, or the negative "reversal" of kataphatic theology. I said it was "the jewel in its crown,"[5] inasmuch as it abandons representational thinking (all concepts: univocal, analogical, or equivocal; all propositions: *affirmative or negative*; all arguments, transcendent or transcendental), all language, all *différance*, in order to be admitted into a simpler, non-discursive, non-linguistic, non-spatial, timeless, unitative experience of divine things. That at least is its desire. So nothing is gained from my point of view by pointing out that mystical theology, which leaves *all* propositions behind, also leaves *negative* propositions behind. It leaves the God of onto-theo-logic at the door *precisely in order to* enter into a deeper relation with the Godhead beyond all representational discourse, positive or negative. So the more the mystical renunciation of affirmation and negation mount up, as in the text Carlson cites, the more purified is the soul for union with God. The more the soul empties itself of creatures, the more room it makes for God. The soul does not get more lost, more *destinerrant*, in this kenosis, but more profoundly fit to become one with the One, united with God, having divested itself of everything that blocks such union. So if the soul is without understanding, without will, and without being, if it is stripped naked and made absolutely poor, if it dares enter this eerie desert kenosis, then it is made simple and empty enough for God's advent. The lovely passage from the *Mystical Theology* that Carlson cites belongs precisely to this register; the longer such texts are strung out, the more purified and fit is the soul for the wordless timeless *pati divina*.

The roof of this is exactly the one that Derrida brings up in "Violence and Metaphysics." Suppose you called Gregory of Nyssa or Pseudo-Dionysius on the carpet—as actually happened to Meister Eckhart and as frequently happens to mystics—for leading the faithful astray. You are lost, the Inquisitors thunder, and if the faithful listen to you they will also get lost. The response that Meister Eckhart made to such charges, after a little name-calling in return, was to insist that the effect of his most extreme locutions was ultimately to raise the praise of God up a notch. When I said that the world was nothing in itself, not even a little droplet of water, Eckhart says, I spoke the orthodox truth, because if the world were anything at all *in itself* that would mean that God is not the creator of all things on heaven and in earth, for this little droplet of water would stand there without God, would subsist, in open defiance of God's omnipotence.[6] By the same token, "when I have said God is not a being and is above being, I have not thereby denied him being; rather I have exalted it in Him."[7] So these extreme formulations are ways to signal the extreme depth and greatness of God, of God beyond being, without being, otherwise than being, even as the best way that "Brother Thomas" (Aquinas) found to praise the incomprehensibility of God was to speak of *ipsum esse per se subsistens*. That is how the mystical economy works. We are lost for words, but we are not lost; we are lost for ways to describe the surpassing greatness of God, but that is a higher, more eloquent, more learned (*docta*) and knowing way to be lost than just wandering about two headed in the world of appearances.

Now there are days, good days, when I feel the same way as Eckhart, Dionysius, and the Christian Neoplatonists. I am certainly not trying to make them look bad, although I am in a certain way telling them, in the most technical sense possible, to get lost, at least a little. Carlson is right, and I cannot fathom how he has divined this (relatively) absolute secret, but I am a lover of a good horse race. Now while I do not want my horse to get lost halfway through the race and wander off the track in confusion, neither do I want the race to be rigged in anyone's favor nor do I gain any pleasure from always betting on the winner. That, I wager, is how a horse lover who is also a deconstructionist would apply the idea of undecidability to his favorite passion. Life is something of horse race, a gamble, risk, a *beau risque*, and there is the real possibility that the night through which Gregory and Dionysius, Eckhart and Angelus Silesius, lead us is night indeed and that is all and there is no way out. That is the condition of faith, but mystical theology *as such*, in its first and dominant voice, just in so far as it really is mystical and really *theo*logical, tends to trump faith with mystical union, just as Thomas

Aquinas said that if his five proofs actually work then on this precise point of God's existence we do not need faith, even as the blessed in heaven do not need faith.[8]

My idea is to knock mystical theology off its horse, displace it, expose it to a Nietzschean night, throw it into a sea of undecidability. The God beyond God is not *khora*, which is but the faceless spacing of our lives, the disjoining disjuncture which leaves things out of joint, but the God beyond God is a limit experience that is exposed at a certain remove to an undecidable confusion with *khora*. As Levinas says, the *illéité* of God's transcendence, which is other than the other one (*autre qu'autrui*), is such that it "falls into a possible confusion with *il y a*."[9] That I think is the work of undecidability on behalf of which I am pleading. I would have the mystical theologians treat this khoral night not as a provisional renunciation, a station on the way of the cross of mystical union, but as an inescapable aporia. I want them to be a little lost, to have no standing, not to know from whence they speak when they say that the cause of all is neither knowledge nor truth, light nor being, being nor non-being, truth nor falsity, instead of treating this economy of neither/nor as so many ways to purify and prepare the soul for unity with God. I side with Levinas when he confesses a certain isomorphism, or iso-amorphism, between *il y a* and illeity, with Derrida when he presses an iso-amorphism between *khora* and *agathon* (and many centuries ago, with David of Dinant, who earned the scorn of Thomas Aquinas by pressing the iso-amorphism of God and prime matter!) The idea would be to press this iso-amorphism to the limit, to the point of "possible confusion," so that the two, the God beyond Being and the *khora* beneath Being, would waver in undecidability, and we would confess that we are lost. Had that been the case, then Eckhart would have said to his Inquisitors, "Well, I do not know what is happening. I believe in God, but I am more than one and so I must also respect the atheist within me." That is not exactly the best defense to make when the forces of radical Orthodoxy have descended upon you. At that point, mystical theology, which is ready to confess a certain "bedazzlement," would have to confess that it is lost and confused, or, to use a more precise and technical vocabulary, unhorsed. Being unhorsed belongs to the most sublime structure of religious life: for it just when I am blind that faith is really faith, just when I in despair that hope is really hope (against hope), and just when I am faced with my enemy that I really need love.

Tom Carlson and I are agreed about many, perhaps most things, about Derrida and theology, including that mystical theology has more than one voice. The opening line of "*Sauf le nom*," which is a dialogue of several voices (*voix*), confesses the several voices of mystical theology, which are also its several ways (*voies*).[10] If its first voice is assured and authoritative, and even in league with a political dangerous esotericism and absolutism, the second voice is unhinged and lost. But I do not believe that one makes any headway in this second more khoral direction by pointing out that *beyond* apophaticism, the things that Neoplatonic mystics say about the First Cause or the Godhead are meant to transcend *both* apophatic and kataphatic discourse. That is exactly what I think high ousiology is and what it always does: it transcends the sphere of propositional discourse, both affirmative *and negative*. But the point is it *transcends* this sphere, *surpasses* it, *overcomes* it, get *beyond* it. That is the high, the exaltation, the heights of hyperousiology. But that is not the second more khoral voice I seek or that I think Derrida is talking about. It is a further example of mystical theology feeling its oats rather than being unhorsed. It is precisely a voice of "assurance," not the voice of someone confused, lost, and uncertain. For when Dionysius says the Neoplatonic First Cause is neither this nor that, *where is he standing*? With what *authority* does he speak? How does he come by this un-knowing? How else than by standing *in* the *Ursache*, in the very heart of the divine truth, reaching a point of super-saturation, where our intentions are flooded with fulfillment and words fail us?

In the second voice, we are indeed lost for words in a rather different way. It shows up not so much in Neoplatonic theology as in poems and spiritual autobiographies when men and women of prayer record experiences like the "dark night of the soul" described by John of the Cross. There the soul reaches a point where she does not think she so much as believes in God, where she experiences a desert "aridity"in which she becomes convinced that she is a faithless, unbelieving, good for nothing atheist. Then we do not make positive assertions about God, or negative ones, nor do we say that God surpasses both positive and negative assertions. We just do not believe in God at that moment and at that moment we are passing for an atheist, perhaps quite rightly. At that point passing for a believer, rightly passing for a believer, is all one could hope for; it would be the answer to one's prayers. But one cannot pray or say a thing. Then you see the porous intermingling of faith and doubt of which I spoke in commenting on the Derrida interview. Then, in such times of spiritual "aridity," as opposed to during her periods of exaltation or "consolation," the soul is forced to go it on faith, on faith without faith, the faith of one who in her heart no longer thinks she really believes in God, who prays and weeps, "Lord, I do believe, help thou my unbelief."

Imagine how difficult it is to pray if you are convinced there is no God. Then you would need to pray to be able to pray, and how could that ever get started? How can you pray for faith if prayer presupposes faith? All you can do is start praying, cast yourself into the circle of prayer, and pray that the faith that there is some point to prayer would come later. We read of religious people who sustain their religious commitment for many years convinced in their heart that they have lost their faith. It is there, in that dark night, when faith, the soul, and God all seem like so many cruel fantasies and impossible illusions, that things really get going. Tom Carlson and I are agreed that there is (at least) a second voice in mystical theology. But I am saying that it is a voice of ruins, deposition, being lost and struck down, whereas the voice he invokes seems to me still the same strong soaring Neoplatonic voice of *transcendence*, the voice that is riding high, that speaks from a point in which both apophatic and kataphatic discourse are stilled, suspended and *superceded*; it still speaks, as Carlson says, of the "cause *beyond* speech and knowledge . . . ," of a God who "surpass[es] speech, mind, and being itself." That is supra-positional not depositional, hyperbolic not elliptical, speaking from a place of exaltation in the *agathon* not of displacement in *khora*. In the second voice, one is not *beyond* anything, but crushed, dispirited, deposed, unhorsed, too lost even for prayer. It is, it seems, impossible to pray, which of course is when the most authentic prayer will—should? may?—take place, the impossible condition that makes it possible.

What happens when the second, more khoral tropic of negativity starts to bleed into the first and higher one and their undecidability asserts itself? Then the *oui, oui* of deconstruction, the desire beyond desire of the mystical theologian for the face to face, and the prophet calling for heart in a heartless world, begin to look like so many differing ways to answer a call coming from who knows where, calling for who knows what. The call summons us towards something to come, something impossible and unforeseeable, forcing us to construe the call as our different times and circumstances permit. We would none of us be able to tell which call is the translation of which, or whether they are all examples of some archi-call still to be named, the call of the secret,[11] or whether there is an archi-call at all, or whether we are just hearing the distant thunder of Nietzsche's cosmic dance. Then, in that impossible situation, when it is impossible to make a move, when we are left without a prayer, things would begin to happen, including prayer.

Maybe. *Peut-être. Il faut croire.*

Notes

1. See his astute *Indiscretion: Finitude and the Naming of God* (Chicago: University of Chicago Press, 1999).

2. It is worth noting that when Derrida used this phrase "religion without religion," he was speaking about Marion and Ricoeur and others, but not about himself or about deconstruction; see GD, p. 49.

3. *Meister Eckhart: Sermons and Treatises*, 3 vols. trans. and ed. M. O'C. Walshe (London: Elements Books, 1981), vol. 2, p. 152.

4. See John D. Caputo,"Fundamental Themes in Eckhart's Mysticism," *The Thomist*, 42 (1978), 197–225.

5. See HE, p. 272; PT, p. 11.

6. *Meister Eckhart: The Essential Sermons, Commentaries, Treatises and Defense*, trans. Edmund Colledge and Bernard McGinn (New York: Paulist Press, 1981), p. 75.

7. *Meister Eckhart: Sermons and Treatises*, p. 151). See PT, §1 for a discussion.

8. See HE, pp. 269–271.

9. Levinas, "God and Philosophy," in *Basic Philosophical Writings*, ed. Adriaan Peperzak et al. (Bloomington: Indiana University Press, 1996), p. 141.

10. Jacques Derrida, ON, p. 35

11. Ibid., p. 29.

12 THE PRAYERS AND TEARS OF JACQUES DERRIDA: ESOTERIC COMEDY AND THE POETICS OF OBLIGATION

CLEO McNELLY KEARNS

One of the pleasures of John D. Caputo's *The Prayers and Tears of Jacques Derrida* is its susceptibility to literary appreciation as well as philosophical reflection, to a way of reading supported or supplemented by an informed awareness of rhetoric and diction, genre, tone, and narrative persona. True, these are matters of art rather than matters of argument, and as such they lie to some extent beyond philosophical dispute. Nevertheless, as Nietzsche long ago argued, the formation of literary taste, old-fashioned as that enterprise may sound, does have a bearing on philosophy and may even have something to contribute to its discourse. In a passage to which Derrida has drawn attention, Nietzsche noted that we must proceed by the apparently circuitous path of cultivation of language, by what he called "self-discipline in . . . [the] mother tongue," in order to make a world worth inhabiting. Literary criticism is the formal expression of that cultivated taste for language, and Caputo's work, like Derrida's, is steeped in literary values which yield in interesting ways to its discipline. Caputo's mother-tongue and literary tradition are, however, quite different from either Nietzsche's Germanic style or Derrida's French one, and that difference is significant both for Caputo's argument and for its impact on his readers in ways that literary criticism can perhaps help to measure. Granted, a literary perspective can be a means of evading as well as of illumining the propositional issues a given text raises. Where, as here, there is a question of the degree of faithfulness a work demonstrates to the texts that have occasioned it and on which it builds, criticism is often mute just where comment seems needed. Likewise, where there are questions of truth-value, critics often precind from these in ways that can be frustrating. The literary-critical ear does not often lend itself, except in a very special sense, to determining whether texts are faithful to their sources of inspiration, or whether they 'have legs' as philosophical statements. Critics often finesse, for example, the question of whether Keats has a sound understanding of Shakespeare, much less whether either of them offers well-formed propositions about the nature of ultimate reality. A rush to judgment on these matters can also, however, be a mode of evasion, foreclosing a more expansive response to meanings generated in subtler ways. Certain texts, and not only strictly literary ones, may have the power, if savored for a while in the spirit of the willing suspension of disbelief, to reorient the very position or starting point from which their propositional merits are approached. This reorientation does not obviate the need for a "moment of truth" at the propositional level, but that moment will be different once such a change in orientation has been allowed to occur. As T. S. Eliot liked to say, "a philosophical theory which has entered into poetry is established, for its truth or falsity in one sense ceases to matter, and its truth in another sense is proved." In this sense, the reserve of literary criticism with respect to the faithfulness of a text to its precursors or its truth-value as a propositional statement may offer readers a certain strategic advantage that a strictly philosophical approach cannot.

To obviate the appearance of evasion here, however (and to approach my own line of argument in a different way) let me say from the outset that I think Caputo reads Derrida faithfully, and that the result is a shared—though not identical—position of great cogency with respect to the analysis of the structure and mode of religious discourse in the West. Caputo interprets Derrida's work as a supremely acute critique of that discourse, but he sees Derrida as engaging religious questions less around the issue of negative theology, as has often been argued, than around the problems posed by the messianic tendency running through the three religions of the book: Judaism, Christianity, and Islam. Caputo finds Derrida attempting to delineate the general structure of messianism, which is to say the structure formed by the terms, conditions, and implications of an apocalyptic encounter with what continental philosophy has come to call the tout autre. Derrida finds the anticipation of some such encounter, with its implications of millennial justice, to be the ineluctable presupposition of human communication. In the interests of a better understanding of Derrida and of furthering the cause of social justice to which he is devoted, Caputo isolates, simplifies and wholeheartedly endorses this view in ways that are useful and compelling, if at times less nuanced than might be.

Caputo's rendering of Derrida, however, also raises difficult issues, issues of which both are well-aware. Among other things, trying to make a distinction between a general structure and a particular instantiation of the messianic, between messianicite and messianism, leads to some concern as to what extent the three religions of the book are just different examples of a common structure or to what extent they are singularities, sources of the pattern they reveal. In the first case, these religions might be approachable in a general way as surface reflections of something deeper and as reducible to a common pattern. In the second, they could not be so approached or reduced, and would have to be understood, as the anthropologists say, "from within." We have here a particular case of the general paradox of exemplarity to which both Derrida and Caputo have drawn attention; both stress the fundamental indeterminacy of this paradox and the necessity for accepting and dealing with it, but this advice can seem inadequate when the issues at stake determination are so grave. Surely each assumption and its resulting approach has merits, and each offers a different kind of interpretive payoff, but each also has its constraints and dangers, and it is difficult to bring them both into focus at the same time.

There is also the problem Richard Kearney has raised with respect both to Derrida and Caputo, the problem created by their extreme emphasis on the entire unpredictability and unprogrammatic quality of the revelation of the *tout autre*, the messianic moment. Derrida's phrase for this emphasis— "*tout autre est tout autre*," which might be translated as "every other is completely other"—lays a double insistence both on the singularity of every encounter and on the extremity of its difference. Caputo highlights every moment in which Derrida stresses the impossibility of controlling or containing the revelation of the sacred messianic otherness of the other by means of conceptual or ethical schemata in advance. This insistence serves to discountenance established ecclesiastical, political, and cultural structures as tending to inhibit the uniqueness of the encounter with the other, and as such it expresses a welcome libertarian impulse. As Kearney points out, however, it also tends to deprive us of important resources for discerning the difference between one kind of tout autre and another. It's all very well to welcome the other unconditionally—to say, with the prophet, "Maranatha, Come O Lord"—provided that what is welcomed, however outwith established categories of life and thought, is indeed the millenial kingdom of justice and peace. But this is not the only tout autre on offer in our world; there are encounters with darkness as well as encounters with light. The emphasis on the complete newness, the total unpredictability and extra-schematic singularity of the apocalyptic moment in Derrida and Caputo, and on the futility of attempts to anticipate or domesticate it, tends to discount the schooling effects of cultural tradition, ethical structure and religious observance as aids to discernment, hence leaving us potentially in thrall, among other things to the kind of bogus apocalypticism with which our popular culture is at the moment rife.

Kearney implies, though he does not argue, that this discountenance of established categories of life and thought vis-à-vis the apocalyptic moment may not be quite as ineluctable as Caputo and Derrida seem to claim. Indeed, the critical cultivation of these resources may play a positive as well as negative role in the approach to the tout autre, contributing not just to the domestication and routinization of that otherness, but to the discernment required to say maranatha!—"Come O Lord"—in the right direction, at the right time, and in the right tone. That right and wrong tones are always ready-to-hand and that no pre-ordained stance of ethics, politics or aesthetics, no program of religion or culture can ever fully guarantee the correct reception in advance is a point well taken, and Caputo rightly emphasizes it in his reading of Derrida. But to take that point to an extreme of ascesis which allows in view only the most schematic dimensions of art, politics, ethics and religion, suppressing thereby all the surprises and quirks of these notoriously unstable and unpredictable discourses, seems at times both reductionistic and purist, suggesting a too sharp separation between cultural tradition and that unprecedented response to the event of the future for which the messianic promise awakens our desire.

But to argue these matters exclusively at the propositional level is to miss the very point I would like to raise, which has to do with the great importance of literary and cultural values in reading and assessing texts such as those found in the work of both Derrida and Caputo. I want therefore to talk here about the poetics of Caputo's work, and to place it less in a philosophical than in a literary context. For Caputo has taken great pleasure in developing a unique literary persona and style in his writing, and in shaping to his own textual purposes a wide range of genres from parody to polemic, from irony to lyric, from pastiche to revelation, and the results are not only pleasurable but profitable to observe. The direction of Caputo's voice and style are hinted at in his early work, but his persona begins to emerge from behind the conventions of contemporary scholarship and public academic discourse most discernably first in *Against Ethics*. This book, in some ways a predecessor to *Prayers and Tears*, offers to the reader's amused delectation a narrative persona of a deceptively humble, awkward, rather rabbinical cast of mind who, he opines, simply wishes to lodge a few marginal objections to the triumphal onward march of Hegelian philosophy. That these objections amount to a full scale indictment of a certain reading of German idealism, Christian piety, and Graeco-Roman universality dawns on us gradually, as the book mounts at points to open polemic. This indictment is based on a broadly political and at times tendentious reading of Levinas and Derrida deeply informed by, though never subsumed to, Catholic social justice theology. *Against Ethics* is, however, primarily a work of deconstructive criticism; like Blake, it "uses corrosives" to cleanse the doors of perception.

In *Prayers and Tears* Caputo allows this narrative persona more scope, and approaches more nearly to a constructive alternative position, though not without an even more extensive deployment of his ironic stance. His persona here becomes less a minor scribe at the margins of a European tradition than a genuinely American iconoclast, expansive yet self-scrutinizing, naive yet canny, on an Emersonian journey toward religious truth based on direct confrontation with its radical undecidability. To carry that journey forward, Caputo assumes a variety of poses, among them that of the inept cartographer, the portentous schoolmaster, the sententious homilist, all to draw attention to the ironies of explicating what consistently and systematically resists explication both in Derrida and in the problems he charts. Here is Caputo gently preparing us to undergo our immersion in this sea of uncertainties:

For a philosopher like Derrida, who is so much taken with aporias and impasses, who thinks that you are really getting somewhere only when you are paralyzed and it is impossible to advance, only when there is no plannable, programmable way to proceed, there is a fitting irony in supplying a map, a little "Michelin's Guide to Jacques Derrida," which is something like giving the Cartesian coordinates of the Promised Land (*Foi*, 15). Still, a map gives the tourist and casual visitor to the country who has a few days to take in everything a chance to see the major sights. What follows is an altogether excellent map, a bit of flawless cartography, I assure the reader, but for a few minor faults: I am not sure, for example, that all of these roads have been finished (they have all been promised) or that many of the places mentioned here actually exist. (PT, xxvii)

Whatever else it may be, this is a self-consciously democratic, open and homespun voice, far from the stylish, refined and aristocratic cut of Derrida's jib. It isn't the only voice Caputo will assume in this book, but it is the base line from which he works, and it has substantive as well as formal implications for his argument. As this voice goes on, the Derridean themes of differance and messianicite, the vexed concepts of the *khora* and the tout autre who is tout autre, almost as arcane in French as in English, are rendered fathomable, if not familiar, in a very American lingo. Derrida's messianicite becomes a line from a frontier hymnal, a "Promised Land," and his Platonic and classicizing *khora* evokes a Sonoma desert in full bloom. Caputo's vital and plainspoken voice, while it mimics at times Derrida's own stylistic bravura, is far more errant than his; from the point of view of stylistics, it drifts more quickly and further, floats higher, and touches down more earthily than Derrida tends to do. It's hard to imagine Derrida remarking that "we are all stuck in the same place pulling on the pants of textuality one leg at a time," (PT, 111) though the point is a very Derridean one. At several points, Caputo's lightness of being even makes Derrida look owlish, though a second later *Prayers and Tears* will catch Derrida's tone exactly, coining the semi-parodic phrase "abocular egalitarian polity," for instance, surely a worthy counterpart to Derrida's "carnephallogocentrism," both of them only slightly tongue-in-cheek (PT, 111).

That this style is not the only possible or only effective one in responding to Derrida is evident from the work of Robert Magliola, whose books follows the same trajectory of an early and acute understanding of the theological and religious as well as the philosophical issues at stake in Derrida and a later, more overtly confessional apprehension of their import. In his *Derrida on the Mend*, Magliola develops a highly wrought metaphysical style to render the striking analogues between deconstruction and certain recondite schools of Buddhism (and the analogues of both to his own highly original and disseminated doctrine of the Trinity). Magliola fully realizes the pathos of these connections. "This Pre/face bears a tear . . ." Magliola begins, "The tear is not ineffable, though you cannot name it" (ix). Later, in his moving book *On Deconstructing Life-Worlds,* which tells the story of a lifetime's study and practice of Buddhism and Christianity and a lifetime's scholarship in continental philosophy, Magliola adapts that same style, though with a lighter hand, to a more directly confessional mode. Magliola's debt to Derrida is both great and greatly realized, and he is especially adept at capturing a Derridean point of view in a highly wrought, punning and allusive style. Indeed, he has developed a mode of writing, even at points a mode of thinking, that Derrida might almost, you could imagine, countersign. Caputo's is a very different practice, relying less on pathos than on comic irony, the creation of personae, the generation of texts within texts, the displacement of lines of filiation through a range of artificially assumed tones from satire to parody and back, above all a resolute ascesis, a renunciation so to speak of the apocalyptic tone in order to be faithful, faithful unto death, to the truth of textuality. This stylistic difference, not without a pathos of its own, is marked enough to make a substantive point.

To grasp this point, it helps to place Caputo's narrative persona in a literary context. There is to be sure more than a touch of Kierkegaard about this speaker, and at times, when he rises to certain heights of invective, something even of Zarathustra. But this is also, as I have already noted, a good deal of Emerson, some Carlyle, and even a touch of Whitman, here, not to mention, as we shall see, a large dose of Melville. These are analogues closer to the shaping of Caputo's mother tongue than Nietzsche and Kierkegaard, even if they are less explicitly, or even consciously, foregrounded, and they throw into relief aspects of his text that might not otherwise be apparent. Carlyle's, *Sartor Resartus*, for instance, is an extravagant and sometimes joltingly salutary read for those who tend to think deconstruction was born yesterday; and Emerson's supple and skeptical essay on Montaigne shares with

Caputo's work both a similarity of problematic and a self-conscious cultivation of tone. And although the primary persona established in *Prayers and Tears* has a great deal both of Johannes de Silentio and of Emerson's American Scholar about him, he resembles even more the generous, exhilarated and engaged Ishmael of Moby-Dick, a persona, like Caputo's, by turns democratic and esoteric, original and derivative, funny and poignant, mundane and sublime.

Like Caputo, Melville is a master of the deferred messianic, the hyperbolic *tout autre* of the *tout autre*, for which his great white whale is in many ways so great figure, at once animal and divine, mundane and extra-terrestrial. Like Caputo's narrative persona, too, Melville's narrator Ishmael and his patch-work cohort of fellow-seamen are adrift on a great sea of textuality in search of some improbable, probably fictive yet intense truth, "one grand, hooded phantom, like a snow hill in the air" (Moby Dick, 16). But long before Caputo, Melville had discovered the utility of the colloquial style for sublime matter, and of a whole set of discursive devices to indicate both the textuality and the ineluctably projective and deferred *hors-texte* quality of a fantasmic and numinous otherness. Among them was a dizzying array of pseudonymous and invented voices and personae, these generated not only by standard rhetorical conventions, but by a constant playing on the conventions of scholarly discourse and on the oscillations in tone between metaphysical disquisition and full-blown apocalyptic revelation. Caputo's self styled "Edifying Divertissements," interspersing throughout *Prayers and Tears* for our delight and instruction their parodic pedantry, their sermonic admonitions, their open moralizing, follow a highly Melvillian technique, like the textbook discourses on whaling and whales with which Moby Dick frames and calls into question its own reach for the sublime. These divertissements mask as digressions, but in fact speak to the issue by destabilizing the very textual authority they purport to assume.

Both the literary and the philosophical analogues for *Prayers and Tears* also have an ambiguous generic status, moving from fiction to fact, fireside chat to lecture hall, mask to direct address, sometimes in the same chapter. All of them offer not only one stable persona, but an array of attitudes and stances, pseudonyms and dopplegangers, both within and without the text. Texts like these take the reader into a hall of mirrors where authority itself is deeply unsettled. In this and many respects these works are instances of what the critic Steve Helmling has called esoteric comedy. In his theologically informed and critically acute book *The Esoteric Comedies of Carlyle, Newman and Yeats*, Helmling defines this troubled genre as swinging wildly between mask and revelation, between inflation and demystification. It is a genre often deployed, he argues, when a writer is caught between a subject matter in some sense sublime and an audience whose expectations run to the other extreme. Trying to specify the elusive but related and slightly ludic effects of his texts, Helmling is led to characterize esoteric comedy as by turns confessional and polemic, earnest and sarcastic, sentimental and rigorous, and candid and reserved, but always emerging from a stance of rather willful marginality. None of these works can come at its material or its passions quite straight. Carlyle is enthralled with German idealism, but finds himself suspicious of continental philosophy's inflationary style; Newman (like Derrida subject to extraordinarily ungenerous misreadings) is engaged with prayers and tears in a full-scale *apologia pro vita sua* but finds it necessary to adopt a delicate irony in its regard; and Yeats is entranced with spirit-writing but is too much of a writer himself to ignore the issues of textuality it raises. (The parallels with Caputo in matter as well as form here are evident.)

Yet there is a deeply ethical sense at work in this unsettled genre, helping to refine the sensibility not merely in the service of aesthetics, but in the service of a deeply theological concern for the virtue St. Ignatius called the discernment of spirits. In esoteric comedy, as Helmling acutely points out, the writer creates a false voice, a false persona, a false stance—of pretended deferential humility, for instance, or vulgar nicety, or apocalyptic inflation— precisely so that the reader might be brought better to identify the true tone, the real thing, when it comes along. Parody here tries not only to show the limitations of conventional discourse, but also to redeem them. The goal of this esoteric comedy is indeed "apocalyptic in the modern, secular way." It is written, as Helmling suggests, "to change how we see." The esoteric comedian seeks the "making conscious" of the unconscious force of stylistic convention in order, as Shelley put it, to "purge [. . .] from our inward sight the film of familiarity which obscures from us the wonders of our being." Here the deployment of literary technique aspires to become a form of spiritual practice, as well as a defense against charges of soft-headedness or naiveté.

Take, for instance, the point where Caputo speculates, most impudently, that the famous vision which rendered St. Thomas Aquinas mute before the full revelation of presence, and after which he shortly died, might have been no more than a cerebral hemorrhage. This is, he says, with comic irony, "a suggestion that is so heartless and cerebral that I will not even mention it." He goes on to opine, however, that even in this heartless place deconstruction puts a humble little offering in theology's collection plate, a "widowy two cents." It suggests that faith may be found as a tiny flower even in this desert. He then breaks off from discursive argument to call out that such flowers bloom "Like an absolute surprise. / *Oui, oui.*/ Like an experience of something that will, in a manner of speaking, knock us dead." The passage concludes with a prayer which hovers between irony and pleading; the difference—unmarked on the page—is only one of tone: "*Sancte* St. Thomas, *ora pro nobis*" (PT, 61). To raise the reductive question of cerebral hemorrhage is, of course, presumptuous.

But to utter that closing prayer to St. Thomas "for real" as the children say, is to presume in another way. Better to defer that moment of full-throated assent than to get it wrong. Parody and pastiche here become, in their own way, forms of reverence, as well as forms of masque.

In *Prayers and Tears*, the comic-esoteric stance—it is humorous only up to a point—is created by a highly ironic discursive situation. Let me try to describe its structure with a fable. There once was a great but controversial philosopher, whose work insisted that knowledge is dependent exclusively on texts and textuality, and in whose orbit the term theology was used almost exclusively in the pejorative mode. Now along came a disciple of this philosopher, working in a different language and place, but fully alert to the cogency of his work, who had nonetheless evolved a rather eccentric and not very well received interpretation of it as being, in fact, steeped in theology and indeed religious at heart. The disciple was discountenanced, however, by the master's own diabolic reputation and by the incredulity of a host of lesser acolytes who believed he had misread their leader. Taking this discountenance as a challenge, he refined his own work and gave it strength, though that strength relied heavily on an acceptance of that principle of pure textuality the distant master had adumbrated, which allowed him to read a rebours, against the grain of apparent meaning.

Then one morning, the philosopher in question returns from the dead letter of textuality, crosses the ocean, and suddenly decides to speak in propria persona He says, in effect, "guess what, Jack, you were right along—I am a homo religiosus, always have been, and I myself am authorizing you in my own voice to say so and to have the last laugh after all." But the irony of the situation, and it is an irony apparent to all parties, is that to make of this sudden revenant a holy spirit, to read his apparent endorsement as gospel and to erect a new ecclesia on the basis of his revised and authorized version of his own teaching, is to vitiate precisely the line of argument which made his work compelling in the first place. It is to suppose, that is to say, that there is in fact after all an extra-textual pronouncement which can serve as a logocentric guarantee of full and present meaning. Yet not to remark on the confessional supplements would seem churlish indeed, a matter of looking a gift horse in the mouth.

It is Caputo's achievement in *Prayers and Tears* to have negotiated this ironic situation by maintaining his own stylistic equilibrium, by keeping his distance, so to speak, though it is a loving distance, from the apocalyptic tone in Derrida's work. No wonder then, that in one of the more telling moments of *Prayers and Tears*, we have Caputo speaking not in tongues but tongue-in-cheek, speaking what is at one level pure revelation, and yet countersigning it, comically, in an assumed persona, and even footnoting it in a kind of parody of citationality. Thus he composes, for one his chapters, an epigraph which is a moving invocation to the other ("Something coming!") of which the refrain is *"Viens!,"* the great revelatory invitation which Derrida analyzes and revoices in "Of an Apocalyptic Tone" (PT, 69). This is, we are told a "fragment" from the (fictive) Book of Elie. To this lyrical pastiche, Caputo appends the following footnote: "1. The paragraph is a fake, a Derridean supplement of Rev. 22, forged/faked from various sources (cf. Parages, 116;PdS, 70/Points, 65), for which I will assume some responsibility only if I cannot avoid it." The footnote here becomes a curious device of deconstruction, framing the more apocalyptic and self-revealing of rhetorical flights with a jerk toward the figurative ground.

There is gusto in the joyousness and humor of this playful, democratic and accessible voice, but it sometimes seems to lighten, perhaps unduly, the burden of Derrida's linguistic otherness. Derrida's messianicite is not quite the same as Caputo's Promised Land, which latter owes more to the American pulpit than it does to the streets of the Left Bank. From a philosophical perspective, what seems a slight stylistic shift of the notion of messianicite into a poetic American landscape becomes seismic, cascading Derrida's difficult, deferred, even tragic European construct into a lighthearted homegrown practice of good fellowship and good faith which contradicts in some respects its origin. Here again, the work of Magliola offers an interesting contrast, for *On Deconstructing Life Worlds*, also a confessional and autobiographical statement of Derrida's impact, foregoes the plain style, as I have mentioned, for a darker (and more Buddhist?) articulation of the deconstructive moment which displaces both self and society.

It is important to remember, however, that Caputo's work stands, from a literary point of view, directly in line with a heritage that includes not only Melville but Whitman. Indeed, he writes as if he had ringing in his ears the good gray poet's challenge to all his sons and daughters, a challenge to relish, if not quite on its own terms:

> What is this you bring my America?
> Is it uniform with my country? Is it not something that has
>   been better told or done before?
> Have you not imported this or the spirit of it in some
>   ship?
> Is it not a mere tale? a rhyme? A prettiness?—is the good
>   old cause in it?
> Has it not dangled long at the heels of the poets, politi-
>   cians, literats, of enemies' lands?
> Does it not assume that what is notoriously gone is still
>   here?
>   ("By Blue Ontario's Shore," 477–478)

From this Whitmanian perspective, Caputo's Promised Land is less a trans-lation, whether dubious or not, than a term in search of its own originality, in search of what rings true in the mother tongue. However close or distant Caputo may be to his "original" in content, and however he may mime, parody, deconstruct, demarcate, demystify Derrida, what he has written is no mere supplement in the weak sense. Its effects emanate from a space somewhere between "Jack" and "Jacques," disconcerting a monotone read-ing of either. There is pleasure in hearing in counterpoint his open, humor-ous, democratic voice and the European elegance, the aristocratic high-handedness, the witty elaborations of Derrida's. Nor is this counter-point merely instrumental. Caputo's plain style testifies to the willingness of the writer to sacrifice dignity, decorum and respectablity, to forfeit his place among the knights of good conscience, in the name of something he wishes to present, much against the spirit of his times, as of higher value than these. As Helmling remarks, one may be a fool for ideas as well as a fool for love. We might add that one may be a fool for style as well, running the risks of mistranslation in order to serve another's unique voice, unique per-sona, unique mode of being. There is a subtle kenosis or emptying out of the usual functions of rhetoric here, adapted here less to the self-aggran-dizement of the writer than to his occultation.

In this sense, as in many others, *Prayers and Tears* is an instantiation of what *Against Ethics* defines as a poetics of obligation, obligation in this case to the other, not perhaps so tout autre after all, that is Jacques Derrida. And in the end, Caputo knows that one must emerge from behind mask and per-sona, genre trouble and gender trouble, in order to express this obligation. One must write—and read—with prayers and tears that are no less real for being also textual. Of what such prayers entail, no one has written better than Derrida himself, in his "own" (translated) voice:

> In every prayer there must be an address to the other as other; for example—I will say it at the risk of shocking—God. The act of addressing oneself to the other as other must of course mean pray-ing, that is asking, supplicating, searching out. The pure prayer demands that the other hear it, receive it, be present to it, be the other as such, a gift, call, even cause of prayer.

To such a gift we must at some point be able to say, with Abraham, *"me voici."* As its "Conclusion: a Passion for God" makes clear, Caputo's book is in many respects a long prolegomenon to this moment of truth, a moment which is, at the end, still deferred. Who do I love when I love my God? Caputo asks with prayers and tears. The answer is undecidable, except in terms of the passion and pathos which inspire it (331–339). As Caputo puts it,

Can I do anything other than repeat that question day and night, especially night? We do not put the secret to sleep by dreaming of the impossible. On the contrary, the secret impassions the dream and the dream keeps us on the *qui vive.* "My God" keeps me up at night. The secret is first, last, and constant. Literature will have always begun, day and night. . . . For the meaning of the name of God that Derrida would save, the power of the nameless name of God that stirs in his works, is not what the Greeks meant either by meaning or by God—but a passion (334–335).

There is, however, a moment of truth, a kind of realized eschatology in this text, though not the one we perhaps expected. Rather, it is a moment more fraternal than numinous, more earthly than sublime. For Caputo does do something besides repeat the question here; he does say *"me voici,"* and he says it with alacrity. He addresses this affirmation, however, not to the God of the Hebrew scriptures, who is jealous of His name, nor to the Son, to the claims for whom he responds with extreme reserve. Still less does he address it to the Holy Spirit, whose very ineffability, as Derrida's *Of Spirit* has so brilliantly argued, is susceptible to highly sinister misreadings. Rather Caputo directs his affirmation to his friend and colleague, Jacques Derrida himself, to whom he offers the gift of a saving faith in the other's work which marks a singular act of solidarity. *"Me voici,"* Caputo says to that friend: *"viens, viens, oui, amen,* I am here praying and crying with you." Though the term lacks a little of the sulphur and brimstone that makes the more rigorous designation of atheism so alluring, this is the testimony of what might be called either a humane deconstruction or a deconstructed humanism, and it has about it a grace and a mercy sadly lacking in other places. (Perhaps humanism, like literary appreciation, ought to be revived.)

Yet . . . nothing but humanism? Is this fellow-being all that Caputo "loves" when he "loves his God"? Yes, I think so. Unless, of course, by a strange chance, this other, this "you," is the tout autre after all. Caputo several times quotes the New Testament: "Lord, when did we see you hungry and give you to eat, or naked and give you clothes?" The answer is well-known: "whatever you have done unto the least of these My brethren, you have done it unto Me." It has been Caputo's gift—a gift developed through a long practice of literary as well as philosophical close reading—to discern, when very few others did, Derrida's religious hunger. Here he expresses a poetic obligation toward that hunger, clothing and supplementing Derrida's thought in an answering work at once original and dedicated to another's point of view. If a certain theological indeterminacy haunts this supplement, that indeterminacy marks a genuinely open space, one into which others, in their turn, may inscribe other and different marks. May these further inscriptions be as generous as those that have inspired them.

NOT IN TONGUES, BUT TONGUE IN CHEEK:
A RESPONSE TO KEARNS

John D. Caputo

I am deeply indebted indeed to Cleo McNelly Kearns for a particularly striking analysis. She says that her gloss on *Prayers and Tears* represents an
"ancillary discourse rather than a direct engagement" because it is focused
not on the logic or argument but rather the poetics of *Prayers and Tears*. It
so, that raises an interesting point. It is as incisive and illuminating to me as
any response to my texts that concentrates on the arguments and stays steadfastly with my point, my logic, my argument. When the philosophers and theologians who read *Prayers and Tears* or *Against Ethics* read past the
poetics—the style, the tone, the irony—in order to get to the standpoint, I
often find myself remonstrating with them about misconstruing my stand.
Cleo Kearns brings out how deeply the poetics bleeds into the standpoint,
the slightly tilted, tipsy standpoint of one who has been knocked off his
hinges, or, as I said to Tom Carlson, unhorsed. My use of wit, of "esoteric
comedy," to use this excellent formulation, goes to the heart of my argument,
of the point I am pleading, which is to keep laughing through our tears. The
pointed tip of my style/stylus is the tragic-comic point of the "argument" that
I am pursuing. I recognize myself in what Cleo Kearns says as well as in anything else I have read about *Prayers and Tears*. She has explained these texts
to me better than I could to myself. By following instead the lines of force of
a strictly literary analysis, she has read back to me what is happening in this
text in a way that sharpens and enlarges its effect for me. Who could ask for
more than that?

She has had the ears to hear what I thought was my personal secret, the
double voice I have given this persona, which my editor at Indiana University
Press, Janet Rabinowitch, to whom I owe so much, is always "editing." This
unhinged voice is at once Kierkegaardian and Philadelphian, melancholy and
upbeat, religious and aesthetic, reflecting the attempt I am always making to
achieve a polyphonic effect, composed of Kierkegaard's comedic, even caustic
tongue and my mother tongue, my American voice, optimistic, democratic, and
as Kearns says, in a compliment I can only consider an ideal to emulate, Whit-
manesque. I once spoke of an "American prag-grammatology,"[1] a phrase that I

did not persist in using because of my endemic leftish suspicion of nationalism, of just the sort that Rorty decries in *Achieving our Country*. But Kearns is right. I do not want to succumb to northern European brooding, to long winter nights and days deprived of light. I have no desire to be a good European but to see what I can get done in American English (while visiting Europe frequently), and I have nothing but contempt for the ludicrous attempts of American continentalists to write like a bad translation from the French or German, or like good ones for that matter. I write in such a way as to run these two voices together in a new world symphony, ducking and weaving between the continent and the USA, the left bank and Philadelphia, keeping an eye out for the abyss and an upbeat tone throughout. Indeed, it was Heidegger's utter humorlessness, and the humor that he missed in Kierkegaard and Nietzsche, that troubled me so much and is part of the reason I have finally taken them to be much more profound than all Heidegger's self-important rumblings.

It is of no less interest to me that this element of esoteric comedy identified by Cleo Kearns is also close to what Derrida says in the interview in this volume, that he is someone who is always laughing at himself while also sounding prophetic, he being a prophet without prophecy. It is precisely in maintaining these tensions, hilarity and sublimity, comedy and tragedy, this mix of playfulness and prophecy, that a genuinely deconstructive effect can be produced, in Derrida, or in my imported American version of Derrida, in my American Catholic "transplant," as Cleo Kearns rightly calls it. For my concerns, as Cleo Kearns so acutely points out, are not far removed from "Catholic social justice theology," even as they are very close to a "little black and very Arab Jew." I am trying to inhabit the distance between Derrida and *les Catholiques*.

Cleo Kearns has also nicely encapsulated all this for me when she says of the style adopted in *Prayers and Tears* that its author speaks "not in tongues but tongue in cheek." Compare this to what Derrida says in the course of his response to Dooley's question about *khora*, "To good readers, my texts attest to the fact that I am not simply a dogmatic, religious person, and that when I say 'God,' it is said with tongue in cheek." To which I add that I have been insisting all along that speaking of "quite rightly passing for an atheist" also has a tongue in cheek quality about it. How can anyone is who is "more than one"—and who is not?—not speak tongue in cheek, lest the one voice provoke a jealous outburst from the other voices? The important thing, however, in Cleo Kearns's felicitous phrase is that she does not praise speaking tongue in cheek *simpliciter*, without further ado, which could amount to nothing more than maintaining an ironic distance from involvement, but speaking tongue in cheek all the while humbly deferring any claim to the gift of speaking in tongues. But that deferral suggests a little twinge of prophetic stirring—you can hear the breathing of a certain suppressed prophetic aspiration—which is to capture perfectly, according to the logic of the *sans*, the structure of being a prophet without prophecy, which goes to the heart of a religion without religion, whose cheeky prophets speak not in tongues but tongue in cheek.

Cleo Kearns has put her finger on my goal of seeing if a sublime matter can insinuate itself into a colloquial manner. I cannot claim that what she says is true, but it is what I hope is true, what I want to make come true. It is what my prayers and tears, my religion, my *viens, oui, oui*, are all about, and how I love to be read.

NOTES

1. John D. Caputo, "Toward an American Pragrammatology," in *The Very Idea of Radical Hermeneutics*, ed. Roy Martinez (Atlantic Highlands: Humanities Press, 1997), pp. 190–193.

13   WITHOUT WHY, WITHOUT WHOM: THINKING OTHERWISE WITH JOHN D. CAPUTO

EDITH WYSCHOGROD

To think *about* thinking "without why" is not to think without why for to ponder such thinking is to reflect upon the question of *why* thought is to proceed in a specifiable way. By contrast, to think without why is to enter into the negation of the "without" while retaining the affirmation of the thought act. But is thinking without why, *"Ohne Warum,"* thinking at all? To answer this question one must read the works of John D. Caputo for whom such thinking is a transcending of metaphysics, an ethical commitment, and a hermeneutical strategy.

Consider first the meaning of enframing, what Heidegger calls the *Gestell,* "the final push, the collective mobilization (*stellen*) of every being as raw material for an unleashed will to power,"[1] a push that is engendered by the why. To ask why is to encounter that which presents itself in terms of cause and effect, what the totalizing strategies of metaphysics interpret as efficacity, Being's power to bring something about. This relation exhibits its own mode of temporalization, that of before and after, of cause prior to effect. What is thus brought to light in the temporalization of production is a privileging of the antecedence of cause and thus the priority of a past that is made present, the time scheme of the cause as fixed and static agency. In its prioritizing of the past as unchanging, as something that eternally is what it always already was, an aetiological metaphysics that thinks coming-to-be as production loses the sinuosity of time.

As early as the latter half of the fourth century not all was tranquil in the house of metaphysics. Troubled by the difficulty in seizing a moment of time, by its infinite divisibility, Augustine discerned time's never-ending passage even as he retreated to the default position of denying its reality in favor of an unchanging eternity. It is with Heidegger's account of the ecstases of time that time is first perceived as the supreme escape artist, always already ahead of itself. To think without thinking causally is to think futurally, to envisage the past not as motionless and unchanging but as that which, when it was what it was, was already directed towards its future possibilities. Caputo is preeminently a thinker of anteriority as futurity.

THINKING WITHOUT WHY

In an otobiographical—Derridean orthography intended—sketch of his journey in thought, Caputo depicts his early life in philosophy as "consorting with saints and mystics and medieval masters" who disclosed "an astonishing world."[2] In this encounter, he was compelled to think otherwise, not by entering into the miasma of non-thinking but rather by seeing via the revelatory power of thinking an astonishing open-ended world of sacralities. The analysis of the difference between *intellectus* and *ratio* would begin for Caputo a process of release from the bondage of *ratio* just as his study of Heidegger would preclude his identification of thinking with the regnant epistemological theories of Anglo-American philosophy or with what Derrida famously calls the logic of presence. Heidegger's critique of the logic(s) of modernity was well-trodden terrain for Caputo in that he had, in his study of medieval thought, especially of Aquinas, already entered into the piety of thinking in Heidegger's sense.

Heidegger's own philosophical itinerary may have had for Caputo an uncanny ring of familiarity. The relation of the early Heidegger's lectures on religion to his later work became the theme of Caputo's 1978 book, *The Mystical Element in Heidegger's Thought*[3] even before the links between the later work and Heidegger's lectures on such texts as *Galatians*, *I Thessalonians*, or book 10 of Augustine's *Confessions* were subjected to intense scrutiny by recent commentators such as Theodore Kisiel, Thomas Sheehan, and John van Buren. Caputo discerned in the young Heidegger an attentiveness to the vital "centers" of the existent. Does not the *Unter-Schied* betweeen Being and beings in the Heidegger of *Identity and Difference* repeat (differently) the *Ab-geschiedenheit* of God in Eckhart, he asks. Still, Caputo's own love of the medievals did not blind him to the fact that it was to poetry that the later Heidegger turned rather than to the mystical dimension of Meister Eckhart or Angelus Silesius that had once engaged him. For the later Heidegger, Caputo suggests, "The great poets think, the great thinkers think poetically."[4]

Yet there is something unsettling in the poetizing of thought from which Caputo turns without however abnegating Heidegger's hermeneutics of facticity. Acutely disturbed by Heidegger's politics as they came to light in the account of Victor Farias and the more scholarly narrative of Hugo Ott, Caputo nevertheless refused to wield the sledge hammer of simplistic critique. To be sure, his aim in demythologizing Heidegger is precisely to disclose the politics of the *Seinsfrage*, "the ontopolitics of the 1930s [that] emerges from a fateful mythic transformation of the most exciting European philosophizing of the the 1920s"[5] and that mesmerized the best minds of the day. But, in a hermeneutical move more radical and more profound, he deconstructs Heidegger's account of Dasein's being as *Sorge*, as Being-towards-death in its existentiality, facticity and fallenness, not by rejecting that account but by showing that it is fissured by an absence, the absence of *kardia* (heart), of "flesh, disablement, affliction."[6]

In Caputo's 1993 *Against Ethics*, the trope of anthropophagy serves to highlight the body's potential for inflicting and suffering pain: "Flesh succombs to the radical reversibility of the carniverous and the carnal, of consuming and being consumed. Flesh fills metaphysics with anxiety."[7] For Heidegger, pain fails to disclose the world but is rather a theme for psychology, a subjective state requiring mastery, whereas for Caputo, *kardia* is the entering wedge through which is disclosed not the meaning of Being but the imperative of justice. With Levinas, he reads justice not as the theoretical articulation of what is to count as right and wrong but as anarchic, as "that which has to do with the impossible singular."[8] Caputo goes on to say that "far from building from a plan, the projection of justice is utterly withut a plan, uttterly devoid of patterns, heavenly or earthly."[9] One can detect in such passages a certain tone perhaps of supplication that will be taken up later in his depiction of the cries and tears of Jacques Derrida, a certain textual style deriving from Biblical and rabbinic sources, a jeremiad for the oppressed from Derrida/Caputo, men of sorrows and acquainted with grief. In its fissuring of *Sorge*, the *kardia* of Caputo transforms the hermeneutics of facticity. A rift in the life of the Dasein now opens the way for a call from an immemorial past to an unknowable future.

Could it not be argued that Heidegger had already inaugurated the understanding of existence as uncalculating exposure to what is to come? No one has acknowledge this point more forcefully than Caputo. Yet, as he insists, the call that issues from the future becomes in Heidegger a desire for "a pure and primordially Greek beginning."[10] At the same time, Heidegger cuts down the indeterminate call of what is coming to historical size by compressing it into a historical actuality, a homeland. The claims of autochthony intrinsic to Heidegger's telling of the myth of Being, the nostalgic vision of *Heimat*, traduce the indeterminateness of an errant or nomadic future as called for by justice.

Yet, Caputo realizes one is never through with Heidegger for he continues to haunt thinking as both Derrida and Levinas also acknowledge. We must, he insists, "hold Heidegger's hand to the fire of *Being and Time*, to the indeterminate structure of the call of conscience and to the indefinite indeterminateness of the future, to the possible as possible which is also the impossible."[11] One can discern that, for Caputo, Kierkegaard's either/or has not become both/and—each of these alternatives fails the litmus test of without why—but rather an eschatological "perhaps." For Caputo, justice is neither the *Sehnsucht* of a Romantic self-centered longing nor the moral law of Kant, a universal law that is the same for all.

Then whose justice, what rationality—Alasdair McIntyre's phrase intended—summons us? Caputo's anwer is the justice of the jewgreek. As jew, the jewgreek puts the question of the Other to philosophy and thereby puts philosophy into question by interrupting its activity as rational comprehension. As greek, she/he attempts to discursively articulate the question of a justice that first manifested itself as a biblical *cri de coeur* on behalf of the helpless and dispossessed. "The flesh of the Other," Caputo contends, "supplies the site, the locus, the topos of a Jewish poetics of obligation."[12]

But the imperative of justice mandated by a Levinasian ethics does not preclude for Caputo the adoption of a certain Nietzschean stance with its own aporias On the one hand, despite an eros for the labyrinthine cathedrals of systematic reflection that constitute the philosophical tradition, Caputo (with Derrida) examines, deconstructively, the conditions of possibility of philosophical constructs such as the subject, truth, reality. At the same time, he insists that in overcoming metaphysics one can become ever more deeply enmeshed in metaphysics. Thus Caputo writes:

> The point of overcoming metaphysics is "not-to-be-overcome-by-metaphysics," . . . not to suffocate, to perish from the extravagent totalizing tendencies of a maximizing metaphysics. One cannot avoid some metaphysics or another [but one need not] rush headlong into the most extravagent... the most metaphysical form of metaphysics.[13]

In fact, Caputo's work might be viewed as a secret diary of the escape from a metaphysics that remains inescapable but in which goodness works to restrain its wills to power that might otherwise run amok.

It sometimes appears as if Caputo, like the acrobat in Nietzsche's *Zarathustra*, is poised perilously on the tightrope of a deconstructive demystification of the metaphysical tradition that extends from the pre-Socratics to Hegel. But Caputo is less a tightrope walker than a great bungee jumper who dangles from a cord and, like Kierkegaard's Abraham, must leap to where there is neither ground nor clearing from which the revealing and concealing of Being could be thought. Perhaps the secret of this leap is its destabilizing effect, its challenge to the *Da* of Heidegger's *Dasein*. Beneath one's feet there is only the mud, the muck of the pain and suffering of the Other through which one must ultimately slog and that John Bunyan had in the seventeenth century already named the slough of despond. In "a hyper-aesthetics of Being's shining glory" Caputo has discerned an "indifference to the concrete sufferings of historical human beings."[14]

WITHOUT WHOM: THE INDISPENSABLE OTHER

To think without why is, we have seen, to reject the identification of thinking with both explanation and representation. Without why mandates that one divest oneself of the conatus to know how things happen or are produced. Crucial to the without of the without why of thinking is its privative and eliminative force: in the absence of the without of without why, the event of thinking cannot occur. Yet "without" is a polysemic term that can signify not only eliminability but its opposite, indispensability. The lover who says "without you I shall die" expresses the without of indispensability, of necessary inclusion, for the beloved is essential to the lover's existence.

It could be argued that a penumbra of causality clings to this indispensability in that the beloved's absence can become the cause of the lover's death. To be sure, the "without" of what I call the "without whom" signals indispensability, the requisite condition for ethics, the without of inclusion: there would be no ethics without the Other but the Other is in no way the cause of ethics since the Other is irreducible to her/his phenomenality. The Other in this sense cannot be specified save as Other for whom and through whom the event of ethics occurs. Caputo's journey from the "without why" of Heideggerian thought to the "without whom" of Levinasian alterity (and that of Derrida and Lyotard), can be seen as constituting a noticeable *Kehre* in Caputo's oeuvre.

Entering the arena of sullied existence with a vengeance, the vengeance of the prophets against injustice, in his *Against Ethics* Caputo conspires, as it were, with Derrida, Levinas and Lyotard to write an ethics without ethics, an ethics of the Other, that I have called an ethics of "without whom." Despite his refusal to evade the command structure of ethics, Caputo nevertheless avoids the pitfalls inherent in theorizing the ought that would entrap it in the dyad "thou shall't/thou shall't not" intrinsic to much ethical reflection.

Instead, what gives itself to thought is the indecidability of ethics. Is it the Other or an infra-ethical anonymous faceless being, what Levinas calls the *il y a*, that summons? Indecidability cannot be eluded in that ambiguity or doubleness is a prior condition of ethics: the *il y a* and the Other enter into a game of reflections which ethics cannot escape. What then is to be done? Caputo appeals to a primordial obligation, the affirmation of infinite worth attaching us to the least among us, placing our mortal selves at the service of the Other:

"Obligation is like a felt shock or blow that strikes me down . . . lays me low, producing a kind of disequilibrium in me."[15] One continues to be obligated despite the ambiguity of the summons. "Obligation," he writes otobiographically, "is what happens in the midst of a cosmic night, in the middle of a disaster."[16] Such ambiguity need not be equated with the psychological paralysis of permanent fence-straddling but rather as requiring a certain humility before an undecidability that unmoors the epistemic and moral subject.

How does ethics thus understood address one ethically, if it is to be an ethics that resists ethics, when who commands and who is to be commanded remain hidden, a concealedness that cannot be a concealing/revealing in Heidegger's sense. This counter-ethics is, Caputo maintains, written with the hand of Johannes de Silentio "in implacable and ironic opposition to Heidegger's originary ethics."[17] Thus, he sees *Against Ethics* "as a kind of postmodern *Fear and Trembling* that is at once "impish, impudent, impious, perhaps even imprudent,"[18] its purpose, like that of Abraham's journey, shrouded in secrecy, a secrecy that by its nature cannot come to light. To enter into the secret, one can only turn to other secrets, those of the tropes of Derrida's writings—*differance*, arche-writing, *brissure* and the like—and watch the manner in which they are transformed in more recent Derridean texts as, for example, the event of circumcision in essays on this topic.[19]

Is there however a non-place that is the place of the secret for the Derridean jewgreek, a place without being, other than being? Such a place is the *khora* of Plato's *Timaeus*, a matrix, as it were, that is always already there, the abode of the forms. Neither idea nor sensible object, the *khora* is the site where the demiurge presses or cuts images of the intelligible paradigms,"as heterogeneous as the forms and of the same age as they."[20] It is not difficult to see how the model of the *khora* insinuates itself into the semiological memory that Hegel depicts as a crypt or pyramid or into the bytes and pixels of cyberspace or to discern its resemblance to that vast reservoir of forms, the repository of eternal archetypes, the *Alayavijnana*, of the Consciousness Only school of Buddhism.

FAITH WITHOUT FAITH

Unlike apophatic theology that cannot name its referent because its superabundant truth precludes containment in language, the secret is not meant to uncover truth but rather that which is otherwise than truth and being. For the apophasis of negative theology, what renders speech necessary is God, "a name that effaces itself in order to save what it names."[21] Unlike the object of negative theology whose revelation is sought but precluded by the excessiveness of its referent, the secret does not strive for exposure. The challenge of the secret is rather to conceal and reveal, to divulge without divulging itself. In a much cited passage, Derrida writes: "There is a secret of denial and a denial of the secret. The secret as such denies itself as secret separates and already institutes a negativity; it is a negation that denies itself. . . , de-negates itself."[22] This de-negation is "essential and originary," both obscuring itself and appearing to the one with whom it is shared, partitioning itself within itself, denying itself.

If the secret is to appear and not appear, would recourse to cryptography as a model not allow for both the secret's concealment and for its transposability into visible signs? Would decoding the secret not render it effective by allowing it to enter into the chain of signifiers, the meanings and practices of everyday life? Are codes not the language that secrets speak? A code may be understood first as a system of equivalences, of information that can be condensed in transcription, for example, the 1's and 0's of the information culture, the condensed bits that are then decoded in accordance with a system of commensurable items. A code may also be thought of as a system of laws or general rules having normative force that can be applied to individual cases and that function as distillates that must be expanded upon and enlarged through use. The very advantages of each type of code—on the one hand accessibility of the message when the code as a system of signs is mastered and, on the other, the code as a general rule applied to particular circumstances or events—disqualify the code as analogue of the secret. To function as a code is to enter into a universal structure of communication, a system of undeconstructed signifiers.

All theology in which God figures is a theology that is secret in that the name of God cannot be encoded only to be exposed. If it is spoken it can only be said in the modality of denial.[23] Like the utterances of Isaiah whose lips are touched by burning coals so that he cannot not speak, deconstruction in this context is for Caputo enforced speech about what cannot be brought to presence. Similarly, the obligatoriness of ethics "turns on the desire for the *tout autre* about which it does not know how not to speak."[24] In conformity with such a non-foundational account of the ethical, Caputo writes: "Obligation is something that happens . . . without the deep back-up of God." Yet far from eventuating in an autonomous ethic trapped in the deontological/consequentialist dyad, an ethics of obligation, Caputo maintains, leads to "a faith without doctrine, a God without Being, a community that cannot say 'we.' "[25]

It might be asked whether the deconstruction of faith, God, and community as the fundamental gesture of ethics does not constitute an intellectual tour de force in a world whose plethora of ills is too obvious to recount? It is at this point, Caputo reminds us, that Derrida introduces the specter of Marx, a certain reading of Marxism that, despite its historical consequences, Derrida thinks cannot be altogether renounced.[26] In a manner somewhat reminiscent of the Frankfort school or of Foucault, Derridean justice is oriented towards the future, committed to speak without speaking in order to produce new forms of action, practice and organization that will eventuate in a new community. Can there however be a community in the wake of the auto-deconstruction, the unravelling of reason? Is there not implicit in the notion of community a common subject that Derrida renounces? In an essay on Foucault, Caputo endorses as a starting point a hermeneutics of refusal, "a hermeneutics that confesses from the start that we do not know who we are."[27] A communal subject based upon self-knowledge can only be the totalizing subject of economy, polity, and culture, a subject always already imbricated in the violence of a shared history. By contrast, the deconstructed community as described (elliptically) by Caputo cannot become the theme of a discourse but may be seen as the non-subject of an ecclesiology without a church. Such a community loosens the knots of the totality by way of a forgiveness that releases and opens, a community one cannot join but to which one can belong without belonging. Forgiveness undoes the past, renders it moot, nugatory, as though it had not been, and opens the way to a "we" of prayers and tears.

Such an an-ecclesiology can be attributed to a person of faith without faith with a Kierkegaardian passion for the impossible, one who beckons a Messiah, "*Viens*," who will not arrive. Longing and anticipation are the affective modalities of this faith, the same, Caputo believes, as those of Hebrew prophecy. Derrida, heir of Abraham and Amos, has as his self-appointed task the admonishing of a philosophical tradition whose confidence in itself is based upon the self-sufficiency of reason. Like Jean-Luc Marion who turns to *Koheleth (Ecclesiates)* as reducing a pre-redeemed world to vanity, Derrida rebukes philosophy by appealing to a world torn by poverty and violence, not in the interest of the nihilism he is alleged to espouse but rather in order to make a messianic point. As Caputo notes, the text of Derrida as messianic visionary who repeats religion differently as religion without religion is not the way things were meant to turn out according to the many interpreters for whom Derrida was to fulfill the promise of Enlightenment secularism.[28] Instead Derrida exhorts: "*Viens*." Let us await the messiah who will come but who will not arrive. Let us have faith in the impossible, pronounce an eschatological yes, "*Oui, oui*." What is to come is altogether other.

It could be argued against Derrida that the messiah functions semiotically in the manner of a Kantian regulative ideal. To do so would be to read the term "messiah" as having positive content, a claim that Derrida denies. It could also be asserted that Derrida generates a mood of anxious desperation insofar as the advent of the messiah is doomed to disappointment, or so the critics of Caputo's Derrida, like those of Nietzsche's Zarathustra, would have one believe. What has been overlooked by these critics however is that a messiah who actually arrives inaugurates an endtime that is the cessation of time, a termination that entails the loss of hope in that hope is contingent upon time's ongoing character and ergo upon future time. Thus the savior of a Derridean soteriology must be the rescuer, the savior, of time and of hope, one who is called yet does not come. But there is more. "Come" is the call that, in beckoning the messiah, calls forth the event, the call "that starting from which there is any event."[29] That which has not yet happened, the sheer possibility of a future that is not only an ecstasis towards one's end is a future awaited in and as hope, hope for what is to come but that, unlike one's own death, does not arrive.

WITHOUT RETURN: THE GIVING OF THE GIFT

At a 1998 conference organized by Caputo at Villanova University in Villanova, Pennsylvania on the subject of the gift, Derrida and Jean-Luc Marion squared off on the matter of how givenness is to be understood. Derrida maintained that the gift cannot be known in that knowing the gift assures its destruction. However, even if "the gift as such cannot be known . . . it can be thought of. We can think what we cannot know."[30] The adumbration of this difference requires thinking without why in order to breach the totality understood in this context as economy, the all-embracing practices of reciprocal exchange.

Consider first, Derrida's response to Marion's reading of his (Derrida's) gloss on Marcel Mauss. Marion is right, says Derrida, in claiming that, for him (Derrida), when a gift is understood as a gift by donator and recipient, it is reintroduced into the circle of exchange, into economy, but Marion is wrong in maintaining that he (Derrida) has problematized the gift in the horizon of economy. On the latter view, the gift would be rendered impossible *tout court* when, in fact, the gift is impossible only in the sense that it cannot appear as phenomenon. Thus, Derrida asserts: "[I]t is impossible for the gift to exist and appear as such. But I never concluded that there is no gift."[31] Heir of Husserlian phenomenology, Derrida here does not renounce phenomenology but espouses a phenomenology of non-appearing, of the impossible maintaining that "if there is a gift through this impossibility, it must be the experience of this impossibility, and it should appear as impossible."[32]

Agreeing with Derrida that the gift cannot be explained, Marion replies that, contrary to Derrida, the gift is amenable to description. "It would sound absurd to ask what is the cause of the gift, precisely because givenness implies the unexpected, the unforeseeable and the pure surge of novelty." For Marion, a description of the gift is not that of an object or a being but one made possible only in the light of previous pragmatic experience. "We have to commit ourselves by achieving the gift by ourselves, in such a way that we become able to describe it."[33] What is more, from a description of the gift's excessiveness, Marion hopes to derive phenomenological rules that, *mutatis mutandis*, are applicable to other revelatory experiences. This account of the gift is in conformity with Marion's description of the saturated phenomenon, one in which the intention of consciousness is never fulfilled not because of an ontological deficiency but rather because that which is given exceeds what the concept can receive or expose.

Contrasting the bedazzlement of excess with Derridean blindness (positively construed), Caputo maintains that "for Marion the gift is a matter of hypergivenness, while for Derrida it is a matter of never-givenness."[34] In explicating the distinction, Caputo attempts not to adjudicate but rather to expose the difference between givenness and that which is yet to be given, between an overwhelming luminosity and a fumbling blindness that does not signal nihilism and despair but a faith in that which is to come. Although not invoked by Caputo, I should like to think of this difference as one between vision and tactility and to read it in the light of Aristotle's analysis of sense knowledge as the relation of sense organ, medium and object. Aristotle, bewildered by the aporias of touch, observed that there is no medium or specialized organ that conveys the object as required by his theory. Refusing to abandon his account of sense perception, Aristotle is forced to posit the body as a whole as the medium and the heart as the organ of reception of the object. Thus Caputo might want to argue (on the side of Aristotle) that, *malgre nous*, we are returned to the heart, to *kardia*, led back not through sight but, as he recognizes, through "a kenotics of faith, of a groping blindness" to the coming of something that cannot be seen of the *tout autre*.[35]

The exposition of faith without faith, faith in the *tout autre* depicted in *The Prayers and Tears of Jacques Derrida* can be envisaged as the discursive equivalent of the painting, *rechts und links eine Kirche*, by the contemporary German artist, Georg Baselitz. A large androgynous figure, the pink flesh of its legs and its green garment contrasting with the dark night of the backdrop, is suspended head down between two tiny cathedral spires. The viewer, disoriented, may be led to imagine the painting itself as upside down thereby setting the figure to rights but, in so doing, s/he upends the churches' spires. The original position of the figure thwarts the viewer's traditional theological expectations and hints at a topsy turvy world, what Hegel had seen as the upside down world. In somewhat analagous fashion, Caputo's argument deftly unfolds the thought of Derrida along its fault lines further deconstructing these already deconstructed lines by stationing himself both inside and outside Derrida's tropes and critical strategies.

In re-reading Jacques Derrida's readings of texts, Caputo does not generate treatises on Plato, Augustine, Eckhart, Aquinas et al., tasks he has in the past performed with distinction. Instead, reading along with Derrida, he takes up and undoes received interpretations of the tradition. With the adroitness one might expect of a Mark McGuire or a Sammy Sosa coaching a team of Little Leaguers by challenging them to repeat the received moves of the game deconstructively in order better to play, not now but next year, Caputo adjures us to await in fear and hope the game that is always to come. To read Caputo as doing otherwise is not to read Caputo.

NOTES

1. John D. Caputo, DH, p. 12.

2. John D. Caputo, "Of Mystics, Magi and Deconstructionists," in *Portraits of American Continental Philosophers*, ed. James R. Watson (Bloomington, IN: Indiana University Press, 1999), p. 25.

3. First edition (Athens: Ohio University Press, 1978). Reprinted with corrections (New York: Fordham University Press, 1986).

4. John D. Caputo, DH, p. 235.

5. Ibid., p. 41.

6. John D. Caputo, AE, p. 68.

7. Ibid., p. 220.

8. John D. Caputo, DH, p.206. See also "*Sorge* and *Kardia*: The Hermeneutics of Factical Life and the Categories of the Heart," in *Reading Heidegger from the Start: Essays in his Earliest Thought*, Theodore Kisiel and John van Buren (eds.) (Albany, NY: State University of New York Press), pp. 327–343.

9. Ibid., p. 207.

10. Ibid., p. 208.

11. Ibid.

12. John D. Caputo, AE, p. 216.

13. Ibid., p. 221.

14. James R. Watson, *Portraits of American Continental Philosophers*, p. 29.

15. John D. Caputo, AE, p. 27.

16. James R. Watson, *Portraits of American Continental Philosophers*, p. 30.

17. John D. Caputo, AE, p. 133.

18. James D. Watson, *Portraits of American Continental Philosophers*, p. 29.

19. See "Circumfession," in Geoffrey Bennington and Jacques Derrida, *Jacques Derrida* (Chicago: University of Chicago Press, 1991).

20. John D. Caputo, PT, p. 35.

21. Ibid., p. 32.

22. Harold Coward and Toby Foshay eds., *Derrida and Negative Theology with a Conclusion by Jacques Derrida* (Albany, NY: State University of New York Press, 1992), p. 95.

23. John D. Caputo, PT, p. 32.

24. Ibid., p. 3.

25. James R. Watson, *Portraits of American Continental Philosophers*, p. 30.

26. Jacques Derrida takes up the ways in which contemporary discourse assumes and renounces Marx in SoM.

27. "On Not Knowing Who We Are: Madness, Hermeneutics and the Night of Truth," in John D. Caputo and Mark Yount eds., *Foucault and the Critique of Institutions* (University Park, PA: Pennsylvania State University Press, 1993), p. 233.

28. John D. Caputo and Michael J. Scanlon eds. *God, the Gift and Postmodernism* (Bloomington, IN: Indiana University Press, 1999), p. 5.

29. John D. Caputo, PT, p. 95.

30. "On the Gift: A Discussion between Jacques Derrida and Jean-Luc Marion moderated by Richard Kearney" in John D. Caputo and Michael J. Scanlon (eds.), *God, the Gift and Postmodernism*, p. 60.

31. Ibid., p. 59.

32. Ibid.

33. Ibid., pp. 63–64.

34. "Apostles of the Impossible." Ibid., p. 207. The reference to blindness derives from Derrida's *Memoirs of the Blind: The Self-Portrait and Other Ruins*, trans. Pascal-Anne Birault and Michael Naas (Chicago: University of Chicago Press, 1997). Caputo's commentary on this work can be found in PT, pp. 308–329.

35. "Introduction" to *God, the Gift and Postmodernism*, p. 8.

ON BEING ATTACHED TO
PHILOSOPHERS AND PROPHETS:
A RESPONSE TO WYSCHOGROD

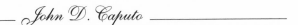

John D. Caputo

The rejoinder I would make to Merold Westphal about *Against Ethics* is to a great extent made on my behalf by Edith Wyschogrod in the present study. Edith Wyschogrod is something of a soulmate of mine, a fellow traveler in a world that is, in Levinas's poignant phrase, "attached to both the philosophers and the prophets."[1] She is someone who wants to station herself, as do I, in the distance between the philosophers and the prophets, which Derrida, citing James Joyce's memorable phrase, described as "Jewgreek."[2] She too wants to be ignited by the sparks that each give off, in a project that is captured perfectly in her exquisite title "saints and postmodernism."[3] Her intuitions about my texts, and especially about *Against Ethics* and *Prayers and Tears*, run deep. She seems to get everything right, to take the words right out of my mouth, perhaps because I have learned so much of them from her in the first place. I have to spend a certain amount of time fending off the misunderstandings created by the impish spin I sometimes put on things, as my rejoinders to Ayres, Kearney, and Westphal make plain, but Edith always catches the spin, seizes the point, is never thrown off track by the tensions I mean to accentuate with my rhetoric. To comment on her lovely text is to say yes, yes, that is what I said and still more, what I did not know I said, for it has been magnified and generously enlarged by her insights and erudition.

So it is no wonder that Edith has seized upon the "without why," an expression used by Angelus Silesius—"The Rose is without why; it blossoms because it blossoms,"—that I have long cherished and held close to my heart, ever since my doctoral dissertation which led to my first book, *The Mystical Element in Heidegger's Thought*, on Heidegger and Eckhart. Silesius's saying, first taken up by Heidegger in *The Principle of Reason* and made the epigraph of Irigaray's interesting critique of Heidegger in *The Forgetting of Air*, goes all the way back to the German sermons of Meister Eckhart, where it was the highest way that Eckhart could name love. Some men love God, Eckhart quipped, the way they love their cow, for its milk (that is what Derrida would call an "economy"), whereas love, the Meister said, is without why, which is

311

what Derrida would call a gift and Eckhart himself called *Gelassenheit*. *Gelassenheit* has (at least) a double value. It is the name for a mode of meditative thinking, one that suspends concepts and propositions, that gives up the search for causes and reasons, in order to enter into a simpler experience of thinking; that was the side that Heidegger seized upon and that I still treasure. I might add, at this point, that it was with Heidegger and Eckhart in mind that I said that in mystical theology one renounces or detaches oneself from *all* propositions, affirmative and negative, both apophatic and kataphatic, a point that comes up in my discussion of Tom Carlson. But Edith Wyschogrod reminds us that *Gelassenheit* was also the name for love in Meister Eckhart, and that was a side of Eckhart that Heidegger simply ignored, with the effect that *Gelassenheit* and *Denken* finally has a strictly poetic sense utterly divested of its prophetic power and biblical resonance. That is what I criticized in Heidegger and what Edith Wyschogrod underlines by taking up the thematics of the body and flesh which she has so insightfully developed in her own work. What concerns us both is how utterly pain and afflicted flesh disappear from Heidegger's view, be that in the absence of an analysis of *Sorge* as *kardia*, as heartfelt care, in *Being and Time*, or the absence of the concrete sufferings of historical human beings from the later "history of Being," in which suffering and injustice simply play no part—except when pain is mystified as a metaphor for the ontological difference.[4]

Heidegger's "call of Being" is I think an aestheticizing secularization of the Shema, which can never take the form of the call for justice that goes to the heart of the work of Levinas and Derrida upon which Edith and I so much depend. The question of justice is formulated by Wyschogrod in her contribution to this volume as the "without whom" of the alterity that is thematized in Levinas, Lyotard, and Derrida, which, as she says in this play of without's, is the subject matter of an ethics without ethics. *Against Ethics* issues in an ethics otherwise, an ethics without rules, where the singular situation is supreme, and an ethics without foundations, where obligation is left on its own, left to speak for itself, without the booming voice of God or of Being or of the Categorical Imperative to back it up. The little voice of obligation sounds in a cosmic night, like a voice crying in the desert of *khora*, in the secret site where the secret is there is no Secret, no unmediated, uninterpreted Fact that silences the conflict of interpretations. Ethics is not a fact but an interpretation, a *beau risque*, Levinas says, the chance that we are making a fool of ourselves.

Now if Merold Westphal thinks that when I talk like this that I have pitched my tent with Nietzsche's merciless play of forces, Edith Wyschogrod—like Cleo Kearns (the women get it right!)—takes all of this "tongue in cheek," as Derrida might say, all by way of a *propaedeutic* to faith. For faith is faith precisely in the face of this faceless *khora*; we need faith just because the call of justice is risky, dark and feint. Such faith is the substance of Derrida's religion without religion, religion with *or* without religion, as I think Edith and I would add. For whatever their institutional shortcomings Edith and I remain attached to our inherited historical faiths, which are the bearers of ancient memories and the guardians of ancient texts, a point that, as regards me at least, may have been obscured by some of the polemics of *Prayers and Tears* about the distinction between the messianic and the concrete messianisms. That is why, in laboring in the distance between the philosophers and the prophets, Edith Wyschogrod and I keep up our correspondence with our respective biblical faiths, she with hers, I with mine, but also she with mine and I with hers. Even as we are both taken by Derrida's formalization of a religion without religion on the basis of the historical religions of the Book, Edith and I have never ceased to be nourished by the Book, which as Levinas argued all his life is indeed a very good book. Saints *and* postmodernism, Levinas *and* Nietzsche, ethics *and* the work of art, obligation *and* the flesh—all ingredient tensions for us both, I think, in a world that is attached to both the philosophers *and* the prophets.

NOTES

1. Emmanuel Levinas, *Totality and Infinity: Essay on Exteriority*, trans. Alphonso Lingis (Pittsburgh: Duquesne University Press, 1969), p. 24.

2. Jacques Derrida, WD, p. 152.

3. Edith Wyschogrod, *Saints and Postmodernism: Revisioning Moral Theory* (Chicago: University of Chicago Press, 1990).

4. This is what my debate with William Richardson is about. See my DH, chs. 3–4, as well as our exchange in this volume.

CONTRIBUTORS

LEWIS AYRES has taught theology and divinity at Trinity College Dublin and at Duke University. He is currently teaching in the Divinity Scool at Emory University. He has published widely on Augustine and scholasticism, including articles in the influential journals *Pro Ecclesia* and *Gregorianum*.

JOHN D. CAPUTO holds the David R. Cook Chair of Philosophy at Villanova University. His most recent publications include *On Religion* (2001), *More Radical Hermeneutics* (2000), *The Prayers and Tears of Jacques Derrida* (1997), *Deconstruction in a Nutshell* (1997), *Against Ethics* (1993), and *Demythologizing Heidegger* (1993). He is also author of the 1986 classic, *Radical Hermeneutics*, as well as *The Mystical Element in Heidegger's Thought* (1978), and *Heidegger and Aquinas: An Essay in Overcoming Metaphysics* (1982). Caputo has edited a series of books for Indiana University Press, based on conferences held at Villanova University around the theme of religion and postmodernism. They include (with Michael J. Scanlon) *God, The Gift, and Postmodernism* (1999), (with Mark Dooley and Michael J. Scanlon) *Questioning God* (2001), and (with Michael J. Scanlon) *Confessions* (Forthcoming). He has served as Executive Co-Director of the Society for Phenomenology and Existential Philosophy, is a past president of the American Catholic Philosophical Association, and was a member of the National Board of Officers of the American Philosophical Association.

THOMAS A. CARLSON is Associate Professor in the Department of Religious Studies at the University of California, Santa Barbara. He is the author of *Indescretion: Finitude and the Naming of God* (1999) and of articles treating deconstruction, phenomenology, and the traditions of apophatic and mystical theology. He is also translator of several works by Jean-Luc Marion, including *God without Being* (1991), *Reduction and Donation* (1998), and *The Idol and Distance* (2000).

W. NORRIS CLARKE, S.J., is Emeritus Professor of Philosophy at Fordham University. He is one of the world's leading Thomist scholars and has authored many landmark books and articles in the area of scholastic philosophy and beyond. The most recent of these include *The One and the Many* (2001), *Explorations in Metaphysics* (1995), and *Person and Being* (1993).

JACQUES DERRIDA is a Director of Studies at the Ecole des Hautes Etudes en Sciences Sociales Paris, and is a Visiting Professor at the University of California–Irvine. His most recent publications translated into English include *On Cosmopolitanism and Forgiveness* (2001), *Of Hospitality* (2000), *Adieu: To Emmanuel Levinas* (1999), and *Monolingualism of the Other OR The Prostesis of the Origin* (1998).

MARK DOOLEY is currently Visiting Research Fellow, Department of Philosophy, University College Dublin. Along with *Questioning Ethics* (1999), which he is coedited with Richard Kearney, Dooley is author of *The Politics of Exodus* (2001). He is also coeditor, with John D. Caputo and Michael J. Scanlon, of *Questioning God* (2001). His forthcoming titles include *The Catastrophe of Memory: On Jacques Derrida* (Acumen), and *After Theism and Atheism: Kierkegaard, Derrida, and Rorty*.

THOMAS R. FLYNN is Samuel Candler Dobbs Professor of Philosophy at Emory University. Among his many influential publications in the area of French philosophy and existentialism are *Sartre, Foucault, and Reason in History* (1997), and *Sartre and Marxist Existentialism* (1986).

RICHARD KEARNEY is Professor of Philosophy at Boston College and University College Dublin. In addition to his award-winning *The Wake of Imagination* (1988), his most recent books include *The God Who May Be* (2001), *Poetics of Imagining* (1998), *Postnationalist Ireland* (1997), and *Poetics of Modernity* (1995). He is also author of the widely acclaimed *Modern Movements in European Philosophy* (1986). He is editor (with Mark Dooley) of *Questioning Ethics* (1999), as well as *Continental Philosophy in the Twentieth Century* (1994). Kearney has published two works of fiction, *Sam's Fall* (1994) and *Walking at Sea Level* (1997), along with a book of poetry, *Angel of Patrick's Hill* (1991). He has just published *On Stories* and *Strangers, Gods, and Monsters*.

CLEO McNELLY KEARNS writes and teaches in the fields of literary criticism, religion, and critical theory. She is the author of *T. S. Eliot: A Study in Poetry and Belief* (1987) and she has written articles on, among others, Julia Kristeva, Jacques Lacan, and Jacques Derrida. Her most recent publication is "Scandals of the Sign: The Virgin Mary as Supplement in the Religions of the Book," in *Questioning God: Religion and Postmodernism 2*, edited by John D. Caputo, Mark Dooley, and Michael Scanlon (2001).

B. KEITH PUTT is Professor of Philosophy at Samford University. He received his doctorate from Rice University, and has written a number of articles (one of which can be found in *Philosophy Today*) on the implications for theology of the work for John D. Caputo.

WILLIAM J. RICHARDSON, S.J., is Professor of Philosophy at Boston College. One of the most eminent members of the American academy, Richardson shot to prominence in 1974 with the publication of the first major study of Heidegger in English, *Heidegger: Through Phenomenology to Thought*. Since then he has beome a leading exponent of Lacanian psychoanalysis. Richardson's work in this area culminated in 1994 with a book coauthored with John P. Muller entitled *Lacan and Language*. He is also the subject of a book of essays edited by Babette Babich published in 1995, *From Phenomenology to Thought, Errancy, and Desire*.

MEROLD WESTPHAL is Distinguished Professor of Philosophy at Fordham University. He has served as President of the Hegel Society of America and the Soren Kierkegaard Society and as Executive Co-Director of the Society for Phenomenology and Existential Philosophy. In addition to two books on Hegel and two on Kierkegaard, he is the author of *God, Guilt, and Death* (1984) and *Suspicion and Faith* (1993). A collection of essays on postmodern philosophy and religion has just appeared from Fordham University Press entitled *Overcoming Onto-Theology*.

EDITH WYSCHOGROD is J. Newton Razor Professor of Philosophy and Religion at Rice University, and has just recently been made a member of the American Academy of Arts and Sciences. Her works include *Saints and Postmodernism* (1990) and *An Ethics of Remembering* (1998). She also authored the acclaimed *Spirit in the Ashes* (1985). Her first book, and the first book in English on Levinas, entitled *Emmanuel Levinas: The Problem of Ethical Metaphysics* has just appeared as a new edition in the Fordham University Press series "Perspectives in Continental Philosophy," edited by John D. Caputo.

INDEX